Get the eBook FREE!

(PDF, ePub, Kindle, and liveBook all included)

We believe that once you buy a book from us, you should be able to read it in any format we have available. To get electronic versions of this book at no additional cost to you, purchase and then register this book at the Manning website.

Go to https://www.manning.com/freebook and follow the instructions to complete your pBook registration.

That's it!
Thanks from Manning!

Pandas Workout

REUVEN M. LERNER

MANNING
SHELTER ISLAND

For online information and ordering of this and other Manning books, please visit
www.manning.com. The publisher offers discounts on this book when ordered in quantity.
For more information, please contact

    Special Sales Department
    Manning Publications Co.
    20 Baldwin Road
    PO Box 761
    Shelter Island, NY 11964
    Email: orders@manning.com

Manning Publications Co.
20 Baldwin Road
PO Box 761
Shelter Island, NY 11964

Development editor:	Frances Lefkowitz
Technical development editor:	Gary Hubbard
Review editor:	Dunja Nikitović
Production editor:	Kathy Rossland
Copy editor:	Tiffany Taylor
Proofreader:	Mike Beady
Technical proofreader:	Ninoslav Cerkez
Typesetter and cover designer:	Marija Tudor

ISBN 9781617299728
Printed in the United States of America

In memory of my father,
Rabbi Barry Dov Lerner (1942–2023), who taught me to

- *be insatiably curious*
- *share everything I learn*
- *believe in other people*
- *do it all with humor*

brief contents

contents

preface

When I started to teach Python at companies around the world, I wasn't surprised by how my students were using the language. They were typically using it the same way I was: for shell scripting in a more expressive language than Bash, writing server-side web applications, developing automated tests, and working with relational databases.

After a while, I found that students were using Python to analyze data—something I hadn't expected. Python was powerful and easy to use, but it was also fairly inefficient. How could people use it for data analysis?

I soon learned what many others already knew: NumPy combined the ease of Python with the efficiency of C. I jumped on the NumPy bandwagon, using it for analysis and teaching courses in it. But NumPy was still a bit too low-level for my tastes.

I was thus delighted to discover pandas, which gave me the speed and efficiency of NumPy but with a rich API that made many of my daily tasks easier. I have often described pandas as being like a car's automatic transmission, which we can contrast with the low-level manual transmission that NumPy provides. Pandas allowed me to read and write data in a variety of formats, to examine and analyze my data, to clean it, and to visualize it—in short, all the functionality I needed. I was hooked.

In the decade since I first encountered pandas, interest in the library has skyrocketed. It's hard to exaggerate the degree to which pandas is now being used; I've personally taught pandas everywhere from government agencies to startups to hedge funds to Fortune 100 companies.

Pandas approaches problems differently than Python. The syntax is the same, but the data structures are different, and the way you structure your solutions is also different. Pandas is so vast that it's easy to lose track of all the techniques. And unlike the core Python language, which tries to adhere to the maxim "There should be only one way to do it," there are often many ways to accomplish the same task in pandas. Knowing which of these ways is fastest to execute and easiest to maintain isn't always obvious, even (or especially) if you're an experienced Python developer.

For all these reasons, I'm a big believer in practice. Only by practicing the use of pandas can you remember its most important functionality and know how to apply it. And it's not enough to practice with pretend, synthetic data; if you want to really get good with pandas, you need to use real-world data with all its problems, warts, missing values, and poor construction.

The exercises in this book all come from classes I've taught over the last decade. Many have gone through iterations and changes along the way as I've seen what problems newcomers to pandas experience and the kinds of problems most likely to trip people up. My goal is to give you an opportunity to practice your pandas skills in a way that sets you up for success when you use pandas at work. Just as every run of a flight simulator makes a pilot more ready to fly an airplane full of passengers, every exercise you do in this book will make you more ready to use pandas to its fullest potential.

acknowledgments

A large number of people have helped me put together *Pandas Workout*.

Although my name appears on the cover, many people at Manning Publications have given me incredible (and patient) support during its creation. Chief among them are associate publisher Mike Stephens, who encouraged me to write a second book, and editor Frances Lefkowitz, who knows how to provide just the right amount of gentle pressure along with useful editorial suggestions. I received helpful comments from technical reviewer Ninoslav Cerkez as well.

Several dozen people signed up to read, review, and comment on the book while it was being written and edited. Their comments definitely helped me improve and sharpen the text, code, examples, and explanations. I also greatly appreciate the many people who bought *Pandas Workout* in the prerelease (MEAP) form and who commented on Manning's liveBook system.

I am grateful to the team that produces the Pandas Tutor website for providing interactive visualization of pandas queries in the same way the Python Tutor site does for Python programs. The link following each exercise in this book takes you to a pandas Tutor page prefilled with my solution. The nature of pandas, and of Pandas Tutor, means I had to make do with truncated data—but the visualization will still help you better understand the solution.

Thank you to all the reviewers—Alain Couniot, Alex Garrett, Alex Lucas, Alexander Kogler, Amilcar de Abreu Netto, Cage Slagel, Dean Langsam, George Mount, Helen Mary Labao Barrameda, Jeff Neumann, Jeff Smith, Juan Delgado, Kiran Anantha, Mikael Dautrey, Miki Tebeka, Răducu Sergiu Popa, Sadhana Ganapathiraju, Salil Athalye, Satej Kumar Sahu, Sruti Shivakumar, Steven Herrera, and Xiangbo Mao—your suggestions helped make this a better book.

Finally, my family has been incredibly patient, somehow believing me every time I told them I had "just a few more things to edit" as I wrote the book over the past three years. Thanks so much to my wife, Shira, and our three children, Atara, Shikma, and Amotz.

about this book

Collecting data used to be a challenge. That's no longer the case, thanks to small, cheap sensors, ubiquitous mobile devices, and the integration of computing into nearly every part of our lives. Now our world is awash in more data than we know what to do with, tracking everything from the steps we take to the effectiveness of advertising to the temperature on nearly any part of the planet.

We're now faced with a new problem: how can we sort through all this data we've collected? How can we make sense of it and use it to make better decisions?

For decades, the go-to choice has been Microsoft Excel. This makes sense; Excel is convenient, graphical, and installed on nearly every computer in the world. Excel makes it fairly easy to import data, clean it, perform calculations with it, and produce fancy, colorful reports, including charts.

In the last few years, though, Excel has faced a new and surprising challenger: pandas. Pandas started as a convenient wrapper for NumPy, a library that combines the speed and efficiency of C with the friendliness of Python. Pandas added many methods to NumPy's offerings, including high-quality support for text strings, date/time data, and visualization. Pandas can also read and write data in a wide variety of formats, including from online resources and relational databases.

All this, along with the underlying power of the Python language, the fact that pandas can handle far larger data sets than Excel, and its ability to run "headless" rather than take up an individual analyst's computer, has increasingly tipped the scales in favor of pandas. I've taught Python and pandas at numerous financial institutions that are moving their analysts away from Excel and toward pandas for these reasons, and I've worked with many companies in other sectors that are increasingly standardizing on pandas.

Of course, Excel isn't the only tool or language for data analysis. People are moving to pandas from programming languages like R and Matlab, too—partly for the price, partly for the performance, and partly for the huge ecosystem of open source Python modules available on the Python Package Index (PyPI).

The problem is that pandas is a *huge* library with thousands of methods and numerous options that you can pass to each of them. And pandas offers numerous ways to accomplish a given task, one of which is often much more performant than the others.

Learning how to work with pandas and how to use it correctly and efficiently frequently means a great deal of trial and error. A shortcut to mastery is to practice on problems specifically meant to help you better understand specific pandas features, much as particular exercises are meant to tone specific muscles.

That's where this book comes in. Across 50 main exercises (and 150 more "Beyond the exercise" challenges, as well as two larger projects), *Pandas Workout* will make you a more fluent, confident user of pandas. Each exercise asks you to load real-world data into pandas and then answer various questions about that data. As you work through the book, you'll learn about the most important parts of pandas—and even more importantly, you'll learn how and when it's appropriate to use them.

Pandas Workout isn't designed to teach you pandas, although I hope you'll learn quite a bit along the way. Rather, this book is meant to help you improve your understanding of pandas, how it works, and how to use it to answer questions based on data.

Please don't just read through the book. It's also a mistake to read an exercise, say to yourself that you know how to solve it, and then move on. Each exercise includes several questions, and many of them are trickier to answer than you may think. Moreover, reading my solutions without having worked on the exercises yourself isn't nearly as effective for internalizing how pandas works. So, please take the time to do the exercises, working through them gradually.

You should especially avoid feeding my questions into ChatGPT and just reviewing the answers it gives. Not only are those answers often wrong, but real learning comes from struggling a bit, getting things wrong, and then learning from your mistakes.

Who should read this book

If you've taken a pandas course but are still searching on Stack Overflow or Google for how to solve problems with pandas, this book is for you. It's not a tutorial but is meant to solidify your understanding of pandas via repeated practice.

Many pandas courses don't emphasize the need for core Python knowledge before learning pandas. I firmly believe you should get a good grounding in Python if you'll be using pandas, and this book reflects that perspective. However, you don't need to know *that* much; I assume you're comfortable with core data types, loops, functions, list comprehensions, and installing modules with `pip`. In a few places (not too many), you can also benefit from knowing about `lambda`.

How this book is organized: A road map

This book has 13 chapters, each focusing on a different aspect of pandas. Exercises in each chapter use techniques from previous chapters and sometimes from later ones. For example, we use string techniques (chapter 9) and `datetime` values (chapter 10) in earlier chapters. Think of the titles as general guidelines, rather than strict rules, for what you'll practice and learn in each chapter.

The chapters cover these topics:

1 *Series*—Understanding what a series is and how we can retrieve selected values from a series.
2 *Data frames*—Constructing data frames and retrieving selected values from a data frame.
3 *Import and export*—Reading and writing files in different formats, including CSV and JSON.
4 *Indexes*—Setting and retrieving indexes and multi-indexes.
5 *Cleaning*—Turning messy, real-world data into a form we can use more easily: for example, identifying duplicates, handling missing values, and removing unnecessary and incorrect data.
6 *Grouping, joining, and sorting*—The core of much pandas functionality: grouping data, joining multiple data frames, and sorting by both indexes and values. These topics are so important that two chapters address them.
7 *Advanced grouping, joining, and sorting*—Deeper examination of the techniques introduced in chapter 6.
8 *Project*—Completing a large project based on the Python developer survey.
9 *Strings*—Working with text data from within pandas.
10 *Dates*—Working with date and time data from within pandas.
11 *Visualization*—Plotting both via the pandas API and using the Seaborn module.
12 *Performance*—Optimizing the speed and memory usage of our data.
13 *Final project*—Completing a large project examining American colleges and universities.

Exercises form the main part of each chapter. Each exercise has five components:

- *Exercise*—A problem statement for you to tackle.
- *Working it out*—A detailed discussion of the problem and how to solve it.
- *Solution*—The solution code and (in most cases) a link to the code on the Pandas Tutor site so you can execute it. Solution code, along with test code for each solution, is also available on the Manning website at www.manning.com/ books/pandas-workout and GitHub at https://github.com/reuven/pandas -workout.
- *Beyond the exercise*—Three additional, related exercises. These questions are neither answered nor discussed in the book, but the code is downloadable along

with all the other solution code from the book. You can also discuss these additional exercises and compare solutions with other *Pandas Workout* readers in the book's online forum on Manning's liveBook platform.

About the code

This book contains a great deal of pandas code. Unlike most books, the code reflects what you are supposed to write rather than what you're supposed to read. If experience is any guide, some readers (maybe you!) will have better, more elegant, or more correct solutions than mine. If this is the case, don't hesitate to contact me.

Solution code for all exercises, including the "Beyond the exercise" questions, is available in these places outside of the book:

- The *Pandas Workout* website (www.manning.com/books/pandas-workout) and GitHub repo (https://github.com/reuven/pandas-workout) have all the code solutions organized by chapter and then by exercise number so you can download the code and run it on your own computer.
- Pandas Tutor (https://PandasTutor.com), an amazing online resource for teaching and learning pandas, allows you to enter nearly any pandas code and see how it works, with visual cues demonstrating transformations. Most of the solutions in this book have a link pointing to the code in the Pandas Tutor so you can run it without typing it into the site. Note that those links generally use small samples of the data.

This book contains many examples of source code, both in numbered listings and in line with normal text. In both cases, the source code is formatted in a fixed-width font `like this` to separate it from ordinary text.

In many cases, the original source code has been reformatted; we've added line breaks and reworked indentation to accommodate the available page space in the book. In rare cases, even this was not enough, and listings include line-continuation markers (➡). Additionally, comments in the source code have often been removed from the listings when the code is described in the text. Code annotations accompany many of the listings, highlighting important concepts.

I hope that the combination of the solution code (in print), explanations, Pandas Tutor links, and downloadable code will help you fully understand each solution and apply its lessons to your own code.

Software/hardware requirements

First and foremost, this book requires that you have both Python and pandas. You can download and install Python most easily from https://python.org. I suggest installing the latest version available. There are also other ways to install Python, including the Windows Store or Homebrew for Mac. This book should work with any version of Python from 3.9 and up; I used 3.12 in the final checks of the code.

You also need to install pandas. I used pandas 2.1.4 by the time the book was done, but most or all of the code should work fine with any 2.1.x version. You can download and install it using `pip install pandas` on the command line.

You aren't required to install an editor or IDE (integrated development environment) for Python, but it will certainly come in handy. Two of the most popular IDEs are PyCharm (from JetBrains) and Visual Studio Code (from Microsoft). I'm a big fan of the Jupyter Notebook, which you can install with `pip install jupyter`.

liveBook discussion forum

Purchase of *Pandas Workout* includes free access to liveBook, Manning's online reading platform. Using liveBook's exclusive discussion features, you can attach comments to the book globally or to specific sections or paragraphs. It's a snap to make notes for yourself, ask and answer technical questions, and receive help from the author and other users. To access the forum, go to https://livebook.manning.com/book/pandas-workout/discussion. You can also learn more about Manning's forums and the rules of conduct at https://livebook.manning.com/discussion.

Manning's commitment to our readers is to provide a venue where a meaningful dialogue between individual readers and between readers and the author can take place. It is not a commitment to any specific amount of participation on the part of the author, whose contribution to the forum remains voluntary (and unpaid). We suggest you try asking the author some challenging questions lest his interest stray! The forum and the archives of previous discussions will be accessible from the publisher's website as long as the book is in print.

about the author

REUVEN M. LERNER is a full-time Python and pandas trainer, teaching both companies and individuals in person and online. Reuven also publishes "Better Developers," a weekly newsletter about Python, and "Bamboo Weekly," with pandas challenges based on current events. Reuven holds a bachelor's degree in computer science from MIT and a PhD in learning sciences from Northwestern. He also wrote *Python Workout*, published by Manning in 2020.

about the cover illustration

The figure on the cover of *Pandas Workout* is "Femme Tongouse," or "Woman of Tunguska, Northern Siberia," taken from a collection by Jacques Grasset de Saint-Sauveur, published in 1788. Each illustration is finely drawn and colored by hand.

In those days, it was easy to identify where people lived and what their trade or station in life was just by their dress. Manning celebrates the inventiveness and initiative of the computer business with book covers based on the rich diversity of regional culture centuries ago, brought back to life by pictures from collections such as this one.

Series

1

If you have any experience with pandas, you know that we typically work with data in two-dimensional tables known as *data frames*, with rows and columns. But each column in a data frame is built from a *series*, a one-dimensional data structure (figure 1.1), which means you can think of a data frame as a collection of series.

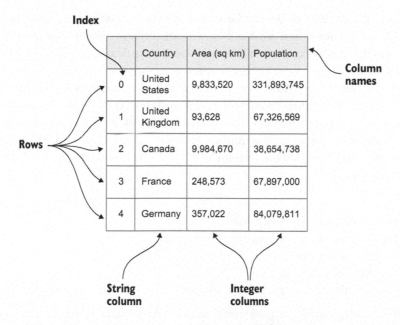

Figure 1.1   Each of a data frame's columns is a series.

This perspective is particularly useful once you learn what methods are available on a series, because most of those methods are also available on data frames—but instead of getting a single result, we get one result for each column in the data frame. For example, when applied to a series, the `mean` method returns the mean of the values in the series (figure 1.2). If you invoke `mean` on a data frame, pandas invokes the `mean` method on each column, returning a collection of mean values. Moreover, those values are themselves returned as a series on which you can invoke further methods.

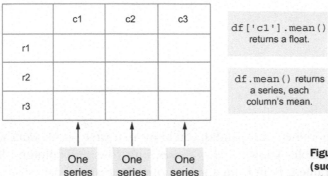

`df['c1'].mean()` returns a float.

`df.mean()` returns a series, each column's mean.

Figure 1.2 Invoking a series method (such as `mean`) on a data frame often returns one value for each column.

A deep understanding of series can be useful in other ways, too. In particular, with a *boolean index* (also known as a *mask index*), we can retrieve selected rows and columns of a data frame. (If you aren't familiar with boolean indexes, see the sidebar "Selecting values with booleans," later in this chapter.)

One of the most important and powerful tools we have as pandas users is the index, used to retrieve values from both series and data frames. We'll look at indexes in greater depth in later chapters, but knowing how to set and modify an index, as well as retrieve values using unique and nonunique values, comes in handy just about every time you use pandas. This chapter will help you better understand how to use indexes effectively.

Naming conventions in this book

I use several variable names throughout this book:

- `s` refers to a series.
- `df` refers to a data frame.
- `pd` is an alias to the pandas library, loaded with `import pandas as pd`.

Although I'm a big fan of using semantically powerful variable names, I use `s` and `df` quite a bit when teaching pandas. Given that we normally work with only one series or data frame at a time, I'll assume its meaning is clear. In the rare cases when I use more than one series or data frame, I'll normally add numbers to `s` and `df`.

I also like to refer to the `Series` and `DataFrame` classes without an initial `pd` before their names. My code thus usually starts with

```
from pandas import Series, DataFrame
```

Useful references

Table 1.1 What you need to know

Concept	What is it?	Example	To learn more
Jupyter	Web-based system for programming in Python and data science	`jupyter notebook`	http://mng.bz/BmYq
f-strings	Strings into which expressions can be interpolated	`f'It is currently {datetime.datetime .now()}'`	http://mng.bz/lWoz and http://mng.bz/a1dJ
data types (aka `dtype`)	Data types allowed in series	`np.int64`	http://mng.bz/gBVR
`pd.Series.astype`	Returns a new series with the same contents, converted to the target dtype	`s.astype(np.int32)`	http://mng.bz/xjVB
`pd.Series.mean`	Returns the arithmetic mean of the series contents	`s.mean()`	http://mng.bz/e1DJ
`pd.Series.max`	Returns the highest value in a series	`s.max()`	http://mng.bz/A8pW
`pd.Series.idxmin`	Returns the index of the lowest value in a series	`s.idxmin()`	http://mng.bz/ZR6Z
`pd.Series.idxmax`	Returns the index of the highest value in a series	`s.idxmax()`	http://mng.bz/RmrP
`np.random.default _rng`	Returns a NumPy random-number generator with an optional seed	`np.random.default _rng(0)`	http://mng.bz/27RX
`g.integers`	Returns a NumPy array of randomly selected integers via the generator	`g.integers(0, 10, 100)`	http://mng.bz/1JZg
`g.random`	Returns a NumPy array of randomly selected floats between 0 and 1 via the generator	`np.random.rand (10)`	http://mng.bz/PRBP
`s.std()`	Returns the standard deviation of a series	`s.std()`	http://mng.bz/Gy4N

Table 1.1   What you need to know *(continued)*

Concept	What is it?	Example	To learn more
`s.loc`	Accesses elements of a series by labels or a boolean array	`s.loc['a']`	http://mng.bz/zXlZ
`s.iloc`	Accesses elements of a series by position	`s.iloc[0]`	http://mng.bz/OK7z
`s.value_counts`	Returns a sorted (descending frequency) series counting how many times each value appears in *s*	`s.value_counts()`	http://mng.bz/WzOX
`s.round`	Returns a new series based on *s* in which the values are rounded to the specified number of decimals	`s.round(2)`	http://mng.bz/8rzg
`s.diff`	Returns a new series based on *s* whose values contain the differences between each value in *s* and a previous row	`s.diff(1)`	http://mng.bz/jP59
`s.describe`	Returns a series summarizing all major descriptive statistics in *s*	`s.describe()`	http://mng.bz/EQ1r
`pd.cut`	Returns a series with the same index as *s* but with categorized values based on cut points	`pd.cut(s, bins=[0, 10, 20], labels=['a', 'b', 'c'])`	http://mng.bz/N2eX
`pd.read_csv` with `squeeze`	Returns a new series based on a single-column file	`s = pd.read_csv ('filename.csv') .squeeze()`	http://mng.bz/D4N0
`str.split`	Breaks strings apart, returning a list	`'abc def ghi' .split() # returns ['abc', 'def', 'ghi']`	http://mng.bz/aR4z
`str.get`	Retrieves a character from a series	`s.str.get(0)`	http://mng.bz/JdWv
`s.fillna`	Replaces `NaN` values with a specified value	`s.fillna(5)`	http://mng.bz/wjrQ

EXERCISE 1 ▪ Test scores

Create a series of 10 elements, random integers from 70 to 100, representing scores on a monthly exam. Set the index to be the month names, starting in September and ending in June. (If these months don't match the school year in your location, feel free to make them more realistic.)

With this series, write code to answer the following questions:

- What is the student's average test score for the entire year?
- What is the student's average test score during the first half of the year (i.e., the first five months)?
- What is the student's average test score during the second half of the year?
- Did the student improve their performance in the second half? If so, by how much?

Working it out

In this first exercise, I asked you to create a series of 10 elements with random integers from 70 to 100. This raises several questions:

- How do we define a series?
- How can we create 10 random integers from 70 to 100?
- How can we set the index of the series to month names?

To define a pandas series, we call `Series`, passing it an iterable—typically a Python list or NumPy array, for example:

```
s = Series([10, 20, 30, 40, 50])
```

Here, I asked you to define the series such that it contains 10 random integers. There are certain areas in which pandas defers to NumPy, including when generating random numbers. We can get a NumPy array of random integers by creating a random-number generator with `np.default_rng` and then invoking `integers` on the object we get back.

Predictable random numbers

The Python standard library's `random` module has a `randint` method that returns a random integer:

```
random.randint(0, 100)
```

In the case of `random.randint`, the returned values range from 0 to 100, *including* 100.

In the world of NumPy, though, we do things differently. First, we create a new random-number generator object:

```
g = np.random.default_rng()
```

With this generator in hand, we can create an array of random integers by invoking `g.integers`:

```
g.integers(0, 100, 10)
```

(continued)

This method differs from Python's `random.randint` function in the following ways:

- It returns a NumPy array rather than a single integer.
- It takes three arguments: the minimum value, the maximum value, and the length of the array that should be returned.
- The second argument is one more than the highest value we can get back.

Because this is a book of exercises, you will likely want to compare your solutions with mine. How can we do that, though, if we're both generating random numbers? We can pass a *random seed*: a number that kicks off the random-number generator when we invoke `np.random.default_rng`. If you and I pass the same argument to `default_rng`, we will see the same sequence of random numbers.

Here's an example of how we can create an array of random integers from 0 to 100:

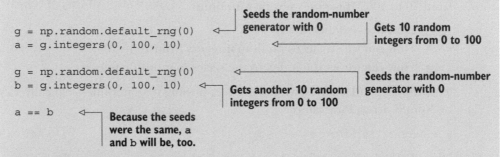

```
g = np.random.default_rng(0)
a = g.integers(0, 100, 10)
```
Seeds the random-number generator with 0

Gets 10 random integers from 0 to 100

```
g = np.random.default_rng(0)
b = g.integers(0, 100, 10)
```
Seeds the random-number generator with 0

Gets another 10 random integers from 0 to 100

```
a == b
```
Because the seeds were the same, `a` and `b` will be, too.

If you're a NumPy old-timer like me, you may wonder about the `np.random.seed` function, which operated similarly to the argument passed to `default_rng`. That function still exists, but the core NumPy developers discourage its use in favor of generator objects.

We can thus get 10 random integers between 70 and 100 with

```
g = np.random.default_rng(0)
g.integers(70, 101, 10)
```
Upper bound of 101 allows for a result of 100.

We can use them to create a series:

```
g = np.random.default_rng(0)
s = Series(g.integers(70, 101, 10))
```

We now have a series of random integers between 70 and 100. But the index contains integers from 0 through 9—much as would be the case in a NumPy array or a Python list. There's nothing inherently wrong with a numeric index, but pandas gives us much more power and flexibility, letting us use a wide variety of data types, including strings.

We can change the index by assigning to the `index` attribute:

```
g = np.random.default_rng(0)
s = Series(g.integers(70, 101, 10))
s.index = 'Sep Oct Nov Dec Jan Feb Mar Apr May Jun'.split()
```

Sure enough, printing the contents of s shows the same values, but with our index:

```
Sep    96
Oct    89
Nov    85
Dec    78
Jan    79
Feb    71
Mar    72
Apr    70
May    75
Jun    95
dtype: int64
```

> **NOTE** You can assign a list, NumPy array, or pandas series as an index. However, the data structure you pass must be the same length as the series. If it isn't, you'll get a `ValueError` exception, and the assignment will fail.

If we know what index we want when we create the series, we can assign it to the `index` keyword parameter:

```
g = np.random.default_rng(0)
months = 'Sep Oct Nov Dec Jan Feb Mar Apr May Jun'.split()
s = Series(g.integers(70, 101, 10),
           index=months)
```

This is my preferred method for creating a series, and I use this style for most of the book. That said, if and when I want to change the index, I can assign a new value to `s.index`.

Now that we've created our series, how can we perform the calculations I asked for? We first want to find the student's average test score for the entire year. We can calculate that with the `mean` method, which runs on any numeric series (Even if the series contains only integers, `mean` will always return a float. That's because in Python, division always returns a float.):

```
print(f'Yearly average: {s.mean()}')
```

Note that we put the call to `s.mean()` inside curly braces in a Python f-string. F-strings (short for *format strings*, although I like to call them *fancy strings*) allow any Python expression inside the curly braces. The result is a string suitable for assigning, printing, or passing as an argument to a function or method.

Next, we want to find the averages for the first and second halves of the school year. To do that, we need to retrieve the first five elements in the series and then the second five elements. There are a few different ways to accomplish this.

If we were using a standard Python sequence, we could use a *slice* by using square brackets along with indications of where we wanted to start and end. For example, given a string s, we can get the first five elements with the slice `s[:5]`. That returns a new series with the elements of s starting with index 0 (the start) up to and not including index 5. Generally, whenever you provide a range in Python—be it in a slice or the `range` built-in—the maximum is always "up to and not including."

It's thus not a surprise that we can retrieve the first five elements from our sequence using this same syntax: `s[:5]`. Because a slice always returns an object of the same type, this slice returns a five-element series. Because it's a series, we can then run the `mean` method on it, getting the mean score for the first semester:

```
s[:5].mean()        ◁──┐  Mean scores for
                       │  the first half
```

What about the second semester? We can get those scores in a similar way, creating a slice from index 5 until the end of the series with `s[5:]` (figure 1.3). It's important not to provide an ending index here because the max index is always one more than we want. If we were to explicitly state `s[5:9]` or `s[5:-1]`, we would miss the final value. And yes, we can say `s[5:10]`, even though there is no index 10, because slices tend to be forgiving in Python:

```
s[5:].mean()        ◁──┐  Mean scores for
                       │  the second half
```

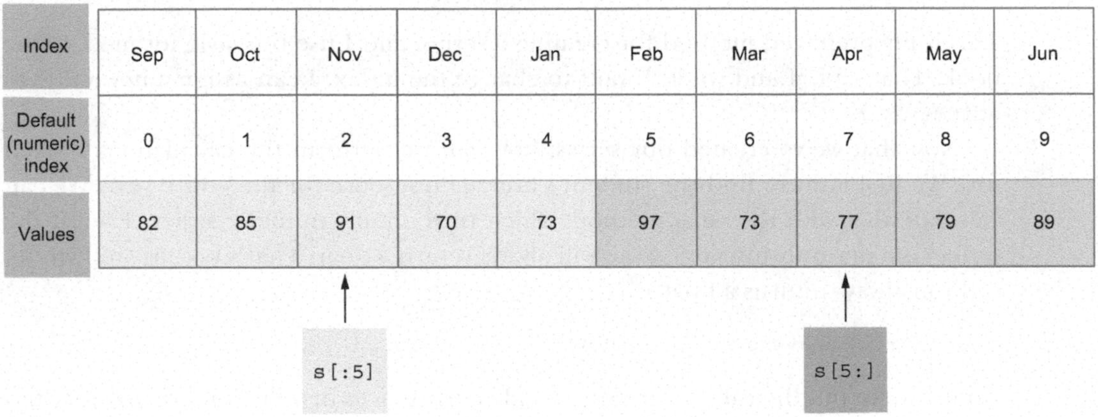

Index	Sep	Oct	Nov	Dec	Jan	Feb	Mar	Apr	May	Jun
Default (numeric) index	0	1	2	3	4	5	6	7	8	9
Values	82	85	91	70	73	97	73	77	79	89

```
                    ↑                        ↑
                  s[:5]                    s[5:]
```

Figure 1.3   Retrieving slices from our series

I would argue that it's even better to use the `.loc` and `.iloc` accessors. Whereas `.loc` retrieves one or more elements based on the index, `.iloc` retrieves based on the numeric position—the default index. Let's start with `.iloc` because its usage is similar to what we've already written:

```
s.iloc[:5].mean()
```

"But wait," you may be saying. "Why are we using the positional, numeric index? Didn't we set an index with the names of the months?" Indeed we did. Moreover, we can use those to get our answers, instead.

Once again, we want to get a slice. And once again, we can do that—pandas is smart enough to let us use the textual index with a slice. We can use the `loc` accessor if we want, which is normally a good idea when working with series and mandatory when working with data frames. It's not mandatory with a series, but it is definitely a good idea to keep your code more readable.

If we want to get the scores from the first five months (September, October, November, December, and January), we can use the following slice:

```
first_half_average = s.loc['Sep':'Jan'].mean()
```

The endpoint of a slice is normally "up to and not including," but in this case, the slice endpoint is "up to and including." That is, our `'Sep':'Jan'` slice *includes* the value for January. What gives?

Simply put, when you use `.loc`, the slice end is no longer "up to and not including" but rather "up to *and* including." This makes logical sense because it's not always obvious what "up to and not including" a custom index would be. But it's often surprising for people with Python experience who are starting to use pandas. It's also different from the behavior we saw on the same series with `.iloc`, using positional indexes.

---

loc vs. iloc vs. head

Most of the time, I prefer to use `.loc`, which is more readable and easier to understand. Plus, `.loc` offers a great deal of flexibility and power when working with data frames. But there is a cost: in some simple benchmarking I performed, pandas took twice as long to get the text-based slice (with `.loc`) as the number-based slice (with `.iloc`).

`.loc` →	Index	Sep	Oct	Nov	Dec	Jan	Feb	Mar	Apr	May	Jun
`.iloc` →	Default (numeric) index	0	1	2	3	4	5	6	7	8	9
	Values	82	85	91	70	73	97	73	77	79	89

Retrieve via the index using `.loc` and via the position using `.iloc`.

I should add that there's another way to get the first and second halves of the year: the `head` and `tail` methods. The `head` method takes an integer argument and returns that many elements from the start of s. (If you don't pass a value, it returns the first 5, which is convenient for our purposes.) We can thus get the mean for the first five months of the year with

```
s.head().mean()
```

If you prefer to be explicit, you can say

```
s.head(5).mean()
```

We can similarly use the `tail` method to get the final five elements from s:

```
s.tail().mean()
```

Again, the default argument value is 5, but we can make it explicit with

```
s.tail(5).mean()
```

Finally, we can check the improvement by subtracting the first half's average from the second half. We assign each half's mean to a variable and then calculate the difference in an f-string:

```
first_half_average = s['Sep':'Jan'].mean()
second_half_average = s['Feb':'Jun'].mean()

print(f'First half average: {first_half_average}')
print(f'Second half average: {second_half_average}')

print(f'Improvement: {second_half_average - first_half_average}')
```

Solution

```
g = np.random.default_rng(0)
months = 'Sep Oct Nov Dec Jan Feb Mar Apr May Jun'.split()
s = Series(g.integers(70, 101, 10),
          index=months)

print(f'Yearly average: {s.mean()}')

first_half_average = s['Sep':'Jan'].mean()
second_half_average = s['Feb':'Jun'].mean()

print(f'First half average: {first_half_average}')
print(f'Second half average: {second_half_average}')

print(f'Improvement: {second_half_average - first_half_average}')
```

You can explore a version of this in the Pandas Tutor at http://mng.bz/27ld.

Beyond the exercise

Here are three additional exercises to help you better understand using `.loc` and `.iloc` to retrieve data from `s`, the series used in this exercise:

- In which month did this student get their highest score? Note that there are at least three ways to accomplish this: you can sort the values, taking the largest one, using a boolean (*mask*) index to find rows that match the value of `s.max()`, the highest value, or invoking `s.idxmax()`, which returns the index of the highest value.
- What were this student's five highest scores?
- Round the student's scores to the nearest 10. (A score of 82 would be rounded down to 80, but a score of 87 would be rounded up to 90.) Be sure to read the documentation for the `round` method (http://mng.bz/8rzg) to understand its arguments and how it handles numbers like 15 and 75.

Understanding mean and standard deviation

Two of the most common and important calculations we can make on a data set are the mean and the standard deviation. Pandas lets us calculate the mean on a series `s` with `s.mean()` and the standard deviation with `s.std()`.

What are these calculations? And why do we care about them so much?

The mean describes the center of a data set. (In a moment, I'll describe where this description can be flawed.) We add all the values and then divide them by the number of values we have. In pandas syntax, we can say that `s.mean()` is the same as `s.sum() / s.count()` because `s.sum()` adds the values and `s.count()` tells us how many non-NaN values are in the series.

Is the mean a truly good measurement of the "middle" of our data? The answer is, it depends. On many occasions, it's useful because it gives us a central point on which we can focus. For example, we can talk about mean height, mean weight, mean age, or mean income in a population, and it will give us a single number that represents the entire population under discussion.

But the mean is flawed because a single large value can skew it. An old statistical joke is that when Bill Gates enters a bar, everyone in the bar is now, on average, a millionaire. For this reason, the mean isn't the only way we can calculate the "middle" of our values. A common alternative is the *median*, which is the value precisely halfway from the smallest to the largest value. (If there is an even number of values, we take the average of the two innermost ones.) In the Bill Gates example, the median income of everyone in the bar will shift slightly when he enters, but it won't change any assumptions we've made about the population.

(continued)

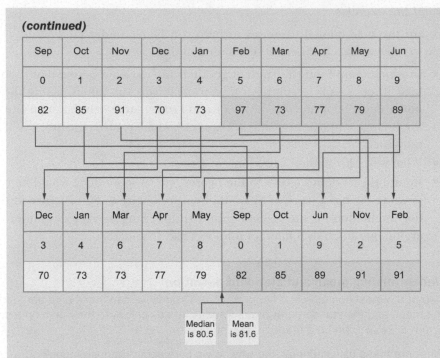

To calculate the median, we first sort the values and then take the middle one.

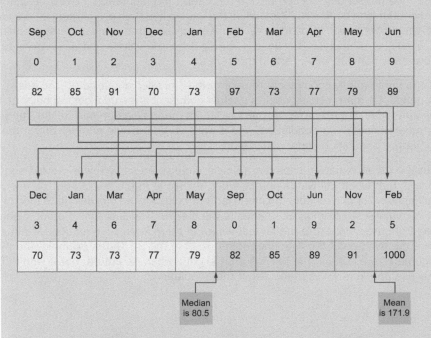

By changing one value, we can see that the mean is more easily affected by outliers than the median.

Whether we're using the mean or the median to find the central point in our data set, we will almost certainly want to know the *standard deviation*: a measurement of how much the values in our data set vary from one another. In a data set with 0 standard deviation, the values are all identical. By contrast, a data set with a very large standard deviation has values that vary greatly from the mean value. The higher the standard deviation, the more the values in the data set vary from the mean.

To calculate the standard deviation on series s, we do the following:
- Calculate the difference between each value in s and its mean.
- Square each of these values.
- Sum the squares.
- Divide by the number of elements in s. This is known as the *variance*.
- Take the square root of the variance, which gives us the standard deviation.

Expressed in pandas, we say

```
import math
math.sqrt(((s - s.mean()) ** 2).sum() / s.count())
```

Given our values of s from before, this results in a value of 8.380930735902785. If we then calculate s.std(), we get . . . uh, oh. We get a different value, 8.83427667918797. What's going on?

By default, pandas assumes that we don't want to divide by s.count() but rather by s.count() - 1. This is known as the *sample standard deviation* and is typically used on a sample of the data rather than the entire population. The pandas authors decided to default to this calculation. (NumPy's std calculation doesn't do this.)

If you want to get the same result that we calculated and that NumPy provides, you can pass a value of 0 to the ddof (*delta degrees of freedom*) parameter:

```
s.std(ddof=0)
```

This tells pandas to subtract 0 (rather than 1) from s.count() and thus match our calculation for standard deviation. In this book, I do not pass this parameter to std, and I use the default value of 1 for the ddof parameter.

In a normal distribution used for many statistical assumptions, we expect that 68% of a data set's values will be within 1 standard deviation of the mean, 95% within 2 standard deviations, and 99.7 within 3 standard deviations. If you invoke np.random.randint (for integers) or np.random.rand (for floats), you'll get a truly random distribution. If you prefer to get a normal distribution in which the randomly selected numbers are centered around a mean and within a particular standard deviation, you can instead use g.normal. This method takes three arguments: the mean, the standard deviation, and the number of values to generate. It returns a NumPy array with a dtype of np.float64, which you can use to create a new series.

In this section, we used several so-called *aggregation methods*, which run on a series and return a single number—for example, sum, mean, median, and std. We'll use these throughout the book, and you can use them in any data-analysis projects you work on.

When sums go wrong

The `sum` method is useful, as you can imagine. You will likely want to use it on numeric series to combine the values. But it turns out that if you run `s.sum()` when `s` is a series of strings, the result is the strings concatenated together:

```
s = Series('abcd efgh ijkl'.split())
s.sum()
```
Returns
'abcdefghijkl'

Things get even weirder when your series contains strings, but those strings are numeric:

```
s = Series('1234 5678 9012'.split())
s.mean()
```
Returns
41152263004.0

Where does this number come from? The values of `s` are added together as strings, resulting in `'123456789012'`. But then `s.mean()` converts this string into an integer and divides it by 3 (the length of the series).

This is one of those cases where the behavior makes logical sense but is almost certainly not what you want. It also appears to have been fixed in Python 3.12, returning a `TypeError` exception.

Understanding dtype

In Python, we constantly use the built-in core data types: `int`, `float`, `str`, `list`, `tuple`, and `dict`. Pandas is a bit different in that we don't use those types much. Rather, we use the types we get from NumPy, which provide a thin, Python-compatible layer over values defined in C.

Every series has a `dtype` attribute, and you can always read from that to know the type of data it contains. Every value in a series is that type; unlike a Python list or tuple, you cannot mix different types in a series. That said, pandas does allow us to define the `dtype` as `object`, meaning a series contains Python objects. When the `dtype` is `object`, we can usually assume that the series contains Python strings; more on that in chapter 9. Storing nonstring objects is rare and should generally be avoided, but there are sometimes good reasons to do so. You'll also have a `dtype` of `object` if there are multiple types in the series.

Several standard types of `dtype` values are defined by NumPy and used by pandas. There are also special pandas-specific types, some of which we'll discuss later in the book. The core NumPy `dtype` values to know are as follows:

- Integers of different sizes—`np.int8`, `np.int16`, `np.int32`, and `np.int64`.
- Unsigned integers of different sizes—`np.uint8`, `np.uint16`, `np.uint32`, and `np.uint64`.
- Floats of different sizes—`np.float16`, `np.float32`, and `np.float64`. (On some computers, you also have `np.float128`.)
- Python objects—`object`.

When you create a series, pandas normally assigns the `dtype` based on the argument you pass to `Series`:

- If all values are integers, the `dtype` is set to `np.int64`.
- If at least one of the values is a float (including `NaN`), the `dtype` is set to `np.float64`.
- Otherwise, the `dtype` is set to `object`.

You can override these choices by passing a value to the `dtype` parameter when you create a series. For example:

```
s = Series([10, 20, 30], dtype=np.float16)
```

If you try to pass a value that's incompatible with the `dtype` you've specified, pandas will raise a `ValueError` exception.

Why should you care about the `dtype`? Because getting the type right, especially if you're working with large data sets, allows you to balance memory usage and accuracy. These are problems we normally don't think about in standard Python, but they are front and center when working with pandas.

For example, The `np.int8` type handles 8-bit signed numbers (i.e., both positive and negative), which means it handles numbers from –128 through 127. What happens if you go beyond those boundaries?

```
s = Series([127], dtype=np.int8)
s+1
```
Returns a one-element series with a value of –128.

That's right: in the world of 8-bit signed integers, 127+1 is –128. It's like the odometer of your car rolling over back to 0 when you've driven it for many years, except you won't have any warning and thus won't know whether your calculations are accurate.

Yes, this is a problem. So, you need to ensure that the `dtype` you use on your series is big enough to store whatever data you're working with, including the results of any calculations you perform. If you're planning to multiply your data by 10, for example, you need to ensure that the `dtype` is large enough to handle that, even if you won't be displaying or directly using such values.

Given this problem, why not go for broke and use 64-bit integers for everything? After all, those are likely to handle just about any value you may have.

Perhaps, but those will also use a lot of memory. Remember that 64 bits is 8 bytes, which doesn't sound like much for a modern computer. But if you're dealing with 1 billion numbers, using 64 bits means the data will consume 8 gigabytes of memory without considering any overhead that Python, your operating system, and the rest of pandas may need. And, of course, you're unlikely to have just only numbers in memory.

As a result, you need to consider how many bits you want and need to use for your data. There's no magic answer; each case must be evaluated on its own merits.

(continued)

What if you want to change the `dtype` of a series after you've already created it? You can't set the `dtype` attribute; it's read-only. Instead, you have to create a new series based on the existing one by invoking the `astype` method:

```
s = Series('10 20 30'.split())
s.dtype                        ⟵—| Returns "object"


s = s.astype(np.int64)
s.dtype                        ⟵—| Returns "np.int64"
```

If you try to invoke `astype` with a type that isn't appropriate for the data, you'll get (as we saw when constructing a series) a `ValueError` exception.

EXERCISE 2 ■ Scaling test scores

When I was in high school and college, our instructors sometimes gave extremely hard tests. Rather than fail most of the class, they would *scale* the test scores, known in some places as *grading on a curve*. They would assume that the average test score should be 80, calculate the difference between our actual mean and 80, and then add that difference to each of our scores.

For this exercise, I want you to generate 10 test scores between 40 and 60, again using an index starting with September and ending with June. Find the mean of the scores and add the difference between the mean and 80 to each of the scores.

Working it out

One of the most important ideas in pandas (and in NumPy) is that of vectorized operations. When we perform an operation on two different series, the indexes are matched, and the operation is performed via the indexes (figure 1.4). For example, consider

```
s1 = Series([10, 20, 30, 40])
s2 = Series([100, 200, 300, 400])

s1 + s2
```

The result is

```
0    110
1    220
2    330
3    440
dtype: int64
```

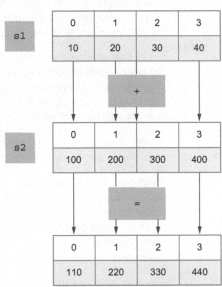

Figure 1.4   When we add two series together, the result is a new series—the result of adding elements at the same index.

What happens if we set an explicit index rather than rely on the default positional index?

```
s1 = Series([10, 20, 30, 40],
    index=list('abcd'))
s2 = Series([100, 200, 300, 400],
    index=list('dcba'))

s1+s2
```

The result is

```
a    410
b    320
c    230
d    140
dtype: int64
```

Again, pandas added the values together according to the index. Notice that this happened even though the index in `s1` was forward (`abcd`), whereas the index in `s2` was backward (`dcba`). The index values determine the value match-ups, not their position (figure 1.5).

But what happens when we try to add not one series and another series but rather a series and a scalar value? Pandas does something known as *broadcasting*—it applies the operator and that scalar value to each value in the series, returning a new series. For example:

```
s = Series([10, 20, 30, 40],
    index=list('abcd'))

s + 3
```

The result is

```
a    13
b    23
c    33
d    43
dtype: int64
```

Notice that we get back from the operation a new series whose index matches those of s and whose values are the result of adding each element of s and the broadcast integer 3 (figure 1.6). We can do this with any

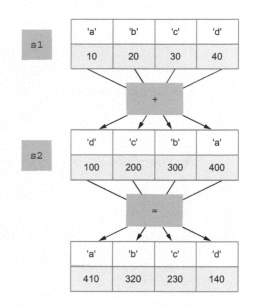

Figure 1.5   Vectorized operations work using the index, not the position.

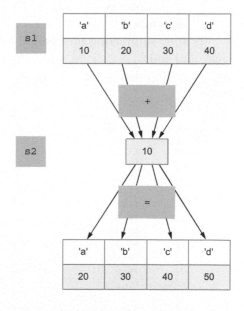

Figure 1.6   Operations involving a series and a scalar value result in *broadcasting* the operation, resulting in a new series.

operator, including comparison operators such as == and <. (The result of the latter is a boolean series, which we can then use as a *mask index* to keep only the rows we want.)

So, if we want to generate 10 test scores between 40 and 60 and then add 10 points to them, we can do the following:

```
g = np.random.default_rng(0)

months = 'Sep Oct Nov Dec Jan Feb Mar Apr May Jun'.split()

s = Series(g.integers(40, 60, 10),
           index=months)

s+10
```

And sure enough, we'll get the following:

```
Sep     62
Oct     65
Nov     50
Dec     53
Jan     53
Feb     57
Mar     59
Apr     69
May     68
Jun     54
dtype: int64
```

That's nice, but the code still doesn't quite do what we want. That's because we don't know how many points we need to add to each score. We must first find the mean of s and then determine how far that is from 80. We can do that by invoking s.mean() and then subtracting the result from 80. Whatever we get back is the scale factor we need to add.

In other words, we can say

```
s + (80-s.mean())
```

And the result?

```
Sep     83.0
Oct     86.0
Nov     71.0
Dec     74.0
Jan     74.0
Feb     78.0
Mar     80.0
Apr     90.0
May     89.0
Jun     75.0
dtype: float64
```

Notice how this solution moves back and forth between scalar values and series, which is common in pandas calculations: The call to s.mean() returns a scalar value. We then calculate 80 - s.mean(), resulting in a scalar value. But then we add s and that number, adding (using broadcast) our series to that scalar value.

> **NOTE** The final series has a dtype of float64, whereas s had a dtype of int64. Why the change? Because whenever we perform an operation on an int and a float, we get back a float, even if there's no need for it, as with addition. And division in Python 3 always returns a float. So the call to s.mean(), because it invokes division, always returns a float. And then when we add (via broadcast) the integer values in s to the floating-point mean, we get a series of floats.

Solution

```
s + (80 - s.mean())
```

You can explore a version of this in the Pandas Tutor at http://mng.bz/1JDV.

Beyond the exercise

Whether you're performing an operation on two series or using broadcasts to combine a series and a scalar, the index is one of the most important ideas in pandas. It dictates how vectorized operations are performed as well as the index of the new series created by the operation. Here are some more exercises having to do with these topics:

- There's at least one other way to scale test scores: by looking at both the mean of the scores and their standard deviation. Anyone who scored within one standard deviation of the mean got a C (below the mean) or a B (above the mean). Anyone who scored more than one standard deviation above the mean got an A, and anyone who got more than one standard deviation below the mean got a D. During which months did our student get an A, B, C, and D?
- Were there any test scores more than two standard deviations above or below the mean? If so, in which months?
- How close are the mean and median to each another? What does it mean if they are close? What would it mean if they were far apart?

EXERCISE 3 ▪ Counting tens digits

In this exercise, I want you to generate 10 random integers in the range 0 to 100. (Remember that the np.random.randint function returns numbers that include the lower bound but exclude the upper bound.) Create a series containing those numbers' tens digits. Thus, if our series contains 10, 25, 32, we want the series 1, 2, 3.

Working it out

Given that we have created our series with np.random.randint(0, 100, 10), we know that the 10 integers will all range from 0 (at the low end) to 99 (at the high end). We know that each number will contain either one or two digits.

To get the tens digit, we can do this:

1 Divide our series by 10, turning the `dtype` into a floating type and moving the decimal point one position to the left.
2 Turn our series back into `np.int8`, removing the fractional part of the number.

If the original number had two digits, we now have the tens digit. And if the original number had one digit, we are left with 0.

Sure enough, this works just fine, resulting in

```
0    4
1    4
2    6
3    6
4    6
5    0
6    8
7    2
8    3
9    8
dtype: int8
```

Notice that the `dtype` here is `int8` (figure 1.7).

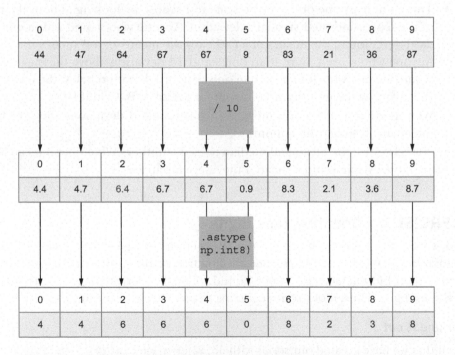

Figure 1.7   Graphical depiction of dividing the series by 10, converting to `np.int8`

But we can do even better than this: Python's // ("floordiv") operator performs integer division. If we divide the series by 10 using //, we'll still get our dtype of int8. That's the approach I'll go with because it reduces the number of operations we need to perform.

There is another way to do this, which involves more type conversions. This time, we convert our series not into floats but rather into *strings*. Why? Because when we turn integers into strings, we can retrieve particular elements from them, such as the second-to-last digit.

To do this, we convert our series of integers (dtype of int8) into a series of strings (dtype of str) using the astype method:

```
s.astype(str)
```

But then what? We'll talk about this more in chapter 8, which discusses strings in depth, but the key is the str accessor that lets us apply a string method to every element in the series. The get method on that accessor works like square brackets on a traditional Python string—so if we say s.astype(str).str.get(0), we get the first character in each integer; and if we say s.astype(str).str.get(-1), we get the final character in each string. (In Python, negative string indexes count from the end.) We can thus get the second-to-last digit, aka the tens digit, with s.astype(str).str .get(-2).

But of course, that's not enough: if we have a one-digit number, what will get(-2) return? It won't give us an error or an empty string, but rather NaN. Fortunately, we can use the fillna method to replace NaN with any other value—for example, '0'. We then get back a series containing one-character strings: the tens digits from our original series. Our code looks like this:

```
s.astype(str).str.get(-2).fillna('0')
```

And the result is

```
0    4
1    4
2    6
3    6
4    6
5    0
6    8
7    2
8    3
9    8
dtype: object
```

As you can see from the dtype, the result is object, which typically means Python strings. Can we turn it back into a series of integers? Yes, by calling astype with an integer argument (figure 1.8). We'll use np.int8 because all of our numbers are small:

```
s.astype(str).str.get(-2).fillna('0').astype(np.int8)
```

And the result is

```
0    4
1    4
2    6
3    6
4    6
5    0
6    8
7    2
8    3
9    8
dtype: int8
```

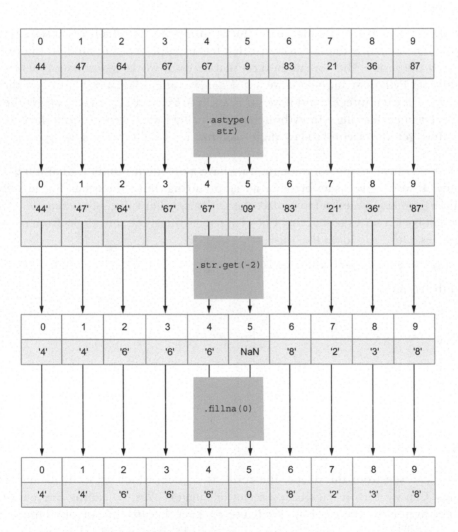

Figure 1.8   **Graphical depiction of turning the series into strings, retrieving the item at index –2, and replacing NaN with 0**

I think this is a cleaner way to do things than the int-to-float technique I showed earlier. But it is also more complex, and if you know you'll only have two-digit data, it may be overkill.

If you think the previous code puts too much on a single line, you can use a sneaky trick popularized by my friend Matt Harrison (www.metasnake.com): Python allows us to split code across lines if we're still inside open parentheses. We can thus open parentheses on purpose and put each method call on a separate line. This can make things easier to read and follow and lets us put comments on each line:

```
(
    s
    .astype(str)      # get a series based on s, with dtype str
    .str.get(-2)      # retrieve the second-to-last character
    .fillna('0')      # replace NaN with '0'
    .astype(np.int8)  # get a new series back dtype int8
)
```

This style gives the same result as the initial one-liner but is often more readable, especially as the code gets more complex.

NOTE Pandas has traditionally used Python strings, and that's what I assume in this book. As of this writing, however, there is an experimental new type, `pd.StringDType`, which aims to replace `str`. This is part of a larger movement in pandas to create new data types, partly so `NaN` will no longer always be a float and can represent a missing value from any type. I wouldn't be surprised if `pd.StringDtype` is a standard, recommended part of pandas in the coming years. There is also increasing support for Apache Arrow, including its string types. For now, though, Python strings are the best-supported version of strings in pandas, and we use them in this book.

Solution

```
g = np.random.default_rng(0)
s = Series(g.integers(0, 100, 10))
s // 10
```

You can explore a version of this in the Pandas Tutor at http://mng.bz/PRY9.

Beyond the exercise

- What if the range were from 0 to 10,000? How would that change your strategy, if at all?
- Given a range from 0 to 10,000, what's the smallest `dtype` you should use for integers?
- Create a new series with 10 floating-point values between 0 and 1,000. Find the numbers whose integer component (i.e., ignoring any fractional part) are even.

Selecting values with booleans

In Python and other traditional programming languages, we select elements from a sequence using a combination of `for` loops and `if` statements. Although you *can* do that in pandas, you almost certainly don't want to. Instead, you want to select items using a combination of techniques known as a *boolean index* or a *mask index*.

Mask indexes are useful and powerful, but their syntax can take some getting used to. First, consider that we can retrieve any element of a series via square brackets and an index:

```
s = Series([10, 20, 30, 40, 50])
s.loc[3]                              ⟵┤ Returns 40
```

Instead of passing a single integer, we can also pass a list (or NumPy array, or series) of boolean values (i.e., `True` and `False`):

```
s = Series([10, 20, 30, 40, 50])
s.loc[[True, True, False, False, True]]    ⟵
```

Notice the double square brackets! The outer pair indicates we want to retrieve from s. The inner pair defines a Python list. Returns a series containing 10, 20, and 50.

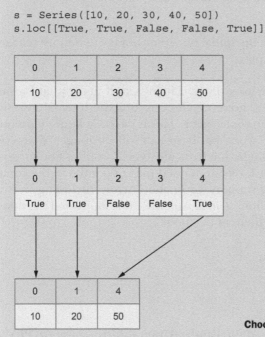

Choosing items via a mask index

Wherever we pass `True`, the value from `s` is returned, and wherever we pass `False`, the value is ignored. This is called a mask index because we're using the list of booleans as a type of sieve, or mask, to select only certain elements. Mask indexes don't transform the data but rather select specific elements from it.

An explicitly defined list of booleans isn't very useful or common. But we can also use a series of booleans—and those are easy to create. All we need to do is use a comparison operator (e.g., `==`), which returns a boolean value. Then we can broadcast the operation and get back a series. For example:

Returns the series containing 10 and 20

```
s.loc[s < 30]    ⟵┘
```

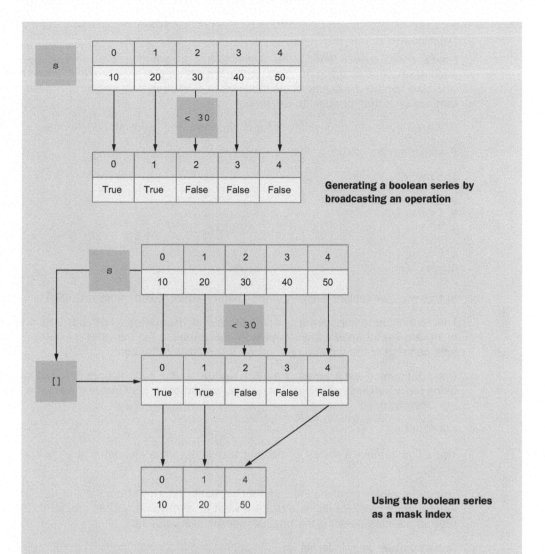

Generating a boolean series by broadcasting an operation

Using the boolean series as a mask index

This code looks very strange, even to experienced developers, in no small part because s is both outside the square brackets and inside them. Remember that we first evaluate the expression inside the square brackets. In this case, it's `s < 30`, which returns a series of boolean values indicating whether each element of s is less than 30. We get back `Series([True, True, False, False, False])`.

That series of booleans is then applied to s as a mask index. Only those elements matching the `True` values are returned—in other words, just 10 and 20.

We can get more sophisticated, too:

```
s.loc[s <= s.mean()]
```
⟵ Returns the series
   containing 10, 20, and 30

(continued)

Now s appears *three* times in the expression: once when we calculate `s.mean()`, a second when we compare the mean with each element of s via broadcast, and a third when we apply the resulting boolean series to s. We can thus see all of the elements that are less than or equal to the mean.

Finally, we can use a mask index for assignment and retrieval. For example:

```
s.loc[s <= s.mean()] = 999
```

The result?

```
0    999
1    999
2    999
3     40
4     50
dtype: int64
```

In this way, we replace elements less than or equal to the mean with 999.

This technique is worth learning and internalizing because it's both powerful and efficient. It's useful when working with individual series, as in this chapter—but it's also applicable to entire data frames, as we'll see later in the book.

One final note: given a series s, you can retrieve multiple items from different indexes using fancy indexing: passing a list, series, or similar iterable inside the square brackets. For example:

```
s.loc[[2,4]]
```

This code returns a series containing two values: the elements at `s.loc[2]` and `s.loc[4]`.

The outer square brackets indicate that we want to retrieve from s using `loc`, and the inner square brackets indicate that we want to retrieve more than one item. Pandas returns a series, keeping the original indexes and values.

Don't confuse fancy indexing with the application of a mask index; in the former case, the inner square brackets contain a list of values from the index. In the case of a mask index, the inner square brackets contain boolean (`True` and `False`) values.

EXERCISE 4 ▪ Descriptive statistics

The mean, median, and standard deviation are three numbers we can use to get a better picture of our data. Adding a few other numbers can give us an even more complete picture. These *descriptive statistics* typically include the mean, standard deviation, minimum value, 25% quantile, median, 50% quantile, and maximum value. Understanding and using descriptive statistics is a key skill for anyone working with data, and in this exercise, you'll practice doing so with the following:

- Generate a series of 100,000 floats in a normal distribution with a mean of 0 and a standard deviation of 100.
- Get the descriptive statistics for this series. How close are the mean and median? (You don't need to calculate the difference; rather, consider why they aren't the same.)
- Replace the minimum value with 5 times the maximum value.
- Get the descriptive statistics again. Did the mean, median, and standard deviations change from their previous values? (Again, it's enough to see the difference without calculating it.) If so, why?

Working it out

In this exercise, we create a slightly different distribution than before: rather than using np.random.randint, we instead use g.normal, which I described in the sidebar "Understanding mean and standard deviation," earlier in this chapter. When we invoke g.normal, we still get random numbers, but they are picked from the normal distribution—and we can specify both the mean and the standard deviation.

We thus create our series as follows:

```
g = np.random.default_rng(0)
s = Series(g.normal(0, 100, 100_000))
```

We can use _ in integers to separate digits.

We could call several different methods to find the descriptive statistics. But fortunately for us, pandas provides the describe method, which returns a series of measurements:

- count—The number of non-NaN values in the series
- mean—The mean, same as s.mean()
- std—The standard deviation, same as s.std()
- min—The minimum value, same as s.min()
- 25%—The value in s you'll choose if you line up the values from smallest to largest and pick whatever is 25% of the way through, same as s.quantile(0.25)
- 50%—The median value, same as s.median() or s.quantile(0.5)
- 75%—The value in s you'll choose if you line up the values from smallest to largest and pick whatever is 75% of the way through, same as s.quantile(0.75)
- max—The maximum value, same as s.max()

You could get each of these values separately—but it's often useful to see and read them all at once.

Here's the result from calling s.describe():

```
count    100000.000000
mean          0.157670
std          99.734467
min        -485.211765
25%         -66.864170
50%           0.172022
```

```
75%              67.343870
max             424.177191
dtype: float64
```

The mean is 0.157670. Not quite zero, which is what I asked for, but these are random numbers picked from a distribution, meaning there will always be wiggle room. The median, aka the 50% quantile, is 0.172022, which is very close to the mean. That makes sense, given that in a normal distribution, half of the numbers are below the mean and half are above it. The standard deviation here is roughly 100, meaning if all goes well, 68% of the values in s will be between –100 and +100.

What happens when we replace the minimum value with 5 times the max value? Moreover, how can we do that?

First, we need to find all the indexes at which the minimum value is located. (The idxmin method would return only one of the locations with this minimum value, but we want to modify as many as may exist.) The easiest way to do that is to first get a boolean series indicating which elements match the minimum value:

```
s == s.min()
```

This returns a boolean series with True wherever the value of s is the minimum. We can then apply this boolean series as a mask index:

```
s.loc[s == s.min()]
```

Now we have a series of only one element whose value is s.min(). We can assign a new value in its place using an assignment. But what do we want to assign? Five times the max value:

```
s.loc[s == s.min()] = 5*s.max()
```

Now that we have modified our series, we can call s.describe() on it again. We want to compare the mean, median, and standard deviations. What do we find?

```
count    100000.000000
mean          0.183731
std          99.947900
min        -465.995297
25%         -66.862839
50%           0.174214
75%          67.345174
max        2120.885956
dtype: float64
```

First, the mean value has gone up a bit—which makes sense, given that we took the smallest value and made it larger than the previously defined largest value. That's why the mean, although valuable, is sensitive to even a handful of very large or very small values.

Second, the standard deviation has also gone up. Again, this makes a great deal of sense, given that we have made a single value that's larger than anything we had before. True, the standard deviation didn't change much, but it reflects that values in our series are spread out more than they were previously.

Finally, the median barely shifted. That's because it tends to be the most stable measurement, even when we have fluctuations at the extremes. This doesn't mean you should only look at the median, but it can be useful. For example, if a country is trying to determine the threshold for government-sponsored benefits, a small number of very rich people will skew the mean upward, thus depriving more people of that help. The median will allow us to say that (for example) the bottom 20% of earners will receive help.

Solution

```
import numpy as np
import pandas as pd
from pandas import Series, DataFrame

g = np.random.default_rng(0)
s = Series(g.normal(0, 100, 100_000))

print(s.describe())

s.loc[s == s.min()] = 5*s.max()

print(s.describe())
```

You can explore a version of this in the Pandas Tutor at http://mng.bz/JdM0.

Beyond the exercise

- Demonstrate that 68%, 95%, and 99.7% of the values in s are indeed within one, two, and three standard distributions of the mean.
- Calculate the mean of numbers greater than s.mean(). Then calculate the mean of numbers less than s.mean(). Is the average of these two numbers the same as s.mean()?
- What is the mean of the numbers beyond three standard deviations?

EXERCISE 5 ▪ Monday temperatures

Newcomers to pandas often assume that a series index must be unique. After all, the index in a Python string, list, or tuple is unique, as are the keys in a Python dictionary. But the values in a pandas index can repeat, making it easier to retrieve values with the same index. If an index contains user IDs, country codes, or email addresses, we can use it to retrieve data associated with specific index values that would otherwise require a messier and longer mask index.

In this exercise, I want you to create a series of 28 temperature readings in Celsius, representing four seven-day weeks, randomly selected from a normal distribution with a mean of 20 and a standard deviation of 5, rounded to the nearest integer. (If you're in a country that measures temperature in Fahrenheit, pretend you're looking at the weather in an exotic foreign location rather than where you live.) The index should start with Sun, continue through Sat, and repeat Sun through Sat until each temperature has a value. The question is, what was the mean temperature on Mondays during this period?

Working it out

This exercise has two parts. First, we need to create a series that contains 28 elements but with a repeating index. Let's start by creating a random NumPy array of 28 elements drawn from a normal distribution in which the mean is 20 and the standard deviation is 5. (This means, as we've seen, that 95% of the values will be within 10 degrees of 20: that is, between 10 and 30. An extreme swing for one month, perhaps, but let's assume it's early spring or late autumn.) We can do this using g.normal, as we've seen before:

```
g = np.random.default_rng(0)
g.normal(20, 5, 28)
```

How can we create a 28-element index with the days of the week? One option is to simply create a list of 28 elements by hand. But I think that we can be a bit more clever than that, taking advantage of some core Python functionality. We can start by creating a seven-element list of strings with the days of the week:

```
days = 'Sun Mon Tue Wed Thu Fri Sat'.split()
```

If we had only seven data points in our series, we could set the index with index=days inside the call to Series. But because we have 28 data points, we want the list to repeat itself. We can create such a 28-element list by multiplying the list by 4, as in days * 4. This is very different behavior than the broadcast functionality of pandas!

We can thus create the series as follows:

```
s = Series(g.normal(20, 5, 28),
           index=days*4)
```
Multiplying a Python list returns a new list with the original list's elements repeated.

But g.normal returns floats (specifically, np.float64 objects). How can we turn this into a series of integers?

One way would be to use astype(np.int8) on our numbers. (The temperature is unlikely to get below –100 degrees or above 100 degrees, so we should be fine.) And that approach would basically work, but it would truncate the fractional part of the values rather than round them. If we want to round them to the nearest integer, we can call round on the series, thus getting back floats with no fractional portion. Then we can call astype(np.int8) on what we get back, resulting in a series of integers:

```
g = np.random.default_rng(0)
s = Series(g.normal(20, 5, 28),
           index=days*4).round().astype(np.int8)
```

We can now start to address the problem of repeated values in the index. Yes, the index can have repeated values—not just integers, but also strings (as in this example) and even other data structures, such as times and dates (as we'll see in chapter 9). Normally, when we retrieve a value from a series via `loc`, we expect to get back a single value. But if the index is repeated, we will get back multiple values. And in pandas, multiple values are returned as a series.

> **NOTE** When you retrieve `s.loc[i]`, for a given index value, you can't know in advance whether you will get a single, scalar value (if the index occurs only once) or a series (if the index occurs multiple times). This is another case in which you need to know your data to know what type of value you'll get back.

In this case, we know that `Mon` exists four times in our series. And thus, when we ask for `s.loc['Mon']`, we'll get back a series of four values, all of which have `Mon` as their index:

```
s.loc['Mon']
```

We get back:

```
Mon    22
Mon    19
Mon    22
Mon    24
dtype: int8
```

Because this is a series, we can run any series methods we like on it. And because we want to know the average temperature on Mondays in this location, we can run `s.loc['Mon'].mean()`. Sure enough, we get the answer: 21.75.

Solution

```
days = 'Sun Mon Tue Wed Thu Fri Sat'.split()

g = np.random.default_rng(0)
s = Series(g.normal(20, 5, 28),
        index=days*4).round().astype(np.int8)

s.loc['Mon'].mean()
```

You can explore a version of this in the Pandas Tutor at http://mng.bz/wjeq.

Beyond the exercise

- What was the average weekend temperature (i.e., Saturdays and Sundays)?
- How many times is the change in temperature from the previous day greater than 2 degrees?
- What are the two most common temperatures in our data set, and how often does each appear?

EXERCISE 6 ■ Passenger frequency

In this exercise, we begin looking at real-world data loaded from a one-column CSV file. We'll take a deeper look at reading from and writing to files in chapter 3, but we start here by invoking `pd.read_csv`, calling `squeeze` on the one-column data frame it returns, and getting back a series.

The data is in the file taxi-passenger-count.csv, available along with the other data files used in this course. The data comes from 2015 data I retrieved from New York City's open data site, where you can get enormous amounts of information about taxi rides in New York City over the last few years. This file shows the number of passengers in each of 100,000 rides.

Your task in this exercise is to show what percentage of taxi rides had only one passenger versus the (theoretical) maximum of six passengers.

Working it out

Let's start with reading the data into our series. `read_csv` is one of the most powerful and commonly used functions in pandas, reading a CSV file (or anything resembling a CSV file) into a data structure. As I mentioned, `read_csv` returns a data frame—but if we read a file containing only one column, we get a data frame with a single column. We can then invoke `squeeze` on that single-column data frame, getting back a series. Because all the values in this file are integers, pandas assumes that we want the series `dtype` to be `np.int64`.

We also set the `header` parameter to `None`, indicating that the first line in the file should not be taken as a column name but rather as data to be included in our calculations:

```
s = pd.read_csv('data/taxi-passenger-count.csv',
        header=None).squeeze()
```

The resulting series has a `name` value of 0, which we can safely ignore.

> **NOTE** Although many methods operate on a series (or data frame), `read_csv` is a top-level function in the `pd` namespace. That's because we're not operating on an existing series or data frame. Rather, we're creating a new one based on the contents of a file.

Once we have read these values into a series, how can we figure out how often each value appears? One option is to use a mask index along with `count`:

```
s.loc[s==1].count()      ◁——┤ Results in 7207
s.loc[s==6].count()      ◁——┤ Results in 369
```

But wait: I asked you to give the proportion of elements in `s` with either 1 or 6. Thus we need to divide those results by `s.count()`:

```
s.loc[s==1].count() / s.count()      ◁——┤ Results in about .720772    Results in
s.loc[s==6].count() / s.count()      ◁——————————————————————————————— about .036904
```

There's nothing inherently wrong with doing things this way, but there's a far easier technique: `value_counts`, a series method that is one of my favorites. If we apply `value_counts` to the series s, we get back a new series whose keys are the distinct values in s and whose values are integers indicating how often each value appeared. Thus, if we invoke `s.value_counts()`, we get

```
1    7207
2    1313
5     520
3     406
6     369
4     182
0       2
Name: 0, dtype: int64
```

Notice that the values are automatically sorted from most common to least common.

Because we get back a series from `value_counts`, we can use all our series tricks on it. For example, we can invoke `head` on it to get the five most common elements. We can also use fancy indexing to retrieve the counts for specific values. Because we're interested in the frequency of one- and six-passenger rides, we can say

```
s.value_counts()[[1,6]]
```

That returns

```
1    7207
6     369
Name: 0, dtype: int64
```

But we're interested in the percentages, not the raw values. Fortunately, `value_counts` has an optional `normalize` parameter that returns the fraction if set to `True`. We can thus say

```
s.value_counts(normalize=True)[[1,6]]
```

which returns the values

```
1    0.720772
6    0.036904
Name: 0, dtype: float64
```

Solution

```
import pandas as pd
from pandas import Series, DataFrame

s = pd.read_csv('data/taxi-passenger-count.csv', header=None).squeeze()

s.value_counts(normalize=True)[[1,6]]
```

You can explore a version of this in the Pandas Tutor at http://mng.bz/qjQw.

Beyond the exercise

Let's analyze the taxi passenger data in a few more ways:

- What are the 25%, 50% (median), and 75% quantiles for this data set? Can you guess the results before you execute the code?
- What proportion of taxi rides are for three, four, five, or six passengers?
- Consider that you're in charge of vehicle licensing for New York taxis. Given these numbers, would more people benefit from smaller taxis that can take only one or two passengers or larger taxis that can take five or six passengers?

EXERCISE 7 ▪ Long, medium, and short taxi rides

In this exercise, we once again look at taxi data—but instead of the number of passengers, we examine the distance (in miles) each taxi ride went. Once again, I'll ask you to create a series based on a single-column CSV file, taxi-distance.csv.

First, load the data into a series. Then modify the series (or create another series) containing category names rather than numbers based on these criteria:

- Short, ≤ 2 miles
- Medium, > 2 miles but ≤ 10 miles
- Long, > 10 miles

Calculate the number of rides in each category.

Working it out

It's not unusual to take numeric values and convert them to named categories. In this exercise, we want to turn taxi distances into short, medium, and long rides. How can we do that?

One approach is to use a combination of comparisons and assignments:

```
categories = s.astype(str)          ⟵┘ Creates a new series
categories.loc[:] = 'medium'        ⟵   the same length as s      Assigns all the
categories.loc[s<=2] = 'short'      ⟵                              values to medium
categories.loc[s>10] = 'long'       ⟵┐  Assigns small values
categories.value_counts()              │ to the string short
                                       Assigns large values to the
                                       string long
```

When we call `value_counts`, we get the following:

```
short    5890
medium   3402
long      707
Name: 0, dtype: int64
```

This certainly works, but as you probably guessed, there is a more efficient approach. The `pd.cut` method allows us to set numeric boundaries and then cut a series into parts (known as *bins*) based on those boundaries. Moreover, it can assign labels to each of the bins.

Notice that `pd.cut` is not a series method but rather a function in the top-level `pd` namespace. We'll pass it a few arguments:

- Our series, `s`
- A list of four integers representing the boundaries of our three bins, assigned to the `bins` parameter
- A list of three strings, the labels for our three bins, assigned to the `labels` parameter

Note that the bin boundaries are exclusive on the left and inclusive on the right. In other words, by specifying that the medium bin is between 2 and 10, that means >2 but < = 10. This means the first boundary needs to be less than the smallest value in `s`. However, we can get around that by passing the `include_lowest=True` keyword argument, which ensures that the lowest value passed to `bins` is included in the first bin.

The result of this call to `pd.cut` is a series the same length as `s` but with the labels replacing the values:

```
pd.cut(s,
       bins=[0, 2, 10, s.max()],
       include_lowest=True,
       labels=['short', 'medium', 'long'])
```

The result, as depicted in Jupyter, is as follows:

```
0          short
1          short
2          short
3          medium
4          short
           ...
9994       medium
9995       medium
9996       medium
9997       short
9998       medium
Name: 0, Length: 9999, dtype: category
Categories (3, object): ['short' < 'medium' < 'long']
```

Notice that the dtype is category. We will discuss categories later in the book.

Shows the relative order of the categories in their description

The task I gave you for this exercise wasn't to turn the ride lengths into categories but rather to determine the number of rides in each category. For that, we need to call on our friend `value_counts`:

```
pd.cut(s,
       bins=[0, 2, 10, s.max()],
       include_lowest=True,
       labels=['short', 'medium', 'long']).value_counts()
```

And sure enough, this gives us the answer we want:

```
short     5890
medium    3402
long       707
Name: 0, dtype: int64
```

Solution

```
import pandas as pd
from pandas import Series, DataFrame

s = pd.read_csv('data/taxi-distance.csv', header=None).squeeze()

pd.cut(s,
       bins=[0, 2, 10, s.max()],
       include_lowest=True,
       labels=['short', 'medium', 'long']).value_counts()
```

You can explore a version of this in the Pandas Tutor at http://mng.bz/7vx9.

Beyond the exercise

- Compare the mean and median trip distances. What does that tell you about the distribution of the data?
- How many short, medium, and long trips were there for trips that had only one passenger? Note that the data for passenger count and trip length is from the same data set, meaning the indexes are the same.
- What happens if you don't pass explicit intervals and instead ask `pd.cut` to just create three bins, with `bins=3`?

Summary

In this chapter, we saw that a pandas series provides powerful tools to analyze data. Whether it's the index, reading data from files, calculating descriptive statistics, retrieving values via fancy indexing, or even categorizing our data via numeric boundaries, we can do a lot. In the next chapter, we'll expand our reach to look at data frames, the two-dimensional data structures that most people think of when they work with pandas.

Data frames 2

Since long before the invention of computers, people have used tables to present data. That's because tables make it easy to enter, display, understand, and analyze data. Each row in a table represents a single record or data point, and every column describes an attribute associated with each point. For example, consider table 2.1 of country names, sizes (in square kilometers), and populations, with data taken from Wikipedia toward the end of 2022.

Table 2.1   Country data

Country	Area (sq km)	Population
United States	9,833,520	331,893,745
United Kingdom	93,628	67,326,569
Canada	9,984,670	38,654,738
France	248,573	67,897,000
Germany	357,022	84,079,811

If it seems obvious to arrange data this way, that's because we've seen it for so long and in so many contexts. Indeed, here are some examples of tables I've seen in just the last few days:

- *Stock-market updates*—The rows are stocks and popular indexes, and the columns are the current value, the absolute change since yesterday, and the percentage change since yesterday.

- *Luggage allowances on international flights*—The rows describe different types of tickets, and the columns indicate how large or heavy our carry-on and checked bags can be.
- *Nutrition information on packaged food*—The rows are different items we want to know about (for example, calories, fat, and sugar), and the columns describe the quantity per 100 grams or for an entire package.

Because each column contains one attribute or category, it typically contains one type of data. However, each row may contain several different types of data because it cuts across several columns. Adding a new column means adding a new dimension, or aspect, to each record. Adding a new row means adding a new record with a value for each column.

Computers have been used to store tabular information for decades, most famously in spreadsheet software such as Excel. Pandas continues this tradition, organizing tables in *data frames*. Each column in a data frame is a pandas series object. The data frame has a single index shared by all of its columns. In many ways, a data frame is a collection of series with a common index.

Because each column in a data frame is its own series, each can have a distinct `dtype`. For example, we can have a data frame with one integer column, one float column, and one string column (figure 2.1).

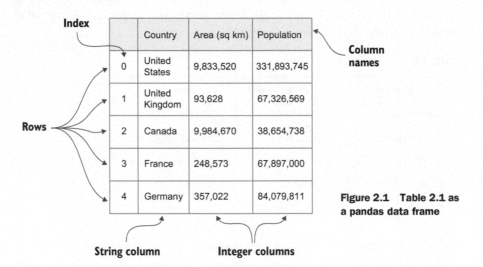

Figure 2.1   Table 2.1 as a pandas data frame

A data frame typically contains more information than we need. Before we can answer any questions, we first need to pare our data down to a subset of its original rows and columns. In this chapter, we practice doing that—retrieving only the rows and columns we want based on criteria appropriate for our query. We see how the `.loc` accessor, boolean indexes, and various pandas methods allow us to work on just the data that we want and need. (In chapter 3, we'll see how to import data from external sources. And in chapter 5, we'll discuss how to clean real-world data so we can use it reliably.)

We'll also practice creating, modifying, and updating data frames. Sometimes we'll do that because we have new information and want the data frame to reflect that change. And sometimes we'll do it because we need to clean our data, removing or modifying bad values.

After this chapter, you'll be comfortable doing the most common tasks associated with data frames. We'll build on these basics in later chapters so you can organize your data in more sophisticated and interesting ways.

Table 2.2 What you need to know

Concept	What is it?	Example	To learn more
DataFrame	Returns a new data frame based on two-dimensional data	DataFrame([[10, 20], [30, 40], [50, 60]])	http://mng.bz/d1xz
s.loc	Accesses elements of a series by labels or a boolean array	s.loc['a']	http://mng.bz/rWPE
df.loc	Accesses one or more rows of a data frame via the index	df.loc[5]	http://mng.bz/V1Pr
s.iloc	Accesses elements of a series by position	s.iloc[0]	http://mng.bz/x4lq
df.iloc	Accesses one or more rows of a data frame by position	df.iloc[5]	http://mng.bz/AoNE
[]	Accesses one or more columns in a data frame	df['a']	http://mng.bz/Zqej
df.assign	Adds one or more columns to a data frame	df.assign(a=df['x']*3)	http://mng.bz/OPln
str.format	Method that works much like f-strings	'ab{0}'.format(5)	http://mng.bz/YR5N
s.quantile	Gets the value at a particular percentage of the values	s.quantile(0.25)	http://mng.bz/RxPn
pd.concat	Joins together two data frames	df = pd.concat([df, new_products])	http://mng.bz/2DJN
df.query	Writes an SQL-like query	df.query('v > 300')	http://mng.bz/1qwZ
pd.read_csv	Returns a new series based on a single-column file	s = pd.read_csv ('filename.csv') .squeeze()	http://mng.bz/PzO2
interpolate	Returns a new data frame with NaN values interpolated	df = df.interpolate()	http://mng.bz/Jgzp
df.dropna	Returns a new data frame without any NaN values	df.dropna()	http://mng.bz/o1PN
s.isin	Returns a boolean series indicating whether each element of a series is in the provided argument	s.isin([10, 20, 30])	http://mng.bz/9DO8

Brackets or dots?

When we're working with a series, we can retrieve values several ways: using the index (and `loc`), using the position (and `iloc`), and using square brackets, which are equivalent to `loc` for simple cases. When we work with data frames, though, we must use `loc` or `iloc` to retrieve rows. That's because square brackets refer to the columns.

For example, let's create a data frame:

```
df = DataFrame([[10, 20, 30, 40],
                [50, 60, 70, 80],
                [90, 100, 110, 120]],
    index=list('xyz'),
    columns=list('abcd'))
```

Given this data frame and the fact that square brackets refer to columns, we can understand how `df['a']` returns the `a` column; and `df[['a', 'b']]`, passing a list of columns inside the square brackets (that is, double square brackets), returns a new, two-column data frame based on `df`. If we ask for `df['x']`, pandas will look for a column `x`, not see one, and raise a `KeyError` exception. To retrieve the row at index `x`, we must say `df.loc['x']` or, if we prefer to retrieve it positionally, `df.iloc[0]`.

But there is an exception to the "square brackets mean columns" rule: if we use a slice, pandas will look at the data frame's rows, rather than its columns. This means we can retrieve rows from `x` through `y` with `df['x':'y']`. The slice tells pandas to use the rows rather than the columns. Moreover, the slice will return rows up to *and including* the endpoint, which is unusual for Python (but typical when using `loc` in pandas).

Another way to work with columns is to use *dot notation*. That is, if you want to retrieve the column `colname` from data frame `df`, you can say `df.colname`.

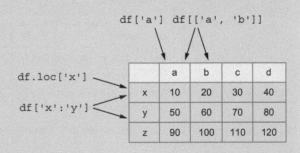

Our data frame

This syntax appeals to many people for a variety of reasons: it's easier to type, it has fewer characters and is thus easier to read, and it seems to flow a bit more naturally.

But there are reasons to dislike it, as well. Columns with spaces and other illegal-in-Python identifier characters don't work. And it's confusing to try to remember whether `df.whatever` is a column named `whatever` or an attribute named `whatever`. There are so many pandas methods to remember, I'll take any help I can get.

So, I use bracket notation and will use it throughout this book. If you prefer dot notation, you're in good company—but keep in mind that there are places you won't be able to use it.

EXERCISE 8 ■ Net revenue

For many pandas users, it's rare to create a new data frame from scratch. We import a CSV file, or we perform transformations on an existing data frame (or several existing series). But sometimes we need to create a new data frame—for example, when assembling data from nonstandard sources or experimenting with new pandas techniques— and knowing how to do so can be useful.

For this exercise, I want you to create a data frame that represents a company's inventory of five products. Each product has a unique ID number (a two-digit integer will do), name, wholesale price, retail price, and number of sales in the last month. You're making it up, so if you've always wanted to be a profitable starship dealer, this is your chance! Once you have created this data frame, calculate the total net revenue from all your products.

Working it out

The first part of this task involved creating a new data frame by passing values to the `DataFrame` class. There are four ways to do this:

- Pass a list of lists (figure 2.2). Each inner list represents one row. The inner lists must all be the same length and fill the columns positionally.
- Pass a list of dictionaries (dicts) (figure 2.3). Each dict represents one row, and the keys indicate which columns should be filled.

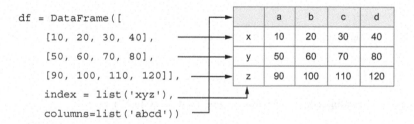

Figure 2.2 Creating a data frame from a list of lists. Each inner list represents one row. Column names are taken positionally.

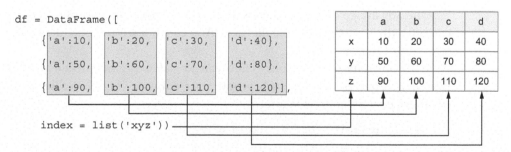

Figure 2.3 Creating a data frame from a list of dicts. Each dict is a row, and the keys indicate column values.

- Pass a dict of lists (figure 2.4). Each key represents one column, and the values (lists) are each column's values.
- Pass a two-dimensional NumPy array (figure 2.5).

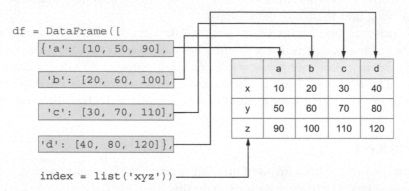

Figure 2.4   Creating a data frame from a dict of lists. Each dict key is a column name, and the list contains values for that column.

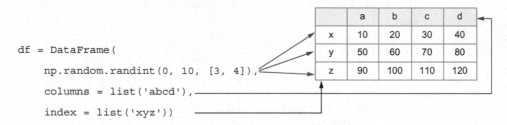

Figure 2.5   Creating a data frame from a two-dimensional NumPy array

Which of these techniques is most appropriate depends on the task at hand. In this case, because we want to create and describe individual products, we decide to use a list of dicts.

One advantage of a list of dicts is that we don't need to pass column names; pandas can infer their names from the dict keys. And the index is the default positional index, so we don't have to set that.

With our data frame in place, how can we calculate our products' total revenue? Doing so requires that for each product, we subtract the wholesale price from the retail price, aka the net revenue:

```
df['retail_price'] - df['wholesale_price']
```

Here, we are retrieving the series `df['retail_price']` and subtracting from it the series `df['wholesale_price']`. Because these two series are parallel to one another, with identical indexes, the subtraction takes place for each row and returns a new series with the same index but with the difference between them.

Once we have that series, we multiply it by the number of sales for each product:

```
(df['retail_price'] - df['wholesale_price']) * df['sales']
```

Without parentheses, the * operator would have had precedence.

This results in a new series that shares an index with df but whose values are the total sales for each product. We can sum this series with the sum method (figure 2.6):

```
((df['retail_price'] - df['wholesale_price']) * df['sales']).sum()
```

Parentheses tell pandas to call sum on the series returned from * rather than directly on df['sales'].

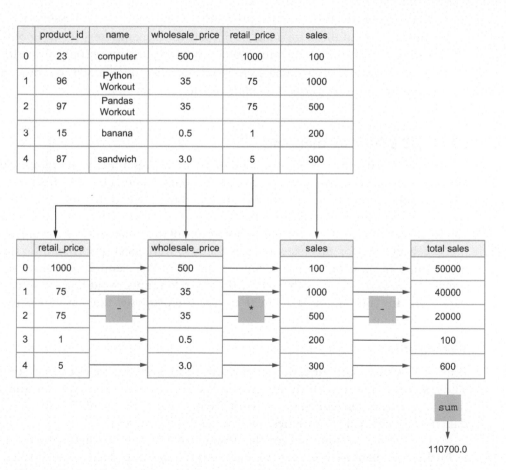

Figure 2.6 Graphical depiction of the solution for exercise 8

Solution

```
df = DataFrame([{'product_id':23, 'name':'computer', 'wholesale_price': 500,
        'retail_price':1000, 'sales':100},
        {'product_id':96, 'name':'Python Workout', 'wholesale_price': 35,
        'retail_price':75, 'sales':1000},
        {'product_id':97, 'name':'Pandas Workout', 'wholesale_price': 35,
        'retail_price':75, 'sales':500},
        {'product_id':15, 'name':'banana', 'wholesale_price': 0.5,
        'retail_price':1, 'sales':200},
        {'product_id':87, 'name':'sandwich', 'wholesale_price': 3,
        'retail_price':5, 'sales':300},
        ])

((df['retail_price'] - df['wholesale_price']) * df['sales']).sum()    ⟵  Returns
                                                                          110700
```

You can explore this in the Pandas Tutor at http://mng.bz/0lAx.

Beyond the exercise

- For what products is the retail price more than twice the wholesale price?
- How much did the store make from food versus computers versus books? (You can retrieve based on the index values, not anything more sophisticated.)
- Because your store is doing so well, you can negotiate a 30% discount on the wholesale price of goods. Calculate the new net income.

EXERCISE 9 ▪ Tax planning

In the previous exercise, you created a data frame representing your store's products and sales. In this exercise, you will extend that data frame (literally). It's pretty common to add columns to an existing data frame, either to add new information you've acquired or to store the results of per-row calculations—which is what you'll do now. A common reason to add a column is to hold intermediate values as a convenience.

The backstory for this exercise is as follows. Your local government is thinking about imposing a sales tax and is considering 15%, 20%, and 25% rates. Show how much less you would net with each of these tax amounts by adding columns to the data frame for your net income under each of the proposed rates, as well as your current net income.

Working it out

If two series share an index, we can perform various arithmetic operations on them. The result is a new series with the same index as each of the two inputs to the operation. Often, as in exercise 8, we perform the operation on two of the columns in our data frame (which are both series, after all) and view the result.

But sometimes we want to keep that result around, either because we want to use it in further calculations or because we want to reference it. In such a case, it's helpful to add one or more new columns to our data frame.

How can we do that? It's surprisingly simple: we assign to the data frame, using the name of the column that we want to spring into being. It's typical to assign a series, but we can also assign a NumPy array or list, as long as it is the same length as the other, existing columns. Column names are unique—so just as with a dictionary, assigning to an existing column replaces it with the new one.

In the previous exercise, we calculated the total sales for each product. To solve the first part of this exercise, we take that calculation and assign the resulting series to a new column in the data frame:

```
df['current_net'] = ((df['retail_price'] - df['wholesale_price'])
    * df['sales'])
```

Adding columns with assign

Another way to add a column to a pandas data frame is the `assign` method, which returns a new data frame rather than modifying an existing one. For example, instead of saying

```
df['current_net'] = ((df['retail_price'] - df['wholesale_price']) *
    df['sales'])
```

we can use

```
df.assign(current_net = (df['retail_price'] - df['wholesale_price']) *
    df['sales'])
```

Keyword arguments passed to `df.assign` result in a new column (with the same name as the keyword argument) whose values are the keyword argument's values.

Using `assign` is often useful if we open parentheses before a query and then chain methods, each on a line by itself, to get a solution. Some people prefer this style, saying that they find it more readable and reproducible than assignment. I personally find that complex queries with numerous steps are often easier to understand using this chained style and that `assign` simplifies writing such queries. Many of the solutions in this book are written using such a multilined, chained style. I encourage you to try writing your queries in this way; many pandas users have found that it results in clearer, easier-to-debug code.

What happens if we're taxed at 15%? This reduces our net by 15%, which we can calculate and then assign to a new column:

```
df['after_15'] = df['current_net'] * 0.85
```

We can then repeat this assignment into two additional columns for the other tax amounts:

```
df['after_20'] = df['current_net'] * 0.80
df['after_25'] = df['current_net'] * 0.75
```

Now our data frame has nine columns: product_id, name, wholesale_price, retail_price, sales, current_net, after_15, after_20, and after_25. Because the final four columns (where we show our net income) are all numeric, we can grab them (with fancy indexing), returning a data frame with the four columns we selected and our five products' rows:

```
df[['current_net', 'after_15', 'after_20', 'after_25']]
```

When we run sum on this data frame, we get back the sum of each column. The result is returned as a series in which the column names serve as the index:

```
current_net     110700.0
after_15         94095.0
after_20         88560.0
after_25         83025.0
dtype: float64
```

We can now clearly see how much we would earn under each tax plan. We can even show the difference between our current net and each of the tax plans, broadcasting the subtraction operation:

```
df['current_net'].sum() - df[['current_net',
    'after_15', 'after_20', 'after_25']].sum()
```

Solution

```
df['current_net'] = ((df['retail_price'] - df['wholesale_price'])
    * df['sales'])
df['after_15'] = df['current_net'] * 0.85
df['after_20'] = df['current_net'] * 0.80
df['after_25'] = df['current_net'] * 0.75
df[['current_net', 'after_15', 'after_20', 'after_25']].sum()
```

You can explore this in the Pandas Tutor at http://mng.bz/K98K.

Beyond the exercise

- An alternative tax plan would charge a 25% tax, but only on products from which you would net more than 20,000. In such a case, how much would you make?
- Yet another alternative tax plan would charge a 25% tax on products whose retail price is greater than 80, a 10% tax on products whose retail price is between 30 and 80, and no tax on other products. Implement and calculate the result of such a tax scheme.
- These long floating-point numbers are getting hard to read. Set the float_ format option in pandas such that floating-point numbers will be displayed with commas every three digits before the decimal point and only two digits after the decimal point. Note that this is tricky because it requires understanding Python callables and the str.format method.

Retrieving and assigning with loc

It's pretty straightforward to retrieve an entire row from a data frame or even replace a row's values with new ones. For example, we can grab the values in the row with index `abcd` with `df.loc['abcd']`. If we prefer to use the numeric (positional) index, we can use `df.iloc[5]` instead. In both cases, we get back a series created on the fly from the values in that row. By contrast, if we retrieve a column, nothing new needs to be created because each column is stored as a series in memory.

What if we want to retrieve only part of a row? More significantly, how can we set values on only part of a row?

We can do this several ways, but I prefer `loc`, with two arguments in square brackets. The first argument describes the row(s) we want to retrieve (*row selector*), and the second describes the column(s) we want to retrieve (*column selector*).

Let's assume we have a 5x5 data frame with index `a-e`, columns `v-z`, and values from 10 through 250. To retrieve row `a`, we can say `df.loc['a']`. But to retrieve the item at index `a` in column `x`, we can say

	v	w	x	y	z
a	10	20	30	40	50
b	60	70	80	90	100
c	110	120	130	140	150
d	160	170	180	190	200
e	210	220	230	240	250

Our sample data frame

```
df.loc['a', 'x']
```

Especially as the arguments become longer and more complex, it can be easier to put them on separate lines:

```
df.loc['a',
       'x']
```
◄───┤ **Row selector**
◄───┐ **Column selector**

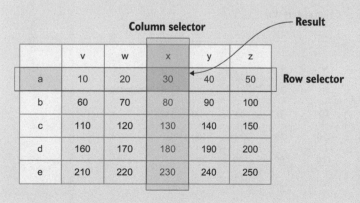

Column selector

	v	w	x	y	z
a	10	20	30	40	50
b	60	70	80	90	100
c	110	120	130	140	150
d	160	170	180	190	200
e	210	220	230	240	250

Result — Row selector

Graphical depiction of `df.loc['a', 'x']`

(continued)

Once you understand this syntax, you can use it in more sophisticated ways. For example, let's retrieve rows `a` and `c` from column `x`:

```
df.loc[['a', 'c'],       ◁—| Row selector
       'x']              ◁— Column
                            selector
```

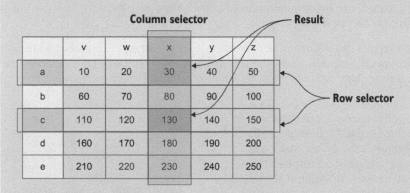

Graphical depiction of `df.loc[['a', 'c'], 'x']`

Notice that we can use fancy indexing to describe the rows we want to retrieve and a regular index (as the second value in the square brackets) to describe the column we want. We can similarly retrieve more than one column. In this example, we retrieve row `a` from columns `v` and `y`:

```
df.loc['a',        ◁—| Row selector
       ['v','y']]   ◁— Column
                       selector
```

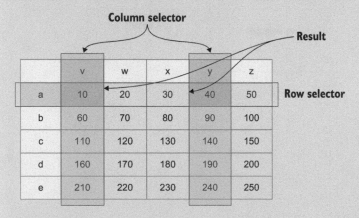

Graphical depiction of `df.loc['a', ['v', 'y']]`

What if we combine these, retrieving rows `a` and `c` from columns `v` and `y`?

```
df.loc[['a', 'c'],      <----| Row selector    | Column
           ['v','y']]   <--                      selector
```

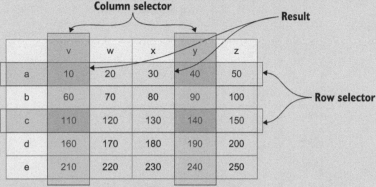

Graphical depiction of `df.loc[['a', 'c'], ['v', 'y']]`

But wait, it gets even better: we can describe rows using a boolean index. We can create a boolean series using a conditional operator (for example, `<` or `==`) and apply it to the rows and/or the columns. For example, we can find all rows in which `x` is greater than 200:

```
df.loc[df['x']>200]    <----| Row selector,
                            | no column selector
```

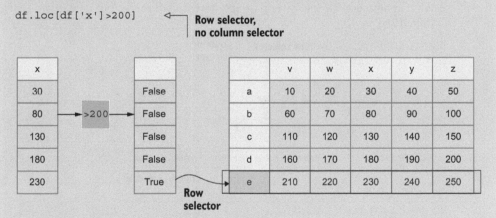

Graphical depiction of `df.loc[df['x']>200]`

Now we can add a second value boolean index after the comma, indicating which columns we want:

```
df.loc[df['x']>200,1((CO9-1))   <----| Row selector
      df.loc['c'] > 135]        <--| Column
                                  | selector
```

(continued)

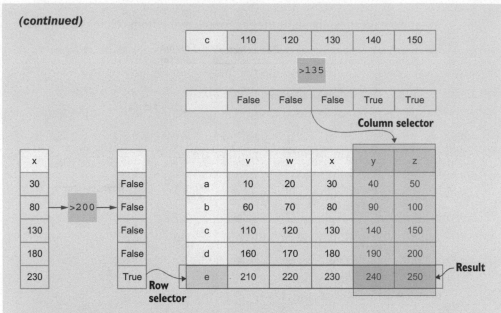

Graphical depiction of `df.loc[df['x']>200, df.loc['c'] > 135]`

This expression returns all rows from `df` in which column `x` is greater than 200 and all columns from `df` in which `c` is greater than 135.

We can also dial it back, saying we're interested in row `b`, but only where `c` is greater than 135:

```
df.loc['b',      ◄——| Row selector  | Column
        df.loc['c']>135]      ◄——          selector
```

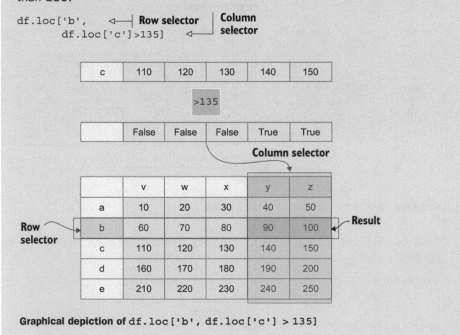

Graphical depiction of `df.loc['b', df.loc['c'] > 135]`

Of course, our conditions can be far more complex than these. But as long as you keep in mind that you want to select based on rows before the comma and based on columns after the comma, you should be fine.

In all these examples, we retrieve values from the data frame. What if we want to *modify* these values? We can do so by putting the retrieval query on the left side of an assignment statement. The only catch is that the value on the right must either be a scalar (in which case it is broadcast and assigned to all matching elements) or have a matching shape (that is, rows and columns).

For example, let's say we want to set the element in row b, column y, to 123. We can do that as follows:

```
df.loc['b',        ⟵┤ Row selector
       'y'       ⟵┐
] = 123          │ Column
                 │ selector
```

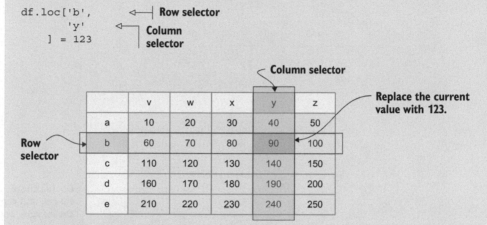

Graphical depiction of `df.loc['b', 'y'] = 123`

What if we want to set new values in row b, where row c is greater than 125? We can assign a list (or NumPy array or pandas series) of three items, matching the three elements our query matches:

```
df.loc['b',        ⟵┤ Row selector    ┐ Column
       df.loc['c'] > 125    ⟵─────────┘ selector
] = [123, 456, 789]
```

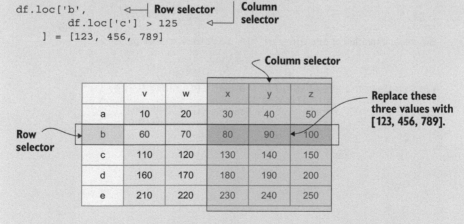

Graphical depiction of `df.loc['b', df.loc['c'] > 125] = [123, 456, 789]`

(continued)

Of course, this requires knowing precisely how many values will be needed. In many cases, you won't know that in advance but will assign based on another column—or even the selection values themselves! For example, the following code doubles the value in row b whenever the corresponding value in row c is divisible by 3:

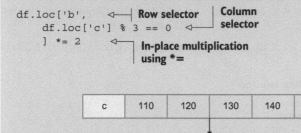

```
df.loc['b',          ◄──┤ Row selector       │ Column
     df.loc['c'] % 3 == 0  ◄──                  selector
   ] *= 2          ◄──┐ In-place multiplication
                      │ using *=
```

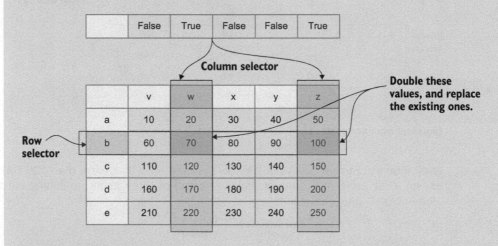

Graphical depiction of `df.loc['b', df.loc['c'] % 3 == 0] *= 2<3>`

We can assign a scalar value to the elements described by `loc`:

```
df.loc[df['v'] > 100,    ◄──┤ Row selector      │ Column
     df.loc['d'] > 180   ◄──                       selector
   ] = 987
```

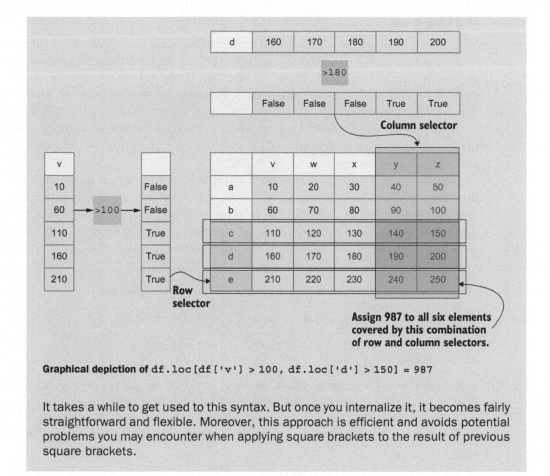

Graphical depiction of `df.loc[df['v'] > 100, df.loc['d'] > 150] = 987`

It takes a while to get used to this syntax. But once you internalize it, it becomes fairly straightforward and flexible. Moreover, this approach is efficient and avoids potential problems you may encounter when applying square brackets to the result of previous square brackets.

EXERCISE 10 ▪ Adding new products

Good news! Your store is making money, and you have decided to add some new products. I'd like you to do that by creating a new data frame and adding it to the existing one. This new data frame should contain three products (including product ID, name, wholesale price, and retail price):

- Phone, with an ID of 24, a wholesale price of 200, and a retail price of 500
- Apple, with an ID of 16, a wholesale price of 0.5, and a retail price of 1
- Pear, with an ID of 17, a wholesale price of 0.6, and a retail price of 1.2

Because these are new products, don't include the `sales` column. And to avoid problems and conflicts, ensure that the indexes of these new products are different from existing product indexes. (In chapter 4, we'll look at some ways to handle index problems more elegantly.)

Once you have added these new products, assign sales figures to each of them. Finally, recalculate the store's total net income, including the new products.

Working it out

We often think of data frames as representing data we've already collected or imported from a file. But data frames are much more fluid than that, allowing us to represent data in various ways and formats. We should expect to modify a data frame over its lifetime, either as we gather data or simply because we want to analyze data from different sources.

In this exercise, I first asked you to create a new data frame representing three new products. This new data frame needs to have all the same values as the previous one, except for the sales column.

The first step is the easiest because it resembles creating a data frame at the start of the chapter. The only difference is that we set the index manually, using Python's built-in range, to avoid collisions between the indexes in our original data frame and this one. Pandas doesn't care whether our index repeats, but we often will care about such a thing, so I decided to include it in the exercise.

We create a new data frame this way:

```
new_products = DataFrame([{'product_id':24, 'name':'phone',
    'wholesale_price': 200, 'retail_price':500},
    {'product_id':16, 'name':'apple', 'wholesale_price': 0.5,
    'retail_price':1},
    {'product_id':17, 'name':'pear', 'wholesale_price': 0.6,
    'retail_price':1.2}], index=range(5,8))
```

With this new data frame in hand, we want to add it to the previously existing one. The pd.concat function does this, and it works a bit differently than you may expect: it's a top-level pandas function and takes a list of data frames to concatenate.

The result of pd.concat is a new data frame, which we then assign back to df (figure 2.7):

```
df = pd.concat([df, new_products])
```

	product_id	name	wholesale_price	retail_price	sales
0	23	computer	500	1000.0	100.0
1	96	Python Workout	35	75.0	1000.0
2	97	Pandas Workout	35	75.0	500.0
3	15	banana	0.5	1.5	200.0
4	87	sandwich	3.0	5.0	300.0
5	24	phone	200.0	500.0	NaN
6	16	apple	0.5	1.0	NaN
7	17	pear	0.6	1.2	NaN

Figure 2.7   **Graphical depiction of** `pd.concat([df, new_products])`

Now we have a data frame containing all our products. But because we didn't include the `sales` column in `new_products`, `sales` is missing some data:

```
product_id              name  wholesale_price  retail_price    sales
0          23          computer            500.0        1000.0    100.0
1          96    Python Workout             35.0          75.0   1000.0
2          97    Pandas Workout             35.0          75.0    500.0
3          15            banana              0.5           1.0    200.0
4          87          sandwich              3.0           5.0    300.0
5          24             phone            200.0         500.0      NaN
6          16             apple              0.5           1.0      NaN
7          17              pear              0.6           1.2      NaN
```

The challenge is to fill in those sales numbers. We can do this several ways. My preferred method is to use `loc` on the data frame, passing a list of rows as the row selector and the `sales` column's name as the column selector:

```
df.loc[[5,6,7], 'sales']
```

This returns

```
5    NaN
6    NaN
7    NaN
Name: sales, dtype: float64
```

Sure enough, we have identified and retrieved all three `NaN` values. Also note that the `dtype` for this column has been changed to `float64`. That's because `NaN` is a float value; whenever pandas wants to use `NaN`, it needs to set the column to have a floating-point `dtype`.

> **NOTE** In NumPy, assigning a float value to an array with an integer `dtype` results in the float being truncated silently. And trying to assign `NaN` (which is a float, albeit a weird float) to an array with an integer `dtype` results in an error, with NumPy indicating that there is no integer value for `NaN`. Pandas, by contrast, tries to accommodate you, changing the `dtype` to `float64` to accommodate your `NaN` value. It doesn't warn you about this, though! You won't lose data, but you may be surprised by the change in `dtype` you didn't explicitly ask for.

How can we set these `NaN` values to integers? One way is to use our `loc`-based retrieval to set values (figure 2.8):

```
df.loc[[5,6,7], 'sales'] = [100, 200, 75]
```

This one line of code is hiding a lot of complexity, so let's go through it:

1 `df.loc` accesses one or more rows from our data frame. In this case, we're using fancy indexing, retrieving three rows based on their indexes.

2 If we stopped here, we would get all the columns for these three rows—meaning we would get back a data frame. But instead, we pass a second argument, which describes the column(s) we want to get back.

3 Because it's only one column, we end up with a three-element series of NaN values.

4 Assigning to this df.loc selection results in the data frame being updated and the NaN values replaced by these numbers.

Note that the dtype does *not* change back to np.int64 automatically.

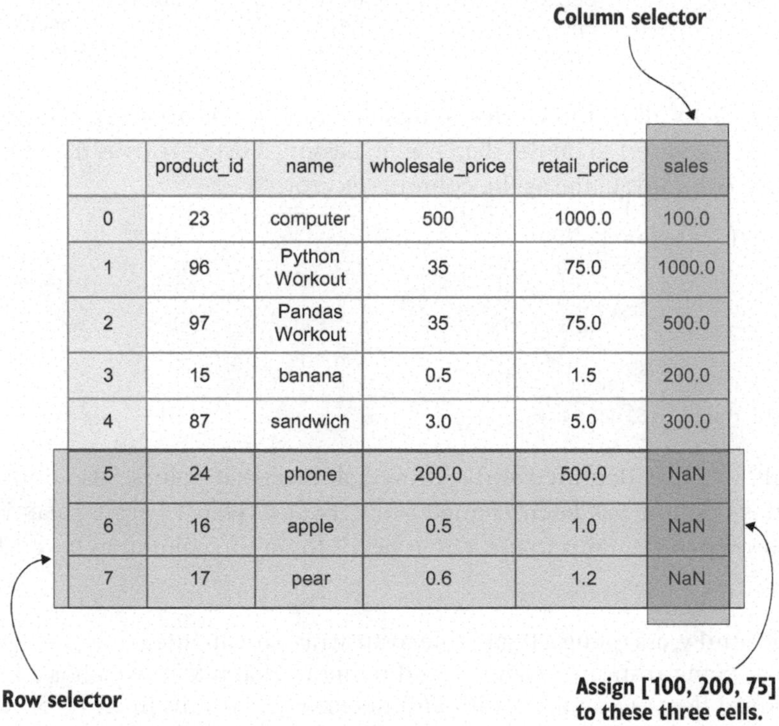

Figure 2.8   Graphical depiction of df.loc[[5,6,7], 'sales'] = [100, 200, 75]

If you're uncomfortable with such en masse assignments, you can do the equivalent in three lines:

```
df.loc[5, 'sales'] = 100
df.loc[6, 'sales'] = 200
df.loc[7, 'sales'] = 75
```

Either way, when we're done with all this, we have ensured that we have sales figures for all our products. And once we've done that, we can calculate the total sales, as we've done before:

```
(df['retail_price'] - df['wholesale_price']) * df['sales'].sum()
```

Solution

```
new_products = DataFrame([{'product_id':24, 'name':'phone',
        'wholesale_price': 200, 'retail_price':500},
                        {'product_id':16, 'name':'apple',
        'wholesale_price': 0.5, 'retail_price':1},
                        {'product_id':17, 'name':'pear',
        'wholesale_price': 0.6, 'retail_price':1.2}],
        index=range(5,8))
```
Creates the data frame of new products

```
df = pd.concat([df, new_products])
```
Adds the old and new products together into a single data frame

```
df.loc[[5,6,7], 'sales'] = [100, 200, 75]
```

```
(df['retail_price'] - df['wholesale_price']) * df['sales'].sum()
```

Assigns sales values for the three new products

Calculates the total net income from all products

You can explore this in the Pandas Tutor at http://mng.bz/9Q4l.

Beyond the exercise

- Add one new product to the data frame without using pd.concat. What's the advantage of pd.concat, and when should you use it?
- Add a new column, department, to the data frame. Place each product in a department. For example, in our data, we would have three departments: electronics, books, and food. Calculate current_net on the data frame, and then show descriptive statistics for the current_net on food products.
- Use the query method (see the following sidebar) to get the descriptive statistics for food items.

Getting answers with the query method

As we have seen, the traditional way to select rows from a data frame is via a boolean index. But there is another way to do it: the query method. This method may feel especially familiar if you have previously used SQL and relational databases.

The basic idea behind query is simple: we provide a string that pandas turns into a full-fledged query. We get back a filtered set of rows from the original data frame. For example, let's say we want all the rows in which column v is greater than 300. Using a traditional boolean index, we would write

```
df[df['v'] > 300]
```

Using query, we can instead write

```
df.query('v > 300')
```

These two techniques return the same results. When using query, though, we can name columns without the clunky square brackets or even dot notation. It becomes easier to understand.

(continued)

What if we want a more complex query, such as one in which column v is greater than 300 and column w is odd? We can write it as follows:

```
df.query('v > 300 & w % 2 == 1')
```

⟵ **& is used for "and" in the query string.**

It's not necessary, but I still like to use parentheses to make the query more readable:

```
df.query('(v > 300) & (w % 2 == 1)')
```

Note that query cannot be used on the left side of an assignment.

On smaller data frames, query can not only be overkill but also slow your code. However, when you work on data frames with more than 10,000 rows, query can be significantly faster than the traditional way of writing queries. Moreover, it can use far less memory. We'll look at query in greater depth in chapter 12.

EXERCISE 11 ▪ Bestsellers

You're going to use the online store for one final exercise. This time, I want you to find the IDs and names of products that have sold more than the average number of units.

Working it out

Pandas is all about analyzing data. And a major part of the analysis we do in pandas can be expressed as "Where *this* is the case, show me *that*." The possibilities are endless:

- Show me the stocks in our portfolio that have performed poorly this year.
- Show me the people on our team who have fixed the most bugs.
- Show me the three highest-scoring sports teams in the league.

In this exercise, I asked you to show the product_id and name columns for products that have sold better than average. As usual with pandas, there are several ways to do this—but I believe the easiest system to remember and work with involves the use of loc. (See "Retrieving and assigning with loc," earlier in this chapter.)

When we work with loc, we are, by definition, starting with the rows. We are interested in rows whose sales values are greater than the minimum. We can thus create a boolean series with the following query:

```
df['sales'] > df['sales'].mean()
```

We can then use that series as a boolean index on our data frame, returning only those rows where the sales figures were better than average:

```
df.loc[df['sales'] > df['sales'].mean()]
```

⟵ **Uses the boolean series as a row selector**

However, we aren't interested in all the columns in the data frame. We only want the `product_id` and `name` columns. We list the columns we want in the second argument to `loc` in our column selector:

```
df.loc[
    df['sales'] > df['sales'].mean(),      The boolean series
                                           is our row selector.
    ['product_id', 'name']                 The list of columns
    ]                                      is our column selector.
```

Sure enough, this produces the desired output (figure 2.9).

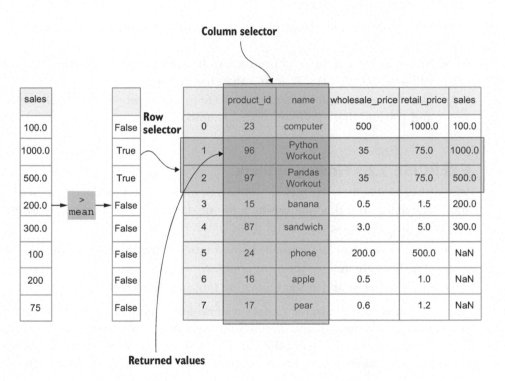

Figure 2.9 Graphical depiction of `df.loc[df['sales'] > df['sales'].mean(),` `['product_id', 'name']]`

It's also possible to solve this problem with the `query` method. Here's how we can get the appropriate rows:

```
df.query('sales > sales.mean()')
```

To get only the `product_id` and `name` columns, we need to apply square brackets to the result of `df.query`:

```
df.query('sales > sales.mean()')[['product_id', 'name']]
```

Solution

```
df.loc[
    df['sales'] > df['sales'].mean(),
    ['product_id', 'name']
]
```

You can explore this in the Pandas Tutor at http://mng.bz/j1zx.

Beyond the exercise

Here are some additional exercises that go beyond the task here. In each case, practice using both `loc` and `query`:

- Show the ID and name of products whose net income is in the top 25% quantile.
- Show the ID and name of products with lower-than-average sales numbers and whose wholesale price is greater than the average.
- Show the name and wholesale and retail prices of products with IDs between 80 and 100 and that sold fewer than 400 units.

EXERCISE 12 ▪ Finding outliers

We've already seen how the mean, standard deviation, and median can help us understand our data. They describe the bulk of our data, trying to summarize where most values lie. But sometimes it's useful to look at the unusual values:

- Which users had an unusually high number of unsuccessful login attempts?
- Which products were the most popular?
- On which days and at what times are our sales the lowest?

These questions aren't unique to data science. For example, bars have been offering "happy hour" for many years, discounting their products at a time when they have fewer customers. Data science allows us to ask these questions more formally, to get more precise answers, and then to check whether our changes have had the desired results.

> **NOTE** The term *outliers* doesn't have a precise, standard definition. Many people define it using the *interquartile range* (IQR), which is the value at the 75% point (aka `quantile(0.75)`) minus the value at the 25% point (aka `quantile(0.25)`). Outliers are then values below the 25% point $-1.5 * IQR$ or values above the 75% + 1.5 * IQR. We use that definition here, but you may find that a different definition—say, anything below the mean – two standard deviations, or above the mean + two standard deviations—is a better fit for your data.

In this exercise, you are to create a two-column data frame from the taxi data we looked at in exercise 6. The first column will contain the passenger count for each trip, and the second column will contain the distance (in miles) for each trip. Once you have created this data frame, I want you to

- Count how many trip distances were outliers.
- Calculate the mean number of passengers for outliers. Is it different from the mean number of passengers for all trips?

Working it out

We have to do four things:

1 Create the data frame based on the individual series.
2 Calculate the IQR.
3 Find the outliers.
4 Use the outliers we have found to analyze passenger counts.

To start, we want to create the data frame based on two separate series. We've already seen how to create each of these series, which we here assign to two separate variables:

```
trip_distance = pd.read_csv('data/taxi-distance.csv', header=None).squeeze()
passenger_count = pd.read_csv('data/taxi-passenger-count.csv',
    header=None).squeeze()
```

How can we turn these series into a data frame? The easiest technique is to create the data frame as a dict in which the keys are strings naming the columns and the values are the series themselves (figure 2.10). This technique works well when (as here) we have several lists or series containing data. Note that the series must be the same length, as is the case here.

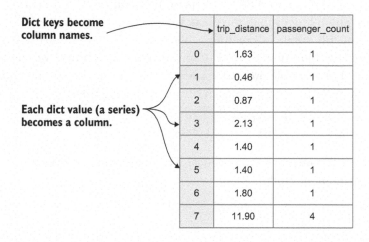

Figure 2.10 Graphical depiction of creating a data frame via a dictionary

Creating the data frame thus requires the following code:

```
df = DataFrame({'trip_distance': trip_distance,
                'passenger_count': passenger_count})
```

With the data frame in place, we can calculate the IQR and thus find our outliers. Remember that the IQR is the difference between the 75th percentile and 25th percentile values. This means if we were to line up all the values, from smallest to largest, we would be looking for the values 25% of the way through and 75% of the way through.

We can find these values using the `quantile` method and pass the point we want to get either 0.25 or 0.75. However, don't make the mistake of calling `quantile` on the data frame! Doing so will return the quantiles for each column; we're only interested in the IQR for the `trip_distance` column. We can thus say

```
iqr = (
    df['trip_distance'].quantile(0.75) -
    df['trip_distance'].quantile(0.25)
)
```

Of course, we didn't have to define an `iqr` variable, but it makes the later calculations easier to understand and read. And with the `iqr` variable defined, we can now find outliers. Let's start with outliers on the low end: distances less than the 25% quantile by at least 1.5 * the IQR. This is how that looks in pandas:

```
df[df['trip_distance'] < df['trip_distance'].quantile(0.25) - 1.5*iqr]
```

The result? There are no outliers! That's probably because so many trips go a short distance, and the lowest distance you can go in a taxi ride is zero miles.

However, there are several outliers at the high end:

```
df[df['trip_distance'] > df['trip_distance'].quantile(0.75) + 1.5*iqr]
```

Of these 10,000 taxi rides, there are 1,889 outliers on the high end! This means about 19% of taxi rides are much longer than the mean ride length.

Notice that we get this result by creating a boolean series and applying it as an index to `df`. However, we don't have to apply it to the entire data frame; we can apply it to a single column. For example, we can apply it to the `passenger_count` column, thus finding the number of passengers in each of the extra-long rides:

```
df['passenger_count'][df['trip_distance'] >
    df['trip_distance'].quantile(0.75) + 1.5*iqr]
```

What if we want to get the mean of these values? This expression returns a series on which we can run the `mean` method:

```
df['passenger_count'][df['trip_distance'] > df['trip_distance'].quantile(
    0.75) + 1.5*iqr].mean()
```

We end up with a value of about 1.70, almost identical to the mean of the entire `passenger_count` column.

Solution

```
trip_distance = pd.read_csv('data/taxi-distance.csv',
        header=None).squeeze()
passenger_count = pd.read_csv('data/taxi-passenger-count.csv',
        header=None).squeeze()

df = DataFrame({'trip_distance': trip_distance,
                'passenger_count': passenger_count})

iqr = (df['trip_distance'].quantile(0.75)
        - df['trip_distance'].quantile(0.25))

df[df['trip_distance']
    < df['trip_distance'].quantile(0.25) - 1.5*iqr]
df[df['trip_distance']
    > df['trip_distance'].quantile(0.75) + 1.5*iqr]
df['passenger_count'][df['trip_distance']
    > df['trip_distance'].quantile(0.75) + 1.5*iqr].mean()
```

There are no low outliers.

There are 1,889 high outliers.

Mean passenger count for outliers

You can explore an abridged version of this in the Pandas Tutor at http://mng
.bz/W1R0.

Beyond the exercise

As I said earlier, there are several ways to define and find outliers. Let's try a few different techniques:

- If you define outliers to be the lowest 10% and highest 10% of values, how many were there? Why is (or isn't) this a good measure?
- How many short, medium, and long trips had only one passenger? Note that data for passenger count and trip length are from the same data set, meaning the indexes are the same. If you're only interested in removing the non-outlier values, you can use the scipy.stats.trimboth function on your series. It takes a second argument: the proportion you want to cut from both the top and bottom.
- The scipy.stats.zscore function rescales and centers (that is, normalizes) the data set. In this case, the mean is set to 0, and values can be above and below that value. Find all the distances for which the absolute value of the z-score is greater than 3.

NaN **and missing data**

So far, we have seen that analyzing data with pandas isn't overly difficult. We need to know what questions to ask and which methods to apply in a given situation—but it's easy to imagine that a data analyst's job isn't too rough.

The time has come to give you some bad news: most data is incomplete. Perhaps the computer responsible for collecting data was down last week. Or maybe the sensors were off. Or possibly we surveyed our users and many decided not to answer.

(continued)

Whatever the reason, it's common for analysts to contend with missing values. (I've often heard analysts and data scientists say that 70%–80% of their job involves cleaning, scaling, and otherwise manipulating data so they can use it.) Although it would be nice to simply ignore those missing values, that's not always possible. If we remove any record with any missing data, we may find ourselves without any data at all, which is a problem.

How do we represent missing values in pandas? It's tempting to use 0, but as you can imagine, that would cause trouble when we tried to calculate mean values. Instead, pandas uses something known as `NaN`, aka *not a number*. You can say either `np.nan` or `np.NaN`; pandas traditionally prefers the second. No matter how you write it, it's still `np.nan`. This strange value is a float that cannot be converted into an integer and is not equal to itself.

Note that, as of this writing, the pandas core developers are suggesting that they will switch from `NaN` to their own `pd.NA` value in the future as part of a larger move to using internal pandas data types that will be more flexible than those from NumPy. However, we continue to use the traditional `NaN` value in this book.

In NumPy, we typically search for `NaN` values with the `isnan` function. Pandas has a different approach, though: we can replace the `NaN` values in a series (or data frame) with the `fillna` method, and we can drop any row with `NaN` values with the `dropna` method.

These methods return a new series or data frame rather than modifying the original object. However, the new object we get back may not have copied the data, meaning assigning to it may produce the famous, dreaded `SettingWithCopyWarning`. If you plan to modify the series or data frame that you get back from `df.dropna`, you should probably invoke the `copy` method, just to be safe:

```
df = df.dropna().copy()
```

This ensures that you can modify `df` without suffering from that warning.

As you can imagine, removing any row containing even a single `NaN` value may be extreme. For that reason, the `dropna` method has a `thresh` parameter to which we can pass an integer: the number of good, non-`NaN` values that a row must contain for it to be kept. You may need to seriously consider how strictly you want to filter your data.

We'll look more closely at how to clean data in chapter 5. For now, remember to look for `NaN` in your data and decide what you want to do with it. Sometimes you'll want to remove the `NaN` values, but other times, such as in exercise 13, you'll want to assign values based on their neighbors.

NOTE The `count` method on a series returns the number of non-`NaN` values. If there are no `NaN` values, the result is the same as the size of the series. The `count` method on a data frame returns a series with the columns' names as the index. If any of the columns have a lower `count` result than the others, it's because they contain `NaN` values.

EXERCISE 13 ■ Interpolation

When data contains missing values, we can remove any row containing even one missing value—but that may be too heavy-handed and may also remove useful data. One alternative is *interpolation*: replacing NaN with plausible values. The values may be wrong, but they will be roughly in the right ballpark.

In this exercise, we load some basic temperature data from New York City from the end of 2018 and the start of 2019. We then simulate a simple recurring equipment failure at 3:00 and 6:00 a.m. preventing us from getting temperature readings at those hours. How well does interpolation help us, and how far off are the interpolated mean and median calculations from the original, true values?

Here are the steps I want you to take:

1 Load the temperature data from New York City (from the nyc-temps.txt file) into a series. The measurements are in degrees Celsius.

2 Create a data frame with two columns: temp, with the temperatures, and hour, representing the hours at which the measurements were taken. The hour values should be 0, 3, 6, 9, 12, 15, 18, and 21, repeated for all 728 data points.

3 Calculate the mean and median values. These are the real values, which we hope to replicate via interpolation.

4 Set all values from 3:00 and 6:00 a.m. to NaN.

5 Interpolate the values with the interpolate method.

6 What are the mean and median of the interpolated data frame? Are they similar to the real values? Why or why not?

Working it out

The first task in this exercise is to read the data into a series. We've done this before, but it can't hurt to review the code:

```
s = pd.read_csv('data/nyc-temps.txt').squeeze()
```

We read the one-column data from nyc-temps.txt and then tell pandas we want it back as a series. (This will change in the next chapter when we start to read in complete data frames.) We can then use that series as one column in a series.

The other column, hour, needs to contain the values 0, 3, 6, 9, 12, 15, 18, and 21, repeated for the length of the data. Because the data contains 728 rows and there are 8 different hours, we can take advantage of some core Python functionality: we multiply the 8-element list of integers by 91 and get a list of 728 elements.

Once we have created our data frame, we remove some of the data to simulate outages at 3:00 and 6:00 a.m. We do this by selecting (with loc) the rows we want along with the temp column and replacing values with NaN with assignment:

```
df.loc[
    df['hour'].isin([3,6]), )        ◁──┐  Row selector, where
    'temp'        ◁──┐  Column            the hour is 3 or 6
] = NaN                  │  selector
```

Notice that this query has several pieces:

- We look for df['hour'] to be either 3 or 6 using isin, getting a boolean series back.
- After the comma, where we choose columns, we pass temp.
- We then use loc not to retrieve rows but rather to assign NaN to them en masse.

Finally, we call df.interpolate, which returns a new data frame (figure 2.11). In theory, all the columns will be interpolated—but in reality, there is missing data only in the temp column. We then assign the new data frame back to df.

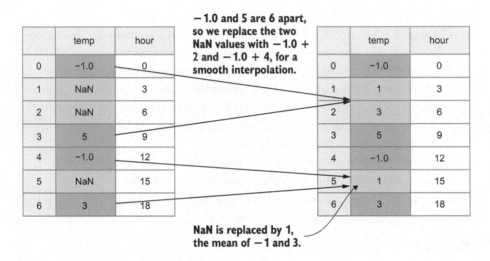

Figure 2.11 Graphical depiction of interpolate

By default, interpolate fills any NaN value with the average of the numbers that come before and after it. So if row 3 has a temperature of –1, row 4 is NaN, and row 5 has a temperature of 5, interpolate will replace NaN with a value of 2.0. If you have two NaN values in a row, interpolate will replace each NaN with half the distance between the preceding non-NaN value and the succeeding non-NaN value.

> **NOTE** By passing a value to the method parameter, you can instruct interpolate to use a different system for interpolation. For example, if you pass method='nearest', NaN values will be replaced by the closest non-NaN value. Other methods are discussed in the documentation at http://mng.bz/MBo7.

Because temperature values don't vary much from hour to hour and can be assumed to rise and fall on a continuum, we use the default *linear* method, which is probably close to the actual values. By contrast, hourly temperature readings from the oven in your kitchen cannot be interpolated reliably this way. Before you use interpolate, consider whether it's an appropriate way to fill in NaN values.

Solution

```
s = pd.read_csv('data/nyc-temps.txt').squeeze()
df = DataFrame(
    {'temp': s,
     'hour': [0,3,6,9,12,15,18,21] * 91})
df.loc[
    df['hour'].isin([3,6]),
    'temp'
] = NaN

df = df.interpolate()

df['temp'].describe()
```

Reads the disk file into a series

Creates a data frame using the series and the hours

Sets everything at hours 3 and 6 to NaN

Runs df.interpolate, and assigns back to df

Gets the descriptive statistics to check the mean and median (among others)

You can explore an abridged version of this in the Pandas Tutor at http://mng .bz/84vP.

Beyond the exercise

- How does the behavior of `interpolate` change if you use `method='nearest'`?
- Let's assume the equipment works fine around the clock but fails to record readings at −1 degrees and below. Are the interpolated values similar to the real (missing) values they replace? Why or why not?
- A cheap solution to interpolation is to replace `NaN` values with the column's mean. Do this (with the missing values from −1 and below), and compare the new mean and median. Again, why are (or aren't) these values similar to the original ones?

EXERCISE 14 ■ Selective updating

In this exercise, I want you to create the same two-column data frame as in the last exercise. Then, update the values in the `temp` column so that any value less than 0 is set to 0.

Working it out

If you're like many pandas users, you may have thought about an approach like this:

1. Get a boolean index for when `df['temp']` is less than 0.
2. Apply that boolean index to the data frame.
3. Retrieve the column by using `['temp']` on the data frame.
4. Assign the new value.

The code would look like this:

```
df[df['temp'] < 0]['temp'] = 0
```

Logically, this makes perfect sense. There's just one problem: you cannot know in advance whether it will work. That's because pandas does a lot of internal analysis and optimization when it's putting together queries. Thus, you cannot know whether your assignment will change the `temp` column on `df`, or—and this is the important thing—whether pandas has decided to cache the results of your first query, applying `['temp']` to that cached, internal value rather than to the original one.

As a result, it's common—and maddening!—to get a `SettingWithCopyWarning` from pandas. It looks like this:

```
<ipython-input-2-acedf13a3438>:1: SettingWithCopyWarning:
A value is trying to be set on a copy of a slice from a DataFrame.
Try using .loc[row_indexer,col_indexer] = value instead
```

When you get this warning, it's because pandas is trying to be helpful, telling you that your assignment may have no effect. The warning, by the way, isn't telling you that the assignment *won't* work, because it may. It all depends on the amount of data you have and how pandas thinks it can or should optimize things.

The telltale sign that you may get this warning is the use of double square brackets—not nested, with one pair inside the other, but with one right after the other. Whenever you see `] [` in pandas queries, you should try hard to avoid it because it may spell trouble when you assign to it. Retrieving with this syntax will also be less efficient than using `loc` with the "row selector, column selector" selection syntax we've seen and discussed.

So, how *should* we set these values? It's pretty straightforward:

1 Use `df.loc` to start.
2 Put our boolean index for the rows inside the square brackets, as before.
3 Put our column selector, which is `'temp'` in this case, inside the same square brackets, following a comma.
4 Assign to that value.

Here it is, broken up across lines:

```
df.loc[
    df['temp'] < 0,          ◁──┐ Row selector:
    'temp'          ◁──┐        │ a boolean series
] = 0               └─── Column selector:
                         a column name
```

If you use this syntax for all your assignments, you will never see that dreaded `SettingWithCopyWarning` message. You'll be able to use the same syntax for retrieval and assignment. And you can even be sure things are running pretty efficiently.

Solution

```
df.loc[df['temp'] < 0, 'temp']  = 0
```

You can explore an abridged version of this in the Pandas Tutor at http://mng.bz/ E9zJ.

Beyond the exercise

- Set all the odd temperatures to the mean of all the temperatures.
- Set the even temperatures at hours 9 and 18 to 3.
- If the hour is odd, set the temperature to 5.

Summary

In this chapter, we started to work with data frames—creating them, adding data to them, retrieving data from them, analyzing them, and even cleaning up when data is missing. These techniques and those from the previous chapter are the building blocks on which we work with data in pandas. In the next chapter, we'll tackle more complex scenarios using data from the real world.

Importing and exporting data

So far, we've been creating data frames manually or using random values. In the real world, data frames contain actual, useful values, typically imported from CSV files, Excel spreadsheets, or relational databases. Similarly, when we're done analyzing data, we want to share our analysis by saving data to files in those (or other) formats.

In this chapter, we explore how to import data from various formats, emphasizing CSV files because they're so common. We look at ways in which we can not only read from such files but also customize the reading either to improve the quality of our data or optimize the process.

Table 3.1   What you need to know

Concept	What is it?	Example	To learn more
`pd.read_csv`	Returns a new data frame based on CSV input	`df = pd.read_csv ('myfile.csv')`	http://mng.bz/wvl7
`df.to_csv`	Writes a data frame to a CSV-formatted file or string	`df.to_csv ('myfile.csv')`	http://mng.bz/7Dzx
`pd.read_json`	Returns a new data frame based on JSON input	`df = pd.read_json ('myfile.json')`	http://mng.bz/mV4n
`df.corr`	Shows the correlations among the columns	`df.corr()`	http://mng.bz/6DQG
`df.dropna`	Returns a new data frame without any `NaN` values	`df.dropna()`	http://mng.bz/o1PN

Table 3.1 **What you need to know** *(continued)*

Concept	What is it?	Example	To learn more
df.loc	Retrieves selected rows and columns	df.loc[df['trip_ distance'] > 10, 'passenger_count']	http://mng.bz/nWPv
pd.read_html	Returns a list of data frames based on HTML input	df = df.read_html ('https://a-site.com')	http://mng.bz/vnxx
s.value_counts	Returns a sorted (descending frequency) series counting how many times each value appears in s	s.value_counts()	http://mng.bz/yQyJ
s.round	Returns a new series based on s in which the values are rounded to the specified number of decimals.	s.round(2)	http://mng.bz/QPym
df.memory_usage	Indicates how many bytes are being used by a data frame and its associated data	df.memory_usage()	http://mng.bz/XNPY
pd.Series.idxmin	Returns the index of the lowest value in a series	s.idxmin()	http://mng.bz/ZR6Z
pd.Series.idxmax	Returns the index of the highest value in a series	s.idxmax()	http://mng.bz/RmrP
pd.DataFrame.agg	Invokes one or more aggregation methods on a data frame	df.idxmax(['min', 'max'])	http://mng.bz/27QX

CSV, the nonstandard standard

Computer scientist Andrew S. Tanenbaum once said, "The good thing about standards is that there are so many to choose from." In many ways, the same can be said for files in comma-separated values (CSV) format, which are the overwhelming favorite in the world of data. Sure, plenty of people use Excel and relational databases, but if you download a data set from the internet, odds are it's a CSV file.

At its heart, CSV assumes that your data can be described as a two-dimensional table. The rows are represented as rows in the file, and the columns are separated by . . . well, they're separated by commas, at least by default. CSV files are text files, meaning you can read (and edit) them without special tools.

For all its popularity, CSV doesn't have a formal specification. There is a Request for Comments (RFC; 4110, available at https://datatracker.ietf.org/doc/html/rfc4180),

(continued)

but it's informational, from 2005. And although we can generally agree on what constitutes legal CSV, many variants and gray areas make writing and parsing CSV difficult or at least ambiguous.

Rather than take a stand on how CSV files should be formatted, pandas tries to be open and flexible. When we read from a CSV file (with `pd.read_csv`) or write a data frame to CSV (with `df.to_csv`), we can choose from many, *many* parameters, each of which can affect how it is written. Among the most common are these:

- `sep`—The field separator, which is (perhaps obviously) a comma by default but can often be a tab (`'\t'`)
- `header`—Whether there are headers describing column names and on which line of the file they appear
- `index_col`—Which column, if any, should be set to be the index of our data frame
- `usecols`—Which columns from the file should be included in the data frame

For example, we can say

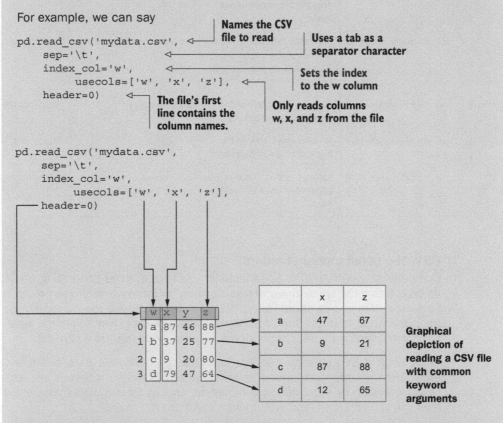

```
pd.read_csv('mydata.csv',
    sep='\t',
    index_col='w',
        usecols=['w', 'x', 'z'],
    header=0)
```

Names the CSV file to read

Uses a tab as a separator character

Sets the index to the w column

Only reads columns w, x, and z from the file

The file's first line contains the column names.

```
pd.read_csv('mydata.csv',
    sep='\t',
    index_col='w',
        usecols=['w', 'x', 'z'],
    header=0)
```

Graphical depiction of reading a CSV file with common keyword arguments

It's worth looking through the documentation for `pd.read_csv`, in no small part because the sheer number of parameters will likely overwhelm you the first time you try to understand what you can configure and how. We'll explore several of these parameters in this book, but many that we don't cover may be useful in your work.

NOTE When teaching data science, I often use the phrase "know your data." That's because it's important to know as much about your data as possible before willy-nilly reading it into memory. You probably don't want to load all the columns into pandas. And you may want to specify the type of data in each column rather than let pandas just guess. Most data sets come with a "data dictionary," a file that describes the columns, their types, their meanings, and their ranges. It's almost always worth your while to examine a data dictionary when starting to analyze the data. In many cases, the dictionary will give you insights that will help you decide what and how you want to read into pandas.

EXERCISE 15 ■ Weird taxi rides

When I was growing up, taking a taxi in New York City was pretty simple: you hailed a cab and told the driver where you wanted to go. When you got there, you paid whatever was on the meter, added a tip, and got a receipt. Of course, the payment was in cash.

Nowadays, things are a bit different: New York taxis have TV screens on which they show advertisements and something resembling entertainment. But those screens aren't just there to annoy you; they also function as credit card terminals, allowing you to use your card to pay for your trip and even add a tip. The screens are also computers, storing information about the trip and sending it to the Taxi and Limousine Commission (TLC), the city department that regulates taxis. The TLC then uses this information to make decisions regarding transportation policy.

Fortunately for the world of data science, the data collected by New York taxis is also available to us, the general public. We can retrieve information about every trip made over the last decade or so, learning where people went, how much they spent, how they paid, and even how much they tipped. This is one of my favorite data sets, so we'll use it quite a bit in this book. In particular, we'll look at several columns from the data set:

- `passenger_count`—The number of passengers who took that taxi ride.
- `trip_distance`—The distance traveled in miles.
- `total_amount`—The total owed to the driver, including the fare, tolls, taxes, and tip.
- `payment_type`—An integer number describing how the passenger paid for the trip. The most important values are 1 (credit card) and 2 (cash).

For this exercise, I want you to create a data frame from the CSV data for January 2019:

1. Load the CSV file into a data frame using only the four columns mentioned earlier: `passenger_count`, `trip_distance`, `payment_type`, and `total_amount`.
2. How many taxi rides had more than eight passengers?
3. How many taxi rides had zero passengers?
4. How many taxi rides were paid for in cash and cost over $1,000?
5. How many rides cost less than $0?
6. How many rides traveled a below-average distance but cost an above-average amount?

> **NOTE**   Why do we read CSV files with the `pd.read_csv` function rather than with a method on an existing data frame? Because the goal of `read_csv` is to create (and return) a new data frame based on the contents of the CSV file, not to modify or update the contents of an existing one.

Working it out

To solve this problem, we first need to create a new data frame from the CSV file. Fortunately, the data is formatted in such a way that `pd.read_csv` works fine with its defaults, returning a data frame with named columns. But this file contains a lot of data—7,667,792 rides, to be exact—and if we only keep the columns we need, we reduce the memory footprint a lot. (I found that loading only the columns I asked for reduced memory usage from 2.4 GB to 234 MB. We'll talk more about optimizing and measuring memory usage in Chapter 10.)

The `usecols` parameter to `pd.read_csv` allows us to select which columns from the CSV file will be kept around. The parameter takes a list as an argument, which can either contain integers (indicating the numeric index of each column) or strings representing the column names. I generally prefer to use strings because they're more readable, and that's what I did here.

The result was a data frame with four columns and more than 7.6 million rows, each representing one taxi ride in New York City during January 2019. With that data in hand, we can start answering the questions asked by this exercise.

For starters, we wanted to know how many taxi rides had more than eight passengers. The standard way to get this information is to create a boolean series with our query and then apply it as an index. We can find all rows in which there were more than eight passengers with

```
df['passenger_count'] > 8
```

We can then apply the boolean series as a mask index to the entire data frame via the `loc` accessor:

```
df.loc[df['passenger_count'] > 8]
```

We can even run the `count` method on every column in the data frame:

```
df.loc[df['passenger_count'] > 8].count()
```

Counting (and ignoring) NaN

When we run `count` on a series, we get back a single integer indicating how many non-NaN values are in that series. When we run it on a data frame, we get back a series in which the index represents the data frame's columns and the numbers indicate how many non-NaN values are in each column. For example:

```
s = Series([10, 20, np.NaN, 40, 50])
s.count()
```

The result of this code is 4. However, the result of the following code is a series:

```
df = DataFrame([[10, 20, np.NaN, 40],
                [50, np.NaN, np.NaN, np.NaN],
                [np.NaN, 60, 70, 80]],
    index=list('abc'),
    columns=list('wxyz'))
df.count()
```

The series shows the number of non-NaN values in each column:

```
w    2
x    2
y    1
z    2
dtype: int64
```

Right now, we're only interested in the passenger_count column and in calculating how many such rides there were. We can thus trim the columns by using loc:

```
df.loc[df['passenger_count'] > 8,          ◄—
    'passenger_count'              ◄—
    ].count()   ◄—
```

Row selector: only rows with more than nine passengers

Column selector: only the passenger_count column

How many non-NaN values are there?

Sure enough, this tells us that in January 2019, there were nine trips with more than eight people, as we can see in figure 3.1. (I hope they took place in larger-than-usual taxis.)

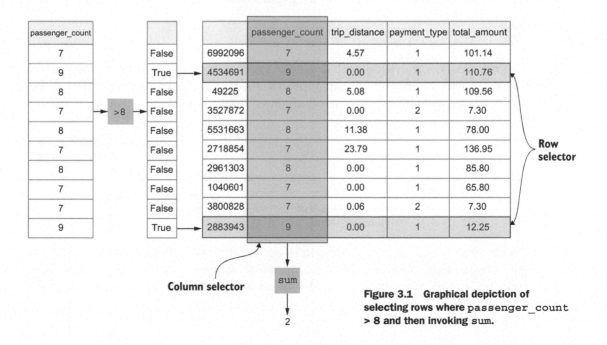

Figure 3.1 Graphical depiction of selecting rows where passenger_count > 8 and then invoking sum.

Next, how many taxi rides in January 2019 had zero passengers? I would guess that if there aren't any passengers, the taxi is being used as a package-delivery service. Or perhaps the driver simply neglected to enter that information; the data dictionary provided by New York City indicates that the number of passengers is entered manually by the driver, which makes it far more error-prone.

Once again, we can query `passenger_count`:

```
df['passenger_count'] == 0
```

This gives us a boolean series, which we can use in another query that uses `loc` and a column selector, along with a call to `count`:

```
df.loc[df['passenger_count'] == 0,     ←──┐  Row selector, looking
    'passenger_count'         ←─────────────┐ for zero passengers
    ].count()    ←──┐ How many non-NaN      │ Column selector: just
                      values are there?       passenger_count
```

There were 117,381 such rides. This sounds like a lot, but it turns out to be only 1.5% of all rides taken that month.

Although it's true that most people pay for taxi rides using credit cards, some still pay cash for various reasons. How many rides that month were paid for in cash and had a `total_amount` of more than $1,000?

This question is a bit harder to answer because we need to combine two different boolean series. The first will find rides in which the payment method was cash (i.e., 2), and the second will find `total_amount` greater than 1,000. We can then join the two together using `&`:

```
(df['payment_type'] == 2) & (df['total_amount'] > 1000)
```

This returns a boolean series with a value of `True` for every index where both are `True` and `False` everywhere else. We can apply it to the data frame using `loc`, retrieving the `total_amount` column via the second argument and then calling `count` on it (figure 3.2):

```
                                              Row selector: looking for cash
                                              payments of at least $1,000
df.loc[(df['payment_type'] == 2) & (df['total_amount'] > 1000),    ←──
    'passenger_count'      ←──────────────┐  Column selector: looking
    ].count()    ←──┐ How many non-NaN     │ for passenger count
                      values are there?
```

I got a result of 5. I may be extreme in using very little cash, but I was still shocked to discover that there were *any* rides paid for in cash with such a large amount of money. Granted, it's only a handful of taxi rides, but still—can you imagine pulling $1,000 out of your wallet to pay for a taxi?

But I digress.

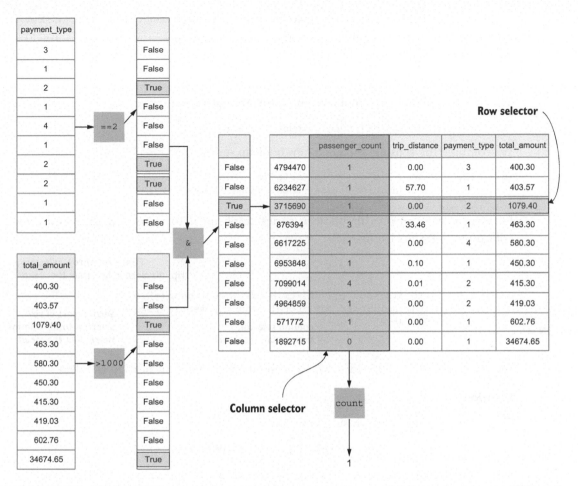

Figure 3.2   Graphical depiction of selecting rows where `payment_type == 2` and `total_amount > 1000`, and counting the elements of `passenger_count`

Next, I asked you to find rides that cost less than \$0. This would presumably mean the rider got a refund, but there could be other reasons, such as overpayment for a previous ride. How many such rides took place in January 2019?

Once again, we use a query to create a boolean series:

```
df['total_amount'] < 0
```

We apply this boolean series as a mask index on the `total_amount` column and run `count`:

```
df.loc[df['total_amount'] < 0, 'total_amount'].count()
```

The total is 7,131, meaning only .01% of all taxi rides gave money back. These are better odds than the lottery, but probably not a good idea if you're looking for a new career.

Finally, I asked how many trips traveled a below-average distance but cost an above-average amount. To solve this, we once again need to find all the trips that traveled a below-average distance:

```
df['trip_distance'] < df['trip_distance'].mean()
```

Then we find all the trips that cost an above-average amount:

```
df['total_amount'] > df['total_amount'].mean()
```

We combine them using `&` to get a new boolean series:

```
(df['trip_distance'] < df['trip_distance'].mean()) &
    (df['total_amount'] > df['total_amount'].mean())
```

Finally, we use `loc` on this boolean series, applying it to `trip_distance` and then counting the results (figure 3.3):

First part of row selector: trip_distance is less than the mean

```
df.loc[(df['trip_distance'] < df['trip_distance'].mean()) &
    (df['total_amount'] > df['total_amount'].mean()),
    'trip_distance'
].count()
```

Count the non-NaN value

column selector, trip_distance column

Second part of row selector, total_amount is more than the mean

We get a total of 411,255 rides, which is about 5% of the total rides in the data set.

Solution

```
df = pd.read_csv('../data/nyc_taxi_2019-01.csv',
                usecols=['passenger_count', 'trip_distance',
                         'total_amount', 'payment_type'])

df.loc[df['passenger_count'] > 8, 'passenger_count'].count()
df.loc[df['passenger_count'] == 0, 'passenger_count'].count()
df.loc[(df['payment_type'] == 2) & (df['total_amount'] > 1000),
       'passenger_count'].count()
df.loc[df['total_amount'] < 0, 'total_amount'].count()
df.loc[(df['trip_distance'] < df['trip_distance'].mean()) &
       (df['total_amount'] > df['total_amount'].mean()), 'trip_distance'].cou
    nt()
```

You can explore this in the Pandas Tutor at http://mng.bz/0lvN.

Beyond the exercise

- Repeat this exercise using the `query` method rather than a boolean index and `loc`.
- How many rides that cost less than $0 involved either a dispute (`payment_type` of 4) or a voided trip (`payment_type` of 6)?
- I stated earlier that most people pay for taxi rides using a credit card. Show this, and find what percentage normally pays in cash versus a credit card.

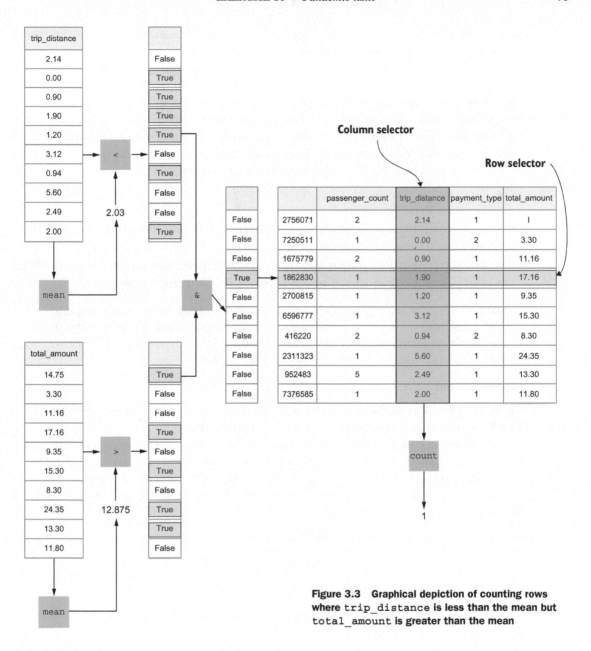

Figure 3.3 Graphical depiction of counting rows where `trip_distance` is less than the mean but `total_amount` is greater than the mean

EXERCISE 16 ■ Pandemic taxis

Not surprisingly, the coronavirus pandemic that caused widespread illness, death, and economic havoc around the world starting in early 2020 affected taxi rides in New York. In this exercise, we look at how we can load data from multiple files into a single data frame and then make some simple comparisons between data before the pandemic and while New York was in the middle of it.

In this exercise, I want you to create a data frame from two different CSV files containing New York taxi data: one from July 2019 (before the pandemic) and a second from July 2020 (near the height of the pandemic, at least in New York). The data frame should contain three columns from the files: `passenger_count`, `total_amount`, and `payment_type`. It should also include a fifth column, `year`, which should be set to 2019 or 2020, depending on the file from which the data was loaded.

With that data in hand, I want you to answer a few questions:

- How many rides were taken in 2019 and 2020, and what is the difference between these two figures?
- How much money (in total) was collected in 2019 and 2020, and what was the difference between these two figures?
- Did the proportion of trips with more than one passenger change dramatically?
- Did people use cash (i.e., `payment_type` of 2) less in 2020 than in 2019?

NOTE There are some great techniques in pandas having to do with grouping and date-time parsing that would make it easier to solve these problems. We'll discuss those techniques in chapters 6, 7, and 10, respectively. For now, see if you can answer the questions without such assistance.

Working it out

There are countless ways to measure the pandemic's effect on our lives and our world. I find that this data set provides some interesting insights.

For starters, I wanted you to take information from two different files and join them into a single data frame. We saw in Chapter 1 how to use `pd.concat` to combine two existing series objects into a single series. It turns out you can also use `pd.concat` on data frames, which is what we want to do here. We can load the data into two separate data frames and combine them:

```
df_2019_jul = pd.read_csv('../data/nyc_taxi_2019-07.csv',
              usecols=['passenger_count',
                    'total_amount', 'payment_type'])

df_2020_jul = pd.read_csv('../data/nyc_taxi_2020-07.csv',
              usecols=['passenger_count',
                    'total_amount', 'payment_type'])

df = pd.concat([df_2019_jul, df_2020_jul])
```

If we were only interested in getting aggregate answers, that would be enough. But we want to separate the answers by year via a `year` column. My preferred solution is to add a new column to each of the file-based data frames and then concatenate them (figure 3.4):

```
df_2019_jul = pd.read_csv('../data/nyc_taxi_2019-07.csv',
              usecols=['passenger_count',
```

```
                                'total_amount', 'payment_type'])
    df_2019_jul['year'] = 2019
```

Adds a year column
with a value of 2019
to all rows from 2019

```
    df_2020_jul = pd.read_csv('../data/nyc_taxi_2020-07.csv',
                usecols=['passenger_count',
                         'total_amount', 'payment_type'])
    df_2020_jul['year'] = 2020
```

Adds a year column
with a value of 2020
to all rows from 2020

```
    df = pd.concat([df_2019_jul, df_2020_jul])
```

Creates df,
combining both
data frames

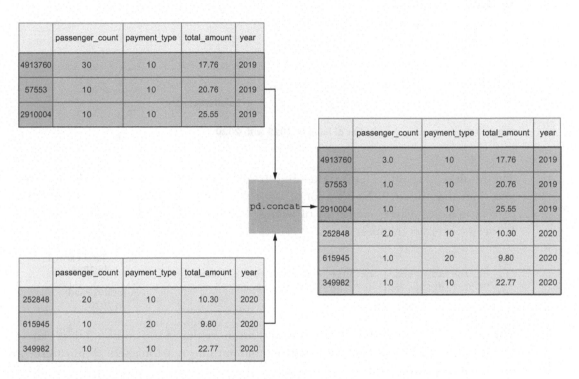

Figure 3.4   Concatenating two data frames into a single one

Once we have done that, we have a single data frame, df, to ask questions. For starters, we want to know how many rides were taken in 2019 versus 2020. That can be done by invoking count on any of our columns, subtracting the 2020 count from the 2019 count (figure 3.5):

```
(
    df.loc[df['year'] == 2019, 'total_amount'].count() -
    df.loc[df['year'] == 2020, 'total_amount'].count()
)
```

Number of
rides in 2019

Number of
rides in 2020

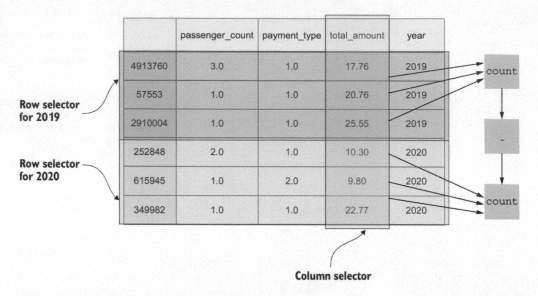

Figure 3.5   Comparing the number of rides in 2019 with 2020

The result is 5,510,007. That's right—in July 2020, New Yorkers took 5.5 million fewer taxi rides than in 2019. That's a lot of taxi rides. But how much less money did taxi drivers make as a result? Instead of using `count`, we use `sum` to total the numbers before we subtract them:

```
(
    df.loc[df['year'] == 2019, 'total_amount'].sum() -     ← Total earned in 2019
    df.loc[df['year'] == 2020, 'total_amount'].sum()     ← Total earned in 2020
)
```

The answer that I get is 108848979.24000001, or more than $108 million. I don't know about you, but I look at that huge number and am simply astonished. (You can see a graphical depiction of this in figure 3.6.)

> ### Rounding floats
> If you're bothered by the long number of numbers after the decimal point, you can use the `round` method on a series to limit it to two digits:
>
> ```
> df.loc[df['year'] == 2019, 'total_amount'].sum().round(2) -
>     df.loc[df['year'] == 2020, 'total_amount'].sum().round(2)
> ```

It makes sense that the number of trips declined during the pandemic. However, we may ask if people's behavior changed, as well. For example, given that the pandemic was in full swing during July 2020 and there wasn't yet a vaccine, people were avoiding

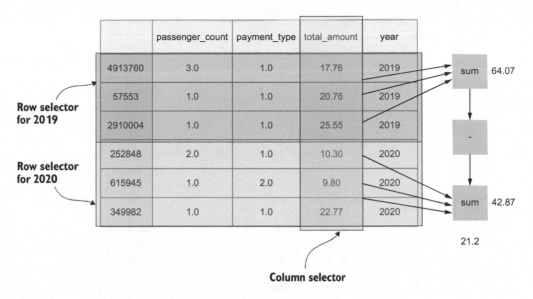

Figure 3.6 Comparing the total amount earned in 2019 with 2020

each other to a large degree. As a result, we may wonder whether people were less likely to take taxis with other people. The next question asked you to compare the proportion (not a raw number) of multiperson taxi rides in 2019 with those in 2020. To do that, we can divide the number of multiperson rides by the number of overall rides. Here's how we do that:

```
                                                         Number of rides in 2019
                                                              with > 1 passenger
df.loc[
    (df['year'] == 2019) &
    (df['passenger_count'] > 1), 'passenger_count'].count() /
        df.loc[df['year'] == 2019, 'payment_type'].count()
```

Total number of rides in 2019

```
                                                         Number of rides in 2020
                                                              with > 1 passenger
df.loc[
    (df['year'] == 2020) &
    (df['passenger_count'] > 1), 'passenger_count'].count() /
        df.loc[df['year'] == 2020, 'payment_type'].count()
```

Total number of rides in 2020

I get about 28% in 2019 and 21% in 2020, meaning people were less likely to share a taxi during the pandemic. Another interpretation would be that there were fewer family vacations and trips in New York, raising the proportion of single passengers commuting to work.

Finally, we want to know whether people were more or less likely to use cash during the pandemic, given that we were trying to avoid physical contact. Here's how we can calculate that (figure 3.7):

```
df.loc[
    (df['year'] == 2019) &
```

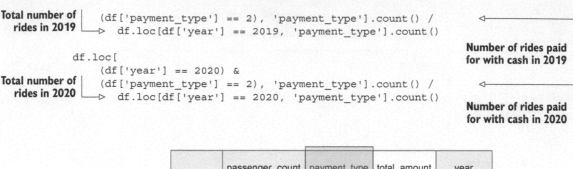

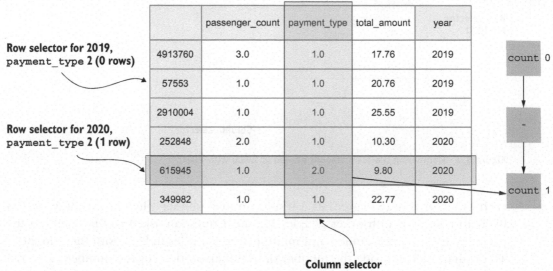

Figure 3.7 Comparing the number of cash payments in 2019 with 2020

Here, the answer is a bit surprising. In July 2019, about 29% of the trips were paid for in cash. But in July 2020, that number went up to 32%—exactly the opposite direction of what I expected, given that many people preferred contactless payment. One theory, floated by members of my family, is that the only people going to work during the pandemic were those who had to do so, the so-called "essential workers." They tend to earn less money and use more cash. Regardless of the reason, the numbers bear out the increased use of cash.

Solution

```
df_2019_jul = pd.read_csv('../data/nyc_taxi_2019-07.csv',
                usecols=['passenger_count',
                    'total_amount', 'payment_type'])
df_2019_jul['year'] = 2019

df_2020_jul = pd.read_csv('../data/nyc_taxi_2020-07.csv',
                usecols=['passenger_count',
                    'total_amount', 'payment_type'])
df_2020_jul['year'] = 2020
```

```
df = pd.concat([df_2019_jul, df_2020_jul])

df.loc[df['year'] == 2019, 'total_amount'].count() - df.loc[df['year'] ==
2020, 'total_amount'].count()
df.loc[df['year'] == 2019, 'total_amount'].sum() - df.loc[df['year'] ==
2020, 'total_amount'].sum()

df.loc[(df['year'] == 2019) &
       (df['passenger_count'] > 1), 'passenger_count'].count() /
          df.loc[df['year'] == 2019, 'payment_type'].count()
df.loc[(df['year'] == 2020) &
       (df['passenger_count'] > 1), 'passenger_count'].count() /
          df.loc[df['year'] == 2020, 'payment_type'].count()

df.loc[(df['year'] == 2019) &
       (df['payment_type'] == 2), 'payment_type'].count() /
          df.loc[df['year'] == 2019, 'payment_type'].count()
df.loc[(df['year'] == 2020) &
       (df['payment_type'] == 2), 'payment_type'].count() /
          df.loc[df['year'] == 2020, 'payment_type'].count()
```

You can explore this in the Pandas Tutor at http://mng.bz/g7jE.

Beyond the exercise

- Use the `corr` method on `df` to find the correlations among the columns. How would you interpret these results?
- Show, with a single command, the difference in descriptive statistics for `total_amount` between 2019 and 2020. Round values to use no more than two digits after the decimal point.
- If we assume that zero-passenger trips are for delivering packages, how were those affected during the pandemic? Show the proportion of such trips in 2019 versus 2020.

Data frames and dtype

In Chapter 1, we saw that every series has as `dtype` describing the type of data it contains. We can retrieve this data using the `dtype` attribute, and we can tell pandas what `dtype` to use when creating a series using the `dtype` parameter when we invoke the `Series` class.

In a data frame, each column is a separate pandas series and thus has its own `dtype`. By retrieving the `dtypes` (notice the plural!) attributes from a data frame, we can determine the `dtype` of each column. This information and additional details about the data frame are also available by invoking the `info` method on our data frame.

When we read data from a CSV file, pandas tries to infer each column's `dtype`. Remember that CSV files are really text files, so pandas has to examine the data to choose the best `dtype`. It will choose one of three types:

- If the values can all be turned into integers, it chooses `int64`.

(continued)

- If the values can all be turned into floats—which includes NaN—it chooses float64.
- Otherwise, it chooses object, meaning core Python objects.

However, there are several problems with letting pandas analyze and choose the data this way. First, although these default choices aren't bad, they can be overly large for many values. We often don't need 64-bit numbers, so choosing int64 or float64 will waste memory.

The second problem is much more subtle: if pandas is to correctly guess the dtype for a column, it must examine all the values in that column. But if a column has millions of rows, that process can use a huge amount of memory. For this reason, read_csv reads the file into memory in pieces, examining each piece in turn and then creating a single data frame from all of them. You normally won't know it's happening; pandas does this to save memory.

This can potentially lead to a problem, if pandas finds (for example) values that look like integers at the top of the file and values that look like strings at the bottom. In such a case, you end up with a dtype of object and with values of different types. This is almost certainly bad, and pandas warns you about it with a DtypeWarning. If you load the New York City taxi data from January 2020 into pandas without specifying usecols, you may well get this warning—I often did, on my computer.

One way to avoid this mixed-dtype problem is to tell pandas not to skimp on memory and that it's okay to examine all the data. You can do that by passing a False value to the low_memory parameter in read_csv. By default, low_memory is set to True, resulting in the behavior I've described here. But remember that setting low_memory to False may use lots of memory, a potentially big problem if your data set is large.

A better solution is to tell pandas that you don't want it to guess the dtype and that you would rather tell it explicitly. You can do that by passing a dtype parameter to read_csv with a Python dictionary as its argument. The dict's keys will be strings, the names of the columns being read from disk, and the values will be the data types you want to use. It's typical to use data types from pandas and NumPy, but if you specify int or float, pandas will simply use np.int64 or np.float64. And if you specify str, pandas will store the data as Python strings, assigning a dtype of object.

For example:

```
df_2019_jul = pd.read_csv('../data/nyc_taxi_2019-07.csv',
                usecols=['passenger_count',
                      'total_amount', 'payment_type'],
                dtype={'passenger_count':np.int8,
                      'total_amount':np.float32,
                      'payment_type':np.int8})
```

Finally, it's often tempting to set an integer dtype. But remember that if the column contains NaN, it cannot be defined as an integer dtype. Instead, you'll need to read the column as floating-point data, remove or interpolate the NaN values, and then convert the column (using astype) to the integer type you want.

EXERCISE 17 ■ Setting column types

Once again, I want you to create a data frame based on New York taxi data from January 2020. This time, however, I want to ensure that the data is in the most appropriate and compact form it can be and will use as little memory as possible when being loaded. So, I want you to do the following:

- Specify the `dtype` for each column as you read it in.
- Identify rows containing `NaN` values. Which columns are `NaN`, and why?
- Remove any rows containing any `NaN` values.
- Set the `dtype` for each column to the smallest, most appropriate value.

Working it out

Although this exercise is ostensibly about setting the `dtype` when reading from files, there is much more to it—in particular, we begin to see that cleaning data and setting appropriate data types can be a multistep process.

We start by reading the data from January 2020, much as we did before, with `read_csv`. However, this time I want you to specify the `dtype` of each column. In theory, the best choices for the `dtype` assignments are `int8` for both `passenger_count` and `payment_type`, because both are integers that won't ever go above 128.

But if we try to set the `dtype` for `passenger_count` and `payment_type` to `int8`, we quickly discover a problem: pandas raises an error, indicating that there are `NaN` values in those columns. Because `NaN` is a float that cannot be converted into an integer, we need to keep those columns as floats. So, we can use `float32` for now and then switch it back to `int8` when we're done removing `NaN` values.

It may seem odd to set the `dtype` to a not-quite-correct value. Why not just let pandas guess, as we have done so far, and then change it afterward? Because in a large data set, we risk having multiple `dtype` values for a single column. That's a result of pandas reading our file in chunks and choosing a `dtype` for each chunk. If all chunks have the same `dtype`, the entire column matches. If not, the column is set to a `dtype` of `object`, meaning a collection of Python objects.

> **NOTE** The chunking I'm describing here is done automatically as pandas reads data from the file. Separate functionality allows us to read files in chunks; we'll discuss that in Chapter 12.

Why would `passenger_count` and `payment_type` contain `NaN` values? Perhaps because both of them are manually set by the driver. However, it doesn't happen very often: out of 6.4 million taxi rides in our data set, only 65,441 had `NaN` values, which works out to about 1%. It doesn't seem unreasonable for drivers to neglect to indicate the number of passengers in 1 out of every 100 rides.

Regardless, to change those two columns' `dtype` to be `int8`, we need to remove the `NaN` values. We can do that with `df.dropna()`, which returns a new data frame identical to df but without rows containing NaN. We can assign the result of df.dropna() back to df (figure 3.8):

```
df = df.dropna()
```

	passenger_count	payment_type	total_amount
1989781	1.0	1.0	10.296875
6355241	NaN	NaN	25.546875
6234861	1.0	1.0	75.812500
4320340	1.0	1.0	16.562500
1847070	3.0	1.0	9.296875
211378	2.0	1.0	25.703125
3581544	1.0	1.0	15.359375
3568409	1.0	1.0	15.953125
1057067	1.0	2.0	5.300781
5894087	2.0	1.0	23.156250

dropna()

	passenger_count	payment_type	total_amount
1989781	1.0	1.0	10.296875
6234861	1.0	1.0	75.812500
4320340	1.0	1.0	16.562500
1847070	3.0	1.0	9.296875
211378	2.0	1.0	25.703125
3581544	1.0	1.0	15.359375
3568409	1.0	1.0	15.953125
1057067	1.0	2.0	5.300781
5894087	2.0	1.0	23.156250

Figure 3.8   Removing rows containing NaN with dropna

Even though df.dropna() returns a new data frame, its data may be shared with other data frames for the sake of efficiency. Modifying our data frame may thus result in a SettingWithCopyWarning. To avoid that, we can use the copy method on our data frame to ensure that there isn't any shared data behind the scenes:

```
df = df.dropna().copy()
```

If you don't use copy, you may get the warning, which may be harmless, but it also may mean any changes you make won't stick.

Now that we have removed all the NaN values, we can finally assign the dtype values we wanted to use all along:

```
df['passenger_count'] = df['passenger_count'].astype(np.int8)
df['payment_type'] = df['payment_type'].astype(np.int8)
```

```
=== Solution
```

```
df = pd.read_csv('../data/nyc_taxi_2020-01.csv',
                 usecols=['passenger_count',
                          'total_amount' , 'payment_type'],
                 dtype={'passenger_count':float32,
                        'total_amount':float32,
                        'payment_type':float32})

    df.count() 2((CO11-2))
    df = df.dropna().copy()

df['passenger_count'] = df['passenger_count'].astype(np.int8)
df['payment_type'] = df['payment_type'].astype(np.int8)
```

Uses df.count to determine which columns may contain NaN

We use float32 for all columns because two of them contain NaN values

Removes all rows containing even one NaN, copies into a new data frame, and assigns back to df

Uses the loc assignment with : to indicate "all rows"

You can explore this in the Pandas Tutor at http://mng.bz/eEKv.

Beyond the exercise

- Create a data frame from four other columns (VendorID, trip_distance, tip_amount, and total_amount), specifying the dtype for each. What types are most appropriate? Can you use them directly, or must you first clean the data?
- Instead of removing NaN values from the VendorID column, set it to a new value: 3. How does that affect your specifications and cleaning of the data?
- We'll talk more about this in Chapter 11, but the memory_usage method allows you to see how much memory is being used by each column in a data frame. It returns a series of integers in which the index lists the columns, and the values represent the memory used by each column. Compare the memory used by the data frame with float16 (which you've already used) and when you use float64 instead for the final three columns.

EXERCISE 18 ▪ passwd to df

As we've seen, CSV is a very flexible format. Many files that you wouldn't necessarily think of as being CSV files can be imported into pandas with read_csv, thanks to a huge number of parameters that you can assign.

In this exercise, I want you to create a data frame from a file that you wouldn't normally think of as CSV but that fits the format fine: the Unix passwd file. This file, which is standard on Unix and Linux systems, contains usernames and passwords. Over the years, it has evolved such that it no longer contains the actual passwords. Although MacOS is based on Unix, it doesn't use the passwd file for most user logins.

Specifically, do the following:

1   Create a data frame based on linux-etc-passwd.txt. Notice that this file contains comment lines (starting with #) and blank lines (which you should ignore). The field separator is :.

2   Add column names: `username`, `password`, `userid`, `groupid`, `name`, `homedir`, and `shell`.

3   Make the `username` column the data frame's index.

Don't worry if you know nothing about Unix or the `passwd` file—the point is to explore `read_csv` and its many options.

Working it out

For this exercise, we pull out all the stops, passing more arguments to `read_csv` than ever before. Each is necessary to parse the `passwd` file correctly, turning it into a data frame we can query. Over time, you'll discover that certain parameters to `read_csv` are used in nearly every project, making it easier to remember them.

Let's review each keyword argument that we pass to `read_csv`, look at what it does, and see how the value we pass allows us to read `passwd` into a data frame. For starters, CSV files are named for the default field separator, the comma. By default, pandas assumes that we have comma-separated values. It's fine if we want to use another character, but then we need to specify that in the `sep` keyword argument. In this case, our separator is :, so we pass `sep=':'` to `read_csv`.

Next, we deal with the fact that this `passwd` file contains comments. Comments all start with # characters and extend to the end of the line. Not many companies put comments in their `passwd` files, but given that some do, we should handle them. And `read_csv` does this elegantly, letting us specify the string that marks the start of a comment line. By passing it `comment='#'`, we indicate that the parser should ignore such lines.

The next keyword argument is `header`. By default, `read_csv` assumes that the first line of the file is a header containing column names. It also uses that first line to figure out how many fields will be on each line. If a file contains headers but not on its first line, we can set `header` to an integer value, indicating which line `read_csv` should look for them. But /etc/passwd isn't really a CSV file, and it definitely doesn't have headers. Fortunately, we can tell `read_csv` that there is no header with `header=None`.

What about the blank lines? We get off easy here because `read_csv` ignores blank lines by default. If we want to treat blank lines as `NaN` values, we can pass `skip_blank_lines=False` rather than accepting the default value of `True`.

The final keyword argument we pass is `names`. If we don't give any names, the data frame's columns will be labeled with integers starting with 0. There's nothing technically wrong with this, but it's harder to work with data. Besides, it's easy to pass the names we want to give our columns as a list of strings. Here, we pass the same list of strings we described in the exercise description (figure 3.9).

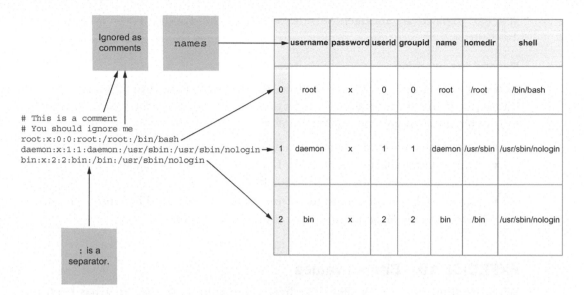

Figure 3.9   Turning the `passwd` file into a data frame

With this in place, the `passwd` file can easily be turned into a data frame. And along the way, I hope your conception of a CSV file has become more flexible.

Field separators and regular expressions

I'm often asked if we can specify more than one separator. For example, what if fields can be separated by either `:` or by `,`? What do we do then?

Pandas has a great solution: if `sep` contains more than one character, it is treated as a regular expression. So if you want to allow for either colons or commas, you can pass a separator of `[:,]`. If that looks reasonable to you, congratulations: you probably know about regular expressions. If you don't know them, I strongly encourage you to learn! Regular expressions are extremely useful to anyone working with text, which is nearly every programmer. If you're interested, I have a free tutorial on regular expressions using Python at https://RegexpCrashCourse.com.

Normally, pandas parses CSV files using a library written in C. If your field separator uses regular expressions, it needs to use a parser written in Python, which executes more slowly and uses more memory. Consider whether you need this functionality and the performance hit the Python-based parser creates.

Solution

```
df = pd.read_csv('../data/linux-etc-passwd.txt',
        sep=':', comment='#', header=None,
          names=['username', 'password', 'userid', 'groupid', 'name',
              'homedir', 'shell'])
```

You can explore an abridged version of this in the Pandas Tutor at http://mng .bz/G9lv.

Beyond the exercise

Now that we've seen how parameters to `read_csv` can help us turn CSV files into data frames, here are a few exercises to further help you understand how to massage `passwd` file into various types of data frames:

- Ignore the `password` and `groupid` fields so they don't appear in the data frame.
- Unix systems typically reserve user IDs below 1000 to special accounts. Show the nonspecial usernames in this `passwd` file.
- Immediately after logging into a Unix system, a command interpreter known as a *shell* fires up. What are the different shells in this file?

EXERCISE 19 ▪ Bitcoin values

When we think about CSV files, it's often in the context of data that has been collected once and that we now want to examine and analyze. But there are numerous examples of computer systems that publish updated data regularly and make their findings known via CSV files. It thus shouldn't come as a surprise to discover that `read_csv`'s first argument, which we normally think of as a filename, can contain several different types of values:

- Strings containing filenames (as we have already seen in this chapter)
- Readable file-like objects, typically the result of calling `open`, but also including `StringIO` objects
- Path objects, such as instances of `pathlib.Path`
- Strings containing URLs

This last case is the most interesting and will be the focus of this exercise. We can pass a URL to `read_csv`, and assuming the URL returns a CSV file, pandas will return a new data frame. The rest of the parameters are the same as any other call to `read_csv`. The only difference is that we're reading from a URL rather than from a file on a filesystem.

Why is this important and useful? Because numerous systems produce hourly or hourly reports, publishing in CSV format to a URL that doesn't change. If we retrieve data from that URL, we're guaranteed to get a CSV file reflecting the latest and greatest data. Thanks to the URL provisions of `read_csv`, we can include pandas in our daily reporting routine, summarizing and extracting the most important data from this report.

Using "requests"

In many cases, CSV files published to a URL require authentication via a username and password. In some cases, sites allow you to include such authentication details in the URL. For those that don't, you can't retrieve directly via `read_csv`. Rather, you need to retrieve the data separately, perhaps using the excellent third-party `requests` package, and then create a `StringIO` with the contents of the retrieved data.

For example, you can say

```
import requests
from io import StringIO
```

```
r = requests.get('https://data_for_you.com/data.csv')      ◄──| Example URL
s = StringIO(r.content.decode())                      ◄──┐ Turns the content into a string
df = pd.read_csv(s)    ◄──┐ Passes the StringIO to   │ and uses it to create a StringIO
                         │ read_csv, returning
                         │ a data frame
```

In this exercise, I want you to retrieve the dates and values for Bitcoin over the most recent year as of when you read this. (For that reason, your results will look different from mine, even if you use the same code.) Once you have retrieved this data, I want you to produce a report showing

- The closing price for the most recent trading day
- The lowest historical price and the date of that price
- The highest historical price and the date of that price

As of this writing, you can retrieve Bitcoin's price history in CSV format at https://api.blockchain.info/charts/market-price?format=csv.

NOTE Many stock-history sites require that you register and log in before retrieving data, but as of this writing, the URL I provided here does not.

Working it out

What always amazes me about using `pd.read_csv` is how easy it is to read CSV data from a URL. Other than the fact that the data comes from the network, it works the same as reading from a file. Among other things, we can select which columns we want to read using the `usecols` parameter.

We can read the CSV file into memory by passing a URL to `pd.read_csv`. There are only two columns to read, but there are no headers—so we have to say `header=None`. Then we give names to the columns, `date` and `value`:

```
df = pd.read_csv('https://api.blockchain.info/charts/market-price?format=csv',
          header=None,
          names=['date', 'value'])
```

Once we have created our data frame, we want to retrieve the closing price for the most recent day. Given that this kind of program can be run daily to automatically summarize market information, it's important to standardize how we retrieve the most recent information. A quick look at the data, especially via `pd.head()` and `pd.tail()`, shows that the file is in chronological order with the newest data at the end. We can thus retrieve the most recent record with `pd.tail(1)`. If we run this program every day, `pd.tail(1)` will always contain the most recent data.

But I didn't ask you to display all the data from the most recent update. Rather, we only want to see the `value`. How can we get that? By realizing that we get a data frame back from `df.tail(1)`. We can request a particular column from that data frame: `value`.

Want just the value?

`df.tail(1)` returns the final row of `df`, which contains both the `date` and `value` columns. What if we only want `value`?

One option is to think of `df.tail(1)` as a one-row data frame. Each column of a data frame is a series, so we can retrieve the value with

```
df.tail(1)['value']
```

Sure enough, we get a one-element series back. But remember that we can retrieve more than one column from a data frame by passing a list of columns—that is, in double square brackets. What if we use double square brackets but list only one column?

```
df.tail(1)[['value']]
```

The result is a data frame containing one row (same as `df.tail(1)`) and one column (`value`).

Which syntax you choose depends on what you want to do with the data. In this particular case, it doesn't matter.

Next, I asked you to find the minimum and maximum values and to show the corresponding `date` and `value`. We can use a boolean index to find the rows—or, more likely, a single row—that matches the minimum closing price. We then pass a second value to `.loc`, allowing us to choose which columns are displayed. Notice that we look for the minimum value of `value` and then find all the rows equal to that, effectively finding the row with the `min` value. In theory, two rows may both have the same value, in which case we show both of them. We then repeat this for the `max` value (figure 3.10):

```
df.loc[df['value'] == df['value'].min(), ['date', 'value']]
df.loc[df['value'] == df['value'].max(), ['date', 'value']]
```

However, there is another, more elegant approach: if we turn the `date` column into the data frame's index, we can then invoke `idxmin` and `idxmax` on the data frame. These method calls return not just the minimum/maximum values but also the indexes associated with these values—that is, the dates:

```
df.set_index('date').idxmin()
df.set_index('date').idxmax()
```

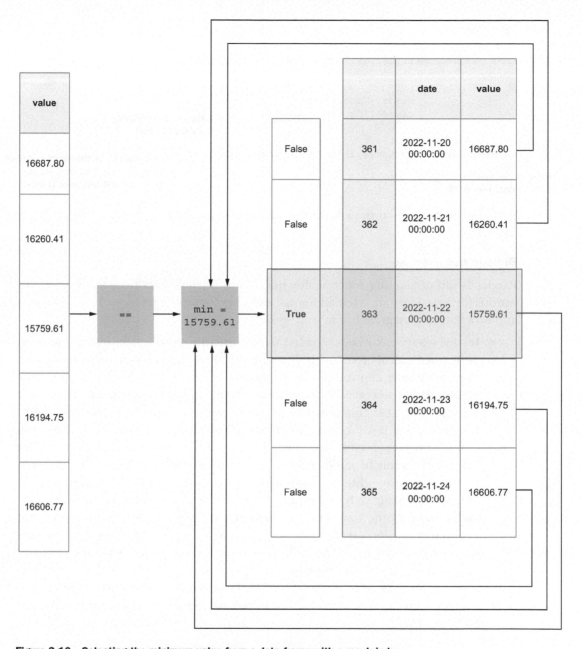

Figure 3.10 Selecting the minimum value from a data frame with a mask index

But why stop there? We can use the `agg` method to invoke more than one aggregation method on a data frame, passing the methods as a list of strings. We can set the data frame's index to be the `date` column and then run `agg` for both `idxmin` and `idxmax` in a single line:

```
df.set_index('date').agg(['idxmin', 'idxmax'])
```

Solution

```
import pandas as pd
from pandas import Series, DataFrame

df = pd.read_csv('https://api.blockchain.info/charts/market-price?format=csv',
                 header=None,
                 names=['date', 'value'])            ⟵  Names the columns
df.tail(1)[['value']]                                     date and value
df.set_index('date').agg(['idxmin', 'idxmax'])      ⟵  Sets date to be the index and then
                                                         find the rows (index + value)
Retrieves the value column                               with the min and max values
from the final row of df
```

You can explore an abridged version of this in the Pandas Tutor at http://mng
.bz/YRXB.

Beyond the exercise

Pandas is full of amazing functionality that lets us retrieve data from the internet in
various formats. Here are a few additional exercises for you to try to see how this works
and how you can integrate it into your workflow:

- In this exercise, you downloaded the information into a data frame and then
  performed calculations on it. Without assigning the downloaded data to an
  interim variable, can you return the current value? Your solution should consist
  of a single line of code that includes the download, selection, and calculation.
- The `pd.read_html` function, like `pd.read_csv`, takes a file-like object or a URL.
  It assumes that it will encounter HTML-formatted text containing at least one
  table. It turns each table into a data frame and then returns a list of those data
  frames. With this in mind, retrieve one year of historical S&P 500 data from
  Yahoo Finance (https://finance.yahoo.com/quote/%5EGSPC/history?p=%
  5EGSPC), looking only at the `Date`, `Close`, and `Volume` columns. Show the date
  and volume of the days with the highest and lowest `Close` values. Note that
  Yahoo seems to look at the `User-Agent` header in the HTTP request, which cannot be set in `read_html`. So you'll need to use `requests` to retrieve the data, setting `User-Agent` to a string equal to `'Mozilla 5.0'`. Turn the content of the
  result into a `StringIO`, and then feed that to `read_html` and retrieve the data.
- Create a two-row data frame with the highest and lowest closing prices for the
  S&P 500. Use the `to_csv` function to write this data to a new CSV file.

EXERCISE 20 ▪ Big cities

There's no doubt that CSV is an important, useful, and popular format. But in some
ways, it has been eclipsed by another format: JSON, aka JavaScript Object Notation.
JSON allows us to store numbers, text, lists, and dictionaries in a text format that's
both readable and writable with various programming languages. Because it's easier to

work with, smaller than XML, and more expressive than CSV, it's no surprise that JSON has become a common format for storing and exchanging data. JSON has also become the standard format for internet APIs, allowing us to access various services in a cross-platform manner.

Just as we can retrieve CSV-formatted data with `pd.read_csv`, we can retrieve JSON-formatted data with `pd.read_json`. In this exercise, I want you to read in data about the 1,000 largest cities in the United States. (This data is from 2013, so if your hometown doesn't appear here, I apologize.) Once you have created a data frame from this city data, I want you to answer the following questions:

- What are the mean and median populations for these 1,000 largest cities? What does that tell you?
- Along these lines, if you remove the 50 most populous cities, what happens to the mean population? What happens to the median?
- What is the northernmost city, and where does it rank?
- Which state has the largest number of cities on this list?
- Which state has the smallest number of cities on this list?

Working it out

Reading a JSON file into a data frame doesn't have to be difficult; in this case, it's easy. That's partly because this particular JSON file is an array of objects, or what Python people call a "list of dicts." When `read_json` sees this file, it sees each dict as a record, using the keys as column names. In many ways, reading this kind of JSON file is similar to creating a data frame with a list of dicts, something we saw in chapter 2. Once we have created the data frame, we can work with it like any other.

First, I asked you to compare the mean and median city populations. We can do that with `describe` in the `population` column, which returns a series. Because we're only interested in two elements from that series, we can limit the output to the `mean` and `50%` (i.e., median) values:

```
df['population'].describe()[['mean', '50%']]
```

The mean population is 131,132, and the median is 68,207. This means a few big values pull the mean higher than the median. And indeed, the United States has a few very large cities and many medium- and small-size cities. By definition, half of these 1,000 cities have populations less than 68,207.

The next question asks, what if we ignore the 50 largest cities? What does that do to the mean and median? For that, we use a slice along with `loc`:

```
df.loc[50:, 'population'].describe()[['mean', '50%']]
```

Remember that when we pass `loc` two values, the first describes what rows we want, and the second describes what columns we want. Here, we indicate that we want all the rows starting with index 50. And we only want one column: `population`. Once again, we run `describe` and then grab only the mean and median values. We find that the mean has dropped a lot, to 87,027, and the median has dropped to 65,796—a much smaller difference. This shows the power of the median; it isn't affected nearly as much as the mean if there are a few large or small values in the data set.

Next, I asked you to find the northernmost city. That means the maximum positive value for `latitude`. We can find that by getting the max latitude and finding which rows of `df` have that value. Once again, we use `loc` to retrieve only those rows and then pass a list of columns to retrieve only those values:

```
df.loc[df['latitude'] == df['latitude'].max(), ['city', 'state', 'rank']]
```

The result, not surprisingly, is Anchorage, Alaska, which is the 63rd largest city in the United States—a much higher rank than I expected!

Finally, I asked you to find the states with the largest and smallest number of cities on this list. This is a perfect use of `value_counts` on the `state` column. California, with 212 cities, is the clear winner:

```
df['state'].value_counts().head(1)
```

Remember that, by default, `value_counts` sorts the results from most common to least common. We thus know that the item at `head(1)` is the most popular, assuming the next-most-common state doesn't have the same value. (As far as I know, there isn't a good way to avoid such problems.)

What about the states with the fewest cities on this list? We use `tail(10)` to look at the 10 lowest-ranked states and find that the bottom 5 states (including Washington, DC) all have a single city in the list:

```
df['state'].value_counts().tail(5)
```

Solution

```
filename = '../data/cities.json'
df = pd.read_json(filename)

df['population'].describe()[['mean', '50%']]
df.loc[50:, 'population'].describe()[['mean', '50%']]
df.loc[df['latitude'] == df['latitude'].max(), ['city', 'state', 'rank']]
df['state'].value_counts().head(1)
df['state'].value_counts().tail(5)
```

> Grabs just the mean and 50% values for the population descriptive statistics

> Grabs just the mean and 50% values for the population descriptive statistics for rows 50 and up

> Finds the maximum latitude value and gets only the city, state, and rank for it

> One state has the most cities, which we can see here.

> Five states have only 1 city in the top 1,000.

You can explore an abridged version of this in the Pandas Tutor at http://mng .bz/z0oB.

Beyond the exercise

- Convert the `growth_from_2000_to_2013` column into a floating-point number. Then find the mean and median changes in city size between 2000 and 2013. If a city has no recorded growth, set it to 0.

- How many cities had positive growth in this period, and how many had negative growth?
- Find the city or cities with latitudes more than two standard deviations from the mean.

Summary

In this chapter, we started to work with real-world data. We read data from CSV, JSON, and even HTML tables and saw how pandas provides parameters that can control and modify how file inputs are parsed and read. Given that the overwhelming majority of our data comes from such files, it's worthwhile to learn how to read data from them— specifying the `dtype` for each column and even which columns we want to see.

Indexes 4

My parents introduced me to the wonders of the public library at a young age. It held an immense number of books on every subject you could imagine.

But wait: with so many books on so many subjects by so many authors, how can you possibly find what you want or even know what's available? The answer is an index. In those days, libraries typically had three different indexes found in the card catalog (hundreds of drawers full of index cards). These cards allowed you to find books (a) by author, (b) by title, or (c) by subject. Beyond that, the books were shelved according to their subjects, using either the Dewey decimal system or the Library of Congress system. If you were familiar with these systems, you could easily find what you were looking for: a particular book that had been mentioned in the newspaper, books written by your favorite author, or books on a particular subject you were researching for school. Nowadays, of course, the indexes are computerized, allowing you to find books more flexibly and easily than we ever imagined in the days of the card catalog.

Could you have a library without an index? Yes, but it would be much less useful. It would be harder to find what you want, and every search would take significantly longer. How to best catalog information so it's easily findable is so important that an entire branch of academia, library science, is dedicated to it.

Just as an index can help us find books in a library, it can help us find data in pandas. We've already seen that a series has one index (for its elements) and a data frame has two (one for the rows and a second for the columns). We've seen how .loc, along with row selectors and column selectors, can be powerful.

But indexes in pandas are far more flexible than we've seen so far: we can make an existing column into an index or turn an index back into a regular column. We can combine multiple columns into a hierarchical *multi-index* and then perform searches on specific parts of that hierarchy. Indeed, knowing how to create, query, and manipulate multi-indexed data frames is key to fluent work with pandas. We can also create *pivot tables* in which the rows and columns reflect not our original data, but rather aggregate summaries of that data.

In this chapter, we'll practice using all these techniques to better understand how to create, modify, and manipulate various types of indexes. After working through these exercises, you'll know how to use pandas indexes to retrieve data more flexibly and easily.

Table 4.1 What you need to know

Concept	What is it?	Example	To learn more
`pd.set_index`	Returns a new data frame with a new index	`df = df.set_index ('name')`	http://mng.bz/MBd2
`pd.reset_index`	Returns a new data frame with a default (numeric, positional) index	`df = df.reset_index()`	http://mng.bz/a1RJ
`df.loc`	Retrieves selected rows and columns	`df.loc[:, 'passenger_count'] = df['passenger_ count']`	http://mng.bz/e1QJ
`s.value_counts`	Returns a sorted (descending frequency) series counting how many times each value appears in s	`s.value_counts()`	http://mng.bz/Y1r7
`s.isin`	Returns a boolean series indicating whether a value in s is an element of the argument	`s.isin(['A', 'B', 'C')`	http://mng.bz/9D08
`df.pivot`	Creates a pivot table based on a data frame *without* aggregation	`df.pivot(index='mont h', columns= 'year', values='A')`	http://mng.bz/zXjZ
`df.pivot_table`	Creates a pivot table based on a data frame, *with* aggregation, if needed	`df.pivot_table(index ='month', columns= 'year', values='A')`	http://mng.bz/0K4z
`s.is_monotonic _increasing`	Contains `True` if values in the series are sorted in increasing order	`s.is_monotonic_ increasing`	http://mng.bz/Ke2n
`slice`	Python builtin for creating slices	`slice(10, 20, 2)`	http://mng.bz/278g

Table 4.1 What you need to know *(continued)*

Concept	What is it?	Example	To learn more
`df.xs`	Returns a cross-section from a data frame	`df.xs(2016, level='Year')`	http://mng.bz/jPg9
`df.dropna`	Returns a new data frame without any `NaN` values	`df.dropna()`	http://mng.bz/o1PN
`IndexSlice`	Produce an object for easier querying of data frames using `xs`	`IndexSlice[:, 2016]`	http://mng.bz/WzPX

EXERCISE 21 ▪ Parking tickets

We have already seen numerous examples of retrieving one or more rows from a data frame using `loc`. We don't necessarily *need* to use the index to select rows from a data frame, but it does make things easier to understand and yields clearer code. For this reason, we often want to use one of a data frame's existing columns as an index. Sometimes we want to do this permanently, and other times we want to do it briefly to clarify our queries.

In this exercise, I'll ask you to perform some queries on another data set from New York City: one that tracked all parking tickets during the year 2020—more than 12 million of them. You could, in theory, perform these queries without modifying the data frame's index. However, I want you to get some practice setting and resetting the index. We're going to do that a lot in this chapter, and you'll likely do it a great deal as you work with pandas with real-life data sets.

With that in mind, I want you to do the following:

1 Create a data frame from the file nyc-parking-violations-2020.csv. We are only interested in a handful of the columns:
   - `Date First Observed`
   - `Plate ID`
   - `Registration State`
   - `Issue Date` (a string in MM/DD/YYYY format, always followed by `12:00:00 AM`)
   - `Vehicle Make`
   - `Street Name`
   - `Vehicle Color`
2 Set the data frame's index to the `Issue Date` column.
3 Determine what three makes were most frequently ticketed on January 2, 2020.
4 Determine the five streets on which cars got the most tickets on June 1, 2020.
5 Set the index to `Vehicle Color`.
6 Determine the most common make of vehicles that were either red or blue.

Working it out

We have already seen that to retrieve rows from a data frame that meet a particular condition, we can use a boolean series as a mask index. Often, especially if we are looking for specific values from a column, it makes more sense to turn that column into the data frame's index, reducing our code's complexity and length. Pandas makes it easy to do this with the `set_index` method. In this exercise, I asked you to make several queries against the data set of New York City parking tickets in 2020 and set the index to do this.

First, we read the data from a CSV file, limiting the columns from the input file:

```
filename = '../data/nyc-parking-violations-2020.csv'

df = pd.read_csv(filename,
                 usecols=[
                     'Date First Observed',
                     'Registration State', 'Plate ID',
                     'Issue Date', 'Vehicle Make',
                     'Street Name', 'Vehicle Color'])
```

Once the data frame is loaded, we perform several queries based on the parking tickets' issue date. So, it makes sense to set the index to the `Issue Date` column, as shown in figure 4.1:

```
df = df.set_index('Issue Date')
```

Notice that `set_index` returns a new data frame based on the original one, which we assign back to `df`. As of this point, if we make queries that involve the index (typically using `loc`), they will be based on the value of the issue date. Also, as far as the data frame is concerned, there is no longer an `Issue Date` column! Its identity as a named column is largely gone. Some pandas methods (e.g., `groupby`) can find and work with an index via its original name, but many others cannot.

> **NOTE** As of this writing, the `set_index` method (along with many others in pandas) supports the `inplace` parameter. If you call `set_index` and pass `inplace=True`, the method will return `None` and will modify the data frame on which it was invoked. The core pandas developers have warned that this is a bad idea because it makes incorrect assumptions about memory and performance. They say there is no benefit to using `inplace=True`. Moreover, getting a new data frame back allows for method chaining, making long queries more readable. As a result, the `inplace` parameter will probably go away in a future version of pandas. Thus, although it may seem wasteful to call `set_index` and then assign its result back to `df`, this is the preferred, idiomatic way to do things.

With this index in place, it's relatively straightforward to find all the tickets issued on January 2:

```
df.loc['01/02/2020 12:00:00 AM']
```

	Plate ID	Registration State	Issue Date	Vehicle Make	Street Name	Date First Observed	Vehicle Color
725518	JFG4137	NY	07/16/2019 12:00:00 AM	DODGE	PACIFIC STREET	0	WHT
247136	DPH1199	NY	07/01/2019 12:00:00 AM	NISSA	160th St	0	BK
1628916	8D45B	NY	08/06/2019 12:00:00 AM	FORD	NB BAYCHESTER AVE @	0	YW
6757299	67974JV	NY	12/11/2019 12:00:00 AM	ISUZU	95th St	0	WHITE
4482906	JBN3055	NY	10/13/2019 12:00:00 AM	DODGE	SWINTON AVE	0	GRY
12331922	CKS1861	GA	06/17/2020 12:00:00 AM	Jeep	NB OCEAN PKWY @ AVE	0	GRAY
1723597	58388MG	NY	08/08/2019 12:00:00 AM	CHEVR	E 38th St	20190808	WH
2474539	AP628T	NJ	08/26/2019 12:00:00 AM	INTER	1st Ave	0	WHITE

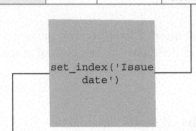

`set_index('Issue date')`

	Plate ID	Registration State	Vehicle Make	Street Name	Date First Observed	Vehicle Color
Issue date						
07/16/2019 12:00:00 AM	JFG4137	NY	DODGE	PACIFIC STREET	0	WHT
07/01/2019 12:00:00 AM	DPH1199	NY	NISSA	160th St	0	BK
08/06/2019 12:00:00 AM	8D45B	NY	FORD	NB BAYCHESTER AVE @	0	YW
12/11/2019 12:00:00 AM	67974JV	NY	ISUZU	95th St	0	WHITE
10/13/2019 12:00:00 AM	JBN3055	NY	DODGE	SWINTON AVE	0	GRY
06/17/2020 12:00:00 AM	CKS1861	GA	Jeep	NB OCEAN PKWY @ AVE	0	GRAY
08/08/2019 12:00:00 AM	58388MG	NY	CHEVR	E 38th St	20190808	WH
08/26/2019 12:00:00 AM	AP628T	NJ	INTER	1st Ave	0	WHITE

Figure 4.1   Graphical depiction of turning `Issue Date` from a column into the index

However, this also returns all the columns. And the first question we're trying to answer with this newly reindexed data frame is which vehicle makes received the most tickets on January 2. Let's limit the results of our query to the `Vehicle Make` column:

```
df.loc['01/02/2020 12:00:00 AM', 'Vehicle Make']
```

Once again, we see that the two-argument form of `loc` means first passing a row selector and then passing a column selector. In this case, we're only interested in a single column, `Vehicle Make`.

But we're still not done: how can we find the three most commonly ticketed vehicle makes on January 2? We use the `value_counts` method:

```
df.loc['01/02/2020 12:00:00 AM', 'Vehicle Make'].value_counts()
```

This returns a series in which the index contains the different vehicle makes and the values are the counts, sorted from highest to lowest. We can limit our results to the three most common makes by adding `head(3)` to our call:

```
df.loc['01/02/2020 12:00:00 AM', 'Vehicle Make'].value_counts().head(3)
```

Once we have this information, we can also check other columns. For example, on what five streets were the most tickets issued on June 1?

```
df.loc['06/01/2020 12:00:00 AM', 'Street Name'].value_counts().head(5)
```

Again, we select rows via the index and then select a column. We pass this to `value_counts` and get the top five results.

But now we want to make queries against the `Vehicle Color` column. We thus need to remove `Issue Date` as the index and put `Vehicle Color` in its place. We could, in theory, do this in two lines of code:

```
df = df.reset_index()
df = df.set_index('Vehicle Color')
```

Thanks to method chaining, we can do it in a single line of code:

```
df = df.reset_index().set_index('Vehicle Color')
```

We could equivalently split it up across several lines, using parentheses (see figure 4.2):

```
df = (
    df
    .reset_index()
    .set_index('Vehicle Color')
    )
```

The information in our data frame hasn't changed, but the index has—thus giving us easier access to the data from this perspective. That will come in handy when answering the next question, which asks which vehicle make received the most parking tickets, if we only consider blue and red cars.

Issue Date	Plate ID	Registration State	Vehicle Make	Street Name	Date First Observed	Vehicle Color
07/16/2019 12:00:00 AM	JFG4137	NY	DODGE	PACIFIC STREET	0	WHT
07/01/2019 12:00:00 AM	DPH1199	NY	NISSA	160th St	0	BK
08/06/2019 12:00:00 AM	8D45B	NY	FORD	NB BAYCHESTER AVE @	0	YW
12/11/2019 12:00:00 AM	67974JV	NY	ISUZU	95th St	0	WHITE
10/13/2019 12:00:00 AM	JBN3055	NY	DODGE	SWINTON AVE	0	GRY
06/17/2020 12:00:00 AM	CKS1861	GA	Jeep	NB OCEAN PKWY @ AVE	0	GRAY
08/08/2019 12:00:00 AM	58388MG	NY	CHEVR	E 38th St	20190808	WH
08/26/2019 12:00:00 AM	AP628T	NJ	INTER	1st Ave	0	WHITE

reset_index()

	Plate ID	Registration State	Issue Date	Vehicle Make	Street Name	Date First Observed	Vehicle Color
725518	JFG4137	NY	07/16/2019 12:00:00 AM	DODGE	PACIFIC STREET	0	WHT
247136	DPH1199	NY	07/01/2019 12:00:00 AM	NISSA	160th St	0	BK
1628916	8D45B	NY	08/06/2019 12:00:00 AM	FORD	NB BAYCHESTER AVE @	0	YW
6757299	67974JV	NY	12/11/2019 12:00:00 AM	ISUZU	95th St	0	WHITE
4482906	JBN3055	NY	10/13/2019 12:00:00 AM	DODGE	SWINTON AVE	0	GRY
12331922	CKS1861	GA	06/17/2020 12:00:00 AM	Jeep	NB OCEAN PKWY @ AVE	0	GRAY
1723597	58388MG	NY	08/08/2019 12:00:00 AM	CHEVR	E 38th St	20190808	WH
2474539	AP628T	NJ	08/26/2019 12:00:00 AM	INTER	1st Ave	0	WHITE

set_index
('Vehicle
Color')

Vehicle Color	Plate ID	Registration State	Vehicle Make	Issue Date	Street Name	Date First Observed
WHT	JFG4137	NY	DODGE	07/16/2019 12:00:00 AM	PACIFIC STREET	0
BK	DPH1199	NY	NISSA	07/01/2019 12:00:00 AM	160th St	0
YW	8D45B	NY	FORD	08/06/2019 12:00:00 AM	NB BAYCHESTER AVE @	0
WHITE	67974JV	NY	ISUZU	12/11/2019 12:00:00 AM	95th St	0
GRY	JBN3055	NY	DODGE	10/13/2019 12:00:00 AM	SWINTON AVE	0
GRAY	CKS1861	GA	Jeep	06/17/2020 12:00:00 AM	NB OCEAN PKWY @ AVE	0
WH	58388MG	NY	CHEVR	08/08/2019 12:00:00 AM	E 38th St	20190808
WHITE	AP628T	NJ	INTER	08/26/2019 12:00:00 AM	1st Ave	0

Figure 4.2 Graphical depiction of returning `Issue Date` **from the index to a column and making** `Vehicle Color` **the new index**

First, we need to find only those cars that are blue or red. We can do that by passing a list to `loc`:

```
df.loc[['BLUE', 'RED']]
```

Once we've done that, we can apply a column selector:

```
df.loc[['BLUE', 'RED'], 'Vehicle Make']
```

This returns all the rows in the data frame that have a blue or red car, but only the `Vehicle Make` column. With that in place, we can use `value_counts` to find the most common make and restrict it to the top-ranking brand with `head(1)`:

```
(
    df
    .loc[['BLUE', 'RED'], 'Vehicle Make']
    .value_counts()
    .head(1)
)
```

Solution

Sets the data frame's index
to be the Issue Date column

Finds all rows on January 2
and just the Vehicle Make
column, then gets the first
three elements from the
resulting series

```
filename = '../data/nyc-parking-violations-2020.csv'

df = pd.read_csv(filename,
    usecols=['Date First Observed', 'Registration State', 'Plate ID',
        'Issue Date', 'Vehicle Make', 'Street Name', 'Vehicle Color'])
df = df.set_index('Issue Date')
df.loc['01/02/2020 12:00:00 AM',
        'Vehicle Make'].value_counts().head(3)
df.loc['06/01/2020 12:00:00 AM',
        'Street Name'].value_counts().head(5)
df = df.reset_index().set_index('Vehicle Color')
df.loc[['BLUE', 'RED'],
        'Vehicle Make'].value_counts().head(1)
```

Finds all rows on January 2 and
just the Street Name column,
then gets the first five elements
from the resulting series

Removes Vehicle Make from
being an index and then sets
Vehicle Color to be the index

Finds all rows with a color of
red or blue and gets the Vehicle
Make column, then gets the
most common make

You can explore a version of this in the Pandas Tutor at http://mng.bz/1JWX.

Beyond the exercise

Just as changing your perspective on a problem can often help you solve it, setting (or resetting) the index on a data frame can dramatically simplify the code you need to write. Here are some additional problems based on the data frame we created in this exercise:

- What three car makes were most often ticketed from January 2 through January 10?

- How many tickets did the second-most-ticketed car get in 2020? (And why am I not interested in the most-ticketed plate?) What state was that car from, and was it always ticketed in the same location?

Working with multi-indexes

Every data frame has an index, giving labels to the rows. We have already seen that we can use the `loc` accessor to retrieve one or more rows using the index. For example, we can say

```
df.loc['a']
```

to retrieve all the rows with the index value `a`. Remember that the index doesn't necessarily contain unique values; `loc['a']` may return a series of values representing a single row, but it also may return a data frame whose rows all have the index value `a`.

This sort of index often serves us well. But in many cases it's not enough. That's because the world is full of hierarchical information, or information that is easier to process if we make it hierarchical.

For example, every business wants to know its sales figures. But getting a single number doesn't let you analyze the information in a useful way. So you may want to break it down by product to know how well each product is selling well and which contributes the most to the bottom line. (We saw a version of this in exercise 8.) However, even that isn't enough; you probably want to know how well each product is selling per month. If your store has been around for a while, you may want to break it down even further than that, finding the quantity of each product sold per month, per year. A multi-index will let you do precisely that.

For example, let's create some random sales data for three products (cleverly called A, B, and C) over the 36 months from January 2018 through December 2020:

```
# let's assume 3 products * 3 years * 12 months = 108 sales figures

g = np.random.default_rng(0)
df = DataFrame(g.integers(0, 100, [36,3]),
               columns=list('ABC'))
df['year'] = [2018] * 12 + [2019] * 12 + [2020] * 12
df['month'] = """Jan Feb Mar Apr May Jun
                 Jul Aug Sep Oct Nov Dec""".split() * 3
```

Triple-quoted strings allow newlines in strings

We could set the index, based on the `year` column, as follows:

```
df = df.set_index('year')
```

But that wouldn't give us any special access to the month data, which we would like to have part of our index. We can create a multi-index by passing a list of columns to `set_index`:

```
df = df.set_index(['year', 'month'])
```

	A	B	C	year	month
0	44	47	64	2018	Jan
1	67	67	9	2018	Feb
2	83	21	36	2018	Mar
3	87	70	88	2018	Apr
4	88	12	58	2018	May
5	65	39	87	2018	Jun
6	46	88	81	2018	Jul
7	37	25	77	2018	Aug
8	72	9	20	2018	Sep

```
df.set_index(
    ['year',
    'month'])
```

year	month	A	B	C
2018	Jan	44	47	64
2018	Feb	67	67	9
2018	Mar	83	21	36
2018	Apr	87	70	88
2018	May	88	12	58
2018	Jun	65	39	87
2018	Jul	46	88	81
2018	Aug	37	25	77
2018	Sep	72	9	20

Graphical depiction of creating a multi-index from the year **and** month **columns**

Remember that when creating a multi-index, we want the most general part to be on the outside and thus be mentioned first. If you create a multi-index with dates, you use year, month, and day, in that order. If you create a multi-index for your company's sales data, you might use region, country, and city to retrieve all rows for a given region, country, or city relatively easily. Usually (but not always), a multi-index reflects a hierarchy.

(continued)

With this in place, we can retrieve one or more parts of the data frame in a variety of different ways. For example, we can get the sales data for all products in 2018:

```
df.loc[2018]
```

We can get all sales data for just products A and C in 2018:

```
df.loc[2018, ['A', 'C']]
```

Notice that we're still applying the same rule we've always used with `loc`: the first argument describes the row(s) we want, and the second argument describes the column(s) we want. Without a second argument, we get all the columns.

We have a multi-index on this data frame, which means we can break the data down not just by year but also by month. For example, what did it look like for all three products in June 2018?

```
df.loc[(2018, 'Jun')]
```

We're still invoking `loc` with square brackets. However, the first (and only) argument is a tuple (i.e., round parentheses). Tuples are typically used in a multi-index situation when we want to specify a specific combination of index levels and values. For example, we're looking for 2018 and June—the outermost level and the inner level—so we use the tuple `(2018, 'Jun')`. We can, of course, retrieve the sales data just for products A and C:

```
df.loc[(2018, 'Jun'), ['A', 'C']]
```

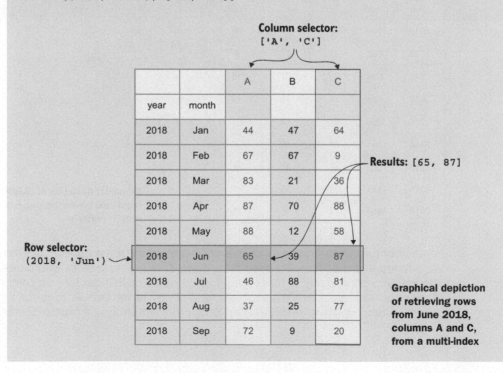

Graphical depiction of retrieving rows from June 2018, columns A and C, from a multi-index

What if we want to see more than one year at a time? For example, let's say we want all data for 2018 and 2020:

```
df.loc[[2018, 2020]]
```

And if we want all data for 2018 and 2020, but only products B and C?

```
df.loc[[2018, 2020], ['B', 'C']]
```

What if we want to get all the data from June in both 2018 and 2020? It's a little complicated:

- We use square brackets with `loc`.
- The first argument in the square brackets describes the rows we want (i.e., a row selector).
- We want all columns, so there isn't a second argument to `loc`.
- We want to select multiple combinations from the multi-index, so we need a list.
- Each year-month combination is a separate tuple in the list.

The result is

```
df.loc[[(2018, 'Jun'), (2020, 'Jun')]]
```

What if we want to look at all values from June, July, or August across all three years? We could, of course, do it manually:

```
df.loc[[(2018, 'Jun'), (2018, 'Jul'), (2018, 'Aug'),
        (2019, 'Jun'), (2019, 'Jul'), (2019, 'Aug'),
        (2020, 'Jun'), (2020, 'Jul'), (2020, 'Aug')]]
```

This works well, but it seems wordy. Is there another, shorter way? You might guess that we could tell pandas we want all the years (2018, 2019, and 2020) and only three months (June, July, and August) by writing the following:

```
df.loc[([2018, 2019, 2020], ['Jun', 'Jul', 'Aug'])]
```

But this won't work! It's rather surprising and confusing to find that it doesn't work, when it seems obvious and intuitive, given everything else we know about pandas. What's missing is an indicator of which columns we want:

```
df.loc[([2018, 2019, 2020], ['Jun', 'Jul', 'Aug']),
       ['A', 'B', 'C']]
```

Although the second argument (our column selector) is generally optional when using `loc`, here it isn't: we need to indicate which column, or columns, we want, along with the rows. Typically, you won't want all the columns because the analysis you'll want to do will involve a subset of the full data frame.

We can do this explicitly, as we did earlier, or we can use Python's "slice" syntax:

```
df.loc[([2018, 2019, 2020], ['Jun', 'Jul', 'Aug']),
       'A':'C']
```

(continued)

For all columns, use a colon by itself:

```
df.loc[([2018, 2019, 2020], ['Jun', 'Jul', 'Aug']),
       :]
```

Assuming the index is sorted, we can even select the years using a slice:

```
df.loc[(:, ['Jun', 'Jul', 'Aug']), 'A':'B']          ⟵┐ This won't
                                                        │ work!
```

Oh, wait—actually, we can't do that here, because Python only allows the colon within square brackets. We tried to use the colon within a tuple, which uses regular, round parentheses. Instead, we can use the builtin `slice` function with `None` as an argument for the same result:

```
df.loc[(slice(None), ['Jun', 'Jul', 'Aug']), 'A':'B']
```

And sure enough, that works. You can think of `slice(None)` as a way of indicating to pandas that you are willing to have all values as a wildcard.

As you can see, `loc` is extremely versatile, allowing us to retrieve from a multi-index various ways.

EXERCISE 22 ▪ State SAT scores

Setting the index can make it easier to create queries about our data. But sometimes our data is hierarchical in nature. That's where the pandas concept of a multi-index comes into play. With a multi-index, we can set the index not just to a single column but rather to multiple columns. Imagine, for example, a data frame containing sales data: we may want sales broken down by year and then further broken down by region. Once you use the phrase "further broken down by," a multi-index is almost certainly a good idea. (See the earlier sidebar "Working with multi-indexes" for a fuller description.)

In this exercise, we look at a summary of scores from the SAT, a standardized university admissions test widely used in the United States. The CSV file (sat-scores.csv) has 99 columns and 577 rows describing all 50 US states and three nonstates (Puerto Rico, the Virgin Islands, and Washington, DC) from 2005 through 2015.

In this exercise, I want you to

1 Read in the scores file, only keeping the `Year`, `State.Code`, `Total.Math`, `Total.Test-takers`, and `Total.Verbal` columns.
2 Create a multi-index based on the year and the two-letter state code.
3 Determine how many people took the SAT in 2005.
4 Determine the average SAT math score in 2010 from New York (`NY`), New Jersey (`NJ`), Massachusetts (`MA`), and Illinois (`IL`).

5 Determine the average SAT verbal score in 2012–2015 from Arizona (AZ), California (CA), and Texas (TX).

Working it out

In this exercise, you begin to discover the power and flexibility of a multi-index. I asked you to load the CSV file and create a multi-index based on the `Year` and `State.Code` columns. We can do this in two stages, first reading the file, including the columns we want, into a data frame and then choosing two columns to serve as our index:

```
filename = '../data/sat-scores.csv'

df = pd.read_csv(filename,
                 usecols=['Year', 'State.Code',
                 'Total.Math', 'Total.Test-takers',
                 'Total.Verbal'])
df = df.set_index(['Year', 'State.Code'])
```

As always, the result of `set_index` is a new data frame, which we assign back to `df`.

You may remember that `read_csv` also has an `index_col` parameter. If we pass an argument to that parameter, we can tell `read_csv` to do it all in one step—reading in the data frame and setting the index as the column we request. We can pass a list of columns as the argument to `index_col`, thus creating the multi-index as the data frame is collected. For example:

```
filename = '../data/sat-scores.csv'

df = pd.read_csv(filename,
                 usecols=['Year', 'State.Code',
                 'Total.Math', 'Total.Test-takers',
                 'Total.Verbal'],
                 index_col=['Year', 'State.Code'])
```

Now that we have loaded our data frame, we can explore our data and answer some questions.

First, we want to know how many people took the SAT in 2005. This means finding all rows from 2005 and the column `Total.Test-takers`, which tells us how many people took the test in each year, for each state, and summing those values:

```
df.loc[2005,          ◁──┤ Row selector
       'Total.Test-takers'   ◁──┐ Column
       ].sum()                  │ selector
```

Next, we want to determine the mean math score for students in four states—New York, New Jersey, Massachusetts, and Illinois—in 2010. As usual, we can use `loc` to retrieve the data that's of interest to us. But we need to combine three things to create the right query:

- From the first part (`Year`) of the multi-index, we only want 2010.

- From the second part (`State.Code`) of the multi-index, we only want NY, NJ, MA, and IL.
- From the columns, we are interested in `Total.Math`.

When retrieving from a multi-index, we need to put the parts together inside a tuple. Moreover, we can indicate that we want more than one value by using a list. The result is

```
df.loc[(2010, ['NY', 'NJ', 'MA', 'IL']),          Multi-index row selector for rows
       'Total.Math'].mean()                        in 2010 from four specific states

                                                   Column selector, indicating
                                                   just the Total.Math column
```

This query retrieves rows with a year of 2010 coming from any of those four states. We only get the `Total.Math` column, on which we then calculate the mean (figure 4.3).

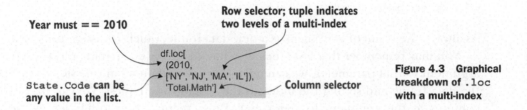

Figure 4.3 Graphical breakdown of `.loc` with a multi-index

The next question asks for a similar calculation but on several years and several states. Once again, that's not a problem if we think carefully about how to construct the query:

- From the first part (`Year`) of the multi-index, we want 2012, 2013, 2014, and 2015.
- From the second part (`State.Code`) of the multi-index, we want AZ, CA, and TX.
- From the columns, we are again interested in `Total.Math`.

The query then becomes

```
df.loc[([2012,2013,2014,2015], ['AZ', 'CA', 'TX']),     Multi-index row selector
       'Total.Math'].mean()                              for rows in 2012–2015
                                                         and three specific states

                                                   Column selector, indicating
                                                   just the Total.Math column
```

Notice how pandas figures out how to combine the parts of our multi-index so we get only the rows matching both parts.

Solution

```
filename = '../data/sat-scores.csv'

df = pd.read_csv(filename,
                 usecols=['Year',
                          'State.Code',
                          'Total.Math',
```

```
                              'Total.Test-takers',
                              'Total.Verbal'])
df = df.set_index(['Year', 'State.Code'])
df.loc[2005, 'Total.Test-takers'].sum()

df.loc[(2010, ['NY', 'NJ', 'MA', 'IL']),
       'Total.Math'].mean()

df.loc[([2012,2013,2014,2015],
       ['AZ', 'CA', 'TX']),
       'Total.Math'].mean()
```

Sets the index to be a combination of Year and State.code

Retrieves rows with 2005 and the column Total.Test-takers and then sums those values

Retrieves rows with 2010 and any of those four states and the column Total.Math and then gets the average

Retrieves rows from 2012–2015 with those three states and the column Total.Math and then gets the average

You can explore a version of this in the Pandas Tutor at http://mng.bz/PRpw.

Beyond the exercise

- What were the average math and verbal scores for Florida, Indiana, and Idaho across all years? (Don't break out the values by state.)
- Which state received the highest verbal score, and in which year?
- Was the average math score in 2005 higher or lower than that in 2015?

Sorting by index

When we talk about sorting in pandas, we're usually referring to sorting the data. For example, we may want the rows in our data frame sorted by price or regional sales code. We'll talk more about that kind of sorting in Chapters 6 and 7.

But pandas also lets us sort data frames based on the index. We can do that with the `sort_index` method, which (like so many others) returns a new data frame with the same content as the original, with rows sorted based on the index's values. We can thus say

```
df = df.sort_index()
```

If your data frame contains a multi-index, the sorting will be done primarily along the first level, then along the second level, and so forth.

In addition to having some aesthetic benefits, sorting a data frame by index can make certain tasks easier or possible. For example, if you try to retrieve a slice, such as `df.loc['a':'c']`, pandas will insist that the index be sorted, to avoid problems if `a` and `c` are interspersed.

If your data frame is unsorted and has a multi-index, performing some operations may result in a warning:

```
PerformanceWarning: indexing past lexsort depth may impact performance
```

This is pandas trying to tell you that the combination of large size, multi-index, and an unsorted index is likely to cause you trouble. You can avoid the warning by sorting your data frame via its index.

(continued)

If you want to check whether a data frame is sorted, you can check this attribute:

```
df.index.is_monotonic_increasing
```

Saying that the index is "monotonically increasing," by the way, simply means it only goes up. Similarly, if the values only go down, we say it's "monotonically decreasing," which we can check with `is_monotonic_decreasing`. Note that these are *not* methods but rather boolean attributes. They exist on all series objects, not just on indexes. Some older documentation and blogs mention the method `is_lexsorted`, which has been deprecated in recent versions of pandas.

EXERCISE 23 ▪ Olympic games

The modern-day Olympic games have been around for more than a century, and even people like me who rarely pay attention to sports are often excited to see a variety of international competitions take place. Fortunately, the Olympics aren't only about sports; they also generate a great deal of data, which we can enjoy and analyze using pandas.

In the previous exercise, we initially looked at building and using a multi-index. A multi-index doesn't have to stop at just two levels; pandas will, in theory, allow us to set as many as we want. Consider a large corporation that has broken down sales reports by region, country, and department; a multi-index would make it possible to retrieve that data in a variety of different ways, be it from the top of the hierarchy or by reaching "inside" the multi-index and creating a cross-regional departmental report.

In this exercise, we're going to build a deep multi-index, allowing us to retrieve data from various levels and in several ways. Specifically, I want you to do the following:

1 Read the data file (olympic_athlete_events.csv) into a data frame. We only care about some of the columns: `Age`, `Height`, `Team`, `Year`, `Season`, `City`, `Sport`, `Event`, and `Medal`. The multi-index should be based on `Year`, `Season`, `Sport`, and `Event`.

2 Answer these questions:

   – What is the average age of winning athletes in summer games held between 1936 and 2000?

   – What team has won the most medals in all archery events?

   – Starting in 1980, what is the average height of the "Table Tennis Women's Team" event?

   – Starting in 1980, what is the average height of both "Table Tennis Women's Team" and "Table Tennis Men's Team"?

   – How tall was the tallest-ever tennis player in Olympic games from 1980 until 2016?

Working it out

In this exercise, we create a multi-index with four levels and then use those levels to ask and answer a variety of questions. The exercise shows you how powerful multi-indexes can be.

First, we have to load the data. As before, we load a subset of the columns and use four of them as a multi-index:

```
filename = '../data/olympic_athlete_events.csv'

df = pd.read_csv(filename,
            index_col=['Year', 'Season',
                       'Sport', 'Event'],
            usecols=['Age', 'Height', 'Team',
                     'Year', 'Season', 'City',
                     'Sport', 'Event', 'Medal'])
df = df.sort_index()
```

Specifies the components and order of the multi-index in index_col

Reads the CSV file into a data frame with nine columns, four of which are used in our index

Sorts the rows of the data frame according to the index

By passing a list of columns to the index_col parameter, we create the multi-index while creating the data frame, rather than doing it in a separate second step (see figure 4.4).

Multi-index

Year	Season	Sport	Event	Age	Height	Team	City	Medal
1996	Summer	Athletics	Athletics Men's 10,000 meters	27.0	178.0	United States	Atlanta	NaN
1992	Winter	Biathlon	Biathlon Women's 15 kilometers	22.0	NaN	China	Albertville	NaN
2012	Summer	Fencing	Fencing Men's Foil, Team	29.0	180.0	China	London	NaN
1988	Winter	Cross-Country Skiing	Cross-Country Skiing Men's 50 kilometers	24.0	174.0	Sweden	Calgary	NaN
1900	Summer	Rowing	Rowing Men's Coxed Eights	21.0	NaN	Germania Ruder Club, Hamburg	Paris	NaN
2006	Winter	Biathlon	Biathlon Men's 4 x 7.5 kilometers Relay	28.0	180.0	Czech Republic	Torino	NaN
2004	Summer	Cycling	Cycling Men's Mountainbike, Cross-Country	22.0	178.0	Spain	Athina	NaN
1912	Summer	Gymnastics	Gymnastics Men's Team All-Around	20.0	NaN	Germany	Stockholm	NaN
1952	Summer	Rowing	Rowing Men's Coxless Fours	26.0	186.0	Norway	Helsinki	NaN
1994	Winter	Ski Jumping	Ski Jumping Men's Large Hill, Team	23.0	175.0	Italy	Lillehammer	NaN

Figure 4.4 Graphical depiction of our data frame with four columns in its multi-index

We then use `sort_index`, which returns a new data frame containing the same data we read from the CSV file but with the rows ordered according to the multi-index. When running `sort_index` on a multi-indexed data frame, we first index on the first level (i.e., `Year`), then on `Season`, then on `Sport`, and finally on `Event`.

> **NOTE** You can invoke `set_index` with `inplace=True`. If you do, `set_index` will modify the existing data frame object and return `None`. But as with all other uses of `inplace=True` in pandas, the core developers strongly recommend against doing this. Instead, you should invoke it regularly (i.e., with a default value of `inplace=False`) and then assign the result to a variable—which could be the variable already referring to the data frame, as we do here.

Although we don't necessarily need to sort our data frame by its index, certain pandas operations will work better if we do. Moreover, if we don't sort the data frame, we may get the `PerformanceWarning` mentioned earlier in this chapter. So, especially when we're doing operations with a multi-index, it's a good idea to sort by the index at the outset.

Now that we have our data frame, we can answer the questions I posed. For starters, I asked you to find the average age of winning athletes who participated in summer games held between 1936 and 2000. This means we want a subset of the years (i.e., the first level of our multi-index) and a subset of the seasons (i.e., just the games for which the second level of the multi-index, the `Season` column, has a value of `Summer`). We want all the values from the third and fourth levels of the multi-index, which means we can ignore them in our query; by ignoring them, we get all the values.

In other words, we want our query to retrieve the following (see figure 4.5):

- All years from 1936 to 2000, which we can express as `slice(1936,2000)`
- All games in which `Season` is set to `Summer`
- The `Age` column from the resulting data frame

Finally, we want to find the mean of those ages. We can express this as

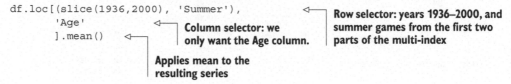

```
df.loc[(slice(1936,2000), 'Summer'),
       'Age'
      ].mean()
```

Column selector: we only want the Age column.

Row selector: years 1936–2000, and summer games from the first two parts of the multi-index

Applies mean to the resulting series

The answer is a float, 25.026883940421765.

Next, I asked you to find which team won the most medals in all archery events. How do we construct this query? We need to think through each level in our multi-index:

- We're interested in all years, so we specify `slice(None)` for the first index level.
- Archery is only a summer sport, so we can either indicate `Summer` for the second level or use `slice(None)`.
- In the third level, we explicitly specify `Archery` so we only get rows for archery events.
- We ignore the fourth level, effectively making it a wildcard.

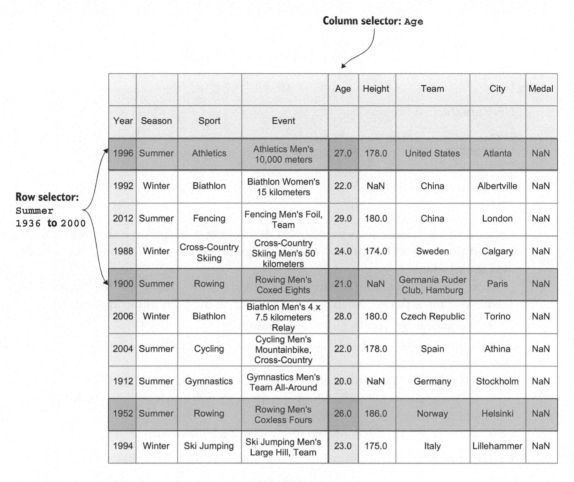

Figure 4.5   Graphical depiction of applying our multi-index row selector

We're interested in calculating which team won the most medals. So, we ask for the `Team` column. Then we can run `value_counts` to identify which team won the most events. The query thus looks like this:

```
df.loc[(slice(None), 'Summer', 'Archery'),
       'Team'
      ].value_counts()
```

- Row selector: all years, summer games, all competitions within archery
- Column selector: we only want the Team column.
- Applies value_counts to the resulting series

But wait: this counts *all* participants in archery events. We are only interested in the medalists. We can thus start our query by removing all rows in which `Medal` contains a `NaN` value, calling `dropna` and passing `subset='Medal'`. It's probably easier to understand if we use method-chaining syntax and formatting:

```
(
    df
    .dropna(subset='Medal')
    .loc[(slice(None), 'Summer', 'Archery'), 'Team']
    .value_counts()
)
```

Here are the first five results:

```
Team
South Korea          69
Belgium              52
France               48
United States        41
China                19
```

Because `value_counts` sorts its values in descending order, we see that South Korea has had the most archery medalists, with Belgium, France, the US, and China in the next few places.

Next, I asked you to find the average height of athletes in one specific event: "Table Tennis Women's Team." Again, we can consider all the parts of our multi-index:

- We want to get results from 1980 onward.
- Table tennis is only played in the summer games, so we can specify either `Summer` or `slice(None)`.
- The sport is "Table tennis," so we can specify that if we want to—but given that all these events fall under the same sport, we can also leave it as a wildcard with `slice(None)`.
- We specify "Table Tennis Women's Team" for the event.

We are only interested in the `Height` column, so our query looks like this:

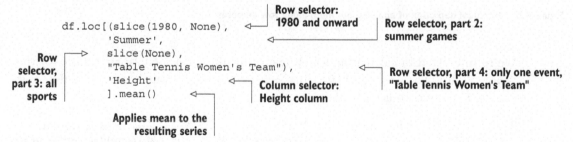

The answer from our data set is the float 165.04827586206898, or just over 165 cm.

For the next query, we expand our population, looking at not just the women's team version of table tennis but also the men's version. Our first three selectors are identical to what we did before, but the final (fourth) multi-index selector is a list rather than a string:

```
df.loc[(slice(1980, None),
       'Summer',
```

Row selector, part 3: all sports

```
slice(None),
["Table Tennis Men's Team",
 "Table Tennis Women's Team"]),
'Height'
].mean()
```

Row selector, part 4: two events: "Table Tennis Women's Team" and "Table Tennis Men's Team"

Column selector: Height column

Applies mean to the resulting series

Given that men are generally taller than women, it's not a surprise that adding men's events has greatly increased the average athlete's height. The answer is 171.26643598615917.

Finally, I was curious to know the height of the tallest-ever tennis player from 1980 until 2020. Once again, let's go through our query-building process:

- We want years from 1980 through 2016. This can be handled most easily with `slice(1980,2016)`.
- Because tennis is only at summer games, it doesn't matter whether we specify the `Season` selector as `Summer` or use `slice(None)`.
- We specify "Tennis" as the sport
- We'll allow any events, so we don't need to pass a fourth element in the tuple.

Finally, we're looking for the `Height` column, so we specify that in our query. And we want the maximum value for `Height`, so we use the `max` method. The final query looks like this:

Row selector: years 1980–2016

Row selector, part 2: summer games

```
df.loc[(slice(1980,2016),
        'Summer',
        'Tennis'),
        'Height'
].max()
```

Row selector, part 3: only tennis

Column selector: Height column

Applies max to the resulting series

The tallest-ever tennis player was 208 cm tall—known in some countries as 6 feet, 10 inches. That's pretty tall!

Solution

```
filename = '../data/olympic_athlete_events.csv'

df = pd.read_csv(filename,
            index_col=['Year', 'Season',
                       'Sport', 'Event'],
            usecols=['Age', 'Height', 'Team',
                     'Year', 'Season', 'City',
                     'Sport', 'Event', 'Medal'])
df = df.sort_index()
df.loc[(slice(1936,2000), 'Summer'), 'Age'].mean()
df.dropna(subset='Medal').loc[
    (slice(None), 'Summer', 'Archery'),
        'Team'].value_counts()
df.loc[(slice(1980, None), 'Summer', slice(None),
    "Table Tennis Women's Team"),
```

Sorts the rows of the data frame according to the index

Reads the CSV file into a data frame with nine total columns, four of which are used in our index

Gets the average age of summer athletes from 1936 to 2000

Which teams got the most medals in all archery events?

```
        'Height'].mean()
df.loc[(slice(1980, None),
        'Summer', slice(None),
        ["Table Tennis Men's Team",
        "Table Tennis Women's Team"]),
        'Height'].mean()
df.loc[(slice(1980,2016),
        'Summer',
        'Tennis'), 'Height'].max()
```

What was the average height of participants in "Table Tennis Women's Team" events from 1980?

What was the average height of participants in both "Table Tennis Women's Team" and "Table Tennis Men's Team" events from 1980?

How tall was the tallest tennis player from 1980 to 2016?

You can explore a version of this in the Pandas Tutor at http://mng.bz/JdXo.

Going deep

As we have already seen, `loc` makes retrieving data from multi-indexed data frames pretty straightforward. However, sometimes we may want to use a multi-index differently. Pandas provides two other methods: `xs` and `IndexSlice`.

Because multi-indexed data frames are both common and important, pandas provides several ways to retrieve data from them. Let's start with `xs`, which lets us accomplish what we did in exercise 23: find matches for certain levels within a multi-index. For example, one question in the previous exercise asked you to find the mean height of participants in the "Table Tennis Women's Team" event from all Olympics years. Using `loc`, we had to tell pandas to accept all values for `Year`, all values for `Season`, and all values for `Sport`—in other words, we only checked the fourth level of the multi-index: the event. Our query looked like this:

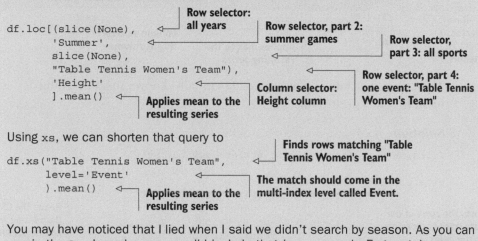

```
df.loc[(slice(None),
        'Summer',
        slice(None),
        "Table Tennis Women's Team"),
        'Height'
        ].mean()
```

Row selector: all years

Row selector, part 2: summer games

Row selector, part 3: all sports

Row selector, part 4: one event: "Table Tennis Women's Team"

Column selector: Height column

Applies mean to the resulting series

Using `xs`, we can shorten that query to

```
df.xs("Table Tennis Women's Team",
        level='Event'
        ).mean()
```

Finds rows matching "Table Tennis Women's Team"

The match should come in the multi-index level called Event.

Applies mean to the resulting series

You may have noticed that I lied when I said we didn't search by season. As you can see in the `loc`-based query, we did include that in our search. Fortunately, we can handle that by passing a list of levels to the `level` parameter and a tuple of values as the first argument:

```
df.xs(('Summer', "Table Tennis Women's Team"),
        level=['Season', 'Event']).mean()
```

Passes a two-element tuple to match two levels of the multi-index

The argument passed to level indicates which levels need to match.

Notice that `xs` is a method and is thus invoked with round parentheses. By contrast, `loc` is an accessor attribute and is invoked with square brackets. And yes, it's often hard to keep track of these things.

You can, by the way, use integers as the arguments to `level` rather than names. I find column names far easier to understand, though, and I encourage you to use them.

A more general way to retrieve from a multi-index is `IndexSlice`. Remember when I mentioned earlier that we cannot use `:` inside round parentheses and thus need to say `slice(None)`? Well, `IndexSlice` solves that problem: it uses square brackets and can use slice syntax for any set of values. For example, we can say

Years 1980–2016, all seasons, and all sports from "Swimming" to "Table tennis"

```
from pandas import IndexSlice as idx
df.loc[idx[1980:2016, :, 'Swimming':'Table tennis'], :]
```

This code allows us to select a range of values for each level of the multi-index. We no longer need to call the `slice` function. Now we can use the standard Python `:` syntax for slicing within each level. The result of calling `IndexSlice` (or `idx`, as we aliased it here) is a tuple of Python `slice` objects:

```
(slice(1980, 2016, None),
 slice(None, None, None),
 slice('Swimming', 'Table tennis', None))
```

In other words, `IndexSlice` is syntactic sugar, allowing pandas to look and feel more like a standard Python data structure, even when the index is far more complex.

One final note: a data frame can have a multi-index on its rows, its columns, or both. By default, `xs` assumes the multi-index is on the rows. If and when you want to use it on multi-index columns, pass `axis='columns'` as a keyword argument.

Beyond the exercise

- Events occur in either summer or winter Olympic games, but not both. As a result, the `"Season"` level in our multi-index is often unnecessary. Remove the `"Season"` level, and then find (again) the height of the tallest tennis player between 1980 and 2016.
- In which city were the most gold medals awarded from 1980 onward?
- How many gold medals were received by the United States since 1980? (Use the index to select the values.)

Pivot tables

So far, we have seen how to use indexes to restructure our data, making it easier to retrieve different slices of the information it contains and thus answer particular questions more easily. But the questions we have been asking have all had a single

(continued)

answer. We often want to apply a particular aggregate function to many different combinations of columns and rows. One of the most common and powerful ways to accomplish this is with a *pivot table*.

A pivot table allows us to create a new table (data frame) from a subset of an existing data frame. Here's the basic idea:

- Our data frame contains two columns with categorical, repeating, nonhierarchical data. For example: years, country names, colors, and company divisions.
- Our data frame has a third column that is numeric.
- We create a new data frame from those three columns, as follows:
  - All unique values from the first categorical column become the index or row labels.
  - All unique values from the second categorical column become the column labels.
  - Wherever the two categories match, we get either the single value where those two intersect or the mean of all values where they intersect.

It takes a while to understand how a pivot table works. But once you get it, it's hard to un-see: you start finding uses everywhere.

For example, consider this simple data frame:

```
g = np.random.default_rng(0)
df = DataFrame(g.integers(0, 100, [8,3]),
               columns=list('ABC'))
df['year'] = [2018] * 4 + [2019] * 4
df['quarter'] = 'Q1 Q2 Q3 Q4'.split() * 2
```

This table shows the sales of each product per year and quarter. And you can certainly understand the data if you look at it a certain way. But what if we were interested in seeing sales figures for product A? It may make more sense, and be easier to parse, if we use the quarters (a categorical, repeating value) as the rows, the years (again, a categorical, repeating value) as the columns, and the figures for product A as the values. We can create such a pivot table as follows:

```
df.pivot_table(index='quarter',      ⟵ Rows (index) are unique
               columns='year',          values from quarter.    Columns are unique
               values='A')           ⟵                          values from year.
                                     ⟵ Values are the mean of each
                                       year—quarter intersection.
```

The result, on my computer, is a data frame that looks like this:

```
year     2018    2019
quarter
Q1        44      88
Q2        67      65
Q3        83      46
Q4        87      37
```

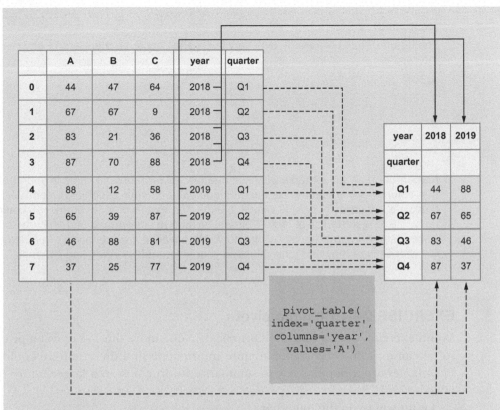

Graphical depiction of creating a pivot table with index `quarter`, **columns** `year`, **and values** `A`

The quarters are sorted in alphabetical order, which is fine here. In some cases, such as using month names for your index, you can pass `sort=False`.

What if more than one row has the same values for year and month? By default, `pivot_table` runs the `mean` aggregation method on all values. (Pandas also offers a `pivot` method, which doesn't do aggregation and cannot handle duplicate values for index-column combinations. I never use it.) To use a different aggregation function, pass an argument to `aggfunc` in your call to `pivot_table`. For example, you can count the values in each intersection box by passing the `size` function:

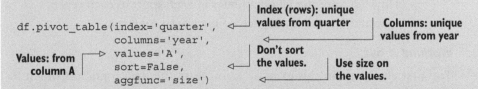

Note that here, it doesn't matter whether we use `size` or `count`, because there aren't any `NaN` values. Generally speaking, `size` includes all values, including `NaN`, and `count` ignores them.

> **(continued)**
>
> The result of this data frame isn't very interesting because there aren't any repeated intersections:
>
> ```
> year     2018    2019
> quarter
> Q1       1       1
> Q2       1       1
> Q3       1       1
> Q4       1       1
> ```
>
> Remember that a pivot table will have one row for each unique value in your first chosen column and a column for each unique value in your second chosen column. If there are hundreds of unique values in either (or, even worse, in both), you could end up with a gargantuan pivot table. This will be hard to understand and analyze and also will consume large amounts of memory. Moreover, if your data isn't very lean (see Chapter 5), you may find junk values in your pivot table's index and columns.

EXERCISE 24 ▪ Olympic pivots

In this exercise, we examine the Olympic data one more time—but using pivot tables, so we can examine and compare more information at a time than we could before. Pivot tables are a popular way to summarize information in a larger, more complex table.

I want you to do the following:

1 Read in our Olympic data again.

   – Only use these columns: `Age`, `Height`, `Team`, `Year`, `Season`, `Sport`, `Medal`.
   – Only include games from 1980 to the present.
   – Only include data from these countries: Great Britain, France, United States, Switzerland, China, and India.

2 Answer these questions:

   – What was the average age of Olympic athletes? In which country do players appear to consistently be the youngest?
   – How tall were the tallest athletes in each sport in each year?
   – How many medals did each country earn each year?

Working it out

The first challenge in this exercise is to create the data frame on which to base our pivot tables. We load the same CSV file as in the previous exercise, but we're interested in fewer rows and columns.

The first step is to read the CSV file into a data frame, limiting the columns we request:

```
df = pd.read_csv(filename,
                 usecols=['Age', 'Height',
                          'Team', 'Year',
                          'Season', 'Sport',
                          'Medal'])
```

Notice that we don't set the index. That's because we ignore the index in this exercise, focusing instead on pivot tables. Because the pivot tables are constructed based on actual columns and not the index, we'll stick with the default numeric index that pandas assigns to every data frame.

Now we want to remove all the rows that aren't from the countries we've named. (I chose these countries because I traveled there in the months before the pandemic. This is not meant to be any sort of representative sample, except where I've done corporate training in Python and data science.) We often keep (or remove) rows with a particular value, but how can we keep rows whose `Team` column is one of several values? We could use a query with | (the boolean "or" operator), but it would be long and complex.

Instead, we can use the `isin` method, which allows us to pass a list of possibilities and get a `True` value whenever the `Team` column equals one of those possible strings. In my experience, the `isin` method is one of those things that seems obvious when you start to use it but is far from obvious until you know to look for it.

We can keep only those countries this way:

```
df = df.loc[df['Team'].isin(['Great Britain', 'France',
                             'United States', 'Switzerland',
                             'China', 'India'])]
```

Now we remove any rows in which `Year` is before 1980. This is a more standard operation, one we've done many times before:

```
df = df.loc[df['Year'] >= 1980]
```

With our data frame in place, we can create pivot tables to examine our data from a new perspective. I first asked you to compare the average age of players for each team, for all sports and all years. As usual, when creating pivot tables, we need to consider what will be the rows, columns, and values:

- The rows (index) will be the unique values from the `Year` column.
- The columns will be the unique values from the `Team` column.
- The values will be from the `Age` column.

Sure enough, we can create our pivot table as follows:

```
df.pivot_table(index='Year',        ◁—┘ Index: unique
               columns='Team',            values of Year in df      ◁—┘ Columns: unique
               values='Age')       ◁—┐                                    values of Team in df
                                       Values: mean of Age for each
                                       year—team combination
```

These numbers are across all sports, and not every country has entrants in every sport. But if we take the numbers at face value, we see that China consistently has younger athletes at Olympic games. Here is the output from the query:

Team	China	France	Great Britain	India	Switzerland	United States
Year						
1980	21.868421	23.524590	22.882507	25.506667	24.557823	22.770992
1984	22.076336	24.369830	24.445423	24.905660	23.589744	24.437118
1988	22.358447	24.520076	25.439560	24.000000	26.218868	24.904977
1992	21.955752	25.140187	25.584055	24.184615	25.413194	25.474866
1994	20.627907	24.601307	25.282051	NaN	25.500000	24.976744
1996	22.021531	25.296629	26.746032	24.629630	27.122093	26.273277
1998	21.784091	25.462069	27.243902	16.000000	25.641509	25.146154
2000	22.515306	25.982833	26.406948	25.400000	27.376812	26.576203
2002	23.127451	25.737805	26.833333	20.000000	26.238710	25.726316
2004	23.006122	26.139073	26.303977	24.728395	27.343284	26.439093
2006	23.457143	26.303226	26.851852	25.200000	26.284848	25.637288
2008	23.903955	26.285714	25.200969	25.402985	27.312500	26.225806
2010	23.239669	25.911458	26.147059	25.666667	26.548387	25.841584
2012	23.894168	26.606635	25.922619	25.637363	27.172131	26.461883
2014	23.400000	25.708995	25.628571	25.000000	25.855814	26.189189
2016	23.873706	27.095238	26.653191	26.100000	25.891892	26.217454

Next, we want to find the tallest players in each sport from each year. Given that we are looking at a large number of sports and a relatively small number of years, it is wise to use the years in the columns this time:

- The rows (index) will be the unique values from the Sport column.
- The columns will be the unique values from the Year column.
- The values will come from the Height column. We're interested in the highest value and will thus provide a function argument to the aggfunc parameter: max.

NOTE   In previous versions of pandas, it was common to specify the aggregation method by passing a NumPy method, such as np.max or np.size. However, pandas now prefers to get a string (e.g., 'max' or 'size'), which translates into an internal function name or reference.

In the end, we create the pivot table as follows:

```
df.pivot_table(index='Sport',      ←──┐ Index: unique
               columns='Year',          values of Sport in df       Columns: unique
               values='Height',   ←─────                            values of Year in df
               aggfunc='max')     ←──  We use max as our
                                       aggregation function.
```

Values: maximum value for Height

From the large number of NaN values, we can see that height information isn't as readily available for all sports and teams as many other measurements. This is not an unusual problem to face with real-world data; sometimes you have to make do with the data that is available, even if it's far from reliable and complete.

Finally, I asked you to determine how many medals each country received at each game. Once again, let's do a bit of planning before creating our pivot table:

- The rows (index) will be the unique values from the Year column.
- The columns will be the unique values from the Team column.
- We want to count the number of medals, not get their average values (as if that's even possible). This means we must provide a function argument to the aggfunc parameter. This can usually be a string referring to a method, such as 'max'. We first have to remove all rows for which Medal has a NaN value indicating that no medal was won.

Our code to create the pivot table can look like this:

```
pd.pivot_table(df.dropna(subset='Medal'),        ← Index: unique           Only uses the
                                                    values of Sport in df    subset of df where
                                                                             Medal isn't NaN
               index='Year',
               columns='Team',
Columns: unique   values='Medal',
values of Team in df   aggfunc='max')             ←                         Values: sum of values
                                                    We use max as our        in the Medal column
                                                    aggregation function.
```

Solution

```
filename = '../data/olympic_athlete_events.csv'

df = pd.read_csv(filename,
                 usecols=['Age', 'Height', 'Team',
                          'Year', 'Season',          ← Loads only five columns;
                          'Sport', 'Medal'])            we ignore the index

df = df.loc[df['Team'].isin(['Great Britain', 'France',      ← Removes rows in which
                             'United States', 'Switzerland',    the team isn't one of the
                             'China', 'India'])]                six we're looking for
df = df.loc[df['Year'] >= 1980]                     ← Removes rows in which
                                                       the year is before 1980
df.pivot_table(index='Year', columns='Team',
               values='Age')                        ← Pivot table from Year (index),
df.pivot_table(index='Sport',                          Team (columns), and mean Age
               columns='Year', values='Height',
               aggfunc='max')                       ← Pivot table from Sport (index), Year
                                                       (columns), and the max value of Height
pd.pivot_table(df.dropna(subset='Medal'),
               index='Year',
               columns='Team',
               values='Medal',                      ← Pivot table from Year (index), Team
               aggfunc='size')                         (columns), and the number of medals
```

You can explore a version of this, in color, in the Pandas Tutor at https://pandastutor.com/vis.html#.

Beyond the exercise

- Create a pivot table that shows the number of medals each team won per year, with the index including the year and the season in which the games took place.

- Create a pivot table that shows both the average age and the average height per year per team.
- Create a pivot table that shows the average age and the average height per year, per team, broken up by year and season.

Summary

In this chapter, we saw that a data frame's index is not just a way to keep track of the rows but one that can be used to reshape a data frame, making it easier to extract useful information. This is particularly true when we create pivot tables, choosing values from an existing data frame for comparison.

Cleaning data 5

In the late 1980s, my employer wanted to know how much rain had fallen in various places. Their solution? They gave me a list of cities and phone numbers and asked me to call each in sequence, recording the previous day's rainfall in an Excel spreadsheet. Nowadays, getting that sort of information—and many other types—is pretty easy. Many governments provide data sets for free, and numerous companies make data available for a price. No matter what topic you're researching, data is almost certainly available. The only questions are where you can get it, how much it costs, and what format it comes in.

You should ask another question, too: how accurate is the data you're using? It's easy to assume that a CSV file from an official-looking website contains good data. But all too often, it will have problems. That shouldn't surprise us, given that the data comes from people (who can make mistakes) and machines (which make different types of mistakes). Maybe someone accidentally misnamed a file or entered data into the wrong field. Maybe the automatic sensors whose inputs were used in collecting the data were broken or offline. Maybe the servers were down for a day, or someone misconfigured the XML feed-reading system, or the routers were being rebooted, or a backhoe cut the internet line.

All this assumes there was data to begin with. Often, we'll have missing data because there wasn't any data to record.

This is why I've heard data scientists say that 80% of their job involves cleaning data. What does it mean to "clean data"? Here is a partial list:

- Rename columns.
- Rename the index.
- Remove irrelevant columns.

131

- Split one column into two.
- Combine two or more columns into one.
- Remove nondata rows.
- Remove repeated rows.
- Remove rows with missing data (aka NaN).
- Replace NaN data with a single value.
- Replace NaN data via interpolation.
- Standardize strings.
- Fix typos in strings.
- Remove whitespace from strings.
- Correct the types used for columns.
- Identify and remove outliers.

We have discussed some of these techniques in previous chapters. But the importance of cleaning your data, and thus ensuring that your analysis is as accurate as possible, cannot be overstated.

In this chapter, we'll look at pandas techniques for cleaning data. We'll see a few ways to handle NaN values. We'll consider how to preserve as much data as possible, even when it's pretty dirty. We'll discuss how to better understand our data and its limitations. And we'll look at a some more advanced techniques for massaging data into a form that's more easily analyzed.

Table 5.1 What you need to know

Concept	What is it?	Example	To learn more
df.shape	A two-element tuple indicating the number of rows and columns in a data frame	df.shape	http://mng.bz/8rpg
len(df) or len(df.index)	Gets the number of rows in a data frame	len(df) or len(df.index)	http://mng.bz/EQdr
s.isnull	Returns a boolean series indicating where there are null (typically NaN) values in the series s	s.isnull()	http://mng.bz/N2KX
s.notnull	Returns a boolean series indicating where there are non-null values in the series s	s.notnull()	http://mng.bz/D420
df.isnull	Returns a boolean data frame indicating where there are null (typically NaN) values in the data frame df	df.isnull()	http://mng.bz/IWGz
df.replace	Replaces values in one or more columns with other values	df.replace('a':{'b':'c'), 'd')	http://mng.bz/Bm2q

Table 5.1 **What you need to know** *(continued)*

Concept	What is it?	Example	To learn more
`s.map`	Applies a function to each element of a series, returning the result of that application on each element	`s.map(lambda x: x**2)`	http://mng.bz/d1yz
`df.fillna`	Replaces `NaN` with other values	`df.fillna(10)`	http://mng.bz/rWrE
`df.dropna`	Removes rows with `NaN` values	`df = df.dropna()`	http://mng.bz/V1gr
`s.str`	Works with textual data	`df['colname'].str`	http://mng.bz/x4Wq
`str.isdigit`	Returns a boolean series, indicating which strings contain only the digits 0–9	`df['colname'].str.isdigit()`	http://mng.bz/AoAE
`pd.to_numeric`	Returns a series of integers or floats based on a series of strings	`pd.to_numeric(df['colname'])`	http://mng.bz/Zq2j
`df.sort_index`	Reorders the rows of a data frame based on the values in its index in ascending order	`df = df.sort_index()`	http://mng.bz/RxAn
`pd.read_excel`	Creates a data frame based on an Excel spreadsheet	`df = pd.read_excel('myfile.xlsx')`	http://mng.bz/2DXN
`pd.read_csv`	Returns a new data frame based on CSV input	`df = pd.read_csv('myfile.csv')`	http://mng.bz/wvl7
`s.value_counts`	Returns a sorted (descending frequency) series counting how many times each value appears in s	`s.value_counts()`	http://mng.bz/1qzZ
`s.unique`	Returns a series with the unique (i.e., distinct) values in s, including `NaN` (if it occurs in s)	`s.unique()`	http://mng.bz/PzA2
`s.mode`	Returns a series with the most commonly found values in s	`s.mode()`	http://mng.bz/7vBm

How much is missing?

We've already seen, on several occasions, that data frames (and series) can contain `NaN` values. One question we often want to answer is, how many `NaN` values are in a given column? Or, for that matter, in a data frame?

(continued)

One solution is to calculate things yourself. There is a `count` method you can run on a series, which returns the number of non-null values in the series. That, combined with the shape of the series, can tell you how many `NaN` values there are:

```
s.shape[0] - s.count()
```
   ◁─┐ **Returns an integer: the
number of null elements**

This is tedious and annoying. And besides, shouldn't pandas provide a way to do this? Indeed it does, in the form of the `isnull` method. If you call `isnull` on a column, it returns a boolean series with `True` where there is a `NaN` value and `False` in other places. You can then apply the `sum` method to the series, which will return the number of `True` values, thanks to the fact that Python's boolean values inherit from integers and can be in place of 1 (`True`) and 0 (`False`) if needed:

```
s.isnull().sum()
```
   ◁─┐ **Calculates the number
of NaN values in s**

If you run `isnull` on a data frame, you get a new data frame back, with `True` and `False` values indicating whether there is a null value in that particular row-column combination. And, of course, you can run `sum` on the resulting data frame to find out how many `NaN` values are in each column:

```
df.isnull().sum()
```
   ◁─┐ **Calculates the number of
NaN values in each column**

Finally, the `df.info` method returns a wealth of information about the data frame on which it's run, including the name and type of each column, a summary of the number of columns of each type, and the estimated memory usage. (We'll talk more about this memory usage in Chapter 12.) If the data frame is small enough, it will also show you how many null values are in each column. However, this calculation can take some time. Thus, `df.info` will only count null values below a certain threshold. If you're above that threshold (the `pd.options.display.max_info_columns` option), you need to tell pandas explicitly to count by passing `show_counts=True`:

```
df.info(show_counts=True)
```
   ◁─┐ **Gets full information about the data
frame df, including the number of
null values in each column**

NOTE Pandas defines both `isna` and `isnull` for both series and data frames. What's the difference between them? There is *no* Difference. If you look at the pandas documentation, you'll find that they're identical except for the name of the method being called. In this book, I use `isnull`, but if you prefer to go with `isna`, be my guest. Note that both are different from `np.isnan`, a method defined in NumPy, on top of which pandas is defined. I try to stick with the methods that pandas defines, which in my experience integrate better into the rest of the system. Rather than using ~, which pandas uses to invert boolean series and data frames, you can often use the `notnull` methods for both series and data frame.

EXERCISE 25 ■ Parking cleanup

In chapter 4, we looked at parking tickets given in New York City in 2020. We were able to analyze that data and draw some interesting conclusions from it. But let's consider that this data was entered by a police officer, a parking inspector, or another person, which means there is a good chance it sometimes has missing or incorrect data. That may seem like a minor problem, but it can mean everything from cars being ticketed incorrectly to bad statistics in the system to people getting out of fines due to incorrect information. (A side note: when you're issued a parking ticket in Israel, it includes a photograph of your car and license plate, taken by the inspector when they issued the ticket. That makes it a bit harder to wriggle out of fines, but people manage to do it anyway.)

In this exercise, we will identify missing values, one of the most common problems you will encounter. We'll see how often values are missing and what effect they may have. Note that for this exercise, we're going to assume that a parking ticket that is missing data may be dismissed; don't blame me if this defense doesn't work when appealing any tickets you get in New York.

I want you to do the following:

1 Create a data frame from the file nyc-parking-violations-2020.csv. We are only interested in a handful of the columns:
    — `Plate ID`
    — `Registration State`
    — `Vehicle Make`
    — `Vehicle Color`
    — `Violation Time`
    — `Street Name`

   How many rows are in the data frame when it is read into memory?
2 Remove rows with any missing data (i.e., a NaN value). How many rows remain after doing this pruning? If each parking ticket brings $100 into the city, and missing data means the ticket can be successfully contested, how much money may New York City lose due to such missing data?
3 Let's instead assume that a ticket can only be dismissed if the license plate, state, car make, and/or street name are missing. Remove rows that are missing one or more of these. How many rows remain? Assuming $100/ticket, how much money would the city lose as a result of this missing data?
4 Now let's assume that tickets can be dismissed if the license plate, state, and/or street name are missing—that is, the same as the previous question, but without requiring the make of car. Remove rows that are missing one or more of these. How many rows remain? Assuming $100/ticket, how much money would the city lose as a result of this missing data?

Working it out

When you're first starting with data analytics, it's reasonable to think you can just toss out imperfect data. After all, if something is missing, you cannot use it, right? In this exercise, I hope you saw not only how to remove rows with missing data but also the potential problems associated with doing that.

For starters, let's load the CSV file into a data frame. We are only interested in a few columns, so loading looks like this:

```
filename = '../data/nyc-parking-violations-2020.csv'

df = pd.read_csv(filename,
                 usecols=['Plate ID',
                          'Registration State',
                          'Vehicle Make',
                          'Vehicle Color',
                          'Violation Time',
                          'Street Name'])
```

We can determine the number of rows in our data frame by getting the first element (i.e., index 0) from the `shape` attribute:

```
df.shape[0]
```

It turns out there's a better way, though: we can invoke the Python builtin `len` on our data frame, thus getting the number of rows:

```
len(df)
```

Not only does this give the same answer, but in my testing, I found that `len` was twice as fast as `shape[0]`. But we can do even better by running `len` on `df.index`:

```
len(df.index)
```

In my tests, I found that `len(df.index)` runs about 45% faster than `len(df)` and about 65% faster than `df.shape[0]`.

> **Counting values**
>
> The `count` method often seems like the most natural, obvious way to count rows. But it has several problems:
>
> - It ignores `NaN` values
> - On a large data frame, it takes a long time to run
>
> If you want to know the number of all values, including `NaN`, you can use the `size` attribute (not a method), which works on both series and data frames. Or invoke `np.size` on the series, as in `np.size(s)`.
>
> However, as I said earlier, I prefer to call `len(df.index)`, which gives me the total length and seems to run fastest.

With that data frame in place, we can start to make a few queries, looking for tickets that could potentially be dismissed for lack of data. Our first query will apply the naive (but well-meaning) approach, in which we remove any rows that have missing data. We can do this with the df.dropna method. That method returns a new data frame, identical to our original df, but without any rows that have any NaN values (figure 5.1):

```
all_good_df = df.dropna()
```

	Plate ID	Registration State	Vehicle Make	Violation Time	Street Name	Vehicle Color
2752511	LHLP99	FL	HYUN	0230P	JACOB RIIS PARK	RED
964568	JXJ1561	PA	TOYOT	0119P	E 58th St	BLUE
5049760	S82HUN	NJ	HONDA	0846A	SB UNIVERSITY AVE @	BK
4248515	HYK8920	NY	FORD	1151A	NB PARK AVE @ E 83RD	GY
353397	KMF8349	PA	NaN	0850P	S/S SEAVIEW AVE	WHITE
2703401	XHXE40	NJ	NaN	1039A	W 43 ST	WH
1434853	TRD7943	OH	NaN	0937A	BASSETT AVE	WH
9585754	76654MK	NY	INTER	NaN	6TH AVE	RED
8915985	HJD9647	NY	ME/BE	NaN	29TH ST	WH
2868914	JHM3686	99	NaN	NaN	NaN	NaN

Figure 5.1　Sample of df, including NaN values

This means, by the way, that if every row in a data frame contains a single NaN value, the result of calling df.dropna will be an empty data frame. Its columns will be identical to your existing data frame but have zero rows (figure 5.2).

	Plate ID	Registration State	Vehicle Make	Violation Time	Street Name	Vehicle Color
2752511	LHLP99	FL	HYUN	0230P	JACOB RIIS PARK	RED
964568	JXJ1561	PA	TOYOT	0119P	E 58th St	BLUE
5049760	S82HUN	NJ	HONDA	0846A	SB UNIVERSITY AVE @	BK
4248515	HYK8920	NY	FORD	1151A	NB PARK AVE @ E 83RD	GY
353397	KMF8349	PA	NaN	0850P	S/S SEAVIEW AVE	WHITE
2703401	XHXE40	NJ	NaN	1039A	W 43 ST	WH
1434853	TRD7943	OH	NaN	0937A	BASSETT AVE	WH
9585754	76654MK	NY	INTER	NaN	6TH AVE	RED
8915985	HJD9647	NY	ME/BE	NaN	29TH ST	WH
2868914	JHM3686	99	NaN	NaN	NaN	NaN

`dropna()`

	Plate ID	Registration State	Vehicle Make	Violation Time	Street Name	Vehicle Color
2752511	LHLP99	FL	HYUN	0230P	JACOB RIIS PARK	RED
964568	JXJ1561	PA	TOYOT	0119P	E 58th St	BLUE
5049760	S82HUN	NJ	HONDA	0846A	SB UNIVERSITY AVE @	BK
4248515	HYK8920	NY	FORD	1151A	NB PARK AVE @ E 83RD	GY

Figure 5.2   Running `dropna` on a data frame removes all `NaN` values and the rows containing them.

Just how many rows did we remove when we used `dropna`? We can calculate that:

```
len(df.index) - len(all_good_df.index)
```

We get a large number as a result: 447,359. That represents about 3.5% of the data in the original data frame—which doesn't sound like much until we consider the next question: how much money New York City would lose if all those tickets were thrown out. Assuming that each parking ticket costs $100, we can calculate the total as follows:

```
(len(df.index) - len(all_good_df.index) ) * 100
```

That works out to a shockingly high number: $44.7 million. I decided to display this result as a string, taking advantage of the fact that Python's f-strings have a special , format code that, when put after : on an integer, puts commas before every three digits:

```
f'${(len(df.index) - len(all_good_df.index) ) * 100:,}'
```

As we can see in this (somewhat contrived) example, removing bad data can give us a better sense of confidence—but even when we remove a small amount (3.5%!), it can add up very quickly.

Next, I asked you to apply a slightly lighter standard, removing rows only if they have `NaN` in one of four columns: `Plate ID`, `Registration State`, `Vehicle Make`, or `Street Name`. But this raises another question: how can we select only particular columns?

One approach is to remember that each column is a series, and we can apply `notnull` to that series, giving us a boolean series. We can combine those four series with `&`, giving us a boolean series in which `True` indicates that all values are non-null. Finally, we can apply that boolean series to our original `df`, giving us a data frame in which most (but not all) data is non-null:

```
semi_good_df = df[df['Plate ID'].notnull() &
                  df['Registration State'].notnull() &
                  df['Vehicle Make'].notnull() &
                  df['Street Name'].notnull()]
```

This works. But there's a better way to do things, using `dropna`. Normally, as we just saw, `dropna` removes rows that contain any `NaN` values. But we can tell it to look in only a subset of the columns, ignoring `NaN` values in any other columns. The result is a much cleaner query (figure 5.3):

```
semi_good_df = df.dropna(subset=['Plate ID',
                                 'Registration State',
                                 'Vehicle Make',
                                 'Street Name'])
```

	Plate ID	Registration State	Vehicle Make	Violation Time	Street Name	Vehicle Color
2752511	LHLP99	FL	HYUN	0230P	JACOB RIIS PARK	RED
964568	JXJ1561	PA	TOYOT	0119P	E 58th St	BLUE
5049760	S82HUN	NJ	HONDA	0846A	SB UNIVERSITY AVE @	BK
4248515	HYK8920	NY	FORD	1151A	NB PARK AVE @ E 83RD	GY
353397	KMF8349	PA	NaN	0850P	S/S SEAVIEW AVE	WHITE
2703401	XHXE40	NJ	NaN	1039A	W 43 ST	WH
1434853	TRD7943	OH	NaN	0937A	BASSETT AVE	WH
9585754	76654MK	NY	INTER	NaN	6TH AVE	RED
8915985	HJD9647	NY	ME/BE	NaN	29TH ST	WH
2868914	JHM3686	99	NaN	NaN	NaN	NaN

```
df[df['Plate ID'].notnull()
              &
       df['Registration
       State'].notnull()
              &
df['Vehicle Make'].notnull()
              &
df['Street Name'].notnull()]
```

	Plate ID	Registration State	Vehicle Make	Violation Time	Street Name	Vehicle Color
2752511	LHLP99	FL	HYUN	0230P	JACOB RIIS PARK	RED
964568	JXJ1561	PA	TOYOT	0119P	E 58th St	BLUE
5049760	S82HUN	NJ	HONDA	0846A	SB UNIVERSITY AVE @	BK
4248515	HYK8920	NY	FORD	1151A	NB PARK AVE @ E 83RD	GY
353397	KMF8349	PA	NaN	0850P	S/S SEAVIEW AVE	WHITE
2703401	XHXE40	NJ	NaN	1039A	W 43 ST	WH

Figure 5.3   Running `dropna` on a data frame, looking at only a subset of columns

Using "thresh" with "dropna"

In this case, we want to ensure that all four columns have non-NaN values. However, passing an integer to the `thresh` keyword argument while we're also passing a list of columns to `subset` allows us to indicate that only some of these columns must be non-NaN. For example, if we're OK with any three of these four columns having non-NaN in them, we can say

```
semi_good_df = df.dropna(subset=['Plate ID',
                                 'Registration State',
                                 'Vehicle Make',
                                 'Street Name'],
                         thresh=3)
```

Of course, this means we'll still have some NaN values in the resulting data frame. But often that is a reasonable trade-off.

How many rows did we remove? And how much money may New York give up if we only remove these rows?

```
f'${(len(df.index) - len(semi_good_df.index) ) * 100:,}
```

According to this calculation, the result is $6,378,500. Still a fair amount of money, but a far cry from what we would have lost had we removed any and all problematic records.

But let's make the rules looser still, mandating only that three of the columns lack NaN values: `Plate ID`, `Registration State`, and `Street Name`. Once again, we can use `df.dropna` along with its `subset` parameter to remove only those rows that lack all three of these columns:

```
loosest_df = df.dropna(subset=['Plate ID',
                               'Registration State',
                               'Street Name'])
```

This removes only 1,618 rows from our original data frame. How much money would that translate into?

```
f'${(len(df.index) - len(loosest_df.index) ) * 100:,}
```

According to this calculation, it works out to $161,800, which seems like a far more reasonable amount of lost revenue.

Solution

```
filename = '../data/nyc-parking-violations-2020.csv'

df = pd.read_csv(filename,
                 usecols=['Plate ID',
                          'Registration State',
                          'Vehicle Make',
                          'Vehicle Color',
                          'Violation Time',      │ Reads the CSV file using
                          'Street Name'])    ◁──┘ only a handful of columns
```

```
all_good_df = df.dropna()          ⟵┐  Removes rows containing
                                      │  any NaN values
len(df.index) - len(all_good_df.index)          ⟵┐  How many rows
                                                    did we remove?
f'${(len(df.index) - len(all_good_df.index) ) * 100:,}'  ⟵┐
                                                            Uses an f-string to
                                                            display potentially lost
                                                            revenue with commas
semi_good_df = df.dropna(subset=['Plate ID',
                                 'Registration State',
Drops rows with NaN in           'Vehicle Make',
any of four columns   ⟶           'Street Name'])   ⟵┐  How many rows did
                                                        we remove now?
len(df.index) - len(semi_good_df.index)          ⟵┘
f'${(len(df.index) - len(semi_good_df.index) ) * 100:,}'  ⟵┐
                                                            Uses an f-string to
                                                            display potentially lost
                                                            revenue with commas
loosest_df = df.dropna(subset=['Plate ID',
                               'Registration State',
                               'Street Name'])    ⟵┐  How many rows did
                     ⟶                                we remove this time?
len(df.index) - len(loosest_df.index)         ⟵┘
f'${(len(df.index) - len(loosest_df.index) ) * 100:,}'  ⟵┐
                                                          Uses an f-string to
                                                          display potentially lost
                                                          revenue with commas
```

Drops rows with NaN in any of three columns

You can explore a version of this in the Pandas Tutor at http://mng.bz/6nlo.

Beyond the exercise

- So far, you have specified which columns must be all non-null. But sometimes it's OK for some columns to have null values, as long as it's not too many. How many rows would you eliminate if you required at least three non-null values from the four columns Plate ID, Registration State, Vehicle Make, and Street Name?

- Which of the columns you've imported has the greatest number of NaN values? Is this a problem?

- Null data is bad, but there is plenty of bad non-null data, too. For example, many cars with BLANKPLATE as a plate ID were ticketed. Turn these into NaN values, and rerun the previous query.

Combining and splitting columns

A common aspect of data cleaning involves creating one new column from several existing columns, as well as the reverse—creating multiple columns from a single existing column. For example, back in exercise 8, we saw how to create a new column, current_net, by calculating the net price of each product and then multiplying that by the quantity sold:

```
df['current_net'] = ((df['retail_price'] -
    df['wholesale_price']) * Df['sales'])
```

This may not seem like "cleaning" to you, but it's a common way to make data clearer and easier to understand. Plus, we can then identify holes and problems in our data and fix them accordingly.

I'll add something I often told my children when they were studying math in school: a large part of mathematics involves finding ways to rewrite problems so they're easier to understand and then solve. The same is true about data structures in programming. And it's also true in data science, where having columns that are clearer and more easily understood can help clarify our analysis.

Perhaps even more frequently, though, cleaning data involves turning one complex column into one or more simpler columns. For example, you can imagine taking a column with a `float64` dtype and turning it into two `int64` columns, one with the integer portion and one with the floating-point portion.

This is especially true in the case of two complex data structures, which we'll have much more to say about in chapters 9 and 10. Let's look at a particularly common example: when we have string data and want to grab certain substrings from within that data. In a normal Python program, we would use a slice to retrieve a substring. For example:

```
s = '00:11:22'
print(s[3:5])    # prints '11'
```

Remember that Python slices are always of the form `[start:end+1]`. So if we want the characters at index 3 and index 4, we ask for `3:5`, which means "starting at 3, up to and not including 5."

Let's assume that `s` isn't a single string but a series containing strings. To retrieve the slice `3:5` from each of those strings, we can use the `str` accessor on the series followed by the `slice` method. The syntax is a bit different than with Python strings, but it should still feel familiar:

```
s.str.slice(3,5)
```

The result of this code is a new series of string objects, of same length as `s`, containing two-element strings taken from indexes 3 and 4 of each row in `s`.

It's common to slice and dice the columns of a data frame this way, retrieving only those parts that are of interest to us. This makes the problem easier to see, understand, and solve and allows us to remove the original (larger) column, saving memory and improving computation speed.

EXERCISE 26 ▪ Celebrity deaths

Sometimes, as in the previous exercise, only a small fraction of the data is unreadable, missing, or corrupt. In other cases, a much larger proportion is problematic—and if you want to use the data set, you'll need to not only remove bad data but also massage and salvage the good data.

For this exercise, we'll look at a (slightly morbid) data set: a list of celebrities who died in 2016 and whose passing was recorded in Wikipedia, including the date of death, a short biography, and the cause of death. The problem is that this data set is messy, with some missing data and some erroneous data that will prevent us from working with it easily.

The goal of this exercise is to find the average age of celebrities who died February–July 2016. Getting there will take several steps:

1 Create a data frame from the file celebrity_deaths_2016.csv. For this exercise, we'll use only two columns:

   – `dateofdeath`

   – `age`

2 Create a new `month` column containing the month from the `dateofdeath` column.

3 Make the `month` column the index of the data frame.

4 Sort the data frame by the index.

5 Clean all nonintegers from the `age` column.

6 Turn the `age` column into an integer value.

7 Find the average age of celebrities who died during that period.

Finding numeric strings

Normally, we can turn a string column into an integer column with

```
df['colname'] = df['colname'].astype(np.int64)
```

However, this will fail if any of the rows in `df['colname']` cannot be turned into integers. That's because the strings either are empty or contain nondigit characters.

We can determine which rows in a column can be successfully turned into integers by applying the `isdigit` method via the `str` accessor:

```
df['colname'].str.isdigit()
```

This returns a boolean series in which `True` values correspond with NaN in `df['colname']` and `False` values correspond to non-NaN values in `df['colname']`. This boolean series can then be applied as a mask index to the original column. This technique comes in handy when working with dirty data—as we are doing here.

Working it out

In this exercise, we create and clean up a two-column data frame. Each column needs to be cleaned differently for us to answer the question I asked: what was the average age of celebrities who died in February through July?

We start by loading the CSV file into a data frame. We are only interested in two of the columns, so we load the file as follows:

```
filename = '../data/celebrity_deaths_2016.csv'

df = pd.read_csv(filename,
                 usecols=['dateofdeath', 'age'])
```

With that in place, we must tackle our two cleaning tasks.

Because we're only interested in celebrity deaths during particular months, wc need to grab the month value from the `dateofdeath` columns. (There are other ways to attack this problem; in chapter 9, we'll discuss a few.) Because `dateofdeath` is a string column, we can use the `slice` method of the `str` accessor to get the months—which happen to be in indexes 5 and 6 of the date string. This means we can retrieve the two-digit month as

```
df['dateofdeath'].str.slice(5,7)
```

and we can assign that value to a new column, `month`, as follows (and figure 5.4):

```
df['month'] = df['dateofdeath'].str.slice(5,7)
```

Notice that we aren't turning the column into an integer. We could, but the leading `0` on the two-digit months makes it trickier. Besides, we don't need to do that, and the data set is relatively small, so we don't have to worry about the memory implications.

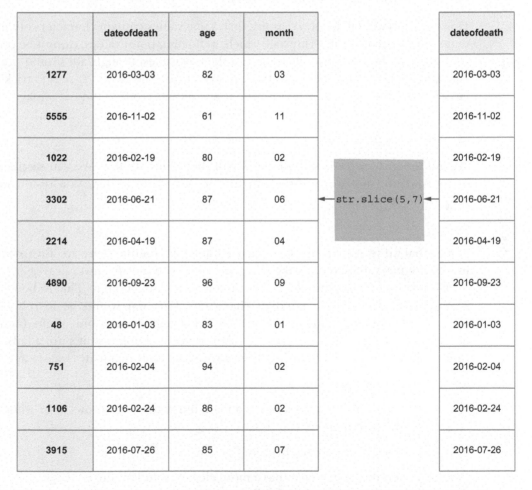

	dateofdeath	age	month		dateofdeath
1277	2016-03-03	82	03		2016-03-03
5555	2016-11-02	61	11		2016-11-02
1022	2016-02-19	80	02		2016-02-19
3302	2016-06-21	87	06	←str.slice(5,7)←	2016-06-21
2214	2016-04-19	87	04		2016-04-19
4890	2016-09-23	96	09		2016-09-23
48	2016-01-03	83	01		2016-01-03
751	2016-02-04	94	02		2016-02-04
1106	2016-02-24	86	02		2016-02-24
3915	2016-07-26	85	07		2016-07-26

Figure 5.4   Adding a new `month` column to our data frame based on the month in `dateofdeath`

Now that we have created the `month` column, we want to turn it into the index:

```
df = df.set_index('month')
```

I next asked you to sort the data frame by the index, meaning we should sort the rows so the index is in ascending order. We do this because we want to retrieve several rows via a slice, and when an index contains repeated values, it needs to be sorted before we can retrieve slices from it. So let's sort by the index:

```
df = df.sort_index()
```

We are now set to retrieve rows from a single month or a range of months. But we're not done yet, because we want to find the average age at which celebrities died in 2016. To do that, we need to turn the `age` column into a numeric value, most likely an integer. We can try like this:

```
df['age'] = df['age'].astype(np.int64)
```

However, this will fail for two reasons: first, some values contain characters other than digits. Second, some values are `NaN`, which, as floating-point values, cannot be coerced into integers. Before willy-nilly removing the `NaN` values, though, we should probably check to see how many there are. We can do that with the `isnull().sum()` trick we've already seen and combine that with the `shape` method to find the percentage of null values:

```
df['age'].isnull().sum() / len(df['age'])
```

We get the answer 0.004, meaning 0.4% of the values are `NaN`. We can sacrifice that many rows and not worry about how much data we're losing. As a result, we can remove the `NaN` values:

```
df = df.dropna(subset=['age'])
```

Notice that we're again using the `subset` parameter. Not that there are any rows in the index with `NaN` values, but it's always a good idea to be specific, just in case.

How can we remove the rest of the troublesome data, though? That is, how can we remove rows that contain nondigit characters? One way would be to rely on the `str.isdigit` method, which returns `True` if a string contains only digits (and isn't empty). (It returns `False` if there is a - sign or decimal point, so it's not a failsafe for finding numbers, but it will work with ages.) We can apply that to `df['age']` as follows:

```
df['age'].str.isdigit()
```

We can then use this boolean series as a mask index to remove rows in `df` whose ages cannot be turned into integers:

```
df = df[df['age'].str.isdigit()]
```

But, as is often the case, pandas has a more elegant solution: the `pd.to_numeric` function. This function—which is defined at the top `pd` level rather than on a series or data frame—tries to create a new series with numeric values. The function attempts to turn the values into integers, but if it cannot, it returns floats instead:

```
df['age'] = pd.to_numeric(df['age'])
```

But wait: it turns out `pd.to_numeric` has some additional functionality, allowing us to skip the step of using `str.isdigit`. By default, `pd.to_numeric` will raise an exception if it encounters a string that cannot be turned into an int or float. But if we pass the keyword argument `errors='coerce'`, it will turn any values it can't convert into `NaN`. We can thus ignore all use of `str.isdigit` and simply say

```
df['age'] = pd.to_numeric(df['age'], errors='coerce')
```

Before we go any further, let's check the numbers we got using `describe`:

```
df['age'].describe()
```

Here's the result:

```
count    6505.000000
mean      100.960338
std       413.994127
min         7.000000
25%        69.000000
50%        81.000000
75%        89.000000
max      9394.000000
Name: age, dtype: float64
```

I don't know about you, but a mean age of 100 seems suspicious. And a maximum age of 9,394 seems a bit high, even if you exercise regularly. This is the result of a string containing the value `'9394'`, which `pd.to_numeric` happily converted into a number.

Let's keep only those people younger than 120 years old:

```
df = df.loc[df['age'] < 120]
```

Our data frame is now ready for our final calculation, which we've been working up to this entire time:

```
df.loc['02':'07', 'age'].mean()
```

Notice that because our index uses strings, we need to specify the slice with strings from `'02'` to `'07'`. The answer we get is 77.1788.

Solution

```
filename = '../data/celebrity_deaths_2016.csv'

df = pd.read_csv(filename,
            usecols=['dateofdeath', 'age'])        ◄───   Loads the CSV into a
                                                           two-column data frame
                                                           Turns month data from
df['month'] = df['dateofdeath'].str.slice(5,7)     ◄──┘    dateofdeath into a new column
df = df.set_index('month')      ◄──┐   Turns the month
                                       column into an index
```

```
df = df.sort_index()            ⟵┐ Sorts the data frame
                                    by the index

df = df.dropna(subset=['age'])  ⟵┐ Removes NaN
                                    values in age
df['age'] = pd.to_numeric(df['age'], errors='coerce')  ⟵┐ Gets a numeric column
                                                           from the strings in age
df.loc['02':'07', 'age'].mean()  ⟵┐ Gets the mean age from
                                     February through July
```

You can explore a version of this in the Pandas Tutor at http://mng.bz/or7d.

Beyond the exercise

- Add a new column, day, from the day of the month in which the celebrity died. Then create a multi-index (from month and day). What was the average age of death from Feb. 15 through July 15?
- The CSV file contains another column, causeofdeath. Load it into a data frame, and find the five most common causes of death. Now replace any NaN values in that column with the string 'unknown', and again find the five most common causes of death.
- If someone asked whether cancer is in the top 10 causes, what would you say? Can you be more specific than that?

EXERCISE 27 ▪ Titanic interpolation

When our data contains NaN values, we have a few options:

- Remove them
- Leave them
- Replace them with something else

What is the right choice? The answer, of course, is "it depends." If you're getting data ready to feed into a machine-learning model, you'll likely need to get rid of the NaN values, either by removing those rows or by replacing them with something else. If you're calculating basic sales information, you may be okay with null values because they aren't going to affect your numbers too much. And of course, there are many variations on these approaches.

If you choose option 3, "replace them with something else," that raises another question: what do you want to replace the NaN values with? A value you have chosen? Something calculated from the data frame itself? Something calculated on a per-column basis? Any and all of these are appropriate under different circumstances.

In this exercise, we will fill in missing data from the famous Titanic data set: a table of all passengers on that famous, doomed ship. Many of the columns in this file are complete, but some are missing data. It will be up to you to decide whether and how to fill in that missing data. We saw in exercise 13 how to use the interpolate method on a data frame to perform this task automatically.

For this exercise, I would like you to do the following:

1 Load the titanic3.xls data into a data frame. Note that this file is an Excel spreadsheet, so you won't be able to use `read_csv`. Rather, you'll have to use `read_excel`.

2 Determine which columns contain null values.

3 For each column containing null values, decide whether you will fill it with a value—and if so, with what value, calculated or otherwise.

Unlike many of the exercises in this book, this one has no obvious right or wrong answer. There are, of course, techniques for calculating values—such as the mean and mode for a column—but I hope you'll consider not just how to make such calculations but also why you would do so and when it's most appropriate.

Working it out

This exercise is practical, but it's also philosophical. That's because there often is no "right" answer to the question of what you should do with missing data. As I often tell my corporate training clients, you have to know your data, which means being familiar with it and how it will be analyzed and used. You also may choose incorrectly or discover that a decision you made was appropriate for one type of analysis but not for another type.

That's one reason it's useful to have your work in a Jupyter notebook or a similar, reproducible format. When you need to, you can modify part of the code, keeping the rest intact.

Let's go through each of the steps in this exercise and see what decisions we could make, as well as the actual decision I made. First, I asked you to create a data frame based on the Excel file titanic3.xls. We do this with the `read_excel` method:

```
filename = '../data/titanic3.xls'
df = pd.read_excel(filename)
```

> **NOTE** Like `read_csv`, `read_excel` is a method we run on `pd` rather than on an individual data frame object. That's because we're not trying to modify an existing data frame but rather to create a new one. Also like `read_csv`, the `read_excel` method has `index_col`, `usecols`, and `names` parameters, allowing us to specify which columns should be used for the data frame, what they should be called, and whether one or more should be used as the data frame's index.

Now that we have created our data frame, we should check for null values. We do that two different ways. First, we use `isnull.sum()` to find out how many NaN values are in each column of the data frame. We can then check to see which columns have a non-zero number of NaN values. This returns a boolean series, which we can then apply as a mask index to `df.columns`:

```
df.columns[df.isnull().sum() > 0 ]
```

We get the following result:

```
Index(['age', 'fare', 'cabin', 'embarked',
       'boat', 'body', 'home.dest'],
    dtype='object')
```

Notice that the column names are stored in an `Index` object, which works similarly to a series object.

We can also run `df.isnull().sum()` by itself to see how many `NaN` values are in each column:

```
df.isnull().sum()
```

We get the following result (figure 5.5):

```
pclass          0
survived        0
name            0
sex             0
age           263
sibsp           0
parch           0
ticket          0
fare            1
cabin        1014
embarked        2
boat          823
body         1188
home.dest     564
dtype: int64
```

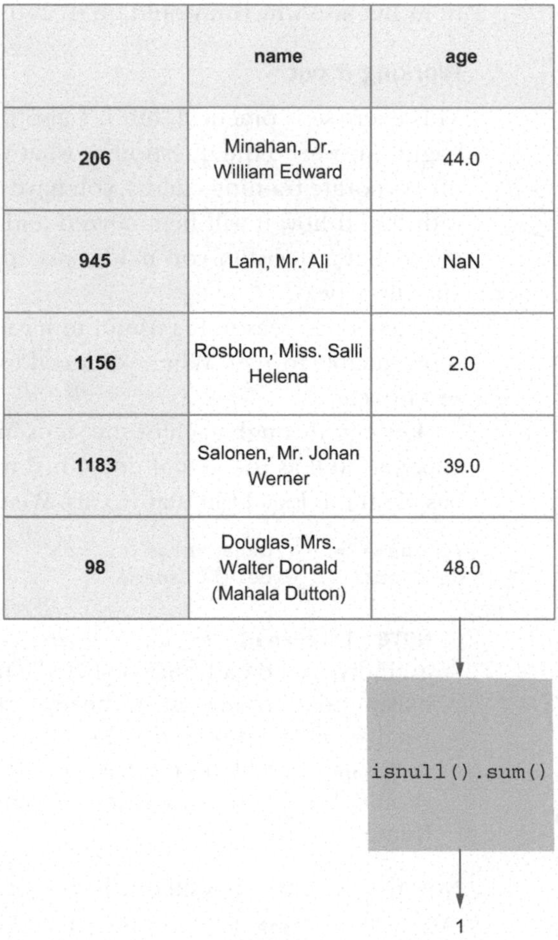

Deciding what to do with each `NaN`-containing column depends on various factors, including the type of data the column contains. Another factor is how many rows have null values. Two cases, `fare` and `embarked`, have one and two null rows, respectively. Given that our data frame has more than 1,300 rows, missing 1 or 2 of them won't make a significant difference. So, I suggest that we remove those rows from the data frame (figure 5.6):

```
df = df.dropna(subset=['fare', 'embarked'])
```

	name	age
206	Minahan, Dr. William Edward	44.0
945	Lam, Mr. Ali	NaN
1156	Rosblom, Miss. Salli Helena	2.0
1183	Salonen, Mr. Johan Werner	39.0
98	Douglas, Mrs. Walter Donald (Mahala Dutton)	48.0

`isnull().sum()`

1

Figure 5.5   Finding the number of NaN values in a column by summing the result of `isnull()`

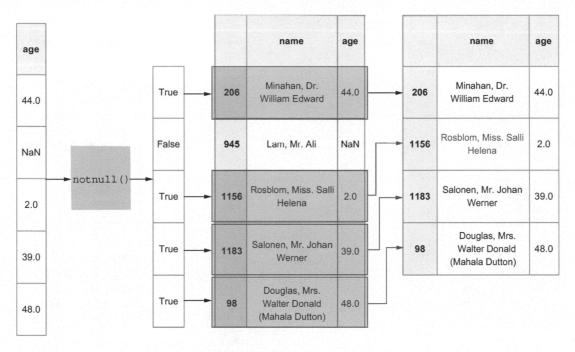

Figure 5.6   Removing rows in which a column contains NaN

When it comes to the age column, though, we want to consider our steps carefully. I'm inclined to use the mean here, but we could use the mode. We could also use a more sophisticated technique, using the mean from within a particular cabin. We could even try to get the complete set of ages on the Titanic and choose from a random distribution built from it.

Using the mean age has some advantages: it won't affect the mean age, although it will reduce the standard deviation. It's not necessarily wrong, even though we know it's not totally right. In another context, such as sales of a particular product in an online store, replacing missing values with the mean can sometimes work, especially if we have similar products with a similar sales history.

In any event, we can replace NaN in the age column as follows (figure 5.7):

```
df['age'] = df['age'].fillna(df['age'].mean())
```

Let's break this into several parts, starting with the expression on the right side:

1 Calculate df['age'].mean(). Pandas ignores NaN values by default, which means this calculation is based on the non-null numeric values in that column. We get a single float value back from this calculation: 29.8811345124283.

2 Run fillna on df['age']. And what value should we put instead of NaN? What we just calculated as the mean of df['age']. And yes, it looks confusing to use df['age'] twice. The result of invoking fillna is a new series identical to

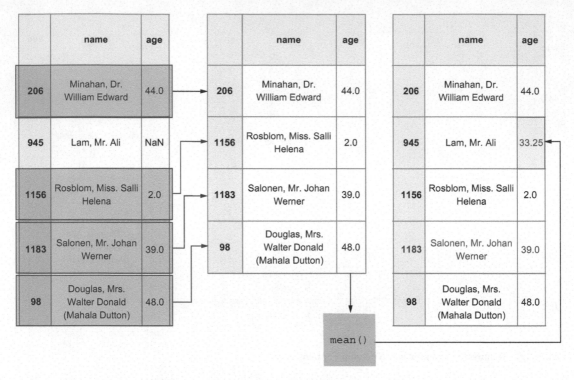

Figure 5.7   Replacing NaN in the age column with the mean of age

df['age'], except the NaN values are replaced with 29.8811345124283, the float we got back in the previous step.

3 The result of df['age'].fillna is a new series, which we assign back to df['age'], replacing the original values.

In the end, we've replaced any NaN values in df['age'] with the mean of the existing values.

Finally, we want to set the home.dest column similarly to what we did with the age column—but instead of using the mean, we'll use the mode (i.e., the most common value). We'll do this for two reasons: first, we can only calculate the mean from a numeric value, and the destination is a categorical/textual value. Second, given no other information, we may be able to assume that a passenger is going where most others are going. We may be wrong, but this is the least wrong choice we can make. We could, of course, be more sophisticated, choosing the mode of home.dest for all passengers who embarked at the same place, but we'll ignore that for now.

Our code looks very similar to what we did for the age column, but using mode instead of mean. And because mode always returns a series, we need to grab its first value with [0] rather than just pass it to fillna:

```
df['home.dest'] = df['home.dest'].fillna(df['home.dest'].mode()[0])
```

Let's break this apart:

1 Calculate `df['home.dest'].mode()`, which returns the most common value from this column. Another way to get the same value would be to invoke `df['home.dest'].value_counts().index[0]`, which counts how often each value appears in `home.dest` and returns a series with this information. We get the index from that series (the different data points from `df['home.dest']` and then get the first (i.e., most common) item from the index.

2 After grabbing the most common destination, we pass it as an argument to `fillna`, which we invoke on `df['home.dest']`. In other words, we replace all null values in `home.dest` with the non-null mode from `home.dest`.

3 Because `fillna` returns a series, we assign the result back to `df['home.dest']`, replacing the original column with the new, null-free, column.

Solution

```
filename = '../data/titanic3.xls'                    Loads all columns
                                                     from Excel
df = pd.read_excel(filename)       ◄───┘
                                                                  Shows how many
                                              Which columns       NaN values each
df.columns[df.isnull().sum() > 0 ]            contain NaN values? column contains
df.isnull().sum()            ◄─────────────────────────────

                                                     Replaces NaN values in the
df['age'] = df['age'].fillna(df['age'].mean())  ◄───┘ age column with the mean age
df = df.dropna(subset=['fare', 'embarked'])
df['home.dest'] = df['home.dest'].fillna(df['home.dest'].mode())[0]   ◄──────
```

Removes null values in   Replaces NaN values in
fare and embarked   home.dest with the mode

You can explore a version of this in the Pandas Tutor at http://mng.bz/n17a.

Beyond the exercise

In these tasks, we will do something I mentioned earlier: replace NaN values in the `home.dest` column with the most common value from that person's `embarked` column. This will take several steps:

1 Create a series (`most_common_destinations`) in which the index contains the unique values from the `embarked` column and the values are the most common destination for each value of `embarked`.

2 Replace NaN values in the `home.dest` column with values from `embarked`. (Because values in `embarked` and `home.dest` are distinct, this is an OK middle step.)

3 Use the `most_common_destinations` series to replace values in `home.dest` with the most common values for each embarkation point.

EXERCISE 28 ■ Inconsistent data

Missing data is a common problem you must deal with when importing data sets. But equally common is inconsistent data, when the same value is represented by several different values.

I once encountered this while doing a project for a university's fundraising department. Their database had been written years before and was a mess. In particular, I remember that the database column for "country" contained all of the following values:

- `United States of America`
- `USA`
- `U.S.A.`
- `U.S.A`
- `United States`
- `US`
- `U.S.`

Although people understand that these refer to the same country, a computer doesn't. If your data is inconsistent, it will be hard for you to analyze it in any sort of serious way. Thus, a big part of cleaning real-world data involves making it more consistent—or, to use a term from the world of databases, *normalizing* it.

In this exercise, we return to the parking tickets database, trying to make it more consistent and thus easier to analyze. (I am sure that even after this exercise, a data set this large will still have some inconsistencies.) Here is what I want you to do:

1. Create a data frame from the file nyc-parking-violations-2020.csv. We are only interested in a handful of the columns:
   - `Plate ID`
   - `Registration State`
   - `Vehicle Make`
   - `Vehicle Color`
   - `Street Name`

2. Determine how many different vehicle colors (the `Vehicle Color` column) there are.

3. Look at the 30 most common colors, and identify colors that appear multiple times but are written differently. For example, the color `WHITE` is also written `WT`, `WT.`, and `WHT`.

4. Prepare a Python dict in which the keys represent the various color-name inputs and the values represent the values you want them to have in the end. I suggest using longer names, such as `WHITE`, rather than shorter ones.

5. Replace the existing (old) colors with your translations. How many colors are there now?

6. Look through the top 50 colors now that you have removed a bunch of them. Are there any you could still clean up? Are there any you cannot figure out? Can you identify some consistent typos and errors in the colors?

Working it out

We're all guilty of typos—but if you make a mistake writing an e-mail, your friend or colleague will (hopefully) forgive you. In the case of data science, typos and other errors are often more insidious, because they take place one at a time as a small and unnoticed drip. When you start to analyze the data, you discover how many mistakes occurred and how many repeated themselves. This is especially true when we're getting data from people rather than from sensors and other automated equipment, although those can cause all sorts of interesting and weird problems, too.

In this exercise, I asked you to look at the colors of the vehicles that received parking tickets in New York City in 2020. As it turns out, there are many opportunities for the people issuing tickets to make mistakes, potentially affecting our analysis (although it's unlikely we would do any serious analysis of the vehicle colors).

Before we can fix the color names, we need to understand what we're dealing with. After all, maybe it isn't even a problem. After reading the data into a data frame, we can quickly check to see how many distinct vehicle colors are listed in the parking-ticket database:

```
len(df['Vehicle Color'].value_counts().index)
```

`value_counts` is a fantastic method for getting the unique values from a series, determining how often each value appears, and sorting them from most to least common. Because `value_counts` returns a series, we can ask for its index and call `len` on it.

We find 1,896 different colors recorded for parking tickets. Color experts may argue that this is a small number of colors compared to what the human eye can distinguish, but it seems a bit high for the purposes of distinguishing cars that have been ticketed.

What were the 30 most common colors in 2020 parking tickets? Let's take a look:

```
df['Vehicle Color'].value_counts().head(30)
```

We can already see that there is little or no standardization and the people giving tickets are wildly inconsistent in how they describe colors. And that's just from looking at the first 30 colors—they've described colors almost 1,900 other ways we haven't even looked at.

To clean this up, we'll create a regular Python dictionary. We could also use a series, but a dict seems like the easiest and most straightforward solution:

```
colormap = {'WH': 'WHITE', 'GY':'GRAY', 'BK':'BLACK',
            'BL':'BLUE', 'RD':'RED', 'SILVE':'SILVER',
            'GR':'GRAY', 'TN':'TAN', 'BR':'BROWN',
            'YW':'YELLO', 'BLK':'BLACK', 'GRY':'GRAY',
            'WHT':'WHITE', 'WHI':'WHITE', 'OR':'ORANGE',
            'BK.':'BLACK', 'WT':'WHITE', 'WT.':'WHITE'}
```

This dict has 18 key-value pairs to standardize 18 color names.

In this dict, the keys are the strings we found describing the colors and the values are the strings that we *want* to see. This sort of translation table is pretty common in data-cleaning pipelines, and over time, you'll likely find yourself adding new key-value pairs as you discover new (and surprisingly creative) ways for people to misspell color names.

By applying the `replace` method to our series (i.e., the `Vehicle Color` column), we can get back a new series. That new series can then be assigned back to `df['Vehicle Color']`, replacing our existing one:

```
df['Vehicle Color'] = df['Vehicle Color'].replace(colormap)
```

> **NOTE** Any values not in `colormap` remain unchanged. The match in `colormap` must be precise, including whitespace, punctuation, and case.

If we check the number of distinct colors again

```
len(df['Vehicle Color'].value_counts().index)
```

we get 1,880, which is 16 less than before. That means at two of the colors didn't change anything. How can that be? Well, it turns out *we* made two mistakes.

First, we said to look for the shortened color name `SILVE` and turn it into `SILVER`. The problem is, the backend system into which parking tickets are entered limits the `Vehicle Color` field to five characters. So changing `SILVE` to `SILVER` didn't combine two color designations into one, because there were no cars with `SILVER` in the original data set. We can thus remove `SILVER` from the `colormap` dictionary because it isn't shortened.

What about `OR`? When we mapped `OR` to `ORANGE`, we accidentally used a six-letter color name. So `OR` was a duplicate, but of `ORANG` rather than `ORANGE`. By changing `colormap` to switch from `OR` to `ORANG`, we reduced the number of different colors by one, uniting all the orange cars under one (very bright and tacky) roof.

Our final working replacement dictionary is as follows:

```
colormap = {'WH': 'WHITE', 'GY':'GRAY',
            'BK':'BLACK', 'BL':'BLUE',
            'RD':'RED', 'GR':'GRAY',
            'TN':'TAN', 'BR':'BROWN',
            'YW':'YELLO', 'BLK':'BLACK',
            'GRY':'GRAY', 'WHT':'WHITE',
            'WHI':'WHITE', 'OR':'ORANG',
            'BK.':'BLACK', 'WT':'WHITE',
        'WT.':'WHITE'}
```

We can then apply `colormap` to the colors using `replace`:

```
df['Vehicle Color'] = df['Vehicle Color'].replace(colormap)
```

The call to `replace` returns a new series in which any value in `df['Vehicle Color']` that matches a key in `colormap` is changed to be the corresponding value in `colormap`. After doing this, we can check to see how many different colors we're now tracking:

```
len(df['Vehicle Color'].value_counts().index)
```

The result is 1,879. If we take the problem of color standardization seriously, we still have a lot of work cut out for us. And this is just for one column in one data set—you can see why data cleaning is both important and time-consuming.

Solution

```
filename = '../data/nyc-parking-violations-2020.csv'

df = pd.read_csv(filename,
                 usecols=['Plate ID',
                          'Registration State',
                          'Vehicle Make',
                          'Vehicle Color',
                          'Street Name'])
len(df['Vehicle Color'].value_counts().index)        ← How many different
df['Vehicle Color'].value_counts().head(30)             colors are listed?
                                                     ← What are the 30 most commonly
                                                        listed colors on parking tickets?

colormap = {'WH': 'WHITE', 'GY':'GRAY',
            'BK':'BLACK', 'BL':'BLUE',
            'RD':'RED', 'GR':'GRAY',
            'TN':'TAN', 'BR':'BROWN',
            'YW':'YELLO', 'BLK':'BLACK',
            'GRY':'GRAY', 'WHT':'WHITE',
            'WHI':'WHITE', 'OR':'ORANG',
            'BK.':'BLACK', 'WT':'WHITE',    ← Creates a dict for translating
            'WT.':'WHITE'}                      bad color names to good ones

df['Vehicle Color'] = df[                    ← Uses replace to apply our colormap
    'Vehicle Color'].replace(colormap)          dict, assigning it back to the column
len(df['Vehicle Color'].value_counts().index)  ← Sees that the number of
df['Vehicle Color'].value_counts().head(50)       colors has indeed declined
                    Looks at the top 50 colors and finds
                    other potential cleanup targets
```

You can explore a version of this in the Pandas Tutor at http://mng.bz/M9EW.

Beyond the exercise

- Run `value_counts` on the `Vehicle Make` column, and look at some vehicle names. (There are more than 5,200 distinct makes, which almost certainly indicates a lot of inconsistency in this data.) What problems do you see? Write a function that, given a value, cleans up the data: putting the name in all caps, removing punctuation, and standardizing whatever names you can. Then use the `apply` method to fix the column. How many distinct vehicle makes are there when you're done?

- How standardized are the street names in the data set? What changes could you apply to improve things?

- Would you need to clean up the `Registration State` column? Why or why not?

Summary

Cleaning data is one of the most important parts of data analysis, although it's not glamorous. In this chapter, we saw that effective data cleaning requires not just knowing the techniques, but also applying judgment—knowing when you can allow null or duplicate values and what you should do with them. pandas comes with a wide variety of tools we can use to clean our data, from removing NaN values to replacing them, replacing existing values, and running custom functions on each row in a series or data frame. The techniques we explored in this chapter, along with the `interpolate` method we saw in exercise 13, are important tools in your data-cleaning toolbox and will likely come up in many of the projects you work on.

Grouping, joining, and sorting

So far, we have looked at how to create data frames, read data into them, clean the data, and then analyze that clean, imported data in a number of ways. But analysis sometimes requires more than just the basics: we often need to break our input data apart, zoom in on particularly interesting subsets, combine data from different sources, transform the data into a new format or value, and then sort it according to a variety of criteria. This type of action is known in the pandas world as *split-apply-combine*, and it is our focus in this chapter. If you have experience with SQL and relational databases, you'll find many similarities, in both principle and name, to functionality in pandas.

For example, a company may want to determine its total sales in the last quarter. It may also want to learn which countries have done particularly well (or poorly). Or perhaps the head of sales would like to see how much each individual salesperson has brought in, or how much each product has contributed to the company's income.

These types of questions can be answered using a technique known as *grouping*. Much like the GROUP BY clause in an SQL query, we can use grouping in pandas to ask the same question for various subsets of our data.

Another common SQL technique is *joining*, which lets us keep our data in small, specific data frames and combine them only when we need to. For example, one data frame may list each sales region and that region's manager, and a second may contain this quarter's regional sales results. To show the monthly sales results for each region along with each region's manager, we'll want to join the data frames together.

A third technique, which you have likely seen in other languages and frameworks, is *sorting*. In chapter 5, we saw how to use sort_index to order a data frame's rows by the values in the index. In this chapter, we'll look at `sort_values`, which reorders the rows based on the values in one or more columns.

You'll want to have these techniques—grouping, joining, and sorting—at your fingertips when solving problems with pandas. In this chapter, you'll see how to use them to solve some of the most common types of problems you'll encounter. These topics are so central to data analysis that one chapter wasn't enough; the next chapter builds on the techniques you'll practice here, showing more advanced uses of the split-apply-combine paradigm.

Table 6.1   What you need to know

Concept	What is it?	Example	To learn more
`s.isnull`	Returns a boolean series indicating where there are null (typically `NaN`) values in the series `s`	`s.isnull()`	http://mng.bz/Jgyp
`df.sort_index`	Reorder the rows of a data frame based on the values in its index, in ascending order	`df = df.sort_index()`	http://mng.bz/wvB7
`df.sort_values`	Reorder the rows of a data frame based on the values in one or more specified columns	`df = df.sort_values('distance')`	http://mng.bz/qrMK
`df.transpose()` or `df.T`	Returns a new data frame with the same values as `df` but with the columns and index exchanged	`df.transpose()` or `df.T`	http://mng.bz/7DXx
`df.expanding`	Lets us run window functions on an expanding (growing) set of rows	`df.expanding().sum()`	http://mng.bz/mVBn
`df.rolling`	Lets us run window functions on a fixed-size window that moves through the data frame	`df.rolling(3).mean()`	http://mng.bz/5wp4
`df.pct_change`	For a given data frame, indicates the percentage difference between each cell and the corresponding cell in the previous row	`df.pct_change()`	http://mng.bz/4DBB
`df.diff`	For a given data frame, indicates the difference between each cell and the corresponding cell in the previous row	`df.diff()`	http://mng.bz/OPDE

Table 6.1 **What you need to know** *(continued)*

Concept	What is it?	Example	To learn more
df.groupby	Allows us to invoke one or more aggregate methods for each value in a particular column.	df.groupby('year')	http://mng.bz/vn9x
df.loc	Retrieves selected rows and columns	df.loc[:, 'passenger_count'] = df['passenger_count']	http://mng.bz/nWzv
s.iloc	Accesses elements of a series by position	s.iloc[0]	http://mng.bz/QPxm
df.dropna	Removes rows with NaN values	df = df.dropna()	http://mng.bz/XN0Y
s.unique	Gets the unique values in a series (Pandas' drop_duplicates is better)	s.unique()	http://mng.bz/yQrJ
df.join	Joins two data frames based on their indexes	df.join(other_df)	http://mng.bz/MBo2
df.merge	Joins two data frames based on any columns	df.merge(other_df)	http://mng.bz/a1wJ
df.corr	Shows the correlation between the numeric columns of a data frame	df.corr()	http://mng.bz/gBgR
s.to_frame	Turns a series into a one-column data frame	s.to_frame()	http://mng.bz/5wp1
s.removesuffix	Returns a new string with the same contents as s but without a specified suffix (if it's there)	s.removesuffix('.csv')	http://mng.bz/6DAD
s.removeprefix	Returns a new string with the same contents as s but without a specified prefix (if it's there)	s.removeprefix('abcd')	http://mng.bz/o1Rr
s.title	Returns a new string based on s in which each word starts with a capital letter	s.title('hello out there')	http://mng.bz/nWzg
pd.concat	Returns one new data frame based on a list of data frames passed to pd.concat	pd.concat([df1, df2, df3])	http://mng.bz/vn9J
df.assign	Adds one or more columns to a data frame	df.assign(a=df['x']*3)	http://mng.bz/YR2A

Table 6.1 What you need to know *(continued)*

Concept	What is it?	Example	To learn more
DataFrame-GroupBy.agg	Applies multiple aggregation methods to a groupby	df.groupby('a')['b'].agg(['mean', 'std'])	http://mng.bz/G9OO
DataFrame-GroupBy.filter	Keeps those rows whose group results in True from an outside function	df.groupby('a').filter(filter_func)	http://mng.bz/z0BQ
DataFrameGroupBy.transform	Modifies those rows based on an outside function	df.groupby('a').transform(transform_func)	http://mng.bz/0l26
df.rename	Renames columns in a data frame	df.rename(columns={'a':'b', 'c':'d'})	http://mng.bz/K9W0
df.drop_duplicates	Returns a data frame whose rows contain distinct values	df.drop_duplicates()	http://mng.bz/9Qv1
df.drop	Removes rows or columns from a data frame, returning a new one	df.drop('a', axis='columns')	http://mng.bz/j1eP

EXERCISE 29 ▪ Longest taxi rides

When I first started to work with relational (SQL) databases, I was surprised that data isn't stored in any particular order. As I soon learned, there are several reasons for this:

- The order in which the rows are stored doesn't affect many queries.
- It's more efficient for the database itself to figure out the order in which rows should be stored.
- There are so many ways in which we may want to sort the data that the database shouldn't guess. Rather, it should allow us to choose how we want to sort and extract the information.

Pandas does keep the rows of our data frame ordered, so it's not exactly like a relational database. But for many types of analysis, the order of the rows doesn't matter. After all, if we're calculating a column's mean, it doesn't matter where we start or end.

If we want to display data—say, sales records, network statistics, or inflation projections—we'll likely want to order it. How we order it depends on the context, though. Sales records may need to be ordered by department, network statistics may need to be ordered by subnets, and inflation projections may need to be ordered chronologically.

Another reason to sort is to get the highest or lowest values from a particular column in the data frame. And in this exercise, I'm asking you to do exactly that. Specifically, I want you to make a few queries using the New York City taxi data from January 2019:

1 Load the CSV file nyc_taxi_2019-01.csv into a data frame using only the columns passenger_count, trip_distance, and total_amount.

2 Using a *descending* sort, find the average cost of the 20 longest (in distance) taxi rides in January 2019.

3 Using an *ascending* sort, find the average cost of the 20 longest (in distance) taxi rides in January 2019. Are the results any different?

4 Sort by ascending passenger count and descending trip distance. (So, start with the longest trip with 0 passengers and end with the shortest trip with 9 passengers.) What is the average price paid for the top 50 rides?

Working it out

When we want to sort a data frame in pandas, we first have to decide whether to sort it via the index or the values. We've already seen that if we invoke `sort_index` on a data frame, we get back a new data frame whose rows are identical to the existing data frame but ordered such that the index is ascending.

In this exercise, we again want to sort the rows of our data frame—but we want to do it based on the values in a particular column rather than the index. You could argue that there isn't much difference between the two; we could take a column, temporarily make it the index, sort by the index, and then return the column back to the data frame. But the difference between `sort_index` and `sort_values` isn't just technical. We're thinking about our data and how to access it in different ways.

`sort_values` is also different from `sort_index` in that we can sort by any number of columns. Again, imagine that a data frame contains sales data. We may want to sort it by price, region, or salesperson—or even a combination of these. When we sort by the index, by contrast, we're effectively sorting by a single column.

In the first part of the exercise, I asked you to create a data frame with our favorite (and familiar) columns, `passenger_count`, `trip_distance`, and `total_amount`:

```
filename = '../data/nyc_taxi_2019-01.csv'

df = pd.read_csv(filename,
            usecols=['passenger_count',
                     'trip_distance',
                     'total_amount'])
```

With the data frame in place, we can start to analyze the data. The first task is to find the 20 longest (in distance) taxi rides in our data set and then find their average cost. We thus need to sort our data set by distance—and I asked you to do that via a descending sort.

To sort our data frame by the `trip_distance` column, we can say

```
df.sort_values('trip_distance')
```

This returns a new data frame identical to `df`, but with the rows sorted according to `trip_distance` in ascending order. Although we could (and will) work with the data in this form, I find it easier in such cases to sort in descending order. We can do that by passing `False` as an argument to the `ascending` parameter (figure 6.1):

```
df.sort_values('trip_distance',
            ascending=False)
```

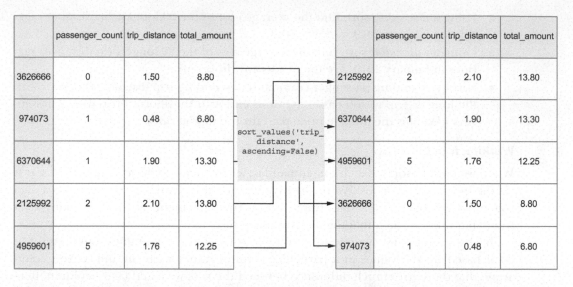

Figure 6.1 Running `sort_values` on a data frame returns a new data frame with the same rows but ordered according to the named column.

Our analysis is of the `total_amount` column. With the data already sorted by `trip_distance`, we can now retrieve just that one column using square brackets (figure 6.2):

```
df.sort_values('trip_distance',
               ascending=False
               )['total_amount']
```

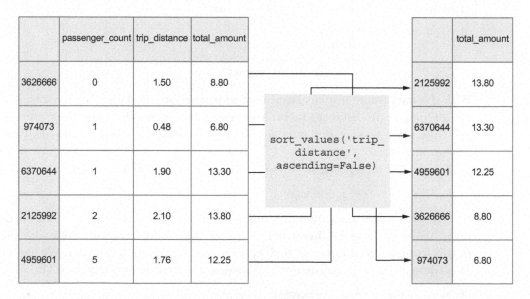

Figure 6.2 Running `sort_values` on a data frame, keeping only one column

But we're not interested in calculating the mean of all rows in total_amount, only those from the 20 longest trips. How can we retrieve the top 20 rows? One way would be to use head(20). Another possibility, which we use here, is to retrieve the first 20 rows via iloc (figure 6.3):

```
df.sort_values('trip_distance',
               ascending=False
              )['total_amount'].iloc[:20]
```

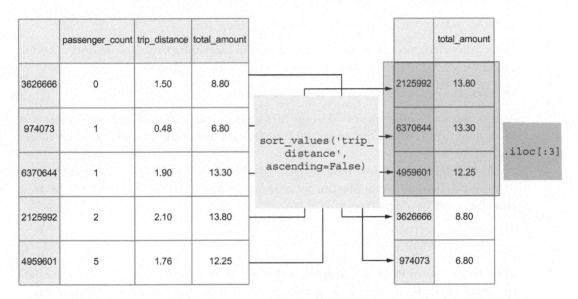

Figure 6.3 Running sort_values on a data frame, then keeping only one column, and then getting only the first rows with iloc

Notice that we have to use iloc here, not loc. That's because loc works with the actual index values—which, now that we've sorted the data frame by trip_distance, are unordered. Asking for loc[:20] will return many more than 20 rows.

Having retrieved total_amount from the 20 longest-distance taxi rides, we can finally calculate the mean value:

```
df.sort_values('trip_distance',
               ascending=False
              )['total_amount'].iloc[:20].mean()
```

We get a result of 290.00999999999993, which I think we can reasonably round to an average of $290 for those 20 longest taxi rides. We could even use the round method to round it to two digits. Here, we rewrite it using line-by-line method chaining for easier reading:

```
(
    df
```

```
         .sort_values('trip_distance',
                      ascending=False)
         ['total_amount']
         .iloc[:20]
         .mean()
         .round(2)
)
```

Next I asked you to make the same calculation but this time do an *ascending* sort. First we sort our data frame by values:

```
df.sort_values('trip_distance')
```

Remember that, by default, `sort_values` sorts in ascending order, so we don't need to specify anything there. We keep only the `total_amount` column:

```
df.sort_values('trip_distance')['total_amount']
```

And again, we're only interested in the 20 longest trips. This time, however, we sort in ascending order, which means the 20 longest trips are at the end of the series rather than at the top.

As before, we have two basic ways to do this. One would be to use `tail(20)` to retrieve the final 20 elements. But we're going to again use `iloc` and get the 20 final rows from our new data frame:

```
df.sort_values('trip_distance')[
    'total_amount'].iloc[-20:]
```

Remember that in Python, a negative index means we count from the end of the data structure rather than from the beginning. Thus index −1 gives us the final element, −2 the second-to-final element, and so forth. Moreover, our slice can be empty on one side, indicating that we want to go through the end of that side. Here, the use of `iloc[-20:]` means we want the final 20 elements in the series.

> **NOTE** Wondering whether it's faster to run `tail` or `iloc` with a slice? Some performance checks I did showed that they were almost exactly the same.

Finally, we invoke `mean()` on the 20 longest-ride fares:

```
df.sort_values('trip_distance')[
    'total_amount'].iloc[-20:].mean()
```

And the result is . . . 290.01000000000005, which is, let's face it, basically the same as 290, our result from before. We can round this result as well, again rewritten to use method chaining:

```
(
    df
    .sort_values('trip_distance')
    ['total_amount']
    .iloc[-20:]
```

```
        .mean()
        .round(2)
)
```

Again, the rounded result is 290.01.

But let's ignore the rounded results and look at the original results, 290.00999999999993 and 290.0100000000001. The differences are slight, but they're real. What is going on here?

The answer, simply put, is that floating-point math is strange and can surprise you. Check out https://0.30000000000000004.com for a good, full explanation of floating-point problems; but is there anything we can do to avoid such problems?

The answer is: sort of. If we use longer (i.e., more bits) floats, such problems will crop up less often. For example, we can instruct pandas to read the `total_amount` column into 128-bit floats, rather than 64-bit floats, which are the default:

```
df = pd.read_csv(filename,
            usecols=['passenger_count',
                  'trip_distance',
                  'total_amount'],
            dtype={'total_amount':np.float128})
```

With this in place, both of our calculations—forward and backward—give the same result: 290.0100000000000076. But, of course, now our column consumes twice as much memory as before.

> **NOTE** If 128-bit floats are the most accurate, why not always use them? First, because they're very large, at 16 bytes (!) per number. If you have 1 million floats, that translates into about 16 MB of data. Not every problem you're trying to solve needs such extreme accuracy. But 128-bit floats can also cause some problems. On my Mac, some pandas methods don't work when my columns have a `dtype` of `np.float128`. And it seems that `np.float128` doesn't even exist on computers running Windows. So if you need the precision and if you're on a platform that supports them, and if the pandas methods you need can use them, then sure—use `np.float128`. But keep in mind that doing so will make your program less portable.

Next, I asked you to sort by two columns. This is something we do naturally all the time without thinking about it. For example, telephone books are—or "were," I guess—sorted first by last name and then by first name, so the names appear in alphabetical order by last name. If more than one person has the same last name, we order the people by first name.

The sort that I asked you to do primarily looked at `passenger_count`, meaning we should sort the rows of `df` in ascending order from the smallest number of passengers to the greatest number of passengers. And in resolving ties between rows with the same passenger count, I asked you to use the `trip_distance` column. However, whereas `passenger_count` is sorted in ascending order, I asked you to sort `trip_distance` in descending order.

Pandas allows us to do this by passing a list of columns as the first argument to `sort_values`. We then pass a list of boolean values to `ascending`, with each element in the list corresponding to one of the sort columns (figure 6.4):

```
df.sort_values(['passenger_count', 'trip_distance'],
                ascending=[True, False])
```

	passenger_count	trip_distance	total_amount
3626666	0	1.50	8.80
974073	1	0.48	6.80
6370644	1	1.90	13.30
2125992	2	2.10	13.80
4959601	5	1.76	12.25

sort_values(['passenger_count', 'trip_distance'], ascending=[True, False])

	passenger_count	trip_distance	total_amount
3626666	0	1.50	8.80
6370644	1	1.90	13.30
974073	1	0.48	6.80
2125992	2	2.10	13.80
4959601	5	1.76	12.25

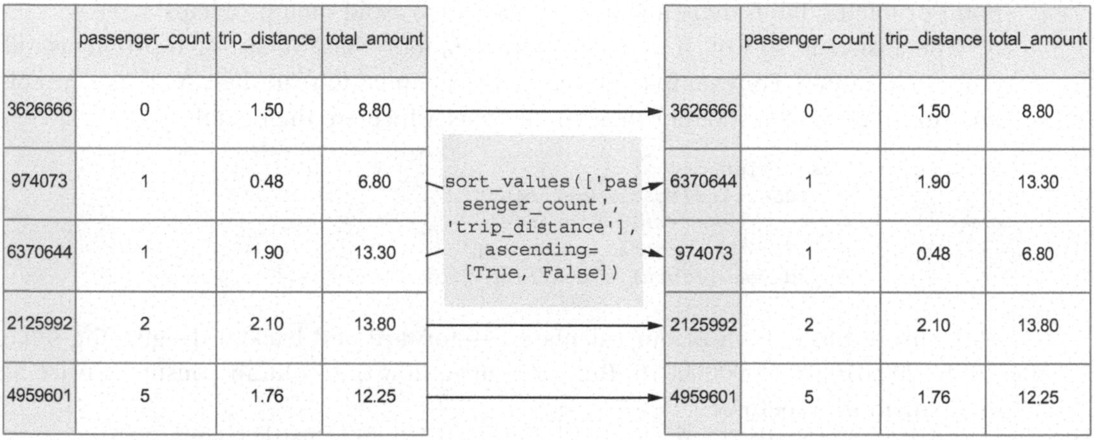

Figure 6.4   Sorting a data frame by `passenger_count` (ascending order) and then `trip_distance` (descending order)

This code returns a new data frame with three columns in which the rows are first sorted by (ascending) `passenger_count` and then by (descending) `trip_distance`. The first row of the returned data frame has the longest trip for the fewest passengers, and its final row has the shortest trip for the most passengers.

We then retrieve the `total_amount` column from the returned data frame, grab its first 50 rows using `iloc` (although we could just as easily use `head(50)` and calculate the mean using method-chaining syntax):

```
(
    df
    .sort_values(['passenger_count',
                  'trip_distance'],
                  ascending=[True, False])
    ['total_amount']
    .iloc[:50]
    .mean()
)
```

We get a result of 135.4974000000001.

Solution

```
filename = '../data/nyc_taxi_2019-01.csv'

df = pd.read_csv(filename,
                 usecols=['passenger_count',
                          'trip_distance',
                          'total_amount'],
                 dtype={'total_amount':np.float128})

df.sort_values('trip_distance',
               ascending=False)[
                  'total_amount'].iloc[:20].mean()    ◁──┐

df.sort_values('trip_distance')[
                  'total_amount'].iloc[-20:].mean()    ◁──┐

(
    df
    .sort_values(['passenger_count',
                  'trip_distance'],
                 ascending=[True, False])
    ['total_amount']
    .iloc[:50]
    .mean()
)    ◁──┘
```

Sorts by descending values of trip_distance, gets only the total_amount column, grabs the first 20 rows, and then calculates their mean

Sorts by ascending values of trip_distance, gets only the total_amount column, grabs the final 20 rows, and then takes their mean

Sorts by ascending passenger_count and then descending trip_distance, gets the total_amount column, grabs the first 50 rows, and takes their mean

You can explore a version of this in the Pandas Tutor at http://mng.bz/W1Z1.

Beyond the exercise

- In which five rides did people pay the most per mile? How far did people go on those trips?
- Let's assume that multipassenger rides are split evenly among the passengers. Given that assumption, in which 10 multipassenger rides did each individual pay the greatest amount?
- In the exercise solution, I showed that we needed to use `iloc` or `head`/`tail` to retrieve the first/last 20 rows because the index was scrambled after our sort operation. But you can pass `ignore_index=True` to `sort_values`: then the resulting data frame has a numeric index starting at 0. Use this option and `loc` to get the mean `total_amount` for the 20 longest trips.

Grouping

We've already seen how aggregate functions, such as `mean` and `std`, allow us to better understand our data. But sometimes we want to run an aggregate function on each piece of our data. For example, we may want to know the number of sales per region, the average cost of living per city, or the standard deviation for each age group in a population. We could, of course, run the aggregate function numerous times, each time retrieving a different group from the data frame. But that gets tedious—and why work hard, when pandas can do it for us?

This functionality, known as *grouping*, should also be familiar if you've worked with relational databases. In this exercise, we'll try to learn whether the number of people

(continued)

taking a taxi affects, on average, the distance the taxi has to travel. In other words, if we're a taxi driver who moonlights as a data analyst (or if you prefer, a data analyst who moonlights as a taxi driver), and we can choose between one rider and a group of riders, which is likelier to go farther—and thus pay us more?

As an example, let's go back to the data frame of products that we created back in chapter 2:

```
df = DataFrame([{'product_id':23, 'name':'computer',
                 'wholesale_price': 500,
                 'retail_price':1000, 'sales':100,
                 'department':'electronics'},
                {'product_id':96, 'name':'Python Workout',
                 'wholesale_price': 35,
                 'retail_price':75, 'sales':1000,
                 'department':'books'},
                {'product_id':97, 'name':'Pandas Workout',
                 'wholesale_price': 35,
                 'retail_price':75, 'sales':500,
                 'department':'books'},
                {'product_id':15, 'name':'banana',
                 'wholesale_price': 0.5,
                 'retail_price':1, 'sales':200,
                 'department':'food'},
                {'product_id':87, 'name':'sandwich',
                 'wholesale_price': 3,
                 'retail_price':5, 'sales':300,
                 'department': 'food'},
               ])
```

As you may have noticed, we've modified the data frame ever so slightly by adding a new column, `department`, that contains a string value. We'll use it in a moment.

To determine how many products we sell in a store (i.e., how many rows are in the data frame), we can use the `count` method:

```
df.count()
```

This is certainly interesting and useful information, but we may want to break it down further. For example, how many products are we selling in each department? To answer that question, we use the `groupby` method on our data frame:

```
df.groupby('department')
```

Notice that the argument to `groupby` needs to be the name of a column. And the result of running the `groupby` method?

```
<pandas.core.groupby.generic.DataFrameGroupBy object at 0x13174f970>
```

We get a `DataFrameGroupBy` object, which is useful because of the aggregate methods we can invoke on it. For example, we can call `count` and thus determine how many items we have in each department:

```
df.groupby('department').count()
```

The result of this code is a data frame whose columns are the same as `df` and whose rows are the different values in the `department` column. Because there are three distinct departments in our store, there are three rows: `electronics`, `books`, and `food`.

Much of the time we don't want all the columns returned to us, just a subset of them. We could, in theory, use square brackets on the result of this code. For example, we could count `product_id`:

```
df.groupby('department').count()['product_id']
```

The result is a series whose index contains the different values in `department` and whose values contain the count of items per department. And the answer is accurate.

However, this code is unnecessarily wasteful. We first apply `count` to the `DataFrameGroupBy` object and only after that remove all columns by `product_id`. It's far more efficient, especially with a large data frame, to apply the square brackets to the `DataFrameGroupBy` object and then invoke our method:

```
df.groupby('department')['product_id'].count()
```

You can see this visually at http://mng.bz/84nw. Again, we get the same results—but this second version runs more quickly.

Although we've used `count` in the examples here, we can use any aggregation method when grouping, such as `mean`, `std`, `min`, `max`, or `sum`. So we can get the average product price per department in our store as follows:

```
df.groupby('department')['retail_price'].mean()
```

What if we want to know both the mean and the standard deviation of prices in our store, grouped by department? We can do that by altering the syntax somewhat: instead of calling an aggregation method directly, we can apply the `agg` method to our `DataFrameGroupBy` object. That method takes a list of methods, each of which is applied to the `GroupBy` object:

```
df.groupby('department')['retail_price'].agg(['mean', 'std'])
```

Notice that we pass a list of strings to `agg`. It used to be common to pass methods, such as `np.mean` and `np.std`, but that has fallen out of favor in recent years; the current standard is to pass strings and let pandas apply the appropriate methods.

Using `agg` this way returns a data frame with two columns (`mean` and `std`) and three rows (for each of the departments in our data frame). We can now determine the mean and standard deviation for the retail prices in each department. You can see this visually in Pandas Tutor at http://mng.bz/E9GO.

What if we want to run multiple aggregations on separate columns? In such a case, we don't need to filter columns via square brackets. Rather, we can pass the entire `DataFrameGroupBy` object to `agg`. We then pass multiple keyword arguments to `agg`:

▪ The key of each keyword argument is the name of an output column.

(continued)

- The value of each keyword argument is a two-element tuple:
  - The first element in the tuple is a string: the name of the column in the original data frame we want to analyze.
  - The second element in the tuple is also a string: the name (yes, as a string) of an aggregation method we wish to run on that column.

For example, we can get the mean and standard deviation of `retail_price` per department as well as find the max sales for each department:

```
df.groupby('department').agg(mean_price=('retail_price', 'mean'),
                             std_price=('retail_price', 'std'),
                             max_sales=('sales', 'max'))
```

Unsorting group keys

Normally, `groupby` sorts the group keys. If you don't want to see this, or if you are concerned that it's making your query too slow, you can pass `sort=False` to `groupby`:

```
df.groupby('department', sort=False)['retail_price'].agg(['mean', 'std'])
```

EXERCISE 30 ▪ Taxi ride comparison

So far, we have taken several looks at our January 2019 taxi data. But we've always examined the overall data or effectively done manual grouping. In this exercise, we're going to use grouping to get a better understanding of the data. Specifically, I'd like you to

1 Load taxi data from January 2019 into a data frame using only the columns `passenger_count`, `trip_distance`, and `total_amount`.
2 For each number of passengers, find the mean cost of a taxi ride. Sort this result from lowest (i.e., cheapest) to highest (i.e., most expensive).
3 Sort the results again by increasing the number of passengers.
4 Create a new column, `trip_distance_group`, in which the values are `short` (< 2 miles), `medium` (≥ 2 miles and ≤ 10 miles), and `long` (> 10 miles). What is the average number of passengers per trip length category? Sort this result from highest (most passengers) to lowest (fewest passengers).

Working it out

Grouping is a simple idea, but it has profound implications. It means we can measure different parts of our data in a single query, producing a data frame that can itself then be analyzed, sorted, and displayed. In this exercise, we load the CSV file nyc_taxi_2019-01.csv into a data frame:

```
filename = '../data/nyc_taxi_2019-01.csv'
```

```
df = pd.read_csv(filename,
                 usecols=['passenger_count',
                          'trip_distance',
                          'total_amount'])
```

I then asked you to find the mean cost of a taxi ride for each number of passengers. When using `groupby`, we have to keep several things in mind:

- On what data frame are we operating?
- Which column will supply the groups? This column is almost always categorical in nature, either with a limited number of string values or with a limited set of integers (as is the case here). The distinct values from this column are the rows in the output from our aggregation method.
- Which column(s) do we analyze? That is, on which columns will we run our aggregation methods?
- Which aggregation method(s) will we be running?

In this case, the question provides all the answers:

- We'll work on the data frame `df`.
- We'll get our groups from `passenger_count`.
- We'll analyze `total_amount`.
- We'll run the `mean` method.

In other words, we're going to do the following:

```
df.groupby('passenger_count')['total_amount'].mean()
```

This returns a series. The index in the series contains each of the unique values in the `passenger_count` column. The values in the series are the result of running `mean` on each subset of `df['total_amount']`. You can think of this as similar to the following:

```
for i in range(df['passenger_count'].max() + 1):
    print(i,
          df.loc[df['passenger_count'] == i,
                 'total_amount'
          ].mean())
```

Prints the current value of passenger_count

Our row selector retrieves rows where passenger_count is i.

Our column selector retrieves the total_amount column.

Calculates the mean of total_amount for one value of passenger_count

This code uses a Python `for` loop to iterate over each value in `df['passenger_count']` and then runs `mean` on that subset of the `total_amount` column. It calculates the same results, but it's far less efficient than using `groupby`. Moreover, it doesn't put the results in a data structure that we can use easily. For these and other reasons, it's almost never a good idea to use a `for` loop on pandas data structures—you should aim to use `groupby` and other native pandas functionality instead. That said, seeing this `for` loop can give us an idea of what's happening inside of the `groupby` and what values we get in the series it returns (figure 6.5).

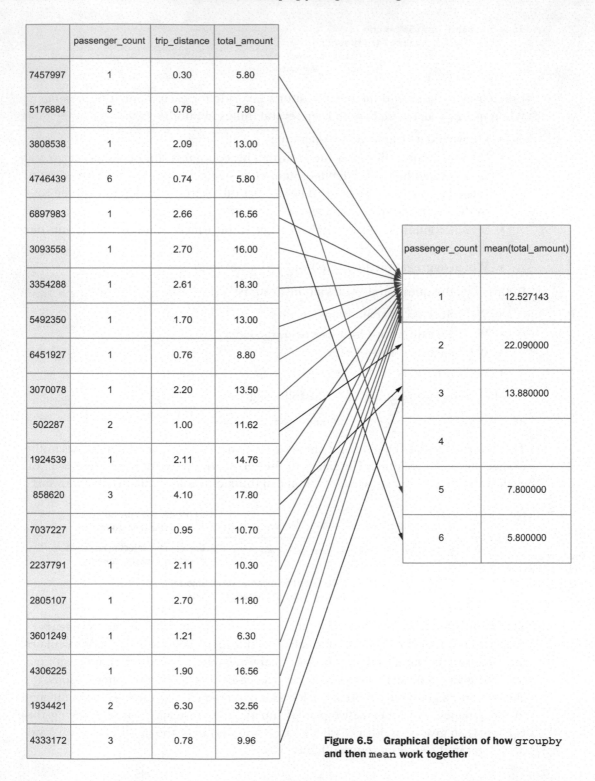

Figure 6.5   Graphical depiction of how `groupby` and then `mean` work together

Now that we have the mean price of a taxi fare for each number of passengers, we want to sort it by value in ascending order. We can do that by applying `sort_values` to the resulting series (figure 6.6):

```
df.groupby('passenger_count')[
    'total_amount'].mean().sort_values()
```

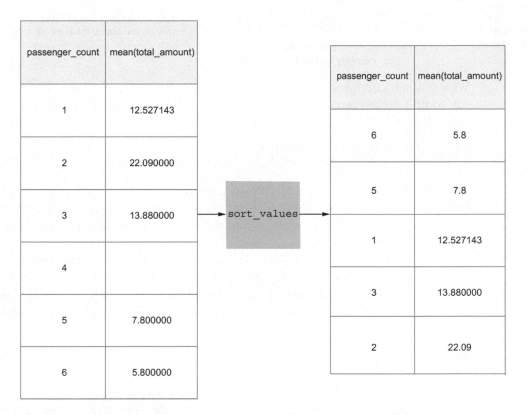

Figure 6.6 Graphical depiction of how you can run `sort_values` on the `groupby` result

The next request was for you to perform the same calculation but to sort the result by the number of passengers in ascending order. Remember that when we invoke `mean` on the grouped result, we get a series. The index of the series contains the unique values from `df['passenger_count']`. To sort by the number of passengers, we need to sort this series by its index:

```
df.groupby('passenger_count')[
    'total_amount'].mean().sort_index()
```

Next, I asked you to create a new column, `trip_distance_group`, whose values are `short`, `medium`, and `long`, corresponding to trips up to 2 miles, from 2 to 10 miles, and greater than 10 miles. We can accomplish this with `pd.cut`, which takes our column and lets us set the values we want to set as separators and the strings to assign to each category:

```
df['trip_distance_group'] = pd.cut(
    df['trip_distance'],
    [df['trip_distance'].min(), 2, 10,
     df['trip_distance'].max()],
    labels=['short', 'medium', 'long'],
    include_lowest=True)
```

Runs pd.cut to get categorical values from numeric ones

Bases the categories on the trip_distance column

Our cut points are the minimum, 2, 10, and max.

Puts values into one of three categories: short, medium, or long

Ensures that the first category includes the left side

With this new column in place, we can use it in a `groupby` query. Specifically, I asked you to find the average number of passengers for each passenger group. We can do this as follows:

```
df.groupby('trip_distance_group')[
  'passenger_count'].mean().sort_values(ascending=False)
```

This says that we want to get the mean passenger count for each distinct value of `trip_distance_group`. We get those results back in a series, where the index is the distinct values of `trip_distance_group` and the values are the means we calculated for each trip-distance category.

Once we're done with those calculations, we sort the values of the resulting data frame in descending order. And in doing so, we find that there's very little difference between these averages. In other words, our moonlighting data scientist/taxi driver has no financial incentive to pick up a large group versus a small one because they'll likely get paid the same.

Solution

```
filename = '../data/nyc_taxi_2019-01.csv'

df = pd.read_csv(filename,
              usecols=['passenger_count',
                       'trip_distance',
                       'total_amount'])

df.groupby('passenger_count')['total_amount'
    ].mean().sort_values()
df.groupby('passenger_count')['total_amount'
    ].mean().sort_index()

df['trip_distance_group'] = pd.cut(
    df['trip_distance'],
       [df['trip_distance'].min(), 2, 10,
        df['trip_distance'].max()],
    labels=['short', 'medium', 'long'])
df.groupby('trip_distance_group')['passenger_count'
    ].mean().sort_values(ascending=False)
```

Returns the mean value of total_amount for each value of passenger_count and then sorts the resulting series by value (i.e., mean of total_amount)

Returns the mean value of total_amount for each value of passenger_count and then sorts the resulting series by index (i.e., value of passenger_count)

Uses pd.cut to get a series of strings back from trip_distance, and assigns it to df['trip_distance_group']

For each value of trip_distance_group, gets the mean of passenger_count and sorts the values in descending order

You can explore a version of this in the Pandas Tutor at http://mng.bz/NVN1.

Beyond the exercise

- Create a single data frame containing rides from both January 2019 and January 2020, with a column `year` indicating which year the ride comes from. Use `groupby` to compare the average cost of a taxi in January from each of these two years.
- Create a two-level grouping, first by year and then by `passenger_count`.
- The `corr` method allows us to see how strongly two columns correlate with one another. Use `corr` and then `sort_values` to find which columns have the highest correlation.

Joining

Like grouping, joining is a concept you may have encountered previously when working with relational databases. The joining functionality in pandas is similar to that sort of a database, although the syntax is different.

Consider, for example, the data frame we looked at earlier in this chapter:

```
df = DataFrame([{'product_id':23, 'name':'computer',
                 'wholesale_price': 500,
                 'retail_price':1000, 'sales':100,
                 'department':'electronics'},
                {'product_id':96, 'name':'Python Workout',
                 'wholesale_price': 35,
                 'retail_price':75, 'sales':1000,
                 'department':'books'},
                {'product_id':97, 'name':'Pandas Workout',
                 'wholesale_price': 35,
                 'retail_price':75, 'sales':500,
                 'department':'books'},
                {'product_id':15, 'name':'banana',
                 'wholesale_price': 0.5,
                 'retail_price':1, 'sales':200,
                 'department':'food'},
                {'product_id':87, 'name':'sandwich',
                 'wholesale_price': 3,
                 'retail_price':5, 'sales':300,
                 'department': 'food'},
               ])
```

But now consider that instead of keeping track of sales numbers in this data frame, we instead break the data into two parts:

- One data frame will describe each of the products we sell.
- A second data frame will describe each sale we make.

Here is a simple example of how we can divide the data:

(continued)

```python
products_df = DataFrame([{'product_id':23, 'name':'computer',
                          'wholesale_price': 500,
                          'retail_price':1000,
                          'department':'electronics'},
                         {'product_id':96, 'name':'Python Workout',
                          'wholesale_price': 35,
                          'retail_price':75, 'department':'books'},
                         {'product_id':97, 'name':'Pandas Workout',
                          'wholesale_price': 35,
                          'retail_price':75, 'department':'books'},
                         {'product_id':15, 'name':'banana',
                          'wholesale_price': 0.5,
                          'retail_price':1, 'department':'food'},
                         {'product_id':87, 'name':'sandwich',
                          'wholesale_price': 3,
                          'retail_price':5, 'department': 'food'},
                        ])

sales_df = DataFrame([{'product_id': 23, 'date':'2021-August-10',
                       'quantity':1},
                      {'product_id': 96, 'date':'2021-August-10',
                       'quantity':5},
                      {'product_id': 15, 'date':'2021-August-10',
                       'quantity':3},
                      {'product_id': 87, 'date':'2021-August-10',
                       'quantity':2},
                      {'product_id': 15, 'date':'2021-August-11',
                       'quantity':1},
                      {'product_id': 96, 'date':'2021-August-11',
                       'quantity':1},
                      {'product_id': 23, 'date':'2021-August-11',
                       'quantity':2},
                      {'product_id': 87, 'date':'2021-August-12',
                       'quantity':2},
                      {'product_id': 97, 'date':'2021-August-12',
                       'quantity':6},
                      {'product_id': 97, 'date':'2021-August-12',
                       'quantity':1},
                      {'product_id': 87, 'date':'2021-August-13',
                       'quantity':2},
                      {'product_id': 23, 'date':'2021-August-13',
                       'quantity':1},
                      {'product_id': 15, 'date':'2021-August-14',
                       'quantity':2}
                     ])
```

What have we done here? We've put all our product information, which is less likely to change, in `products_df`. Every time we add a new product to the store or change the name or price of an existing product, we update that data frame. But each time we make a sale, we don't touch `products_df`. Rather, we add a new row to `sales_df`, describing which product was sold, how many we sold, and when we sold it. You can see these data frames in the following figures.

	product_id	name	wholesale_price	retail_price	department
0	23	computer	500.0	1000	electronics
1	96	Python Workout	35.0	75	books
2	97	Pandas Workout	35.0	75	books
3	15	banana	0.5	1	food
4	87	sandwich	3.0	5	food

Graphical depiction of `products_df`

This is all well and good, but how can we describe how much of each product has been sold? This is where joining comes in: we can combine `products_df` and `sales_df` into a new, single data frame that contains all the columns from both of the input data frames.

But wait a second—how does pandas know which rows on the left should be joined with which rows on the right? The answer, at least by default, is that it uses the index. Wherever the index of the left side matches the index of the right side, it joins them together, giving them a new row that contains all columns from both left and right.

	product_id	date	quantity
0	23	2021-August-10	1
1	96	2021-August-10	5
2	15	2021-August-10	3
3	87	2021-August-10	2
4	15	2021-August-11	1
5	96	2021-August-11	1
6	23	2021-August-11	2
7	87	2021-August-12	2
8	97	2021-August-12	6
9	97	2021-August-12	1
10	87	2021-August-13	2
11	23	2021-August-13	1
12	15	2021-August-14	2

Graphical depiction of `sales_df`

(continued)

This means we need to change our data frames such that both are using the same values for their indexes. The obvious choice here is `product_id`, which appears in both `products_df` and `sales_df` (see the following two figures):

```
products_df = products_df.set_index('product_id')
sales_df = sales_df.set_index('product_id')
```

product_id	name	wholesale_price	retail_price	department
23	computer	500.0	1000	electronics
96	Python Workout	35.0	75	books
97	Pandas Workout	35.0	75	books
15	banana	0.5	1	food
87	sandwich	3.0	5	food

Graphical depiction of `products_df` with `product_id` as the index

Now that our data frames have a common reference point in the index, we can create a new data frame combining the two:

```
products_df.join(sales_df)
```

The result of this join is a new table with 13 rows and 6 columns. The columns combine all the columns from `products_df` and then all the columns from `sales_df`:

- `name`
- `wholesale_price`
- `retail_price`
- `department`
- `date`
- `quantity`

product_id	date	quantity
23	2021-August-10	1
96	2021-August-10	5
15	2021-August-10	3
87	2021-August-10	2
15	2021-August-11	1
96	2021-August-11	1
23	2021-August-11	2
87	2021-August-12	2
97	2021-August-12	6
97	2021-August-12	1
87	2021-August-13	2
23	2021-August-13	1
15	2021-August-14	2

Graphical depiction of `sales_df` with `product_id` as the index

Each row is the result of a match between the index (`product_id`) on the left (from `products_df`) and the index (`product_id`) on the right (from `sales_df`). Because several products have multiple sales, we end up with more rows than either of the original tables contained. The join is shown in the following figure.

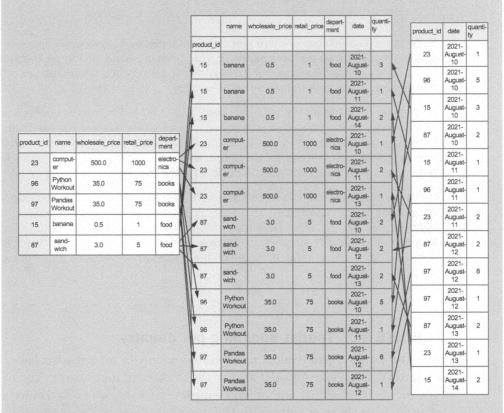

Graphical depiction of joining `products_df` and `sales_df`

We can now perform whatever queries we like on this new, combined data frame. For example, we can determine how many of each product have been sold:

```
products_df.join(sales_df).groupby(
    'name')['quantity'].sum()
```

Or we can determine how much income we get from each product and then sort the products from lowest to highest source of income:

```
products_df.join(sales_df).groupby(
    'name')['retail_price'].sum().sort_values()
```

We can even determine how much income we had on each individual day:

```
products_df.join(sales_df).groupby(
    'date')['retail_price'].sum().sort_index()
```

(continued)

And although our data set is tiny, we can determine how much each product contributed to our income per day:

```
products_df.join(sales_df).groupby(
    ['date','name'])['retail_price'].sum().sort_index()
```

Separating data into two or more pieces so each piece of information appears only a single time is known as *normalization*. There are all sorts of formal theories and descriptions of normalization, but it boils down to keeping the information in separate places and joining data frames when necessary.

Sometimes you'll normalize your own data. But other times, you'll receive data that has been normalized and then separated into separate pieces. For example, many data sets are distributed in separate CSV files, which almost always means you'll need to join two or more data frames to analyze the information. Or you may want to normalize the data yourself to gain flexibility or performance.

One final point: the join I've shown you here is known as a *left join* because values of `product_id` on the left (i.e., in `products_df`) drive which rows are selected on the right (i.e., `sales_df`). More advanced joins called *outer joins* allow us to tell pandas that even if there isn't a corresponding row on the left or the right, we want to have a row in the result, albeit one filled with null values. We'll explore those in exercise 35 in the next chapter.

EXERCISE 31 ■ Tourist spending per country

Before the Covid-19 pandemic, I traveled internationally on a regular basis, both for work (giving classes to companies around the world) and for pleasure. The pandemic, of course, changed all that, with many countries restricting who could enter and leave and under what circumstances.

This was certainly a serious problem for corporate Python trainers. But it was an even bigger problem for the tourism industry. That's because tourists generate a great deal of money to countries around the world. In this exercise, we'll look at prepandemic data from the OECD (Organization for Economic Cooperation and Development), which the *Economist* describes as "a club of mostly-rich countries," to see how much they were earning in tourist dollars. As we'll see, the data covers countries beyond the OECD itself.

Here's what I would like you to do:

1   Load the OECD tourism data (from oecd_tourism.oecd) into a data frame. We're interested in the following columns:
    –   LOCATION—A three-letter abbreviation for the country name
    –   SUBJECT—Either INT_REC (for tourist funds received) or INT-EXP (for tourist expenses).

- TIME—A year (integer)
- Value—A float indicating thousands of dollars

2 Find the five countries that received the greatest amount of tourist dollars, on average, across years in the data set.

3 Find the five countries whose citizens spent the least amount of tourist dollars, on average, across years in the data set.

4 The separate CSV file oecd_locations.csv has two columns: one contains the three-letter abbreviated location name from the first CSV file, and the second is the full country name. Load this into a data frame, using the abbreviated data as an index.

5 Join these two data frames together into a new one. In the new data frame, there is no LOCATION column. Instead, there is a name column with the full name of the country.

6 Rerun the queries from steps 2 and 3, finding the five countries that spent and received the most, on average, from tourism. But this time, get the name of each country, rather than its abbreviation, for your reports.

7 Ignoring the names, did you get the same results as before? Why or why not?

NOTE The column names and values in this data set demonstrate the type of inconsistency that can creep into a project. The SUBJECT column can contain one of two strings, INT_REC or INT-EXP. Why does one use an underscore and the other a hyphen? Good question! Similarly, why are all column names in all caps, whereas Value has only its first letter capitalized? Another good question! This happens in many real-world data sets. Be on the lookout for these sorts of problems when you first see a data set. And if you're creating a data set for others, try to keep things as consistent as possible.

Working it out

In this exercise, we create two separate data frames and then join them. In so doing, we create a report that uses countries' full names rather than three-letter abbreviations. Let's walk through each of the steps to achieve that.

For starters, I asked you to load the OECD tourism data into a data frame. This CSV file includes a number of columns that wouldn't help with our analysis, so I asked you to select a subset of them:

```
tourism_filename = '../data/oecd_tourism.csv'
tourism_df = pd.read_csv(tourism_filename,
                    usecols=['LOCATION',
                            'SUBJECT',
                            'TIME',
                            'Value'])
```

This data frame, tourism_df, contains information about the total amount spent and the total amount received by a number of countries over about a decade. For example, if we want to determine how much money the French economy received in total from tourists during 2016, we can look at the row in which SUBJECT is INT_REC, LOCATION is FRA, and TIME is 2016. That returns a single row from the data frame; if we retrieve the Value column in that row, we learn the total amount of tourism income.

What if we want to determine the average amount of income that countries received in our data set? We can say, using method-chaining syntax,

```
(
    tourism_df
    .loc[tourism_df['SUBJECT'] == 'INT_REC']
    ['Value']
    .mean()
)
```

But this isn't very useful. (You could even say it isn't very "meaningful".) That's because countries differ in how much tourist income they receive. Breaking it apart by country gives many more insights than an overall mean.

How can we get the mean tourist income per country? By grouping the call to mean by the LOCATION column:

```
(
    tourism_df
    .loc[tourism_df['SUBJECT'] == 'INT_REC']
    .groupby('LOCATION')['Value']
    .mean()
)
```

Here's what we do in this code:

1 Select rows in which SUBJECT is INT_REC, for received tourism funds.
2 Group by LOCATION, meaning we'll get one result per value of LOCATION, aka country.
3 Ask for only the Value column.
4 Invoke the mean method on each location's values.

This produces a series: a single column in which the index contains the three-letter country abbreviations and with the values being the mean income per country.

I then asked you to find the five countries that received the most (on average per year) from tourism. To do this, we sort our results in descending order and then use head to get the five top-grossing locations:

```
(
    tourism_df
    .loc[tourism_df['SUBJECT'] == 'INT_REC']
    .groupby('LOCATION')['Value']
    .mean()
    .sort_values(ascending=False)
    .head()
)
```

Next, I asked you to perform a second, similar query, finding the countries that spent the least amount on tourism. In other words, we're now interested in the INT-EXP value from SUBJECT, and we want to look at the five lowest-spending (on average, per year) tourism countries. The solution is

```
(
    tourism_df
    .loc[tourism_df['SUBJECT'] == 'INT-EXP']
    .groupby('LOCATION')['Value']
    .mean()
    .sort_values()
    .head()
)
```

Beyond the difference in the string we're matching in SUBJECT, we also reverse the call to sort_values, using the default of an ascending sort. This way, head retrieves the five least-spending countries.

With these initial queries out of the way, we can now use join to make an easier-to-read report from what we've created. To help with that, we create a two-column CSV file that we can read. However, this CSV file needs massaging if we're going to use it. For one thing, there isn't a header row, so we need to state that and provide our own names.

But we're also planning to use the imported data for joining with tourism_df. We'll want to use the three-letter country abbreviation for joining, so we may as well make that the index of locations_df. Here's what we do:

```
locations_filename = '../data/oecd_locations.csv'
locations_df = pd.read_csv(locations_filename,
                        header=None,
                         names=['LOCATION', 'NAME'],
                        index_col='LOCATION')
```

Now we'll bring this all together by creating a new data frame, the result of joining locations_df and tourism_df. The problem is that although the three-letter abbreviation (i.e., LOCATION) is the index of locations_df, it's just a plain ol' column in tourism_df. And yes, you can join non-index columns in pandas, but having the data frames share index values makes the code shorter and clearer.

We'll thus do the following:

1 Create a new (anonymous) data frame based on tourism_df, whose index is set to LOCATION.
2 Run join on locations_df and the new LOCATION-indexed version of tourism_df.
3 Assign this to a new data frame, which we call fullname_df.

You can see the setting of the indexes for our join in figures 6.7 and 6.8:

```
fullname_df = locations_df.join(tourism_df.set_index('LOCATION'))
```

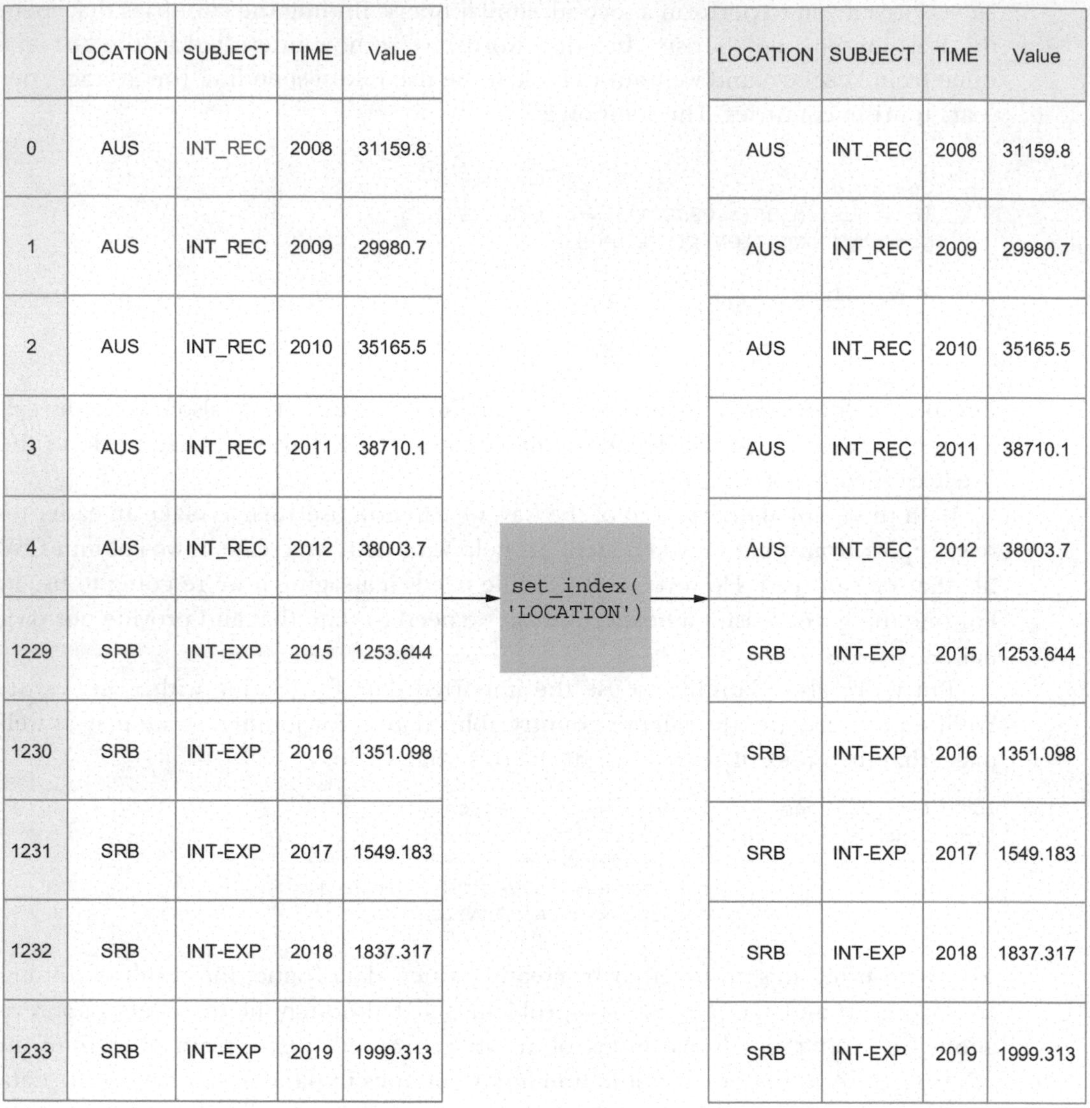

	LOCATION	SUBJECT	TIME	Value		LOCATION	SUBJECT	TIME	Value
0	AUS	INT_REC	2008	31159.8		AUS	INT_REC	2008	31159.8
1	AUS	INT_REC	2009	29980.7		AUS	INT_REC	2009	29980.7
2	AUS	INT_REC	2010	35165.5		AUS	INT_REC	2010	35165.5
3	AUS	INT_REC	2011	38710.1		AUS	INT_REC	2011	38710.1
4	AUS	INT_REC	2012	38003.7		AUS	INT_REC	2012	38003.7
1229	SRB	INT-EXP	2015	1253.644		SRB	INT-EXP	2015	1253.644
1230	SRB	INT-EXP	2016	1351.098		SRB	INT-EXP	2016	1351.098
1231	SRB	INT-EXP	2017	1549.183		SRB	INT-EXP	2017	1549.183
1232	SRB	INT-EXP	2018	1837.317		SRB	INT-EXP	2018	1837.317
1233	SRB	INT-EXP	2019	1999.313		SRB	INT-EXP	2019	1999.313

`set_index('LOCATION')`

Figure 6.7   **Graphical depiction of making the LOCATION column the index of** `tourism_df`

NOTE `fullname_df` is significantly smaller than `tourism_df`—364 rows instead of 1,234. That's because the joined data frame's rows are the result of finding a match between the left and right sides of the join. `locations_df` doesn't include all the countries listed in `tourism_df`, so the result is smaller.

Figure 6.8 Graphical depiction of making the LOCATION column the index of locations_df

The index of `fullname_df` is the three-character country codes. Its columns are

- `NAME`—The full name, which we get from `locations_df`
- `SUBJECT`—Tells us whether we're dealing with income or expenses
- `TIME`—Tells us the year in which the measurement was taken
- `Value`—Tells us the dollar amount that was measured

By using `NAME` for our grouping operations, we can get a report that displays each country's full name rather than the three-letter abbreviation. And indeed, I asked you to rerun our earlier queries on the result of our join (figure 6.9).

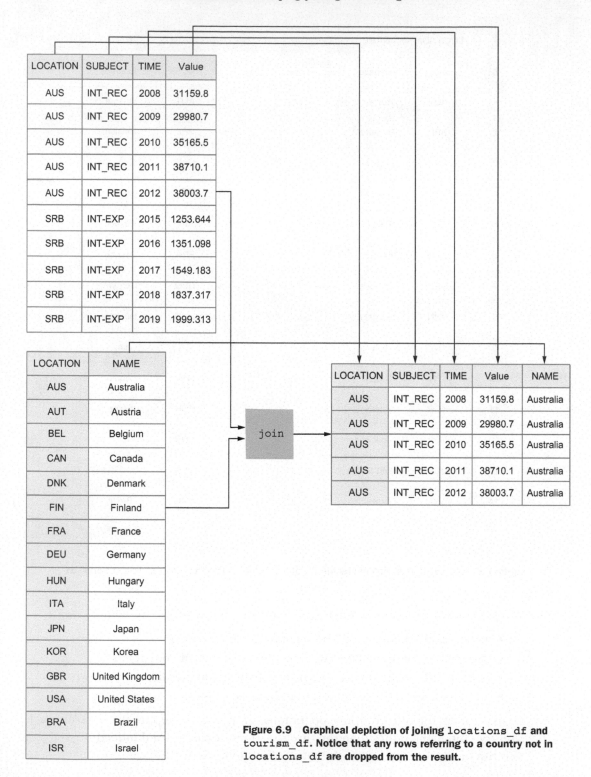

Figure 6.9   Graphical depiction of joining `locations_df` **and** `tourism_df`**. Notice that any rows referring to a country not in** `locations_df` **are dropped from the result.**

Here's how we can get the five countries with the greatest income from tourism, on average, during the years of the data set:

```
(
    fullname_df
    .loc[fullname_df['SUBJECT'] == 'INT_REC']
    .groupby('NAME')['Value']
    .mean()
    .sort_values(ascending=False)
    .head()
)
```

And here are the five countries that spent the least on tourism, on average, during the years of the data set:

```
(
    fullname_df
    .loc[fullname_df['SUBJECT'] == 'INT-EXP']
    .groupby('NAME')['Value']
    .mean()
    .sort_values()
    .head()
)
```

Finally, I asked whether the results are the same as before. Besides the obvious, that these results give the countries' full names rather than their abbreviations, the countries themselves are different. That's a result of locations_df not including all the countries in tourism_df. We lose some data as a result of our join.

Solution

```
tourism_filename = '../data/oecd_tourism.csv'
tourism_df = pd.read_csv(tourism_filename,
                         usecols=['LOCATION',
                         'SUBJECT', 'TIME', 'Value'])
```

⟵ **Creates a data frame from four columns in the tourism data**

```
(
    tourism_df
    .loc[tourism_df['SUBJECT'] == 'INT_REC']
    .groupby('LOCATION')['Value']
    .mean()
    .sort_values(ascending=False)
    .head()
)
```

⟵ **Chooses rows where SUBJECT is INT_REC; for each location (i.e., country), gets the mean value in the data set.; sorts those values in descending order, and takes the top five values**

```
(
    tourism_df
    .loc[tourism_df['SUBJECT'] == 'INT-EXP']
    .groupby('LOCATION')['Value']
    .mean()
    .sort_values()
    .head()
)
```

Chooses rows where SUBJECT is INT-EXP; for each location (i.e., country), gets the mean value in the data set; sorts those values in ascending order, and takes the top five values

```
locations_filename = '../data/oecd_locations.csv'
locations_df = pd.read_csv(locations_filename,
                           header=None,
                            names=['LOCATION', 'NAME'],
                            index_col='LOCATION')
fullname_df = locations_df.join(
        tourism_df.set_index('LOCATION'))
(
    fullname_df
    .loc[fullname_df['SUBJECT'] == 'INT_REC']
    .groupby('NAME')['Value']
    .mean()
    .sort_values(ascending=False)
    .head()
)

(
    fullname_df
    .loc[fullname_df['SUBJECT'] == 'INT-EXP']
    .groupby('NAME')['Value']
    .mean()
    .sort_values()
    .head()
)
```

Creates a data frame from the locations data, setting column names to **LOCATION** and **NAME** and making **LOCATION** the index.

Creates a new data frame, the result of joining tourism_df and locations_df

In the joined data, chooses rows where **SUBJECT** is **INT_REC**; for each location (i.e., country), gets the mean value in the data set; sorts those values in descending order, and takes the top five values

Chooses rows where **SUBJECT** is **INT-EXP**; for each location (i.e., country), gets the mean value in the data set; sorts those values in ascending order, and takes the top five values

You can explore a version of this in the Pandas Tutor at http://mng.bz/D9Yw.

Beyond the exercise

- What happens if you perform the join in the other direction? That is, what if you invoke `join` on `tourism_df`, passing it an argument of `locations_df`? Do you get the same result?
- Get the mean tourism income per year rather than by country. Do you see any evidence of less tourism income during the time of the Great Recession, which started in 2008?
- Reset the index on `locations_df` such that it has a (default) numeric index and two columns (LOCATION and NAME). Now run `join` on `locations_df`, specifying that you want to use the LOCATION column on the caller rather than its index. (The data frame passed as an argument to `join` will always be joined on its index.)

Summary

Once you've read data into a data frame, there are many ways in which you can split, combine, and analyze it. In this chapter, we looked at some of the most common tasks—from grouping for analysis, to grouping for including/excluding rows, to joining and merging data frames. Having these skills at your fingertips makes it easy to perform particularly complex types of analysis. The exercises in this chapter showed you how and when you can use these tools to explore your data in ways that analysts perform on a regular basis, with the "split-apply-combine" approach that's pervasive in pandas. In the next chapter, we'll build on what we've done here, using these techniques in more advanced ways.

Advanced grouping, joining, and sorting

In the previous chapter, we used three of the central tools in pandas: grouping data across different columns, joining multiple data frames, and sorting a data frame by its index or one or more columns. As we saw, each of these techniques gives us a powerful way to manipulate our data into a form that allows for better understanding and interpretation.

In this chapter, we'll explore deeper ways to use these techniques, both by themselves and together. We'll turn multiple CSV files into a single data frame, we'll group and sort by multiple columns, and we'll use the `filter` method to keep and reject rows based on group properties. After going through the exercises in this chapter, you'll have an even stronger understanding of these techniques, how they can help you solve problems, and when it's appropriate to use them.

Table 7.1 What you need to know

Concept	What is it?	Example	To learn more
`s.isnull`	Returns a boolean series indicating where there are null (typically NaN) values in the series s	`s.isnull()`	http://mng.bz/ngYe
`df.sort_index`	Reorders the rows of a data frame based on the values in its index, in ascending order	`df = df.sort_index()`	http://mng.bz/wvB7
`s.isnull`	Returns a boolean series indicating where there are null (typically NaN) values in the series s	`s.isnull()`	http://mng.bz/Jgyp

Table 7.1 What you need to know *(continued)*

Concept	What is it?	Example	To learn more
`df.sort_index`	Reorders the rows of a data frame based on the values in its index, in ascending order	`df = df` `.sort_index()`	http://mng.bz/wvB7
`df.sort_values`	Reorders the rows of a data frame based on the values in one or more specified columns	`df = df.sort_` `values('distance')`	http://mng.bz/qrMK
`df.transpose()` or `df.T`	Returns a new data frame with the same values as `df` but with the columns and index exchanged	`df.transpose()` or `df.T`	http://mng.bz/7DXx
`df.expanding`	Lets us run window functions on an expanding (growing) set of rows	`df.expanding()` `.sum()`	http://mng.bz/mVBn
`df.rolling`	Lets us run window functions on an expanding (growing) set of rows	`df.rolling(3)` `.mean()`	http://mng.bz/5wp4
`df.pct_change`	For a given data frame, indicates the percentage difference between each cell and the corresponding cell in the previous row	`df.pct_change()`	http://mng.bz/4DBB
`df.diff`	For a given data frame, indicates the difference between each cell and the corresponding cell in the previous row	`df.diff()`	http://mng.bz/OPDE
`df.groupby`	Allows us to invoke one or more aggregate methods for each value in a particular column	`df.groupby('year')`	http://mng.bz/vn9x

`df.loc`	Retrieves selected rows and columns	`df.loc[:, 'passen-`
		`ger_count'] = df`
		`['passenger_count']`
			http://mng.bz/nWzv

`s.iloc`	Accesses elements of a series by position	`s.iloc[0]`	http://mng.bz/QPxm
`df.dropna`	Removes rows with NaN values	`df = df.dropna()`	http://mng.bz/XN0Y
`s.unique`	Gets the unique values in a series (`drop_duplicates` is better)	`s.unique()`	http://mng.bz/yQrJ
`df.join`	Joins two data frames based on their indexes	`df.join(other_df)`	http://mng.bz/MBo2

Table 7.1   What you need to know *(continued)*

Concept	What is it?	Example	To learn more
df.merge	Joins two data frames based on any columns	df.merge(other_df)	http://mng.bz/a1wJ
df.corr	Shows the correlation between the numeric columns of a data frame	df.corr()	http://mng.bz/gBgR
s.to_frame	Turns a series into a one-column data frame	s.to_frame()	http://mng.bz/5wp1
s.removesuffix	Returns a new string with the same contents as s but without a specified suffix (if it's there)	s.removesuffix('.csv')	http://mng.bz/6DAD
s.removeprefix	Returns a new string with the same contents as s but without a specified prefix (if it's there)	s.removeprefix('abcd')	http://mng.bz/o1Rr
s.title	Returns a new string based on s in which each word starts with a capital letter	s.title('hello out there')	http://mng.bz/nWzg
pd.concat	Returns one new data frame based on a list of data frames passed to pd.concat	pd.concat([df1, df2, df3])	http://mng.bz/vn9J
df.assign	Adds one or more columns to a data frame	df.assign (a=df['x']*3)	http://mng.bz/1J1V
DataFrameGroupBy.agg	Applies multiple aggregation methods to a groupby	df.groupby('a')['b'].agg(['mean', 'std'])	http://mng.bz/v8o1
DataFrameGroupBy.filter	Keeps rows whose group results in True from an outside function	df.groupby('a').filter (filter_func)	http://mng.bz/z0BQ
DataFrameGroupBy.transform	Modifies rows based on an outside function	df.groupby('a').transform (transform_func)	http://mng.bz/0l26
df.rename	Renames columns in a data frame	df.rename(columns= {'a':'b', 'c':'d'})	http://mng.bz/K9W0
df.drop_ duplicates	Returns a data frame whose rows contain distinct values	df.drop_ duplicates()	http://mng.bz/9Qv1
df.drop	Removes rows or columns from a data frame, returning a new one	df.drop('a', axis='columns')	http://mng.bz/j1eP

EXERCISE 32 ▪ Multicity temperatures

Grouping is one of the most useful and common functions we use when analyzing data. That's because although it's helpful to get an overall view of a data set, it's even *more* useful to learn about the different pieces of the data set so we can compare them with one another. For example, we may want to know how many people voted in the most recent election. But if we're interested in running a campaign that encourages more people to vote, we'll want to count voters from each age range, location, or ethnicity, to target our campaign more effectively.

In this exercise, we're going to get some additional practice with grouping. But I've added another challenge: creating the data frame on which you'll perform the grouping. That's because I want you to create the data frame based on eight different CSV files, each of which contains weather data from a different city. Moreover, the eight cities come from four different US states—and we want the data frame to contain `city` and `state` columns so we can work with them individually in that way.

Each of the files you'll load has the same column names and format. Take advantage of that when loading the data into a data frame.

Specifically, I'd like you to

1 Take the eight CSV files I've provided, containing weather data from eight different cities (spanning four states), and turn them into a data frame. The files are san+francisco,ca.csv, new+york,ny.csv, springfield,ma.csv, boston,ma.csv, springfield,il.csv, albany,ny.csv, los+angeles,ca.csv, and chicago,il.csv.

2 We are only interested in the first three columns from each CSV file: the date and time, the max temperature, and the min temperature.

3 Add `city` and `state` columns that contain the city and state from the filename and allow us to distinguish between rows.

Once you've done all that, answer the following questions:

▪ Does the data for each city and state start and end at (roughly) the same time? How do you know?

▪ What is the lowest minimum temperature recorded for each city in the data set?

▪ What is the highest maximum temperature recorded in each *state* in the data set?

Working it out

One of the most important things I tell newcomers to programming is that your choice and design of data structures has a huge effect on the programs you write. When you're working with Python, you should think carefully about whether you'll use a list, a tuple, a dictionary, or some combination of those.

The pandas analog to this advice is that you should design your data frames such that they include all the information you need to simplify your queries. This sometimes means you'll need to do some additional manipulations and calculations when loading data from files—but for the most part, having your data in a clear and organized data frame opens the door to straightforward, easy-to-understand, and efficient queries.

In this exercise, we need columns for `city` and `state` (where the temperature reports were made), the date and time of the reading, the maximum temperature recorded, and the minimum temperature recorded. We can get the city and state from the filename and the final three values from the rows of the CSV files. We'll aim to create a data frame with these columns from each of the cities and then combine them into one large data frame.

Let's first consider how we can create a data frame from the combination of all these CSV files. We already know how to read in a single CSV file using `read_csv`:

```
one_filename = 'new+york,ny.csv'
one_df = pd.read_csv(one_filename)
```

However, we aren't interested in every column in the CSV file. We thus pass a number of key-value pairs:

- `usecols`, specifying which columns we want to read and use from the CSV file. Here, we specify them using integers.
- `names`, indicating what column names we want in the data frame, ensuring that the names are the same across all files.
- `header`, indicating that the first row (i.e., line 0) of the file contains the header information—mostly so we can ignore the names and replace them with our own.

Our call to `read_csv` ends up like this:

```
one_df = (
    pd
    .read_csv(one_filename,
            usecols=[0, 1, 2],
            names=['date_time', 'max_temp',
                    'min_temp'],
            header=0)
)
```

This code gives us the three columns we want from CSV-file data. However, we still need to extract the city and state info from the filename and add that to the data frame.

First, we remove the .csv suffix:

```
base_filename = one_filename.removesuffix('.csv')
```

The filenames, at least as I've defined them for the Jupyter notebooks we're using for this book, are all in a parallel directory called ../data. So the real filename is ../data/new+york,ny.csv, which means we need to remove both the prefix and the suffix. We can do that in one line via method chaining:

```
one_filename.removeprefix('../data/').removesuffix('.csv')
```

This whole expression returns a string that we could assign to a new variable. But we want to get the city and state from the string, so we'll run the Python `str.split` method, which returns a list of strings based on breaking a string into multiple parts. All we have to do is indicate what character serves as a field delimiter in this string—in this case, a comma:

```
one_filename.removeprefix('../data/').removesuffix('.csv').split(',')
```

Given that we know how these files are named, we can be sure that the result of calling `str.split` is a two-element list in which the first element is the city name and the second element is the two-letter state abbreviation. Thanks to Python's "tuple unpacking" feature, we can assign the elements of this list to two variables:

```
city, state = (
    one_filename
    .removeprefix('../data/')
    .removesuffix('.csv')
    .split(',')
)
```

Just like that, the `city` variable contains the city name from the filename, and the `state` variable contains the state abbreviation.

We now have `one_df` (a variable containing a data frame) and both `city` and `state`. How can we put the values from the variables `city` and `state` into columns `city` and `state` in `one_df`?

One way is to assign a scalar value to a new column, which has the effect of assigning that value to every row in the column:

```
one_df['city'] = city
one_df['state'] = state
```

But there's something wrong here: the city names contain + signs instead of space characters and are written in lowercase letters. Similarly, the state abbreviations are in lowercase letters. We can fix that, using some additional Python string methods:

```
one_df['city'] = city.replace('+', ' ').title()
one_df['state'] = state.upper()
```

Although this code works, we should use method chaining when importing the files. We can do that by using `assign`, which temporarily adds one or more new columns to a data frame. We can say this, using method-chaining syntax:

```
one_df = (
    pd
    .read_csv(one_filename,
              usecols=[0, 1, 2],
              names=['date_time', 'max_temp',
                     'min_temp'],
              header=0)
    .assign(city=city.replace('+', ' ').title(),
            state=state.upper())
)
```

In other words: `read_csv` returns a new data frame based on the city's CSV file. Before returning that data frame to the caller, we add `city` and `state` columns. The result, assigned to `one_df`, is a data frame with the five columns we want.

How can we use this template to read data from all eight CSV files into a single data frame? We can use `pd.concat`, which takes a list of data frames and returns a single, combined data frame. If we can create a list of data frames, each based on a different CSV file, we'll have the data as we need it.

To do that, we use a `for` loop, iterating over the list of filenames returned by `glob.glob`, a function in Python's standard library. We iterate over each filename we get back from `glob.glob`, create a data frame from its contents, add the city and state, and append that data frame to our list. After all the iterations are done, we can use `pd.concat` to combine them:

```python
import glob

all_dfs = []

for one_filename in glob.glob('../data/*,*.csv'):
    print(f'Loading {one_filename}...')

    city, state = (
        one_filename
        .removeprefix('../data/')
        .removesuffix('.csv')
        .split(',')
    )

    one_df = (
        pd
        .read_csv(one_filename,
                  usecols=[0, 1, 2],
                  names=['date_time', 'max_temp',
                         'min_temp'],
                  header=0)
        .assign(city=city.replace('+', ' ').title(),
                state=state.upper())
    )

    all_dfs.append(one_df)
```

In this code, we iterate over each filename that matches the pattern `*,*.csv`. We create a new data frame from that CSV file and add (with `assign`) a new `city` column (based on the city name, which we get from `one_filename`) and a new `state` column (again, based on the state abbreviation, which we also get from `one_filename`).

We append each data frame to `all_dfs`, a list, such that we'll grow the list with one new element per CSV file. When we're done with all the data frames, we then create `df`, the result of concatenating them (figure 7.1). We can then run `pd.concat` and get a single data frame from the list.

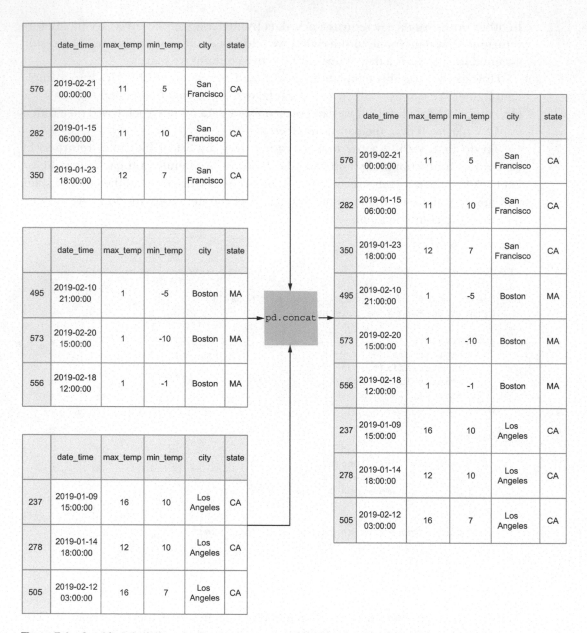

Figure 7.1   Graphical depiction of using `pd.concat` to join separate data frames into a single one

Put that all together, and we have our loading code:

```
df = pd.concat(all_dfs)
```

Now that we have created our five-column data frame with information from all eight cities, we can start to tackle the questions I raised in the exercise. First, I asked whether the data for each city and state starts at roughly the same time. How can we know such a thing? Well, each row has a `date_time` column indicating when the temperature readings were taken. If we can get the minimum and maximum values for each city's rows, we can do a quick comparison.

This, of course, is precisely what `groupby` was designed to do: take a data frame and run an aggregation method (e.g., `min` or `max`) for each of the distinct values in one column.

However, there's a twist. Although we could group by city alone, we're going to group by two different columns: first `state` and then `city`. Why not just `city`? Because several of the city names appear twice. If we grouped results only by city, the information from Springfield, Illinois would be mixed up with that from Springfield, Massachusetts. Also, grouping by both state and city ensures that we get a nice report of our data. The query looks like this:

```
(
    df.groupby(['state', 'city'])['date_time'].min()
    .sort_values()
)
```

In this code, we tell pandas that we want to get the minimum value of `date_time` for each distinct combination of `state` and `city`. We then want to sort the values so we can easily find the earliest one—as well as find out if they're all from the same period of time. We can similarly run `max` on the values, to find the highest one:

```
(
    df.groupby(['state', 'city'])['date_time'].max()
    .sort_values()
)
```

In running these queries, we see that all the data files are from the same period, starting on December 11, 2018, and going through March 11, 2019. As we'll see in chapter 9, pandas allows us to work with actual dates and times, performing calculations and comparisons on them. Here, the `date_time` column is a string, which makes it possible to do some basic queries, but nothing as sophisticated as what we can do with `timestamp` objects, as you'll see.

I then asked you to find the lowest minimum temperature recorded for each city in our data set. Again, we run a `groupby` query, but this time we're interested in the actual values, not just in comparing them with one another. The minimum temperature is located in the `min_temp` column. So if we want to get the lowest minimum temperature for each city-state combination, we can say

```
df.groupby(['state', 'city'])['min_temp'].min()
```

This returns a series in which the index is the combination of state and city and the values are the minimum temperatures in each city. We can see that the data was taken in the winter, given how many of the temperatures are below 0 Celsius.

Finally, I asked you to find the highest maximum temperature recorded during this period, but on a per-state basis rather than a per-city basis. This means grouping just by state:

```
df.groupby('state')['max_temp'].max()
```

Sure enough, we get the maximum temperature for each state. Notice that because we have eight cities but that they're spread across only four states, we get four results rather than eight. The number of results we get from a grouping action reflects the number of unique values in the grouping column (or columns).

Of course, we can also use the agg method to ask for both results:

```
(
    df.groupby(['state', 'city'])['date_time']
    .agg(['min', 'max'])
)
```

Solution

```
import glob

all_dfs = []          ←── Creates an empty list

for one_filename in glob.glob('../data/*,*.csv'):   ←── Uses glob.glob to get all filenames matching this pattern, and iterates over them
    print(f'Loading {one_filename}...')

    city, state = (
        one_filename
        .removeprefix('../data/')
        .removesuffix('.csv')
        .split(',')       ←── Uses str.split to get separate variables
    )

    one_df = (
        pd
        .read_csv(one_filename,
                  usecols=[0, 1, 2],        ←── We only care about the first three columns in each CSV file.
                  names=['date_time',
                         'max_temp',         ←── Assigns names to the three columns we loaded
                         'min_temp'],
                  header=0)       ←── The file's first row (index 0) contains headers.
        .assign(city=city.replace('+', ' ').title(),   ←── Adds a city column to the data frame
                state=state.upper())    ←── Adds a state column to the data frame
    )
    all_dfs.append(one_df)       ←── Appends the new data frame to all_dfs

df = pd.concat(all_dfs)       ←── Creates one data frame from each of the city-specific data frames

df.groupby(['state', 'city'])[
    'date_time'].min().sort_values()      ←── Gets the earliest value of date_time for each city and state

df.groupby(['state', 'city'])[
    'date_time'].max().sort_values()      ←── Gets the latest value of date_time for each city and state
```

```
df.groupby(['state', 'city'])['min_temp'].min()
df.groupby('state')['max_temp'].max()
```

◄───┐ **Gets the minimum temperature for each city**

◄─── **Gets the maximum temperature for each state**

You can explore a version of this in the Pandas Tutor at http://mng.bz/ddQO.

Beyond the exercise

- Run describe on the minimum and maximum temperature for each state-city combination.
- Running describe works, but we only see the first and last few rows from each result. Using pd.set_option to change the value of display_max_rows makes it possible to see all the results in Jupyter. Then reset the option to 10 rows.
- What is the average difference in temperature (i.e., max – min) for each of the cities in our data set?

Window functions

Let's assume that a data frame contains sales information for last year:

```
df = DataFrame({'sales':[100, 150, 200, 250,
                200, 150, 300, 400,
                500, 100, 300, 200],
                'quarters':'Q1 Q2 Q3 Q4'.split()_ 3})
```

We've already seen how we can evaluate the data here a few different ways:

- We can get the mean (and other aggregate information) for all sales quarters by applying mean to the sales column.
- We can use groupby on the quarters column and then run mean on the Data-FrameGroupBy object we get back to find out how well we did, on average, in each quarter.

These are important, common, and useful analyses. But what if we want to determine how much we sold, total, through the current quarter? That is, we want to know how much we sold in Q1, then in Q1+Q2, then Q1+Q2+Q3, and so on, until the final result is df['sales'].sum().

To perform this kind of operation, pandas provides *window functions*. There are several different types of window functions, but the basic idea is that they allow us to run an aggregate function, such as mean, on subsections of our data frame.

What I described earlier—that we would like to know, for each quarter, how much revenue we had through that quarter—is a classic example of a window function. This is known as an *expanding window* because we run the function with an ever-expanding number of lines—first one line, then two, then three . . . all the way up to the entire data frame.

For example, we could run

```
df['sales'].expanding().sum()
```

(continued)

This returns a series whose values are the cumulative sum of values in `sales` up to that point. Because the first four values in the `sales` column are 100, 150, 200, and 250, the output of our call to `expanding` is 100, 250, 450, and 700.

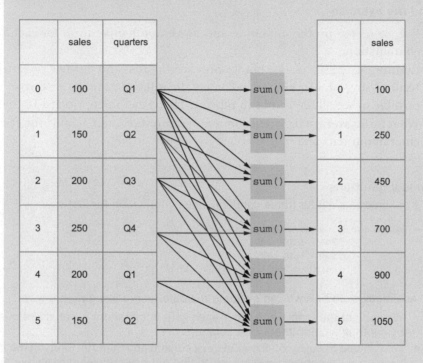

Graphical depiction of an expanding window function with `sum`

Perhaps we don't want to get a cumulative total, but rather a running average of how much we've sold per quarter. We can run `mean` or any other aggregation method:

```
df['sales'].expanding().mean()
```

In this case, the output from `expanding` is 100, 125, 150, and 175.

We can also use a *rolling* window function. In this case, we determine how many rows are considered part of the window. For example, if the window size is 3, we run the aggregation function on row index 0-2, then 1-3, then 2-4, and so on, until we get to the end of the data frame. For example, if we want to determine the mean of rows that are close to each other, we can do it as follows:

```
df['sales'].rolling(3).mean()
```

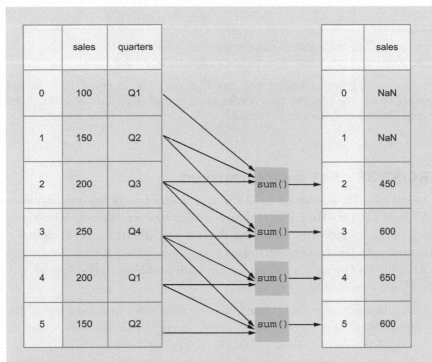

Graphical depiction of a rolling window function (looking at three lines) with `sum`

In this code, `rolling` is how we indicate that we want to run a rolling window function, and the argument 3 indicates that we want three rows in each window. We thus invoke `mean` on rows 0-2, then 1-3, then 2-4, then 3-5, and so on. The series we get back from this call puts the result of `mean` in the same location as the third (and final) row in our rolling window. This means row indexes 0 and 1 have `NaN` values.

A third type of window function is `pct_change`. When we run this on a series, we get back a new series with `NaN` at row index 0. The remaining rows indicate the percentage change from the previous row to the current one:

```
df['sales'].pct_change()
```

For example, the output from this code is

```
0         NaN
1    0.500000
2    0.333333
3    0.250000
```

The result is calculated as (`later_row - earlier_row`) / `earlier_row`:

- Index 0 is always `NaN`.
- Index 1 is the result of calculating (150 – 100) / 100.

(continued)

- Index 2 is the result of calculating (200 − 150) / 150.
- Index 3 is the result of calculating (250 − 200) / 200.

`pct_change` is great for finding how much values go up or down from row to row. If we want to get the raw changes across rows, rather than the percentage changes, we can use the `diff` method, instead.

EXERCISE 33 ▪ SAT scores, revisited

Back in exercise 22, we looked at SAT scores. There have long been accusations that the SAT isn't a fair test for college admissions, because wealthier students generally do better than poorer students. Given the data we have about the SAT, can we conclude that wealthier students do indeed, on average, score better? We will examine the math portion of the SAT, seeing if we can see any such problems in the data.

Here's what I would like you to do:

1 Read in the scores file (sat-scores.csv). This time, you want the following columns: `Year, State.Code, Total.Math, Family Income.Less than 20k.Math, Family Income.Between 20-40k.Math, Family Income.Between 40-60k.Math, Family Income.Between 60-80k.Math, Family Income.Between 80-100k.Math,` and `Family Income.More than 100k.Math`.

2 Rename the income-related column names to something shorter. I recommend `income<20k, 20k<income<40k, 40k<income<60k, 60k<income<80k, 80k<income 100k,` and `income>100k`.

3 Find the average SAT math score for each income level, grouped and then sorted by year.

4 For each year in the data set, determine how much better each income group did, on average, than the next-poorer group of students. Do you see (just by looking at the data) any income group that did worse, in any year, than the next-poorer students?

5 Which income bracket, on average, had the greatest advantage over the next-poorer income bracket?

6 Can we find, in a calculated and automated way, which income levels consistently (i.e., across all years) do worse than the next-poorest group?

Working it out

In this exercise, we use data to gain insight into a real-world problem. (What we do with this analysis is another question entirely.) For starters, we need to load data from our CSV file into a data frame. We're only interested in the math scores—but actually, we're more interested in the math scores when broken down by family income. As a result, we load the CSV file as follows:

```
df = pd.read_csv(filename,
        usecols=['Year', 'State.Code', 'Total.Math',
                'Family Income.Less than 20k.Math',
                'Family Income.Between 20-40k.Math',
                'Family Income.Between 40-60k.Math',
                'Family Income.Between 60-80k.Math',
                'Family Income.Between 80-100k.Math',
                'Family Income.More than 100k.Math'])
```

What I find particularly interesting here is what we *don't* include in the call to
pd.read_csv: first and foremost, we don't assign an index. Although it's often useful
to set an index, the analyses we do here all use grouping. And although we can still
use groupby on a column we've set to be the index, there's no added value. For that
reason, we stick with the default numeric index starting at 0.

I also asked you to change the names of the columns from long, unwieldy names to
something easier to type and read. In theory, we could do so by giving a value to the
name parameter. But if we give names to columns, we need to use integers to indicate
which columns should be imported from CSV. And to be honest, I always find that
hard to read, debug, and understand.

So instead, we load the columns with their full, original names, as per the file. We
then change the column names by assigning to df.columns:

```
df.columns = ['Year', 'State.Code', 'Total.Math',
                'income<20k',
                '20k<income<40k',
                '40k<income<60k',
                '60k<income<80k',
                '80k<income<100k',
                'income>100k',
                ]
```

However, in some older versions of pandas, assigning to df.columns this way runs the
risk of getting the order wrong. As a result, it's better to rename columns using
df.rename, passing the columns keyword argument a dict value in which the keys are
the old column names and the values are the new ones:

```
df = df.rename(
    columns={
    'Family Income.Less than 20k.Math':'income<20k',
    'Family Income.Between 20-40k.Math':'20k<income<40k',
    'Family Income.Between 40-60k.Math':'40k<income<60k',
    'Family Income.Between 60-80k.Math':'60k<income<80k',
    'Family Income.Between 80-100k.Math':'80k<income<100k',
    'Family Income.More than 100k.Math':'income>100k'
    })
```

Now that our data frame has the rows and columns we want and the columns have
easy-to-understand names, we can start to analyze things. First, I asked you to find the
average SAT math score for each income level, grouped and then sorted by year:

```
df.groupby('Year').mean(numeric_only=True).sort_index()
```

This query is similar to what we've done before: we want to invoke `mean` on every column in `df`, grouping the results by year. We can thus say, for each income bracket, what the average SAT math score was across the United States in each year.

Because we're grouping by the `Year` column, it isn't included in our output. But why isn't `State.Code` included in the output? Because we pass `numeric_only=True`, thus removing any non-numeric columns. In previous versions of pandas, non-numeric columns were silently ignored. Now, however, we need to either explicitly choose numeric columns or ask `mean` to do it for us with this keyword argument.

Moreover, because we group by `Year`, the index of the resulting data frame has an index of `Year`. Because the data set comes sorted by `Year`, the results appear to be sorted. But just to be on the safe side, we invoke `sort_index` on the data frame, ensuring that the result we get back is sorted from the earliest year in the data set through the final year in the data set.

But then I asked you to do something else: to find how much *better* each income bracket did than the next-poorer income bracket. That is, first find the average SAT math score for students in the lowest bracket: `income<20k`. Then determine how much better (or worse) the next bracket (i.e., `20k<income<40k`) did. Perhaps we'll see that there's a negligible difference between them, in which case we can say, to some degree, that SAT scores aren't correlated with student income.

How can we make this comparison? We use `pct_change`, described in the "Window functions" sidebar.

We want to compare the scores by year and income brackets. But `pct_change` works on rows, not columns—and right now, our data frame has the brackets as columns. We thus need to flip the data frame on its side so the years are the columns and the income brackets are the rows.

The solution is to use the `transpose` method, more easily abbreviated as `T`, which returns a new data frame in which the rows and columns have exchanged places (figure 7.2):

```
df.groupby('Year')[['income<20k',
            '20k<income<40k',
            '40k<income<60k',
            '60k<income<80k',
            '80k<income<100k',
            'income>100k']].mean().T
```

T, a shortcut for "transpose"

The `transpose` method is invoked like any other method in pandas, using parentheses:

```
df.transpose()
```

Its convenient alias, `T`, is *not* a method and thus should not be invoked with parentheses:

```
df.T
```

In both cases, we get a new data frame back; the original data frame is unmodified.

	Year	State.Code	Total.Math	income<20k	20k<income<40k	40k<income<60k	60k<income<80k	80k<income<100k	income>100k
162	2008	CO	572	555	567	571	578	533	583
428	2013	GA	488	451	470	484	496	426	530
263	2010	AZ	527	491	506	523	531	472	553
490	2014	ME	471	494	520	535	555	468	569
334	2011	MI	605	549	565	590	609	528	626

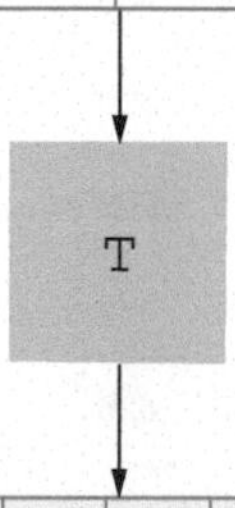

T

	162	428	263	490	334
Year	2008	2013	2010	2014	2011
State.Code	CO	GA	AZ	ME	MI
Total.Math	572	488	527	471	605
income<20k	555	451	491	494	549
20k<income<40k	567	470	506	520	565
40k<income<60k	571	484	523	535	590
60k<income<80k	578	496	531	555	609
80k<income<100k	533	426	472	468	528
income>100k	583	530	553	569	626

Figure 7.2 Example of using T to transpose a data frame

We can now invoke pct_change on this new data frame:

```
(
    df
    .groupby('Year')
    [['income<20k',
      '20k<income<40k',
      '40k<income<60k',
      '60k<income<80k',
      '80k<income<100k',
      'income>100k']]
    .mean()
    .T
    .pct_change()
)
```

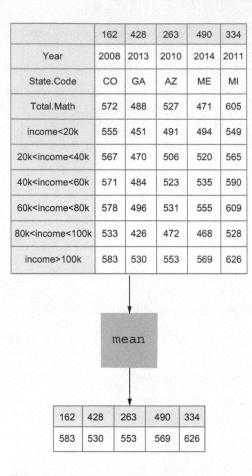

	162	428	263	490	334
Year	2008	2013	2010	2014	2011
State.Code	CO	GA	AZ	ME	MI
Total.Math	572	488	527	471	605
income<20k	555	451	491	494	549
20k<income<40k	567	470	506	520	565
40k<income<60k	571	484	523	535	590
60k<income<80k	578	496	531	555	609
80k<income<100k	533	426	472	468	528
income>100k	583	530	553	569	626

mean

162	428	263	490	334
583	530	553	569	626

Figure 7.3　Get the mean after transposing.

We get back a data frame in which the columns are years (2005 to 2015) and the rows are income brackets. The values in the data frame are floats, with each number indicating the percentage by which the math scores for that income bracket, in that year, differed from the next-poorer income bracket. The lowest income bracket has NaN values, because there is no previous row (figure 7.3).

From a visual scan of the data, we can see that most income brackets did better than the next-lower bracket. Thus, families with an income between $20,000 and $40,000 per year did about 3% to 7% better on their math SAT than people in the lowest bracket. And in families making $40,000 to $60,000 per year, they generally did 2% to 3% better than those in the next-lower bracket.

However, across the years, those earning between $80,000 and $100,000 per year did slightly worse than those than those in the next-lowest income bracket (i.e., between $60,000 and $80,000 per year). What's the reason for this? I'm not sure, but it is consistently true across all the years.

Next, I asked you to determine which income bracket, on average, had the greatest advantage over the next-poorer income bracket. To do this, we start with the result of our call to pct_change. But we want to determine how much better, on average, each bracket did than the next-poorer bracket. To do this, we use mean—but not on the data frame we get back from pct_change. Rather, we retranspose the data frame such that the income brackets are the columns and the years are the rows:

```
(
    df
    .groupby('Year')
    [['income<20k',
      '20k<income<40k',
      '40k<income<60k',
      '60k<income<80k',
      '80k<income<100k',
      'income>100k']]
```

```
    .mean()
    .T
    .pct_change()
    .T
    .mean()
)
```

Changing the axis

Another option would be to pass mean the `axis` keyword argument:

```
df.mean(axis='columns')
```

The default value for `axis` is `'rows'`, giving us a new row with the mean from each column. If we pass `axis='columns'`, we get a new column back with the same index as the data frame.

If the data set isn't too large, I'm fine with transposing twice, which I see as a way to return to the earlier state. But if you feel more comfortable passing the `axis` keyword argument, or if your data set is large enough that transposing will take too much time or memory, you can try that.

We now know how much each income bracket did better, on average, than the next-poorer bracket. Where was the greatest jump in SAT math performance? We can find out by invoking `sort_values` and asking for the values to be in descending order. Then we can invoke `head()` to see the top-ranking income brackets:

```
(
    df
    .groupby('Year')
    [['income<20k',
      '20k<income<40k',
      '40k<income<60k',
      '60k<income<80k',
      '80k<income<100k',
      'income>100k']]
    .mean()
    .T
    .pct_change()
    .T
    .mean()
    .sort_values(ascending=False)
    .head()
)
```

All this is fine, but relying on a visual scan of the data is not a good way to go about things. Rather, we'd like an automated way to find which, if any, of the income brackets did worse than the next-lower bracket. How can we do that?

Well, we know that the result of calling `pct_change` is a data frame. As such, we have all our pandas analysis tools at our disposal. We can, for example, assign the result of `pct_change` to a data frame and then look for values that are ≤ 0:

```
change = (
    df
    .groupby('Year')
    [['income<20k',
      '20k<income<40k',
      '40k<income<60k',
      '60k<income<80k',
      '80k<income<100k',
      'income>100k']]
    .mean()
    .T
    .pct_change()
)

change <= 0
```

We're applying a comparison operator to a data frame, which means we get back a boolean data frame. Just as applying a boolean series to a series only shows the elements corresponding to True values, applying a data frame to a boolean data frame shows the items corresponding to True values. The difference is that the data frame has the same shape—and thus any filtered-out values are replaced with NaN:

```
change[change <= 0]
```

We can then remove any rows that contain any NaN values, showing only rows in which we consistently see a change for the worse as the income level rises:

```
change[change <= 0].dropna()
```

Sure enough, we see that every single income bracket did better, on average, than the income bracket below it.

Solution

```
filename = '../data/sat-scores.csv'

df = pd.read_csv(filename,
 usecols=['Year', 'State.Code', 'Total.Math',
      'Family Income.Less than 20k.Math',
      'Family Income.Between 20-40k.Math',
      'Family Income.Between 40-60k.Math',
      'Family Income.Between 60-80k.Math',
      'Family Income.Between 80-100k.Math',    ⟵⎤ Reads data from
      'Family Income.More than 100k.Math'])  ⟵⎦ the CSV file

df = df.rename(
    columns={
    'Family Income.Less than 20k.Math':'income<20k',
    'Family Income.Between 20-40k.Math':'20k<income<40k',
    'Family Income.Between 40-60k.Math':'40k<income<60k',      Renames the
    'Family Income.Between 60-80k.Math':'60k<income<80k',      columns as per the
    'Family Income.Between 80-100k.Math':'80k<income<100k',    dict, with old names
    'Family Income.More than 100k.Math':'income>100k'          as the keys and new
    })                                       ⟵                 names as the values
```

```
df.groupby('Year').mean(
    numeric_only=True).sort_index()        ◁──┐ Calculates the mean value of
                                               │ each column for each year
                                               │ and then sorts by year
(
    df
    .groupby('Year')
    [['income<20k',
      '20k<income<40k',
      '40k<income<60k',
      '60k<income<80k',
      '80k<income<100k',
      'income>100k']]
    .mean()
    .T                  Transposes the result of grouping and getting the
    .pct_change()       mean, and then uses pct_change to check how much
)                   ◁──┘ better each income group did than the previous one


(
    df
    .groupby('Year')
    [['income<20k',
      '20k<income<40k',
      '40k<income<60k',
      '60k<income<80k',
      '80k<income<100k',
      'income>100k']]
    .mean()
    .T
    .pct_change()
    .T
    .mean()
    .sort_values(ascending=False)
    .head()
)              ◁──┐ Which income bracket had the
                  │ greatest advantage over the
change = (        │ next-highest income bracket?
    df
    .groupby('Year')
    [['income<20k',
      '20k<income<40k',
      '40k<income<60k',
      '60k<income<80k',
      '80k<income<100k',
      'income>100k']]
    .mean()
    .T          Assigns the
    .pct_change() previous output to
)          ◁──┘  a variable, change   Finds all rows of change in
                                      which all columns did worse
change[change <= 0].dropna()     ◁──── than the previous value
```

You can explore a version of this in the Pandas Tutor at http://mng.bz/rj9D.

Beyond the exercise

- Calculate descriptive statistics for all the changes in income brackets. Where do you see the largest difference between income brackets?
- Which five states have the greatest gap in SAT math scores between the richest and poorest students?
- You analyzed math scores. If you perform the same analysis on verbal SAT scores, will you similarly see that wealthier students generally do better than poorer students? Do any income brackets do worse than the next-poorer bracket?

Filtering and transforming

We've already seen how we can use `groupby` to run aggregate methods on each portion of our data to get the average rainfall per city or the total sales figures per quarter. We've also seen, in earlier chapters, how to use a boolean index to filter out rows that fail to match particular criteria.

For example, consider a data frame containing the year-end math scores for each student. The rows of the data frame describe the students. The columns of the data frame, `name`, `year`, and `score`, describe those three student attributes. Here's how we can create a simple form of this data frame:

```
import numpy as np
np.random.seed(0)

df = DataFrame({'name': list('ABCDEFGHIJ'),
                'year': [2018, 2019, 2020]_ 3 + [2021],
                'score':np.random.randint(80, 100, 10)})
```

Our data frame is

```
name  year  score
0     A    2018     92
1     B    2019     95
2     C    2020     80
3     D    2018     83
4     E    2019     83
5     F    2020     87
6     G    2018     89
7     H    2019     99
8     I    2020     98
9     J    2021     84
```

We can perform a number of calculations:

- We can get the mean score by running `df['score'].mean()`. This returns a single floating-point value, 89.0.
- We can get all the students who scored above 90 with `df.loc[df['score'] > 90]`. This returns the original data frame minus students who got less than 90—in our case, row indexes 0, 1, 7, and 8.

- We can get the mean score per year by running `df.groupby('year')` `['score'].mean()`. If the school has eight grades, the result of this query is a series whose index contains the distinct values of `year` from `df` and whose values are the average grades for each year. Here, we get four different results (one for each year).

So far, so good. But consider this: we want to determine which years in our school had an average score of at least 90, and see all the students in those years. We want to filter out specific groups of students based on a per-year aggregate calculation. How can we do that?

The answer, it turns out, is to apply the `filter` method to our `DataFrameGroupBy` object. All we need is to pass `filter` a function that, given a group of rows, returns either `True` or `False`, to indicate whether those rows should be in the result data frame.

In other words,

- We want to decide whether to include or exclude rows based on the `year`, so we run `df.groupby('year')`
- On that `DataFrameGroupBy` object, we run the `filter` method.
- `filter` takes a function as an argument.
- The function we pass is invoked once per group. It receives a data frame—a subset of `df`—as its argument.
- The function must return `True` or `False` to indicate whether rows from that group should be included or excluded in the resulting data frame.
- The function can be a full-fledged Python function (i.e., one defined with `def`), or we can use `lambda` for an inline, anonymous function.

Here's an example of such a function, as well as how we could invoke it:

```
def year_average_is_at_least_90(df):
    return df['score'].mean() > 90

df.groupby('year').filter(year_average_is_at_least_90)
```

The result of running this code is a data frame whose rows all come from `df`, from years in which the average final-exam math score was at least 90. That is only the year 2019, so we get the rows with indexes 1, 4, and 7.

Here are some examples of how to use `filter` in real-world data sets:

- Show all products coming from factories that brought in more than $1 million last year.
- List the staff working for divisions with below-average salaries.
- Find networks whose segments have had more than 10 outages in the last week.

Another, related method we can use on a `GroupBy` object is `transform`. In this case, the point is not to remove rows from the original data frame but rather to transform them in some way. For example, let's say we want to turn the score into a percentage expressed as a float. We can say

```
df.groupby('year')['score'].transform(lambda x: x/100)
```

(continued)

In this example we're grouping by year, so the function is run once for each year:

- It's invoked with a three-element series with all rows from 2018.
- It's invoked with a three-element series with all rows from 2019.
- It's invoked with a three-element series with all rows from 2020.
- It's invoked with a one-element series with the only row from 2021.

The function is expected to return a series with the same dimensions as the input, which happens naturally in our example because our `lambda` function invokes the division (/) operator on the series. Thanks to broadcasting (i.e., that an operation on a series and a scalar is repeated on each element of the series), we're guaranteed to get a result of the correct dimensions. We can then replace the original `score` column with our transformed column:

```
df['score'] = (
    df.groupby('year')['score']
    .transform(lambda x: x/100)
    )
```

But we can do much more than this. After all, our `lambda` function has access to all the rows from each year. This means we can run aggregate functions, such as `sum` or `mean`. For example, let's say that we pass `np.max` as our function:

```
df.groupby('year')['score'].transform(np.max)
```

We want to invoke our function (`np.max`) once for each value of `year` in the data frame. And the input to our function is the column `score`, with the rows for each year. The result is as follows:

```
0    92
1    99
2    98
3    92
4    99
5    98
6    92
7    99
8    98
9    84
Name: score, dtype: int64
```

In the resulting series, the value in each row is the highest value of `score` from that particular year. In other words, we have replaced every score with the maximum score for that year. (This is probably not the best way to evaluate students, I'll admit.)

We can then assign the transformed row back to our data frame:

```
df['score'] = df.groupby('year')['score'].transform(np.max)
```

As you can see, the grouped version of `transform` is useful when we want to transform values in a data frame on a group-by-group basis, much as the grouped version of `filter` is useful when we want to filter values on a group-by-group basis.

Here are some ways to use `transform` with real-world data sets:
- Find the difference between each value in a group and the group's mean.
- Find the proportion that each value in the group has versus the group's sum.
- Calculate the z-score (i.e., the number of standard deviations) that each value is from its group's mean.

NOTE In the case of both `filter` and `transform`, an attribute `name` is added to the `df` parameter with the name of the current group.

NOTE The `filter` method for `GroupBy` is very similar to Python's builtin `filter` function, and the `transform` method for `GroupBy` is very similar to Python's builtin `map` function. They work differently because they're acting on data frames rather than simple iterables, but the usage is similar.

EXERCISE 34 ■ Snowy, rainy cities

One constant theme, wherever I've lived, is that people complain about the weather. In a hot climate, people complain that it's too hot. In a cold climate, people complain that it's too cold. In a city with hot summers and cold winters, they complain about both. And, of course, people tell visitors and newcomers that their city's weather is worse than anywhere else. There isn't much that we can do about people's complaints. But maybe we can use data to determine which city does indeed have the most extreme weather. Because, you know, if someone is complaining about the weather, they want nothing more than to be corrected with hard data.

The calculations we'll make in this exercise all take advantage of the `filter` and `transform` methods on `DataFrameGroupBy` objects. These methods allow us to conditionally keep (`filter`) and modify (`transform`) rows in a data frame while having access to all rows of the group when deciding and calculating.

NOTE The `DataFrameGroupBy` versions of `filter` and `transform` are, in my experience, among the most complex pieces of functionality that pandas provides. It may take you a while to think through what calculation you want to perform and then find the right way to express it in pandas.

In this exercise, I want you to

1 Read in the data frames for the city weather as in exercise 32, reading three columns: `max_temp`, `min_temp`, and `precipMM`.
2 Determine which cities had, on at least three occasions, precipitation of 15 mm or more.
3 Find cities that had at least three measurements of 10 mm of precipitation or more when the temperature was at or below 0° Celsius.
4 For each precipitation measurement, calculate the proportion of that city's total precipitation.

5   For each city, determine the greatest proportion of that city's total precipitation to fall in a given period.

Working it out

In this exercise, we use `filter` and `transform` on `DataFrameGroupBy` objects to work with rows according to their aggregate properties. We start by loading the weather data from six different cities, similarly to how we did it in exercise 32. We want to load three columns: `max_temp`, `min_temp`, and `precipMM` (i.e., the amount of precipitation that fell, in millimeters). Because it's so similar to what we did before, I'll show the code here without comment:

```
import glob

all_dfs = []

for one_filename in glob.glob('../data/*,*.csv'):
    print(f'Loading {one_filename}...')

    city, state = (
        one_filename
        .removeprefix('../data/')
        .removesuffix('.csv')
        .split(',')
    )

    one_df = (
        pd
        .read_csv(one_filename,
                  usecols=[0, 1, 2],
                  names=['max_temp',
                         'min_temp',
                         'precipMM'],
                  header=0)
        .assign(city=city.replace('+', ' ').title(),
                state=state.upper())
    )

    all_dfs.append(one_df)

df = pd.concat(all_dfs)
```

Once we have our data frame in place, we can start to analyze it. For starters, we want to find cities that had measured precipitation of 15 mm or more on at least three occasions. This means

- We need to check measurements on a per-city basis (via `groupby`).
- We'll only keep cities that reported 15 mm of precipitation at least three times (via `filter`).

Let's start with our `groupby`. Because we want to find the precipitation on a per-city basis, you may think we should group by city name:

```
df.groupby('city')
```

However, we can't do this, because there are two different cities with the name "Springfield"—one in Illinois and the other in Massachusetts. For that reason, we need to group not just by city but also by state. We can do so by passing a list of columns to groupby rather than just one:

```
df.groupby(['city', 'state'])
```

This gives us our GroupBy object, which we've previously used to apply aggregate functions on distinct subsets of our data. But here we'll use the groupby object a different way, to include and exclude rows from df based on properties of their city and state. That is, we want to filter out rows, but we want to do it by group—such that for each group, all the rows are included or excluded. (You can think of this as the collective punishment feature of pandas.)

We do this by calling filter on our GroupBy object. filter on a GroupBy works on a group-by-group basis. The argument to filter is a function that expects to get a data frame as its argument. The function is called once for each group in the groupby, and the data frame passed to it is a subset of the original data frame, containing only those rows in the current group.

The function passed to filter should return True or False. If the function returns True, the rows from this subframe are kept. If the function returns False, the rows from this subframe are not included. Because its argument is a data frame with all the rows in the current group, filter can perform all sorts of calculations in determining whether to return True or False.

In this case, we want to preserve rows from cities that had 15 mm of precipitation on at least three occasions. Our function thus needs to determine whether the subframe it is passed contains at least three such rows. Our function can look like this:

```
def has_multiple_readings_at_least(mini_df):
    return mini_df.loc[
        mini_df['precipMM'] >= 15,
        'precipMM'
    ].count() >= 3
```

If we were to invoke this function on a data frame, it would return a single True or False value indicating whether the complete data frame had recorded at least 15 mm of precipitation on at least three occasions. By running it via filter, though, we can determine which cities had such records:

```
(
    df
    .groupby(['city', 'state'])
    .filter(has_multiple_readings_at_least)
)
```

The result of this query is a subset of our original data frame. But my question to you wasn't which rows would pass the filter. Rather, I asked you which cities had such precipitation. One way to do this would be to retrieve just the `city` and `state` columns from the resulting data frame:

```
(
    df.groupby(['city', 'state'])
    .filter(has_multiple_readings_at_least)
    [['city', 'state']]
)
```

However, this gives us the city and state for each row. That's more than we need. We can just run the `drop_duplicates` method on the result, instead:

```
(
    df
    .groupby(['city', 'state'])
    .filter(has_multiple_readings_at_least)
    [['city', 'state']]
    .drop_duplicates()
)
```

This works and gives us the answer we want—namely, that only New York and Los Angeles had three occasions on which at least 15 mm of precipitation fell. However, if you've been programming for any length of time, the `has_multiple_readings_at_least` function may seem odd. Do we really want to hard-code the values "15 mm" and "3 times" into the function? It may make more sense to write a generic function that can take additional arguments.

But how can we do that? After all, we're not calling `has_multiple_readings_at_least` directly. Rather, we're passing it to `filter`, which calls the function on our behalf. There isn't an obvious way for us to pass arguments to our function when it's being invoked via `filter`.

Here, pandas does something clever: any additional arguments passed to `filter` are passed along to our function. This is done using the standard Python constructs of `*args` and `**kwargs`, for arbitrary positional and keyword arguments. (For a tutorial on this subject, check out my blog post at https://lerner.co.il/2021/06/07/python-parameters-primer.)

We can thus rewrite our function as follows:

```
def has_multiple_readings_at_least(mini_df, min_mm, times):
    return mini_df.loc[
        mini_df['precipMM'] >= min_mm,
        'precipMM'
        ].count() >= times
```

Now it looks more like a regular Python function, taking three arguments. The first is still the subframe that was passed before, containing all the rows in the current group. But the second two arguments are assigned indirectly, via `filter`, when it calls our function. We can then say

```
(
    df
```

```
    .groupby(['city', 'state'])
    .filter(has_multiple_readings_at_least,
            min_mm=10,
            times=3)
    [['city', 'state', 'precipMM']]
    .drop_duplicates()
)
```

In this code, we call `filter` and pass it our function, `has_multiple_readings_at_least`. In theory, we could then pass values for `min_mm` and `times` as positional arguments. But if we do that, we'll also have to pass a second positional argument to `filter`, called `dropna`. Rather than calling `filter(func, True, 10, 3)`, we call `filter(func, min_mm=10, times=3)`. This is an aesthetic choice, rather than a technical one, but I think it makes sense here.

Next, I asked you to find cities that had

- At least three measurements of 10 mm precipitation . . .
- . . . when the temperature was below 0° Celsius

We again use `groupby` and then `filter`, using a slightly modified version of our `has_multiple_readings_at_least` function from before:

```
def has_multiple_readings_at_least(mini_df, min_mm, times):
    return mini_df.loc[
        ((mini_df['precipMM'] >= min_mm) &
         (mini_df['min_temp'] <= 0)),
        'precipMM'
        ].count() >= times
```

We can then perform our grouping and filtering in the following way:

```
(
    df
    .groupby(['city', 'state'])
    .filter(has_multiple_readings_at_least, min_mm=10, times=3)
    [['city', 'state']]
    .drop_duplicates()
)
```

Next, I asked you to find the proportion of that city's precipitation that fell with each measurement. If our data frame contains two precipitation measurements for a given city, and we see that 3 mm fell on the first day and 7 mm fell on the second day, we want to find that 30% fell in the first measurement and 70% fell in the second.

In other words, we'll calculate one value for each row. But the value we calculate for each row will depend on an aggregate calculation for the row's group. It's precisely for these situations that pandas provides the `transform` method. Similar to what we did with `filter`, we'll pass a function as the first argument to `transform`. This function is invoked once per group, and the function is passed a series: the column we want to transform. The function must then return a series, of the same length and with the same index, as its argument.

Let's assume that we have a series of numbers, each representing one measurement of precipitation. What function can we write that will return a new series with the same length and index as the original, but whose values indicate the proportion of the whole? It may look like this:

```
def proportion_of_city_precip(s):
    return s / s.sum()
```

Our function takes a series s as input and then returns the result of dividing each row by the sum total of all rows. This is how we would do it if all the values were from the same city. How can we do it, then, if we have many different cities? That's part of the magic—the groupby version of transform takes care of it for us. The rows from each group are passed, one at a time, to the function proportion_of_city_precip. The return value is then a series in which the parallel rows from the input series have their new values. We can assign the resulting series back to the column from which it was transformed, add a new column to a data frame, or just save the transformed column.

The difference between the standard transform method and the groupby version of transform is that in the latter, we have access to the entire series and can thus make calculations using aggregation functions.

Here's how we can write this:

```
df['precip_pct'] = df.groupby('city')[
    'precipMM'].transform(proportion_of_city_precip)
```

Notice that, in this example, we assign the returned series to the data frame as a new column. With this column in place, we can then answer the final question for this exercise: for each city, what was the greatest proportion of that city's total precipitation to fall in a given period? In other words, which measurement reflected the greatest proportion of precipitation we measured?

To answer this question, we use a simple, classic groupby: we apply an aggregate function (max) to each city in our system. Of course, because we have a duplicate city name, we group on both city and state. That gives the following:

```
df.groupby(['city', 'state'])['precip_pct'].max()
```

Solution

```
import glob

all_dfs = []

for one_filename in glob.glob('../data/*,*.csv'):
    print(f'Loading {one_filename}...')

    city, state = (
        one_filename
        .removeprefix('../data/')
        .removesuffix('.csv')
        .split(',')
    )
```

```
    one_df = (
        pd
        .read_csv(one_filename,
                  usecols=[0, 1, 2],
                  names=['max_temp',
                         'min_temp',
                         'precipMM'],
                  header=0)
        .assign(city=city.replace('+', ' ').title(),
                state=state.upper())
    )
```

Appends, one by one, the data frames we load to a list ← `all_dfs.append(one_df)`

`df = pd.concat(all_dfs)` ← **Creates one data frame from all the loaded data frames**

```
def has_multiple_readings_at_least(mini_df):
    return mini_df.loc[
        mini_df['precipMM'] >= 15,
        'precipMM'
        ].count() >= 3
```
← **This function returns True if there are at least three rows with precipMM >= 15.**

```
(
    df
    .groupby(['city', 'state'])
    .filter(has_multiple_readings_at_least)
    [['city', 'state']]
    .drop_duplicates()
)
```
Grouping by city and state, we apply the filter to keep the rainiest cities.

Gets the unique combinations of city and state ← `.drop_duplicates()`

```
def has_multiple_readings_at_least(mini_df, min_mm, times):
    return mini_df.loc[
        ((mini_df['precipMM'] >= min_mm) &
         (mini_df['min_temp'] <= 0)),
        'precipMM'
        ].count() >= times
```
← **This function returns True if precipitation of min_mm has fallen at least times times.**

```
(
    df
    .groupby(['city', 'state'])
    .filter(has_multiple_readings_at_least, min_mm=10, times=3)
    [['city', 'state']]
    .drop_duplicates()
)
```
Uses the new version of has_multiple_readings_at_least to find rainiest cities

Gets the unique combinations of city and state ← `.drop_duplicates()`

```
def proportion_of_city_precip(s):
    return s / s.sum()
```
← **This function returns the proportion of a city's precipitation that fell in one reading.**

```
df['precip_pct'] = df.groupby('city')[
    'precipMM'].transform(proportion_of_city_precip)
```
← **Adds a new column, precip_pct, showing the proportion for each city**

`df.groupby(['city', 'state'])['precip_pct'].max()` ← **Finds the reading showing the greatest proportion of precipitation for that city**

You can explore a version of this in the Pandas Tutor at http://mng.bz/VRA0.

Beyond the exercise

- Implement the first version of `has_multiple_readings_at_least`, which takes a single argument (`df`), but with `lambda`.
- Implement the second version of `has_multiple_readings_at_least`, which takes three arguments (`df`, `min_mm`, and `times`), but with `lambda`.
- Implement our transformation, but replace `proportion_of_city_precip` with a `lambda`. Then find the reading that represented the greatest proportion of rainfall for each city.

EXERCISE 35 ▪ Wine scores and tourism spending

Earlier in this chapter, we used `join` to combine two data frames into a single one. In this exercise, we go deeper into uses for `join`, exploring how we can join more than two data frames, how we can combine joining with grouping, and the different types of joins we can perform. We'll also look for correlations among our joined data sets.

This time, we'll combine several data sets to answer a question I'm sure you've often thought about: does a country that spends more on tourism also make better wines? Our data will come not only from the OECD tourism data we've previously explored but also from more than 150,000 rankings of wines.

To perform this analysis, I'd like you to do the following:

1 Create a data frame, `oecd_df`, from oecd_locations.csv, containing a subset of all OECD countries. The resulting data set should have a single column called `country`. The index should be based on the country's abbreviation.

2 Create a second data frame, `oecd_tourism_df`, from oecd_tourism.csv. You're only interested in four columns: `LOCATION` (which will serve as the index), `TIME` (containing the year in which the measure was taken), `SUBJECT` (the type of spending), and `Value` (the amount spent in each year). You're also only interested in rows where `SUBJECT` has the value `'INT-EXP'`, meaning spending. Once you've kept only the rows with `'INT-EXP'`, you can remove the `SUBJECT` column.

3 Create a new series, `tourism_spending`, in which the index reflects the country names (i.e., not abbreviations) and the value contains the average tourism spending for that country.

4 Create a third data frame, `wine_df`, based on winemag-150k-reviews.csv. You only need two columns: `country` and `points`.

5 Get the mean wine score for each country, across all wine reviews, sorted in descending order.

6 Perform a standard join between the average wine scores per country and the average tourism spending per country. Where do you see `NaN` values? What do those `NaN` values mean?

7 Perform an outer join between the average wine scores per country and the average tourism spending per country. Where do you see NaN values? What do they mean now?

8 Find the correlation between average wine score and average tourism spending. What can you say about these two values? Is there any correlation?

Working it out

This exercise is meant to demonstrate how we can bring together many of the ideas we've seen in this chapter on a grander scale—joining multiple data frames, moving between series and data frames, and even finding correlations across different data sets. The first thing I asked you to do was create oecd_df, a data frame with a subset of OECD members. The input CSV file, as we saw in exercise 31, contains just two columns and doesn't have any headers, which means we need to set the column names to abbrev and country. I asked you to set the input data frame's index column to be abbrev. To do all this, we can use the following code:

```
oecd_df = pd.read_csv('../data/oecd_locations.csv',
                      header=None,
                      names=['abbrev', 'country'],
                      index_col='abbrev')
```

Let's take a look at oecd_df.head():

```
abbrev   country
AUS      Australia
AUT      Austria
BEL      Belgium
CAN      Canada
DNK      Denmark
```

This data frame isn't that useful on its own. The point of loading this is to get a translation table between the country names (the country column) and the country abbreviations (the abbrev column). We will need the country names to work with the wine ratings, but we will need the country abbreviations to work with the tourism spending data. It's not uncommon to have such data frames when working with data from different sources.

With this data frame created and in place, we can create the second one, which we call oecd_tourism_df. This data frame comes from a CSV file that does have headers, so we don't need to name them. However, we are only interested in four of the input columns, so we need to select them using usecols. Then we use one column (SUBJECT) to keep only those rows that have to do with tourist expenses; once we're done with it, we drop it. Finally, I asked that you set the LOCATION column (i.e., the country abbreviation) as the index.

We can do all this with the following code:

```
oecd_tourism_df = (
    pd
```

```
    .read_csv('../data/oecd_tourism.csv',
            usecols=['LOCATION', 'TIME',
                    'Value', 'SUBJECT'],
            index_col='LOCATION')
    .loc[lambda df_: df_['SUBJECT'] == 'INT-EXP']   ◄─┐ Keeps rows where the
    .drop('SUBJECT', axis='columns')   ◄─┐              subject is 'INT-EXP'
)                                         │ Removes the
                                            SUBJECT column
```

Notice that, in this code, we use `lambda` as an argument to `.loc`. Wherever the `lambda` expression returns `True`, the row from the original data frame is kept. We use `df_` as the parameter in the `lambda` expression to indicate that it's a temporary value and to ensure that we don't confuse it with `df`, which is often used for other data frames. Besides, when the `lambda` is being run, the data frame created by `read_csv` hasn't yet been assigned to a variable, so we need to give it a temporary name.

Once we're done using the SUBJECT column to keep only tourist expenses, we can remove it with `drop`. Don't forget that `drop` defaults to using the index; to drop one or more columns, we need to specify that with `axis='columns'`.

Here's the result of invoking `oecd_tourism_df.head()`:

```
TIME     Value
LOCATION
AUS      2008    27620.0
AUS      2009    25629.6
AUS      2010    31916.5
AUS      2011    39381.5
AUS      2012    41632.8
```

We now have two data frames, both of which use the same country abbreviations for their indexes. Never mind that in `oecd_tourism_df`, the index contains repeat values, whereas in `oecd_df`, the index contains unique values; the join system knows what to do in such cases and will handle things just fine. The key (no pun intended) thing here is that the two data frames' indexes contain the same elements. (What happens if one or both of them contains values that aren't in the other? We'll deal with that later in this exercise.)

I next asked you to find the mean tourist spending per country in the OECD subset. That is, we have tourist spending figures from a number of different OECD countries across several years. We want to determine how much each country spent on tourism, on average, across all years in the data set. Moreover, we want the results to show the countries' names, not their abbreviations.

Finding the mean tourist spending per country across all years is a classic use of grouping. We could, for example, do it as follows:

```
oecd_tourism_df.groupby('LOCATION')['Value'].mean()
```

This code says that we want to get the mean of the `Value` column for each distinct LOCATION. (Notice that even though LOCATION is now the index of this data frame, we can still use it for grouping.) However, we don't want LOCATION, containing the country abbreviations. Rather, we want to use the country names, which are in `oecd_df`.

We thus need to join these two data frames. Both use the abbreviations as an index, which makes this possible. (It doesn't matter that the columns have different names; joining typically works on the data frames' indexes.) When we join, we basically say that we want to create a new, wider data frame containing all the columns from the first and all the columns of the second, with the indexes overlapping. So the resulting data frame has a total of four columns: an index containing the location abbreviations, as before, a `country` column (from `oecd_df`), and `TIME` and `value` columns (from `oecd_tourism_df`). The left and right sides are joined wherever the index of `oecd_df` matches the index of `oecd_tourism_df`, which means it's not a problem to have repeated values in the indexes of one or both data frames.

We can join them this way:

```
oecd_df.join(oecd_tourism_df)
```

We invoke `join` on `oecd_df`, which is seen as the left data frame, and we pass `oecd_tourism_df` as an argument to `join`. It is, of course, the right data frame in the join. The result is a new data frame. We run `groupby` on this data frame, grouping by country—the full names of the countries we're looking at. We then retrieve only the `Value` column and calculate the mean:

```
(
    oecd_df
    .join(oecd_tourism_df)
    .groupby('country')['Value'].mean()
)
```

This way, we've again calculated and retrieved the mean tourism spending, per country, over all years in the data set. But the result we get back uses the full country names, rather than the abbreviations. Moreover, because the result has an index (country names) and a single value column, it's returned as a series, rather than as a data frame. I asked you to assign the resulting series to a variable, `tourism_spending`, for easier manipulation later:

```
tourism_spending = (
    oecd_df
    .join(oecd_tourism_df)
    .groupby('country')['Value'].mean()
)
```

Here is the result of invoking `tourism_spending.head()`:

```
country
Australia    36727.966667
Austria      11934.563636
Belgium      20859.883455
Brazil       21564.351833
Canada       40984.633333
Name: Value, dtype: float64
```

Now it's time to load our third CSV file into a data frame. In this case, we're only interested in two columns from the CSV file, country and points:

```
wine_df = pd.read_csv(
    '../data/winemag-150k-reviews.csv',
    usecols=['country', 'points'])
```

Here's the result of running wine_df.head():

```
  country  points
0  US          96
1  Spain       96
2  US          96
3  US          96
4  France      95
```

As soon as we've created this data frame, we want to calculate the mean score (points) that each country received. Once again, we can perform a grouping operation:

```
country_points = (
    wine_df
    .groupby('country')['points'].mean()
)
```

Here's the result of running country_points.head():

```
country
Albania                 88.000000
Argentina               85.996093
Australia               87.892475
Austria                 89.276742
Bosnia and Herzegovina  84.750000
Name: points, dtype: float64
```

This returns a series in which the index contains the country names and the values are the mean points per country. We assign this to a variable, country_points, so we can use it in additional tasks.

The first task we want to do with it is to sort the average scores from highest to lowest. This can be done with a call to sort_values, passing ascending=False to ensure that we sort the values in descending order:

```
country_points.sort_values(ascending=False)
```

We get back a new series showing which countries had the highest average wine scores and which had the lowest. Here are the first five rows from my result:

```
country
England  92.888889
Austria  89.276742
France   88.925870
Germany  88.626427
Italy    88.413664
```

Now we come to the climax of this exercise: joining the wine scores and the tourism spending. How can we do that?

Well, it makes sense that we want to use `join` again, with `country_points` on the left (i.e., as the data frame on which we invoke `join`) and `tourism_spending` on the right (i.e., as the data frame passed as an argument to `join`). There's just one problem: `country_points` is a series, and we can only invoke `join` on a data frame. (We can pass a series as the argument to `join`, though—so a series can be the right side, but not the left side, of a pandas join.)

Fortunately, we can call the `to_frame` method on our series and get back a single-column data frame with the same index we had in the series:

```
country_points.to_frame()
```

With our new data frame in place, we can invoke `join`, passing `tourism_spending` as the argument:

```
country_points.to_frame().join(tourism_spending)
```

Again, it's important to remember that a join links the left data frame with the right one, connecting them along their indexes. In this case, we end up with three columns: `country`, the index column that is shared by the left and right, `points` from the left, and `Value` from the right.

Here's what the first five rows look like after performing this join:

```
country        points              Value
Albania        88.0                NaN
Argentina      85.9960930562955    NaN
Australia      87.89247528747227   37634.433333333334
Austria        89.27674190382729   16673.886363636364
Bos and Herz   84.75               NaN
```

Avoiding duplicate column names

What happens if the left and right data frames have identically named columns? After all, although pandas indexes don't need to have unique elements, column names must be unique. If you try to join frames such that you'll end up with more than one column with the same name, you'll get a `ValueError` exception saying "columns overlap but no suffix specified." And indeed, pandas allows you to specify what the suffixes should be for the left side (`lsuffix`) and right side (`rsuffix`) when you invoke `join`. For example, we can join `oecd_df` with itself (already a wild idea known as a "self join," for which there are practical uses) with

```
oecd_df.join(oecd_df, lsuffix='_l', rsuffix='_r')
```

The data frame we get back has the `abbrev` index and two identical columns named `country_l` and `country_r`.

The good news is that this join worked. But as you look at it, you'll likely notice that there are NaN values in many rows of the `Value` column. That's because the index of the left data frame (in this case, `country_points.to_frame()`) dictates the index of the resulting data frame. As a result, this is known as a *left join*. In a left join, columns from the right frame are missing values (and thus have `NaN`) wherever there was no corresponding row for the left's index.

For example, after performing this join, although we have both `points` and `Value` for Australia and Austria, there is a `NaN` in `Value` (i.e., tourism information) for Albania, Bulgaria, and Chile (among others). That's because although we had wine-quality information for these countries (and thus an entry in the left side's index), we didn't have tourism information (in the right side's index).

There are other types of joins, too. If we want to use the right data frame's index in the result, we can use a *right join*. We can accomplish that in pandas by passing `how='right'` to the `join` method. (By default, the method assumes `how='left'`.) In such a case, we get `NaN` values on columns from the left frame wherever it has no index entry corresponding to the right.

We can also be fancy and do an *outer join*, in which case the output frame's index is the combination of the left's index and the right's index. We may thus end up with `NaN` values in columns from both the left and right, depending on which index value was missing. And so, for the final part, I asked you to perform an outer join:

```
country_points.to_frame().join(tourism_spending,
                               how='outer')
```

The resulting data frame has 54 rows rather than 48, reflecting the union of the indexes from the left and right. And we now have `NaN` values from the left, such as for Belgium and Denmark, along with `NaN` values from the right. Outer joins ensure that you don't lose any data when combining data sources, but they don't automatically interpolate values—so you will almost certainly end up with some null values, which (as we've seen in chapter 5) need cleaning in various ways.

Here are the first five rows from this outer join. Notice that Belgium now appears, with a `NaN` for `points`:

```
points          Value
country
Albania         88.000000           NaN
Argentina       85.996093           NaN
Australia       87.892475     36727.966667
Austria         89.276742     11934.563636
Belgium               NaN     20859.883455
```

Finally, I asked you to determine whether there's any correlation between the scores a country received from the wine magazine's judges and the amount its citizens spend on tourism. To find this, we can use the `corr` method:

```
country_points.to_frame().join(
    tourism_spending, how='outer').corr()
```

This finds how highly correlated each column is to the other columns in the data set. A score of 1 indicates that it's 100% positively correlated, meaning when one column goes up, the other column goes up by the same degree. A score of −1 indicates that it's 100% negatively correlated, meaning when one column goes up, the other goes *down* by the same degree. A score of 0 indicates that there is no correlation at all. Generally speaking, the closer to 1 (or −1) the score, the more highly correlated the two columns are. By default, corr uses the Pearson correlation, but you can change that by passing another value to the "method" keyword argument.

The output from corr is a data frame with an identical index and columns. We can thus see how highly correlated (or not) any two columns are by finding one along the index and the other along the columns. (The data is duplicated; we can do it either way.) Along the diagonal, we always see a correlation of 1, because a column is 100% positively correlated with itself.

Our result? We get 0.288, which points to a weak positive correlation between the two. So yes, countries that spend more on tourism are more likely to have highly rated wines. But the relationship is far from strong, so don't select wine based on tourism expenditures.

Solution

```
oecd_df = pd.read_csv('../data/oecd_locations.csv',
                      header=None,
                      names=['abbrev', 'country'],
                      index_col='abbrev')

oecd_tourism_df = pd.read_csv(
    '../data/oecd_tourism.csv',
    usecols=['LOCATION', 'TIME', 'Value'],
    index_col='LOCATION')

tourism_spending = (
    oecd_df
    .join(oecd_tourism_df)
    .groupby('country')['Value'].mean()
)

wine_df = pd.read_csv(
    '../data/winemag-150k-reviews.csv',
    usecols=['country', 'points'])

country_points = (
    wine_df
    .groupby('country')['points'].mean()
)

country_points.sort_values(ascending=False)
country_points.to_frame().join(tourism_spending)
country_points.to_frame().join(tourism_spending,
    how='outer')
country_points.to_frame().join(tourism_spending,
    how='outer').corr()
```

You can explore a version of this in the Pandas Tutor at http://mng.bz/A8eK.

Beyond the exercise

- Read in the three data frames, but without setting an index. Ensure that the column names in `oecd_tourism_df` are `abbrev`, `TIME`, and `Value` and that the dtype of the `Value` column is `np.int64`.
- Perform the same joins as before, but using `merge` rather than `join`.
- How is the default `merge` different from the default `join` when it comes to `NaN` values?

Summary

In this chapter, we dove even further into the world of split-apply-combine, looking at grouping, joining, and sorting from a variety of new perspectives. It's a rare project that doesn't use these techniques at least a little, so I hope you took the time to review these exercises and compare your answers with mine.

Midway project 8

Congratulations! You've made it halfway through this book. If you've been doing the exercises, I hope you've found your pandas skills improving, little by little. (And if you opened the book to this chapter without doing the exercises first, shame on you!)

Are you forgetting some of the syntax, method names, and parameter names? Are you making frustrating, "stupid" mistakes? That's only natural, and it happens to everyone, no matter how long they've been using pandas or any other large software library. Over time, though, it will become more natural and more obvious, at least when using the functionality that's most common in your work.

The whole point of this book is to gain experience and fluency through practice. Such gains happen incrementally and over time. But they do happen, even if it doesn't always feel that way.

In this chapter, we're taking a break from exercises that concentrate on particular topics and themes. Instead, I'm going to ask you to do a small project that requires you to use many of the parts of pandas that you've learned about in the last few chapters. I hope this project gives you a chance to integrate the different skills you've learned so far.

We'll look at data from the 2020 Python Developer Survey alongside the 2021 survey from Stack Overflow. The Python survey, which is run by JetBrains (the company behind the popular PyCharm editor for Python, among others), is our best snapshot of the global Python community—who they are and what they do. Separately, the well-known programming Q&A site Stack Overflow runs an annual survey of programmers of all types, including those using Python.

Table 8.1   What you need to know

Concept	What is it?	Example	To learn more
`pd.MultiIndex.from_tuples`	Returns a multi-index object from a list of tuples	`pd.MultiIndex.from_tuples(a_list)`	http://mng.bz/ZqnZ
`str.split`	Breaks strings apart, returns a list, and puts extra items on the *right*	`'abc def ghi'.split(None, 1) # returns ['abc', 'def ghi']`	http://mng.bz/aR4z
`str.rsplit`	Breaks strings apart, returns a list, and puts extra items on the *left*	`'abc def ghi'.rsplit(None, 1) # returns ['abc def', 'ghi']`	http://mng.bz/aR4z

Problem

Here is what I'd like you to do:

1 Load the CSV file (called 2020_sharing_data_outside.csv) with results from the Python survey into a data frame. Let's call that `py_df`.
2 Turn the columns into a multi-index. How you do this depends on the column:
   – Most of the columns have the form `first.second.third`, with two or more words separated by `.` characters. Divide the column name into two parts, one before the final `.` and one after. The multi-index column for this example would then be (`'first.second'`, `'third'`). If there were only two parts, it would be (`'first'`, `'second'`).
   – In the case of about 20 columns, the top level should be `general`, and the second level should be the original column name. The columns you should treat this way are
     – `age`,
     – `are.you.datascientist`,
     – `is.python.main`,
     – `company.size`,
     – `country.live`,
     – `employment.status`,
     – `first.learn.about.main.ide`,
     – `how.often.use.main.ide`,
     – `is.python.main`,
     – `main.purposes`
     – `missing.features.main.ide`,
     – `nps.main.ide`,
     – `python.version.most`,

- `python.years,`
- `python2.version.most,`
- `python3.version.most,`
- `several.projects,`
- `team.size,`
- `use.python.most,`
- `years.of.coding`
- Use the function `pd.MultiIndex.from_tuples` to create the multi-index, and then reassign it back to `df.columns`. (Hint: A function, along with a Python `for` loop or list comprehension, will come in handy here.)

3 Sort the columns so they're in alphabetical order. (This isn't technically necessary, but it makes the data easier to see and understand.)

4 Answer these questions:

- What are the 10 most popular Python IDEs?
- Which 10 other programming languages (`other.lang`) are most commonly used by Python developers?
- What were the 10 most common countries from which survey participants came?
- According to the Python survey, what proportion of Python developers have each level of experience?
- Which country has the greatest number of Python developers with 11+ years of experience?
- Which country has the greatest *proportion* of Python developers with 11+ years of experience?

5 Load the Stack Overflow data (so_2021_survey_results.csv) into a data frame. Let's call that `so_df`.

6 Show the average salary for different types of employment. Contractors and freelancers like to say that they earn more than full-time employees. What does the data here show you?

7 Create a pivot table in which the index contains countries, the columns are education levels, and the cells contain the average salary for each education level per country.

8 Create this pivot table again, only including countries in the OECD subset. In which of these countries does someone with an associate's degree earn the most? In which of them does someone with a doctoral degree earn the most?

9 Remove rows from `so_df` in which `LanguageHaveWorkedWith` is NaN.

10 Remove rows from `so_df` in which Python isn't included as a commonly used language (`LanguageHaveWorkedWith`). How many rows remain?

11 Remove rows from `so_df` in which `YearsCode` is NaN. How many rows remain?

12 Replace the string value `Less than 1 year` in `YearsCode` with 0. Replace the string value `More than 50 years` with 51.

13   Turn `YearsCode` into an integer column.

14   Create a new column in `so_df`, called `experience`, which will categorize the values in the `YearsCode`. Values can be
   – Less than 1 year
   – 1–2 years
   – 3–5 years
   – 6–10 years
   – 11+ years

15   According to the Stack Overflow survey, what proportion of Python developers have each level of experience?

Working it out

This project is all about understanding the world of Python developers better, using data from two different surveys. There are hundreds, if not thousands, of other questions we could ask (and answer) using this data; if you find this project of interest, I encourage you to continue the analysis on your own.

LOAD PYTHON SURVEY RESULTS INTO A DATA FRAME

We start by loading the data from the Python community survey into a data frame. On the face of it, this shouldn't be too hard:

```
py_filename = '../data/2020_sharing_data_outside.csv'
py_df = pd.read_csv(py_filename)
```

If you load the data in this way, you'll likely get a warning from pandas indicating that some columns had mixed types. We've seen this problem before; pandas does a good job of guessing a column's `dtype`, but that consumes a great deal of memory. We can either explicitly specify the `dtypes` of our columns in our call to `pd.read_csv` or (if we have sufficient memory) let pandas read all the data in and guess.

   We won't be using many columns in this project, so the real-life, practical solution is to specify columns with `usecols`. However, I want you to get some practice creating a multi-index and also have the data available for further exploration after this project is complete. Thus, we read all the data in and tell pandas to use as much memory as it needs to guess the `dtype` correctly:

```
py_filename = '../data/2020_sharing_data_outside.csv'
py_df = pd.read_csv(py_filename, low_memory=False)
```

> **NOTE**   I'm assuming that your computer has enough memory to load all the columns. If not, you should indeed pass `usecols` to `read_csv`, specifying only the columns used in this exercise. That will reduce the memory usage enough to let pandas guess correctly without over-burdening your computer.

There's nothing technically wrong with using the data frame as is. However, it contains 264 (!) columns, too many for most people to understand and think about.

Moreover, although a CSV file cannot have hierarchical column names, the names were clearly designed to give us a sense of hierarchy. For example, we have `other.lang.Java`, `other.lang.JavaScript`, `other.lang.C/C++`, and so forth—all of which could fit under an `other.lang` category.

Can we take a flat list of columns and turn it into a multi-index, thus making it easier to think about and work with? Yes, but it will take a little work. Notice that each column name is of the type `first.second.third`. If we break the column name apart at the final `.` character, we can create a multi-index in which the primary column becomes `first.second` and the secondary column `third`. We end up with a top-level column of `other.lang` and second-level columns of `Java`, `JavaScript`, `C/C++`, and so on (figure 8.1).

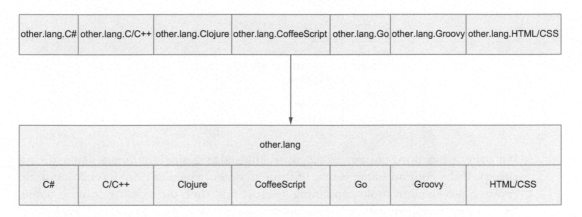

Figure 8.1   Turning a single index row into a multi-index

How can we create such a multi-index and then apply it to our data frame? We can use `pd.MultiIndex.from_tuples`, a function that pandas provides for precisely this purpose. If we pass a list of tuples to this function, it returns a multi-index object, which we can then assign to a data frame's `index` or `columns` attribute, as appropriate. In our case, we want to assign it to `columns`, replacing the existing index object used on the columns.

First, we create the list of tuples. Each tuple's first element contains the text up to the final `.` in the column name, and the second element is the word following that final `.`. We can do this using Python's `str.rsplit` method, which works similarly to `str.split` but from the right rather than the left. By itself, `str.rsplit` won't make a difference. But if we pass a second, integer argument of 1, it returns a list of two elements split from the final `.`:

```
s = 'abcd.efgh.ijkl'
s.rsplit('.', 1)
```

This code returns [`'abcd.efgh'`, `'ijkl'`], perfect for our purposes. (Except that it's a list, not a tuple.)

However, some of the column names don't belong in an overall category. For those, we give a top-level column of `general`. We define those columns in a list:

```python
general_columns = ['age',
                   'are.you.datascientist',
                   'is.python.main',
                   'company.size',
                   'country.live',
                   'employment.status',
                   'first.learn.about.main.ide',
                   'how.often.use.main.ide',
                   'is.python.main',
                   'main.purposes'
                   'missing.features.main.ide'
                   'nps.main.ide',
                   'python.version.most',
                   'python.years',
                   'python2.version.most',
                   'python3.version.most',
                   'several.projects',
                   'team.size',
                   'use.python.most',
                   'years.of.coding'
                   ]
```

We write a function, `column_multi_name`, that takes a single column name (i.e., a string). If the column name is one of those that gets a `general` top-level column, we return a two-element tuple containing `general` and then the existing column name. In all other cases, we return a two-element tuple based on a list we get back from `str.rsplit`:

```python
def column_multi_name(column_name):
    if column_name in general_columns:
        return ('general', column_name)
    else:
        first, rest = column_name.rsplit('.', 1)
        return (first, rest)
```

Splits the tuple into a two-element list →

Should this column have a general prefix?

Returns a two-element tuple starting with general

Returns the elements as a tuple

We invoke this function on each column name in `py_df` and then pass the result to `pd.MultiIndex.from_tuples`. We use a list comprehension:

```python
(
    pd
    .MultiIndex.from_tuples([
    column_multi_name(one_column_name)
    for one_column_name in py_df.columns])
)
```

Runs column_multi_name on the current column name

Goes through each column name in py_df

We then assign the resulting list to `py_df.columns`, replacing the original columns with our multi-index:

```
py_df.columns = (
    pd
    .MultiIndex.from_tuples([
    column_multi_name(one_column_name)
    for one_column_name in py_df.columns ])
)
```

SORT THE COLUMNS ALPHABETICALLY

Most of the time, it doesn't matter whether columns are sorted. But I've found that when working with a multi-index, it's often best to sort the column names, if only to make it easier to skim through them. To do this, we take advantage of the fact that we can pass a list of columns to py_df to get those columns back. If we sort the list before we apply it, we can get the columns back in a particular order. Assigning that back to py_df will thus sort the columns:

```
py_df = py_df[sorted(py_df.columns)]
```

WHAT ARE THE 10 MOST POPULAR PYTHON IDES?

We can determine what IDEs Python developers use most often from the ide top-level column and the main second-level column, by passing a tuple:

```
py_df[('ide', 'main')]
```

We can count how often each IDE appears using value_counts, limiting the output to the 10 top results:

```
(
    py_df[('ide', 'main')]
    .value_counts()
    .head(10)
)
```

WHICH 10 OTHER PROGRAMMING LANGUAGES (OTHER.LANG) ARE MOST COMMONLY USED BY PYTHON DEVELOPERS?

I asked you to find what other languages are most commonly used by Python developers. Non-Python languages were listed under the other.lang top-level index, with the particular language that each developer uses as a second-level index entry. Asking for py_df['other.lang'] thus returns all columns under other.lang as a data frame—one with 54,462 rows (one for each survey respondent) and 24 columns (one for each non-Python language). Each cell contains either the name of the language or NaN (indicating that the survey respondent does not use this language). With this data, how can we calculate the number of people who use each of these languages?

The answer is easier than it may at first appear: the count method returns the number of non-NaN values in a series. When applied to a data frame, the count method returns a series whose indexes are the data frame's columns and whose values are the number of non-null values in that column. In other words, we can run

```
py_df['other.lang'].count()
```

The result is the following series:

```
Bash / Shell    13793
C#               4460
C/C++           11623
Clojure           361
CoffeeScript      319
Go               3398
Groovy            719
HTML/CSS        15469
Java             8109
JavaScript      16662
Kotlin           1384
None             6402
Objective-C       583
Other            3592
PHP              4060
Perl              886
R                2465
Ruby             1165
Rust             1853
SQL             13391
Scala             927
Swift             854
TypeScript       3717
Visual Basic     1604
dtype: int64
```

With this series, we can sort the values in descending order:

```
(
    py_df['other.lang']
    .count()
    .sort_values(ascending=False)
)
```

Finally, we get the 10 first values:

```
(
    py_df['other.lang']
    .count()
    .sort_values(ascending=False)
    .head(10)
)
```

WHAT ARE THE 10 MOST COMMON COUNTRIES FROM WHICH SURVEY PARTICIPANTS CAME?

This information is in the `general` top-level index and the `country.live` second-level index:

```
py_df[('general', 'country.live')]
```

This returns the country name for each survey respondent. To count the number of times each country appears, we can use `value_counts`:

```
py_df[('general', 'country.live')].value_counts()
```

Because `value_counts` sorts results by descending value, we can use `head(10)` to retrieve the 10 most commonly named countries in the survey:

```
py_df[('general', 'country.live')].value_counts().head(10)
```

WHAT PROPORTION OF PYTHON DEVELOPERS HAVE EACH LEVEL OF EXPERIENCE?

Once again, we can turn to `value_counts`, passing `normalize=True` to get the percentage for each level:

```
py_df[
    ('general', 'python.years')
    ].value_counts(normalize=True)
```

The greatest proportion of developers have three to five years of experience, followed by those with less than one year, followed by those with between one and two years. All told, about 75% of the respondents to the survey have been using Python for up to five years, and half of them have been using it for less than two years.

WHICH COUNTRY HAS THE GREATEST NUMBER OF PYTHON DEVELOPERS WITH 11+ YEARS OF EXPERIENCE?

What about the most experienced Python developers? In particular, what countries have the greatest number of Python developers with 11+ years of experience using the language? To find out, we first need to get only those rows of `py_df` in which the experience is 11+ years:

```
py_df[py_df[
    ('general','python.years')] == '11+ years']
```

But wait: we want to group by `country.live`, whose top-level index is `general`—the same as `python.years`. We can thus restrict our query, applying our boolean index only to those columns within `general`:

```
py_df['general'][py_df[
    ('general','python.years')] == '11+ years']
```

Now that we only have the columns in `general`, we can prepare a new query that gives us results on a per-country basis:

```
py_df['general'][py_df[
    ('general','python.years')] == '11+ years'
    ].groupby('country.live')
```

This sets up the grouping query to operate on a per-country basis but doesn't ask any questions. Let's determine how many non-null values each column has for each country:

```
py_df['general'][
    py_df[('general','python.years')] == '11+ years'
    ].groupby('country.live').count()
```

The resulting data frame's rows are country names, and its columns are from `general`. Values are integers indicating how many non-null rows there are for each column for each country. The difference in counts reflects occasional null values. We're interested in finding super-experienced Python developers in each country, allowing us to cut our result down to one column only, `python.years`:

```
(
    py_df['general']
    [py_df[('general','python.years')] == '11+ years']
    ['python.years']
    .groupby('country.live')
    .count()
)
```

This returns a series in which the index contains country names and the values are integers: the number of 11+ year veterans of Python.

To find which country has the most experienced Python developers, we call `sort_values`, asking for results in descending order. Then we apply `head(1)`, returning the name of the country with the most developers, as well as the number itself:

```
(
    py_df['general']
    [py_df[('general','python.years')] == '11+ years']
    .groupby('country.live')
    ['python.years']
    .count()
    .sort_values(ascending=False)
    .head(1)
)
```

WHICH COUNTRY HAS THE GREATEST PROPORTION OF PYTHON DEVELOPERS WITH 11+ YEARS OF EXPERIENCE?

The US, somewhat naturally, has the greatest number of experienced developers. A more interesting question is which country has the greatest *proportion* of Python developers with 11+ years of experience.

We need to find out how many developers are in each country. To do that, we create a new variable called `country_experience`, taken from `py_df['general']` and consisting of two columns—`country.live` and `python.years`:

```
country_experience = (
    py_df['general']
    [['country.live', 'python.years']]
)

all_per_country = (
    country_experience
    ['country.live']
    .value_counts()
)
```

We also need to get the number of senior Python developers in each country. We did that in a previous part of this exercise, but with `country_experience` in place, we have another method for determining this:

```
expert_per_country = (
    country_experience
    .loc[country_experience['python.years'] == '11+ years',
        'country.live']
    .value_counts()
)
```

We now have two series (`expert_per_country` and `all_per_country`) with matching indexes (country names). We can take advantage of the fact that pandas will use the index when dividing one series by another:

```
(expert_per_country / all_per_country
    ).sort_values(ascending=False).dropna().head(10)
```

In this code, we first divide the number of experts by the total number of Python developers per country. We then sort the values in descending order so we can find the country with the greatest proportions of experienced Python developers. To avoid null values, we use `dropna` on the resulting series, getting

```
Norway            0.265432
Ireland           0.225490
Australia         0.225420
Belgium           0.225108
Slovenia          0.224490
New Zealand       0.197917
Sweden            0.194030
Finland           0.190141
United Kingdom    0.186486
Austria           0.186170
Name: country.live, dtype: float64
```

Although the United States certainly has a very large number of senior Python developers, it's not in the top 10 when we take country size into account.

But is the data an accurate portrait of the modern Python community? After all, do one quarter of Norwegian Python developers really have more than a decade of experience? Maybe it's just me, but I'm skeptical. I wonder whether the type of person who fills out such a survey is also more enthusiastic than the average Python developer—and thus skews to a more experienced population.

LOAD THE STACK OVERFLOW DATA INTO A DATA FRAME, SO_DF

Next, we switch gears and look at the Stack Overflow survey. We load the CSV file into a data frame:

```
so_filename = '../data/so_2021_survey_results.csv'
so_df = pd.read_csv(so_filename, low_memory=False)
```

Once again, we pass `low_memory=False`, telling pandas that it should use as much memory as it needs to guess the `dtype` correctly.

SHOW THE AVERAGE SALARY FOR DIFFERENT TYPES OF EMPLOYMENT

The Stack Overflow survey includes a great deal of information about people's jobs and salaries. I asked you to verify whether, based on the data collected here, freelancers and contractors earn more than full-time employees, as is often assumed to be the case. To find this out, we take the data frame and run `groupby` on `Employment`:

```
so_df.groupby('Employment')
```

This means whatever query we run, the rows are the distinct values in the `Employment` column. We're interested in the mean annual salary, reported here in dollars as `ConvertedCompYearly`, per type of employment, which we can calculate as follows:

```
so_df.groupby('Employment')['ConvertedCompYearly'].mean()
```

This is good, but we can make it easier to compare the data points by sorting them:

```
(
    so_df
    .groupby('Employment')['ConvertedCompYearly'].mean()
    .sort_values(ascending=False)
)
```

We can see from these results that according to this survey, people who are employed full time earn the most, followed by retirees, followed by contractors:

```
Employed full-time                                      129913.094086
Retired                                                 120252.500000
Independent contractor, freelancer, or self-employed    111160.260190
I prefer not to say                                      44589.437500
Employed part-time                                       43344.532974
Not employed, and not looking for work                         NaN
Not employed, but looking for work                             NaN
Student, full-time                                             NaN
Student, part-time                                             NaN
Name: ConvertedCompYearly, dtype: float64
```

I find this hard to believe and especially wonder whether it's accurate to say that retirees are earning almost as much as full-time employees.

There's nothing technically wrong with this result, but it's hard to read. We may want to remove the `NaN` values. Plus, dollar figures can generally be rounded to two digits after the decimal point. And maybe we can add commas before every group of three digits.

Dropping `NaN` is easy with `dropna`. But how can we format floating-point values? I would normally use an f-string:

```
x = 12345.6789
print(f'{x:,.2f}')
```
    Prints
    12,345.68

We can't use an f-string directly on each element of a series, but we can use a function to do it for us. In particular, we can use `apply` to run a function on each element and then use `lambda` to create an anonymous function that applies the f-string to each one, thus giving a column of strings:

```
(
    so_df
```

```
    .groupby('Employment')['ConvertedCompYearly'].mean()
    .sort_values(ascending=False)
    .dropna()
    .apply(lambda n: f'{n:,.2f}')
)
```

If you're one of the many Python developers who dislike `lambda`, you can hand `str.format` to `apply`:

```
(
    so_df
    .groupby('Employment')['ConvertedCompYearly'].mean()
    .sort_values(ascending=False)
    .dropna()
    .apply('{:,.2f}'.format)
)
```

Notice that we're not invoking the method, but passing it to `apply`, where it is invoked on each value. There isn't any value preceding the `:` in the curly braces; that's because `str.format` implicitly handles positional arguments.

To display all floats this way, we can set `pd.options.display.float_format`:

```
pd.options.display.float_format = '{:,.2f}'.format
```

This does what we did with `apply`, telling pandas to invoke this method whenever it sees a floating-point value.

Now let's ask a different question: rather than looking at average salaries for different types of work, let's instead look at average salaries for different levels of education. Moreover, let's further divide that by country. What I'm asking for, of course, is a pivot table—one in which the index contains country names, the columns contain the distinct values from `EdLevel`, and the cells contain the mean of `ConvertedCompYearly` for each country-education combination:

```
so_df.pivot_table(index='Country',
        columns='EdLevel',
        values='ConvertedCompYearly')
```

CREATE THIS PIVOT TABLE AGAIN, ONLY INCLUDING COUNTRIES IN THE OECD SUBSET

Next, I asked you to load the subset of OECD countries into a data frame:

```
oecd_filename = '../data/oecd_locations.csv'
oecd_df = pd.read_csv(oecd_filename,
    header=None, index_col=1,
    names=['abbrev', 'Country'])
```

The data frame we create in this code uses the country name for the index. That's because we're next going to use it in a `join` with `so_df`, so the indexes need to be aligned. The country names will act as indexes.

We join our OECD subset data frame with the Stack Overflow data and then recreate our pivot table. The effect is to reduce the number of rows (i.e., countries) in our output. And indeed, once we run our `join`, we get back only 13 rows, one for each country in the OECD subset:

```
(
    oecd_df
    .join(so_df
        .set_index('Country'))
    .pivot_table(index='Country',
            columns='EdLevel',
            values='ConvertedCompYearly')
)
```

Notice that we call `so_df.set_index('Country')` to temporarily set the country to be the index of `so_df`. That allows us to join it with `oecd_df`—and then create the pivot table, which is our ultimate goal.

Now that we know average salaries in all these countries and for all education levels, we can ask some questions of the data. For example, I asked you to determine in which country someone with an associate's degree can expect to earn the most. We could have stored the pivot table to a variable, but instead we chain the relevant methods together:

```
(
    oecd_df
    .join(so_df.set_index('Country'))
    .pivot_table(index='Country',
            columns='EdLevel',
            values='ConvertedCompYearly')
    ['Associate degree (A.A., A.S., etc.)']
    .sort_values(ascending=False)
)
```

After creating the pivot table, we retrieve the column for associate's degrees and sort them from highest to lowest. From the results we see here, it looks like the country that offers the best pay for people with an associate's degree is Australia, followed by Germany and Israel.

What about PhDs? Do countries that pay well for an associate's degree also pay well if you have a PhD or similar post-graduate degree? We can perform a similar query:

```
(
    oecd_df
    .join(so_df.set_index('Country'))
    .pivot_table(index='Country',
            columns='EdLevel',
            values='ConvertedCompYearly')
    ['Other doctoral degree (Ph.D., Ed.D., etc.)']
    .sort_values(ascending=False)
)
```

There does seem to be some overlap; the highest-paying countries for PhDs are Japan, Australia, France, Israel, and Germany.

There may also be some reason to suspect that this data isn't totally accurate; is it really possible that the mean salary in Hungary for someone with an associate's degree is $63,000/year, whereas with a PhD it's only $52,000/year? Or that there is a salary difference of only $12,000/year between Germans with an associate's degree and a PhD?

My point is that data analysis requires more than just number crunching—you also have to ask whether the numbers make sense. And if they don't, you should ask yourself why that may be the case. For example, perhaps the sample sizes are so small that the data isn't truly representative of the total population.

REMOVE ROWS FROM SO_DF IN WHICH LANGUAGEHAVEWORKEDWITH IS NaN

Next we want to analyze Python programmers in the Stack Overflow survey. The LanguageHaveWorkedWith column allows us to identify who they are—but that column contains text, with languages separated from one another with `;` characters. So, someone who works with both Python and JavaScript could have a value of `Python;JavaScript`. If we want people who work with Python, we need to find those who have "Python" in that column. For that, we can use `str.contains` to look inside the string. But there's a problem: some survey respondents didn't fill out this information, which means it's NaN. And trying to run `str.contains` on a NaN value will result in an error.

We thus need to first remove all rows that contain NaN for LanguageHaveWorkedWith. We can do that by running `dropna`, telling it to only look at the LanguageHaveWorkedWith column:

```
so_df = (
    so_df
    .dropna(subset=['LanguageHaveWorkedWith'])
)
```

REMOVE ROWS FROM SO_DF IN WHICH PYTHON ISN'T IN LANGUAGEHAVEWORKEDWITH

Once we've done that, we can be sure all values in LanguageHaveWorkedWith are strings. We apply `str.contains` and look for "Python":

```
so_df = (
    so_df
    .loc
    [so_df['LanguageHaveWorkedWith'].str.contains('Python')]
)
```

We end up with nearly 40,000 people who use Python—a smaller sample than the 54,000 who responded to the Python survey, but still a substantial sample size. Also, although the survey asked what languages people had used in the last year, we don't know whether they used Python once in the last year, every day, or somewhere in between.

Now that we have found the Python developers from Stack Overflow, we would like to compare them with the respondents to the Python community survey. In particular, we'd like to know if they have similar levels of experience. But in the data's original form, it's not possible to determine that: whereas the Python community survey lumps people into categories (e.g., "Less than 1 year" and "1–2 years"), the Stack Overflow survey asks for a specific number of years of experience.

REMOVE ROWS FROM SO_DF IN WHICH YEARSCODE IS NAN

To do this, we first remove all rows in which YearsCode is NaN:

```
so_df = so_df.dropna(subset=['YearsCode'])
```

IN YEARSCODE, REPLACE "LESS THAN 1 YEAR" WITH 0 AND "MORE THAN 50 YEARS" WITH 51

I asked you to create a new column called experience in the Stack Overflow data frame, which turns the raw year numbers into categories. We know we can use pd.cut to accomplish this, but pd.cut works only if all values in a column are numeric—and in this case, two options are non-numeric: Less than 1 year and More than 50 years. Our first task is thus to turn those into numbers:

```
so_df.loc[so_df['YearsCode'] ==
    'Less than 1 year', 'YearsCode'] = 0
so_df.loc[so_df['YearsCode'] ==
    'More than 50 years', 'YearsCode'] = 51
```

With these integer values in place, we can turn YearsCode into an integer column:

```
so_df['YearsCode'] = so_df['YearsCode'].astype(int)
```

CREATE A NEW COLUMN CALLED "EXPERIENCE" IN SO_DF, CATEGORIZING VALUES IN YEARSCODE

Now we can use pd.cut to re-create the same categories we had in the Python community survey:

```
so_df['experience'] = pd.cut(so_df['YearsCode'],
    bins=[-1, 1, 2, 5, 10, 100],
    labels=['Less than 1 year',
    '1-2 years',
    '3-5 years',
    '6-10 years',
    '11+ years'])
```

Remember that pd.cut uses the numbers passed to the bins keyword argument as the extreme edges of the bins it defines—which means if we want to give the first label to a number of 0, we should start the bin at –1. And yes, there is the option of including values on the left (or right), but I decided this is easier and ensures that bins don't overlap.

ACCORDING TO THE STACK OVERFLOW SURVEY, WHAT PROPORTION OF PYTHON DEVELOPERS HAVE EACH LEVEL OF EXPERIENCE?

Next, we want to see the distribution of experience levels in the Stack Overflow survey. We again use value_counts:

```
11+ years       0.373388
6-10 years      0.318589
3-5 years       0.222530
```

```
1-2 years            0.047440
Less than 1 year     0.038054
Name: experience, dtype: float64
```

From this, we can see that Stack Overflow respondents are much more experienced than Python survey respondents. As you may recall, 75% of the Python survey respondents have been using Python for up to five years, whereas in the Stack Overflow survey, the number of new programmers is about 25%. Half of the Python survey respondents have been using it for less than two years, whereas that's true for less than 10% of the Stack Overflow group.

However, we need to think before we say anything too sweeping when comparing these surveys. After all, the Stack Overflow survey asked about all the experience the respondent has had as a programmer, whereas the Python survey asked how long the person had been programming in Python. The same person, filling out both surveys, might have been programming in Java for 20 years and Python for only 2 and would thus have answered the questions differently on each survey. Making such comparisons and integrating data from different sources can be tricky and requires some thought; just joining two data frames isn't sufficient. That said, it is interesting to see just how heavily the Python survey skewed toward newcomers and how heavily Stack Overflow skewed toward experienced developers. The Python community survey might do well to include an "overall programming experience" question in the future, to help with such analysis and to better understand how much Python plays a role in the members of its community.

Solution

```python
py_filename = '../data/2020_sharing_data_outside.csv'
py_df = pd.read_csv(py_filename, low_memory=False)

general_columns = ['age', 'are.you.datascientist',
                   'is.python.main', 'company.size',
                   'country.live', 'employment.status',
                   'first.learn.about.main.ide',
                   'how.often.use.main.ide',
                   'is.python.main', 'main.purposes'
                   'missing.features.main.ide'
                   'nps.main.ide',
                   'python.version.most',
                   'python.years',
                   'python2.version.most',
                   'python3.version.most',
                   'several.projects',
                   'team.size',
                   'use.python.most',
                   'years.of.coding'
                   ]

def column_multi_name(column_name):
    if column_name in general_columns:
        return ('general', column_name)
```

```
        else:
            first, rest = column_name.rsplit('.', 1)
            return (first, rest)

py_df.columns = pd.MultiIndex.from_tuples(
                  [column_multi_name(one_column_name)
                   for one_column_name in py_df.columns])


py_df = py_df[sorted(py_df.columns)]

py_df[('ide', 'main')].value_counts().head(10)

py_df['ide'].value_counts().head(10)

py_df['other.lang'].count().sort_values(ascending=False).head(10)

py_df['general', 'country.live'].value_counts().head(10)

py_df[('general', 'python.years')].value_counts(normalize=True)

(
    py_df['general']
    [py_df[('general','python.years')] == '11+ years']
    .groupby('country.live')['python.years'].count()
    .sort_values(ascending=False)
    .head(1)
)

country_experience = (
    py_df['general']
    [['country.live', 'python.years']]
)

all_per_country = (
    country_experience['country.live']
    .value_counts()
)

expert_per_country = (
    country_experience
    .loc[
        country_experience['python.years'] == '11+ years',
        'country.live']
    .value_counts()
)

(expert_per_country / all_per_country).sort_values(
    ascending=False).dropna().head(10)
```

Is that it? No, not at all! But our printing and formatting system requires that we take a break after 60 lines. And hey, if you've been reading more than 60 lines of code, maybe you should take a break before continuing.

All set? Here's the rest of the code:

```
so_filename = '../data/so_2021_survey_results.csv'
so_df = pd.read_csv(so_filename, low_memory=False)
```

```
so_df.pivot_table(index='Country', columns='EdLevel',
    values='ConvertedCompYearly')

oecd_filename = '../data/oecd_locations.csv'
oecd_df = pd.read_csv(oecd_filename, header=None,
    index_col=1, names=['abbrev', 'Country'])

(
    oecd_df
    .join(so_df
          .set_index('Country'))
    .pivot_table(index='Country',
                 columns='EdLevel',
                 values='ConvertedCompYearly')
)

(
    oecd_df
    .join(so_df.set_index('Country'))
    .pivot_table(index='Country',
                 columns='EdLevel',
                 values='ConvertedCompYearly')
    ['Associate degree (A.A., A.S., etc.)']
    .sort_values(ascending=False)
)

(
    oecd_df
    .join(so_df.set_index('Country'))
    .pivot_table(index='Country',
                 columns='EdLevel',
                 values='ConvertedCompYearly')
    ['Other doctoral degree (Ph.D., Ed.D., etc.)']
    .sort_values(ascending=False)
)

so_df = so_df.dropna(subset=['LanguageHaveWorkedWith'])
so_df = so_df[so_df['LanguageHaveWorkedWith'].str.contains('Python')]

so_df.shape

so_df = so_df.dropna(subset=['YearsCode'])

so_df.shape

so_df.loc[so_df['YearsCode'] ==
    'Less than 1 year', 'YearsCode'] = 0
so_df.loc[so_df['YearsCode'] ==
    'More than 50 years', 'YearsCode'] = 51

so_df['YearsCode'] = so_df['YearsCode'].astype(int)


so_df['experience'] = pd.cut(so_df['YearsCode'],
      bins=[-1, 1, 2, 5, 10, 100],
```

```
       labels=['Less than 1 year',
       '1-2 years',
       '3-5 years',
       '6-10 years',
       '11+ years'])

so_df['experience'].value_counts(normalize=True)
```

Summary

Whew! This was a big, long exercise, meant to help you integrate and use many of the ideas and techniques we've discussed in this book so far. Of course, there are many pieces of pandas that we didn't use in this project—but to be honest, it's a rare project that uses all the capabilities pandas has to offer. That said, we did a lot of things here: loading and cleaning data, joining data frames, analyzing data, and even comparing different data sets and thinking critically about how trustworthy they are. If you felt comfortable with all the techniques in this project, I'd say you're well on your way to internalizing the way pandas does things and using it productively in your projects.

9

Strings

When most people think of pandas or data analysis in general, they think of numbers. And indeed, much of the work that people do with pandas is with numbers. That's why pandas is built on top of NumPy, which takes advantage of C's fast, efficient integers and floats. And that's why so many of the exercises in this book involve working with numbers.

However, we often have to work with textual data—usernames, product names, sales regions, business units, ticker symbols, and company names are just a few examples. Sometimes the text is central to the analysis you're doing—such as when you're preparing data for a text-based machine-learning model—and other times, it's secondary to the numbers and used as a description or categorical data.

It turns out that pandas is also well-equipped to handle text. It does this not by storing string data in NumPy but rather by using fully fledged string objects: either those that come with Python or (more recently) a pandas-specific string class that reduces both ambiguity and errors. (I'll have more to say about these two string types and when to use each one later in the chapter.) In either case, we can apply a wide variety of string methods to our data.

This is normally done via the `str` accessor, available on every pandas series that contains strings. When we invoke a method via `str`, we get back a new series. The returned series can replace the existing one, be assigned to a new variable, or be assigned as a new column alongside the original one.

In this chapter, you'll work through exercises that help you identify and understand how to work with textual data and the `str` accessor in pandas. After going through these exercises, you'll know which string methods are available, feel more comfortable using them, and know how to apply your own custom functions to string columns.

251

Text data types

For many years, pandas used Python's internal string type to store text. This was a big improvement over NumPy, which stores characters in C arrays—more efficient than Python strings but with much more limited functionality. To refer to such Python strings, pandas assigned a `dtype` of `object`. The good news is that this worked fairly well, giving great string functionality within pandas. The bad news was that a series could contain *any* type of Python object, not just strings. This led to bugs because we could accidentally store a list, dictionary, or `None` into such a column without noticing. After all, these are all Python objects, so there was no way for pandas to stop us from adding them.

Pandas 1.0.0 added a new `pd.StringDtype` to solve such problems. As the name indicates, it is meant to be used as a `dtype` on a series. Because it's specific to textual data, we cannot mix it up with other types of objects. Further, the pandas documentation indicates that this will, at some point, be the standard string type for pandas.

But wait—previously, a series with a `dtype` of `object` could be a string and could also be `NaN`. What happens now? After all, `NaN` isn't an instance of `pd.StringDtype` but rather of `float`. The answer is that if you're going to use `pd.StringDtype`, you should also use `pd.NA` instead of `NaN`. You can think of `pd.NA` as a more flexible version of `NaN` that is compatible with all pandas `dtype`s.

Should you use `pd.StringDtype`? As of this writing, the pandas documentation is inconsistent: on the one hand, it lists several benefits of `pd.StringDtype`. On the other hand, it says "`StringDType` is considered experimental. The implementation and parts of the API may change without warning."

In this chapter, I'll assume that you are using the old-fashioned (and definitely stable) `object` type in your columns. However, you will likely need (and want) to switch to `pd.StringDType` in the future. If all goes well, doing so will mean no changes to your programs other than better checking of your values and potentially even better performance.

Table 9.1 What you need to know

Concept	What is it?	Example	To learn more
`s.explode`	Returns a new series with each element on its own line	`s.explode()`	http://mng.bz/RxDP
`str.contains`	Returns a series of booleans, indicating which elements of the input series contain the target string	`s.str.contains('a')`	http://mng.bz/2D2X
`str.get_dummies`	Returns a data frame containing 1s and 0s based on a categorical series	`s['country'].get_dummies(sep=';')`	http://mng.bz/1q2g

Table 9.1   What you need to know *(continued)*

Concept	What is it?	Example	To learn more
str.index	Returns a series of integers, each indicating where the target string was found in the corresponding element of the input series	s.str.index('a')	http://mng.bz/PzEP
str.len	Returns a series of integers indicating the length of each element	s.str.len()	http://mng.bz/JgOv
str.replace	Returns a series based on an existing series, replacing the first argument with the second	s.str.replace('a', 'e')	http://mng.bz/wv6Q
str.split	Returns a series in which each element is a list of strings; the argument specifies the delimiter used to perform the split	s.str.split(';')	http://mng.bz/qrD2
str.strip	Returns a series of Python strings without the argument's characters on either side	s.str.strip('.!?')	http://mng.bz/7D2y
s.isin	Returns a boolean series indicating whether a value in *s* is an element of the argument	s.isin(['A', 'B', 'C'])	http://mng.bz/mVW2
i.intersection	Returns a new index object containing elements in two existing index objects	i.intersection(i2)	http://mng.bz/5w21

The str accessor

Traditional Python strings support a large number of methods and operators ranging from search (str.index) to replacement (str.replace) to substrings (slices) to checks of the string's content (e.g., str.isdigit and str.isspace). But if we have a series containing strings, how can we invoke such a method on every element?

Experienced Python developers would normally use a for loop or perhaps a list comprehension. But in pandas, we do whatever we can to avoid such loops because of their inefficiency. We could use the apply method, invoking a function to every element of a series. And indeed, apply is needed if we want to use a custom function.

In many cases, though, there's a better way: the str accessor. Using str gives us access to a variety of string methods—including, but not limited to, standard Python

(continued)

string methods. A method invoked via `str` is applied to every element in the series. It returns a new series of the same length and with the same index, whose values are the results of invoking the method on each element. For example, we can get the length of a string by invoking the `len` method on the `str` accessor:

```
s = Series('this is a test 123 456'.split())
s.str.len()
```

The result is a new series containing the lengths of the values in `s`:

```
0    4
1    2
2    1
3    4
4    3
5    3
dtype: int64
```

1	this		1	4	
2	is		2	2	
3	a	`str.len()`	3	1	
4	test		4	4	
5	123		5	3	
6	456		6	3	

Getting the lengths of all strings in a series with `.str.len()`

What if we want to find all values in `s` that can be turned into integers?

```
s.str.isdigit()
```

The result is a boolean series indicating which values contain only the characters 0–9:

```
0    False
1    False
2    False
```

```
3       False
4       True
5       True
dtype: bool
```

Because it contains only booleans and shares an index with `s`, it's suitable for use as a boolean (mask) index on `s` to find numeric values:

```
s.loc[s.str.isdigit()]
```

1	this		1	False
2	is		2	False
3	a	`str.isdigit()`	3	False
4	test		4	False
5	123		5	False
6	456		6	False

Finding which elements of a series contain only digits

The `str` accessor supports methods beyond those available in Python's `str` class. For example, we can search in a string using `contains`. However, `contains` allows us to use a regular expression. We can thus find all words containing either *a* or *e*:

```
s.str.contains('[ae]')
```

This query returns the following series:

```
0       False
1       False
2       True
3       True
4       False
5       False
dtype: bool
```

(continued)

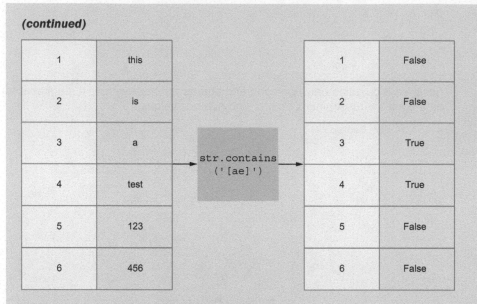

Finding which elements of a series contain either *a* or *e*:

Applied to our original series `s`, we can find all words that contain either *a* or *e*:

```
s.loc[s.str.contains('[ae]')]
```

This results in

```
2    a
3    test
dtype: object
```

Note that although `str.contains` currently (as of this writing) defaults to treating its argument as a regular expression, there are plans for that default value to change. It's thus a good idea to be explicit about your intentions by passing `regex=True` so the string isn't taken literally:

```
s[s.str.contains('[ae]', regex=True)]
```

The `str` accessor makes it easy to use pandas to call string methods and work with textual data. However, you should spend some time reviewing the list of string methods in the pandas documentation to get a good sense of what they are and what they can do.

EXERCISE 36 ■ Analyzing Alice

In this exercise, we'll look at the famous book *Alice in Wonderland*, the text of which is made freely available via Project Gutenberg and included with the data files for this book. Here is what I'd like you to do:

1 Open the file alice-in-wonderland.txt, and read it into a pandas series or data frame such that each word is a separate value. (If you choose to read it as a data frame, that's fine. I'll refer to the "series" or "column" when describing the data in this exercise.)

2 Answer these questions:
   – What are the 10 most common words in the book?
   – Does this change if you count the words without regard to case?
   – Does this change if you remove all the punctuation (as defined in `string .punctuation`) from the beginning and end of each word?
   – How many capitalized words does the book contain?
   – If you ignore punctuation and quotes before the start of a word, how many capitalized words does the book contain?
   – Count the number of vowels (a, e, i, o, and u) in each word. What is the average number of vowels per word?

Working it out

In this exercise, we use the string functionality in pandas in a variety of ways. To begin, I asked you to read the contents of *Alice in Wonderland* into a series. Normally, we don't read text files into pandas—although to be honest, a library such as pandas has so many users and use cases that it's possible people do this on a regular basis. If you were to feed `open(filename)` into `Series`, the series would contain the lines from alice-in-wonderland.txt. Instead of that, I asked you to create a series containing the separate words from the file.

To turn the file into a series of words, we need to do the following:

1 Read the entire file into Python as a string with the `read` method.
2 Break the string into a list of strings with the `str.split` method.
3 Turn the resulting list into a series.

Here's the code we use to do this:

```
filename = '../data/alice-in-wonderland.txt'
s = Series(open(filename).read().split())
```

NOTE The `read` method returns a string containing the contents of the file. What if the file contains several terabytes of data? Unless the IT department at your company is unusually generous, you'll find yourself running out of memory. Normally, I suggest that people *not* read an entire file into memory at once and instead iterate over its lines. In this particular case, I know the file is small and there won't be any problems with reading it all at once.

With our series in place, we can analyze the text it contains. First, I asked you to find the most common words. As we've seen countless times before, `value_counts` will help us here. Invoking it on our series returns a new series whose index contains our words (i.e., the values from `s`) and whose values (sorted in descending order) are integers describing how many times each word appears in `s`:

```
s.value_counts()
```

Not surprisingly, the most common words are *the, and, a,* and *to.* But what if these words appeared at the start of a sentence? They would be capitalized and wouldn't be included in our count. How can we transform all the words to lowercase and then find how common they are? We can use the str accessor to run the lower method on our series. That returns a new series of strings on which we can run value_counts:

```
s.str.lower().value_counts().head(10)
```

But wait a second—because of the way we create our series, using whitespace characters to indicate the boundary between words, it's possible that the words have punctuation marks before or after their letters. I thus asked you to repeat the query for the 10 most common words, but only after removing/ignoring punctuation characters. This turns out to be easier than you may imagine using the str.strip method. This method is typically use to remove whitespace from the start or end of a string:

```
s = '  abc  '
s.strip()          ◁─┤ Returns 'abc'
```

But we can also pass a string argument to str.strip, removing any characters that appear in that argument from the start or end of the string:

```
s = ':;:;abc:;:;'      │ Returns 'abc' after removing all occurrences
s.strip(':;')      ◁─┘ of : and ; from the start and end of s
```

The string module provides a number of predefined strings, including string.punctuation, which comes in handy on such occasions:

```
import string
s = ':;:;abc:;:;'
s.strip(string.punctuation)    ◁─┤ Returns 'abc'
```

Given a series s containing strings, we can get a new series containing those same strings, but without leading and trailing punctuation, by invoking split via the str accessor:

```
s.str.strip(string.punctuation)
```

To find the 10 most common words in s, ignoring punctuation, we can thus say

```
(
    s
    .str
    .strip(string.punctuation)
    .value_counts()
    .head(10)
)
```

And although I didn't ask you to do this, we could get the 10 most common words, ignoring both case and punctuation:

```
(
    s
    .str
    .lower()
    .str
    .strip(string.punctuation)
    .value_counts()
    .head(10)
)
```

Notice that we use `str` twice here: once to run `lower` on the original series `s` and a second time to run `strip` on the series of strings returned by `str.lower`. We'll see more examples of this as we review the other parts of this exercise.

Next, I asked you to count the number of capitalized words in the book. This means finding all words that begin with a capital letter, from *A* through *Z*. There are several ways to do this, but my favorite is to use a regular expression. Given that the pandas string method `str.contains` supports regular expressions, we can say the following:

```
s.str.contains('^[A-Z]\w*$',
        regex=True)
```

◁— **Words starting with a capital letter followed by zero or more alphanumeric characters**

This returns a boolean series with the same index as `s`. The value is `True` whenever the word starts with a capital letter (anchored to the start of the string with `^`) and contains zero or more alphanumeric characters (`\w*`) through the end of the word. (We have to allow for zero or more characters because of single-letter capitalized words such as *A* and *I*.)

With this in hand, we can apply the boolean series to `s`:

```
(
    s
    .loc[s.str.contains('^[A-Z]\w*$', regex=True)]
)
```

Then we can apply the `count` method to find how many values the series contains:

```
(
    s
    .loc[s.str.contains('^[A-Z]\w*$', regex=True)]
    .count()
)
```

But wait: what if the word has a punctuation mark, such as quotes, before the initial capital letter? To get an accurate count, we need to remove punctuation from both ends of the words and look for which are capitalized. Here's how we can do that:

```
(
    s
    .loc[s.str.strip(string.punctuation )
    .str
```

```
        .contains('^[A-Z]\w*$', regex=True)]
        .count()
)
```

Here we first remove punctuation from the start and end of each word and feed the
resulting series into str.contains with our regular expression. That returns a boolean series we can apply back to s, thus finding the total number of capitalized words.

Next, I asked you to calculate the mean number of vowels in each word. This
requires first finding a way to calculate the number of vowels in each word and then
calculating the mean value. The easiest way to do this is with the apply method, which
lets us run a function of our choice on each element of the series. We start by writing a
function that counts vowels:

```
def count_vowels(one_word):
    total = 0
    for one_letter in one_word.lower():
        if one_letter in 'aeiou':
            total += 1

    return total
```

This is a simple Python function that takes a string as an argument, counts the vowels
in it, and returns an integer. We can apply this function to every element of our series
s, getting a new series back:

```
s.apply(count_vowels)
```

I asked for the mean number of vowels in each word. Because we now have a series of
integers, we can get that back with

```
s.apply(count_vowels).mean()
```

Solution

```
filename = '../data/alice-in-wonderland.txt'        Creates a series based
s = Series(open(filename).read().split())           on the words in the file

s.value_counts().head(10)                            Which 10 words          If we ignore case,
s.str.lower().value_counts().head(10)                appear most often?      which 10 words
s.str.strip(string.punctuation).value_counts().head(10)                      appear most often?

                                                     If we ignore punctuation before
                                                     and after the word, which 10
(                                                    words appear most often?
    s
    .loc[s.str.contains('^[A-Z]\w*$', regex=True)]
)
                                                     How many capitalized
                                                     words appear in the book?
(
    s
    .loc[s.str.contains('^[A-Z]\w*$', regex=True)]   Ignoring leading and trailing
    .count()                                         punctuation, how many
)                                                    capitalized words appear?
```

```
def count_vowels(one_word):
    total = 0
    for one_letter in one_word.lower():
        if one_letter in 'aeiou':
            total += 1

    return total

s.apply(count_vowels).mean()
```

Defines a function that returns the number of vowels in a given string

What is the mean number of vowels in our words?

You can explore a version of this in the Pandas Tutor at http://mng.bz/y82d.

Beyond the exercise

- What is the mean of all integers in *Alice*?
- What words in *Alice* don't appear in the dictionary? Which are the five most common such words? (For the purposes of this exercise, I used a version of Linux's dictionary file available from http://mng.bz/MZWB.)
- What are the minimum and maximum number of words per paragraph?

EXERCISE 37 ■ Wine words

If you're like me, you may enjoy having a glass of wine with your dinner. On occasion, you may even read the wine's description on the back of the bottle, where the wine-maker uses flowery language to describe the winemaking process and the flavors you may detect when drinking the wine. I know I'm not the only person who sometimes raises an eyebrow at the words used in these descriptions. I decided to use pandas to better understand what words are used in describing wine and whether we can find any interesting insights from these words.

We looked at the wine-review database earlier, in exercise 35. In this exercise, we'll examine the words that reviewers use to describe the wines and see if particular words are more likely to occur related to specific provinces and varieties. Along the way, we'll find ways to use pandas to analyze text in some new ways. Here's what I want you to do:

1 Open the file winemag-150k-reviews.csv, and read it into a data frame. You only need the columns `country`, `province`, `description`, and `variety`.
2 Answer these questions:
  - What are the 10 most common words containing five or more letters in the wine descriptions? Turn all words into lowercase and remove all punctuation and symbols at the start or end of each word for easier comparison. Also remove the words *flavors*, *aromas*, *finish*, *palate*, and *drink*.
  - What are the 10 most common words for non-California wines?
  - What are the 10 most common words for French wines?
  - What are the 10 most common words for white wines? For our purposes, look for Chardonnay, Sauvignon Blanc, and Riesling.

– What are the 10 most common words for red wines? For our purposes, look for Pinot Noir, Cabernet Sauvignon, Syrah, Merlot, and Zinfandel.

– What are the 10 most common words for rosé wines?

3 Show the 10 most common words for the five most common wine varieties.

Working it out

First, I asked you to create a data frame with the wine information. We only need four columns, so we can load just those:

```
filename = '../data/winemag-150k-reviews.csv'
df = pd.read_csv(filename,
                usecols=['country','province',
                  'description', 'variety'])
```

Next I wanted to start performing some analysis on the words. But because we'll be running the same type of analysis on different subsets of the data frame, we can benefit from writing a function. What does this function need to do?

- Accept a series of text (i.e., wine descriptions)
- Turn the text into lowercase (for easier comparison)
- Turn that into a series of individual words
- Remove leading and trailing punctuation
- Remove words with fewer than five letters
- Remove common wine-related words
- Find the 10 most commonly occurring words

Fortunately, it's not difficult to write such a function, which we call `top_10_words`. The function expects to receive one argument, a pandas series of strings, which we call `s`. Each string in the series is assumed to contain multiple words separated by whitespace.

The first thing we want to do is turn all the strings in the series to lowercase for easier counting. We can do that using the `str` accessor and the `lower` method:

```
words = (
    s
    .str
    .lower()
    )
```

We next want to turn our series of sentences into a series of words. That is, instead of having multiple words in each row, we want a single word in each row. This means we'll create a series that's larger—potentially *much* larger—than the input series `s`.

If you're familiar with Python string methods, you won't be surprised that we use the `split` method here via the `str` accessor. (Note that this means we need to specify `str` a second time so we can run `split` on each element of the series returned from `str.lower()`.) `split` takes a string and breaks it apart wherever it encounters a delimiter such as : or ,. In this case, we don't specify a delimiter, so split uses any whitespace—space, tab, newline, carriage return, or vertical tab—to break the strings apart:

```
words = (
        s
        .str
        .lower()
        .str
        .split()
)
```

The good news is that we have separated the words from one another. The bad news is that our series still contains the same number of rows as before. Now each row contains a list of strings rather than a single string.

Fortunately, the explode method takes a series containing an iterable of objects (e.g., a list of strings) and returns a new series in which each object has its own row. We can thus get each word in its own row as follows:

```
words = (
        s
        .str
        .lower()
        .str
        .split()
        .explode()
)
```

We could stop there, but let's clean things up a bit more by removing any punctuation characters at the beginning or end of any word. That will avoid problems when counting words that come at the start or end of a sentence; otherwise we might include leading and trailing punctuation. The easiest way to do this is with the Python str.strip method. We normally think of strip as a method that removes whitespace at the start or end of a string, but that's just the default behavior. We can pass a string containing characters we want to remove from the beginning and end of each string. The result is a new series in which the strings don't have any of these characters at their start or end:

```
words = (
    s
    .str
    .lower()
    .str
    .split()
    .explode()
    .str
    .strip(',$.?!$%')
)
```

We now have in words a series containing individual, lowercase words without any leading or trailing punctuation. Next we want to remove words that have fewer than five letters. We can do that using a boolean index based on the output from the `len` method on the `str` accessor:

```
words.loc[(words.str.len()>=5)]
```

But that's not the only filter we want to put on `words`. We also want to remove a number of common words that crop up in nearly every wine description or review. We can use the `isin` method in a series, passing a list of strings as an argument, to determine which rows are and aren't in that list:

```
common_wine_words = ['flavors', 'aromas', 'finish', 'drink', 'palate']
~words.isin(common_wine_words)
```

We can combine these two mask indexes to get only words that contain at least five characters and don't appear in `common_wine_words`:

```
(
    words
    .loc[(words.str.len()>=5) &
        (~words.isin(common_wine_words))]
)
```

Note that we use `~`, the boolean "not" operator in pandas, to flip the boolean index that we get back from `words.isin`.

Our function is called `top_10_words` because it's supposed to return the 10 most common words found in the wine reviews. Given that `words` is now a series of words, we can run `value_counts`, followed by `head(10)`, and return the 10 words most commonly found:

```
return (
    words
    .loc[(words.str.len()>=5) &
        (~words.isin(common_wine_words))]
    .value_counts()
    .head(10)
)
```

With this, we have a complete function, `top_10_words`, that we can apply to any series of words:

```
def top_10_words(s):
    common_wine_words = ['flavors', 'aromas',
            'finish', 'drink', 'palate']

    words = s.str.lower().str.split(
        ).explode().str.strip(',$.?!$%')

    return (
        words
        .loc[(words.str.len()>=5) &
            (~words.isin(common_wine_words))]
        .value_counts()
```

```
    .head(10)
)
```

We can apply our function to all wines in the review database:

```
top_10_words(df['description'])
```

I asked you to find the 10 most common words used in French wine reviews. We need to extract the description column for wines made in France:

```
df.loc[df['country'] == 'France', 'description']
```

We can pass the resulting series to top_10_words:

```
top_10_words(
    df
    .loc[df['country'] == 'France',
        'description']
        )
```

Next, I asked you to find the words most commonly associated with wines made outside of California. We need to search on the province column and then apply the != operator to find those from outside of that state:

```
top_10_words(
    df
    .loc[df['province'] != 'California',
    'description']
    )
```

Notice that in this data set, you have to pay attention to the province column, which is distinct from the country column. Additional columns allow you to zero in on a particular region within a country; as you may know, different regions are known for producing not only different types of wines but also distinctive flavors specific to those regions.

Next, I thought it would be interesting to compare the words used most often for white, red, and rosé wines. I gave a (very nondefinitive) list of wines of each type and asked you to find the top 10 words used in each of their descriptions. The queries are identical except for the lists:

```
top_10_words(
    df.loc[df['variety']
        .isin(['Chardonnay',
            'Sauvignon Blanc',
            'Riesling']),
        'description'])

top_10_words(
    df.loc[df['variety']
        .isin(['Pinot Noir',
            'Cabernet Sauvignon',
            'Syrah', 'Merlot',
```

```
                    'Zinfandel']),
            'description'])

top_10_words(
    df.loc[df['variety'] == 'Rosé',
            'description'])
```

Notice how the `isin` method allows us to perform an "or" search—one that we could certainly do with pandas boolean operators and a mask index but that is shorter and more readable with `isin`.

Finally, I asked you to find the 10 most common words for the five most commonly mentioned wine varieties. To do that, we first need to determine the five most-mentioned varieties:

```
(
    df['variety']
    .value_counts()
    .head(5)
    .index
)
```

Here we run `value_counts` on the varieties to determine how common each variety is in the database. We use `head(5)` to find the five most common varieties. We can then find all reviews for one of these varieties using `isin`:

```
(
    df
    .loc[df['variety']
        .isin(df['variety']
                .value_counts()
                .head(5)
                .index),
        'description']
)
```

Notice that we couldn't just use `isin` on the values we got back from `value_counts`, because those would be numbers. Instead, we have to check the index of the resulting series, which contains words.

Finally, we can find the top 10 words used in reviews for these varieties by again applying our function, `top_10_words`:

```
top_10_words(
    df
    .loc[df['variety']
        .isin(df['variety']
                .value_counts()
                .head(5)
                .index),
        'description']
)
```

Solution

```python
filename = '../data/winemag-150k-reviews.csv'
df = pd.read_csv(filename,
                 usecols=['country','province',
                     'description', 'variety'])


def top_10_words(s):
    common_wine_words = ['flavors', 'aromas',
            'finish', 'drink', 'palate']

    words = (
        s
        .str.lower()
        .str.split()
        .explode()
        .str.strip(',$.?!$%')
        )

    return (
        words
        .loc[(words.str.len()>=5) &
            (~words.isin(common_wine_words))]
        .value_counts()
        .head(10)
    )

top_10_words(df['description'])
top_10_words(df.loc[df['country'] ==
    'France', 'description'])

top_10_words(df.loc[df['province'] !=
    'California', 'description'])

top_10_words(
    df.loc[df['variety']
            .isin(['Chardonnay',
                    'Sauvignon Blanc',
                    'Riesling']),
            'description'])

top_10_words(
    df.loc[df['variety']
            .isin(['Pinot Noir',
                    'Cabernet Sauvignon',
                    'Syrah', 'Merlot',
                    'Zinfandel']),
            'description'])

top_10_words(
    df.loc[df['variety'] == 'Rosé',
            'description'])

top_10_words(
    df
    .loc[df['variety']
        .isin(df['variety']
```

```
                    .value_counts()
                    .head(5)
                    .index),
    'description']
)
```

You can explore a version of this in the Pandas Tutor at http://mng.bz/aE4m.

Beyond the exercise

- Which country's wines got the highest average score?
- Create a pivot table in which the index contains countries, the columns contain varieties, and the cells contain mean scores. Include only the top 10 varieties.
- What is the correlation between the number of wines offered by a country and the mean score for that country? That is, does a country that submits more wines to competitions get, on average, a higher score than one that submits fewer wines to competitions?

EXERCISE 38 ▪ Programmer salaries

In the Stack Overflow survey we examined in chapter 8, developers indicated which programming languages they're currently using. Unfortunately, the languages are in a single text column separated by semicolons. In this exercise, you'll work with that data, extracting and analyzing it in a variety of ways:

1. Open the file so_2021_survey_results.csv, and read it into a data frame. You only need the columns `LanguageHaveWorkedWith`, `LanguageWantToWorkWith`, `Country`, and `CompTotal`.
2. Answer these questions:
   - What are the different programming languages that developers currently use?
   - What are the 10 programming languages most commonly used today?
   - What are the 10 programming languages people most want to use?
   - What languages are on both top-10 lists?
   - What languages in the top 10 have people worked with but *don't* want to work with in the future?
   - What is the most popular (current) language used by people in each country?
   - What is the mean number of languages used in the last year?
   - What is the greatest number of languages people listed as having used in the last year?
   - How many people chose that largest number?
   - How many people in the survey claim salaries of $2 million or more?
3. Remove rows in which salaries are less than $2 million.
4. Turn the `LanguageHaveWorkedWith` column into "dummy" columns in `df` such that each language is its own column.

5 Determine what combination is best if you want to maximize your salary and have to choose two languages from Python, JavaScript, and Java.

Working it out

In this exercise, we look at one of the most useful and interesting parts of the Stack Overflow survey: the list of programming languages that participants marked themselves as having used in the last year. The good news is that we have rich data that can give us insights into developers from around the world. The bad news is that these languages are all in a single column of the original CSV, making the data challenging to work with. This exercise uses a number of techniques to work with such data.

To begin with, we load the Stack Overflow data by reading it all into a data frame:

```
filename = '../data/so_2021_survey_results.csv'
df = pd.read_csv(filename,
    usecols=['LanguageHaveWorkedWith',
             'LanguageWantToWorkWith',
             'Country', 'CompTotal'])
```

To reduce memory usage and allow pandas to correctly determine what type of data should be in each column, we specify which columns we want to load into the data frame.

The first question we want to answer is which programming languages programmers currently use. The answers are all in `LanguageHaveWorkedWith`, a text (string) column. However, people answering the survey could provide more than one answer—which explains why this field contains numerous subfields separated by semicolons. For example, here are five rows from the file:

```
0       C++;HTML/CSS;JavaScript;Objective-C;PHP;Swift
9                               C++;Python
11  Bash/Shell;HTML/CSS;JavaScript;Node.js;SQL;Typ...
12                          C;C++;Java;Perl;Ruby
16          C#;HTML/CSS;Java;JavaScript;Node.js
```

Notice that in the third row, the respondent indicated so many programming languages that pandas doesn't even display all of them by default, ending the string with ... (an elipsis).

Pandas display options

You can change the maximum width of a column displayed by pandas by setting the `display.max_colwidth` option. For example:

```
pd.set_option('display.max_colwidth', 100)
```

You can set it back to the original value with `pd.reset_option`:

```
pd.reset_option('display.max_colwidth')
```

Full documentation about pandas display options is at http://mng.bz/gvYv.

To query the data frame based on which programming language(s) people used, we need to be able to treat these strings as separate fields, not just as large strings. The best way to do that, as we saw in exercise 37, is to first run `split` on our string column (resulting in a series of Python lists) and run the `explode` method on the result (figure 9.1):

```
(
    df['LanguageHaveWorkedWith']
    .str.split(';')
    .explode()
)
```

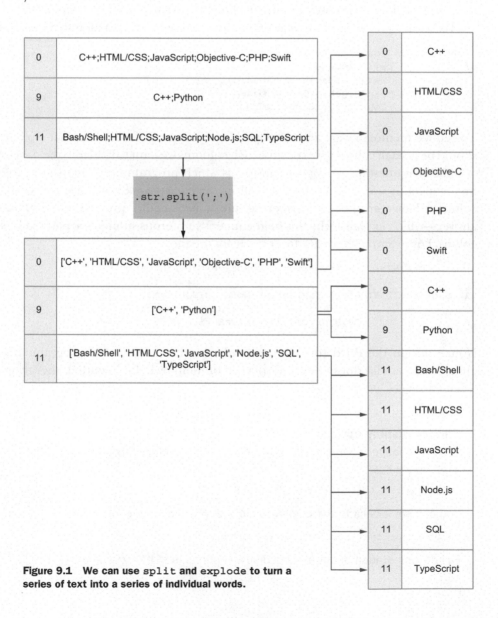

Figure 9.1 We can use `split` and `explode` to turn a series of text into a series of individual words.

The result of this query is a series of strings—all the different strings the Language-HaveWorkedWith column contained. But now, each programming language is in a separate row. This allows us to count them using `value_counts`:

```
(
    df['LanguageHaveWorkedWith']
    .str.split(';')
    .explode()
    .value_counts()
)
```

This way, we can see how many times each language was mentioned, sorted from the most popular (JavaScript) to the least popular (APL). We're only interested in the 10 most commonly found languages, so we cut off the result after the top 10:

```
(
    df['LanguageHaveWorkedWith']
    .str.split(';')
    .explode()
    .value_counts()
    .head(10)
)
```

We're actually less interested in the numbers than in the names of those languages. We can thus request the index from the returned series:

```
(
    df['LanguageHaveWorkedWith']
    .str.split(';')
    .explode()
    .value_counts()
    .head(10)
    .index
)
```

Finally, we assign that to a variable, `have_worked_with`, because we'll need these values shortly and it's easier to work with them from a variable than a long, repeated query:

```
have_worked_with = (
    df['LanguageHaveWorkedWith']
    .str.split(';')
    .explode()
    .value_counts()
    .head(10)
    .index
)
```

Next, we perform the same query on the column `LanguageWantToWorkWith` containing the answers to the question "What language do you hope to work with in the next year?" Other than the name of the column and the variable to which we assign the results, the query is the same:

```
want_to_work_with = (
    df['LanguageWantToWorkWith']
    .str.split(';')
    .explode()
    .value_counts()
    .head(10)
    .index
)
```

Next, I asked what languages are on both top-10 lists. Because pandas index objects are similar to series, we could run the `isin` method, asking which elements of `want_to_work_with` are in `have_worked_with` and using the resulting boolean index on `want_to_work_with`:

```
(
    want_to_work_with
    .loc[want_to_work_with.isin(have_worked_with)]
)
```

But it turns out that pandas makes it easy to do this with the `intersection` method. Note that this method works on index objects and not on series:

```
want_to_work_with.intersection(have_worked_with)
```

Next, I asked you to determine which languages in the top 10 people have worked with but *don't* want to work with in the coming year. We can again use `isin` to find which elements of `have_worked_with` are in `want_to_work_with`:

```
have_worked_with.isin(want_to_work_with)
```

This returns a boolean index. We can reverse it with ~ to find which elements of `have_worked_with` are *not* in `want_to_work_with`:

```
~have_worked_with.isin(want_to_work_with)
```

Now we can apply the resulting boolean index to `have_worked_with`:

```
(
    have_worked_with
    [~have_worked_with.isin(want_to_work_with)]
)
```

And we discover that despite their current popularity, people aren't excited about working with either shell scripts or C++ in the future. (I understand and agree!)

Next, I asked you to find out which language is most popular in each country. That is, we've already found that JavaScript is the most popular programming language overall—is this universally true? Our data frame has a `Country` column, so it stands to reason that we can use `groupby` to find the most popular language per country. But there's a problem: the languages are all in the `LanguageHaveWorkedWith` column. If we use `explode` to put each language on its own row, the resulting series is a different length than `df`, meaning we cannot add it as a new column.

However, the series we get back from `explode` has the same index as the original series on which it was run. So if the original column had an index of 0 and mentioned both Python and JavaScript, the resulting series has two rows, both with an index of 0, one with Python and the other with JavaScript. This means although we cannot assign the exploded series as a column, we can use `join` to merge the series onto the data frame.

First, let's create a new series, `all_languages`, containing the programming languages. We don't need to do this, but it will make the join easier to understand:

```
all_languages = (
    df
    ['LanguageHaveWorkedWith']
    .str.split(';')
    .explode()
)
```

Then we can perform our join. Note that although `join` is a method on data frames (not series), we can pass either a data frame or a series as the argument to it. In other words, we can say

```
df.join(all_languages)
```

Actually, this code doesn't work: we get an error because the data frame that results from this join would have two columns named `LanguageHaveWorkedWith`. There are several ways to solve this problem: we could set `LanguageHaveWorkedWith.name` to a different value, or we could pass a value to one or both of the `lsuffix` or `rsuffix` parameters, adding a suffix to joined columns from the left or right and thus avoiding a clash. But I think the easiest approach is to realize that we really only care about the `Country` column in the data frame, meaning we can run `join` on it and it alone:

```
df[['Country']].join(all_languages)
```

Notice that we use double square brackets around `'Country'` to ensure that the result is a data frame rather than a series. Now that we've created this new data frame, we can use `groupby` on it:

```
(
    df[['Country']]
    .join(all_languages)
    .groupby('Country')
)
```

This gives us a `groupby` object, but now we have to apply a method. And what aggregation method should we use? The normal choices are `mean`, `count`, and `std`, but here we want the value that appears the most, often known as the *mode*. However, there isn't any `mode` method we can apply—at least, no such method is provided directly. However, we can use the method `pd.Series.mode`, applying it by passing it to the `agg` method on our `groupby` object:

```
(
    df[['Country']]
    .join(all_languages)
    .groupby('Country')
    .agg(pd.Series.mode)
)
```

The result is a one-column data frame whose index contains country names and whose values represent the most popular language in each country. We can even find the relative popularity of different languages with `value_counts`:

```
(
    df[['Country']]
    .join(all_languages)
    .groupby('Country')
    .agg(pd.Series.mode)
    .value_counts()
)
```

Next, I asked you to find the mean number of languages that developers used in the last year. What we can do is break `LanguageHaveWorkedWith` into pieces and then run `len` on that list. That gives us a series of integers on which we can run `mean`:

```
(
    df['LanguageHaveWorkedWith']
    .str.split(';')
    .str.len()
    .mean()
)
```

Notice that we have to use the `str` accessor twice here: first to run the `split` method, turning our series of strings into a series of lists, and a second time to run `len` on each element, giving us a series of integers—on which we can run `mean`. And yes, we're using the `str` accessor to run `len` on lists; the accessor will try to run the method on whatever data it has, and because lists also support `len`, we're fine.

Next, I wanted you to determine the greatest number of languages anyone indicated they used in the last year. We can do that by running `max`:

```
(
    df['LanguageHaveWorkedWith']
    .str.split(';')
    .str.len()
    .max()
)
```

At least one person said they worked with 38 different programming languages in the last year—out of the 38 listed on the survey questionnaire. This leads me to wonder if they simply checked all the boxes. Maybe others did the same thing. I asked you to determine how many people marked that same number of languages:

```
(
    df
```

```
    .loc[df['LanguageHaveWorkedWith']
        .str.split(';')
        .str.len() == 38,
      'LanguageHaveWorkedWith']
    .count()
)
```

Here we use the length of the post-split list in a comparison, resulting in a boolean index. We apply the boolean index to the column `LanguageHaveWorkedWith` and apply `count` to find out how many rows match.

Next, I asked you to look at developer salaries as reported in the survey. First, how many developers are making more than $2 million/year?

```
(
    df
    .loc[df['CompTotal'] >= 2_000_000]
    ['CompTotal']
    .count()
)
```

Wow—2,369 people reported that kind of salary! Let's remove them from our data, because otherwise it will be skewed:

```
df = (
    df
    .loc[df['CompTotal'] < 2_000_000]
)
```

We'll get back to salaries in a moment. Now we take the `LanguageHaveWorkedWith` column and turn it into multiple columns to so we can analyze the individual languages more easily. Doing this is known as creating *dummy columns*. Instead of a column containing the string `'JavaScript;Python'`, we create one column called `JavaScript` and another called `Python`, putting 1s where the person marked themselves as using JavaScript and 0s where they indicated they did not.

We can create a new data frame of dummy values based on `LanguageHaveWorked-With` using the `str.get_dummies` method:

```
(
    df['LanguageHaveWorkedWith']
    .str.get_dummies(sep=';')
)
```

But how can we integrate this new data frame into our existing one? The answer is `pd.concat`, which we've used before. The difference is that we want to join the data frames horizontally (i.e., combining them left and right, rather than top and bottom). To tell `pd.concat` this, we need to indicate `axis='columns'`, similar to what we've done with other methods in the past, such as `df.drop`. We can then assign the result of the concatenation back to `df`:

```
df = (
    pd.concat([df,
```

```
        df['LanguageHaveWorkedWith']
        .str.get_dummies(sep=';')],
        axis='columns')
)
```

With these dummy columns in place, we can ask questions about salaries and language knowledge. First, what was the average salary of someone who knows Python and JavaScript but not Java?

```
df['CompTotal'][(df['Python'] == 1) &
               (df['JavaScript'] == 1) &
               (df['Java'] == 0)].mean()
```

We get a result of $126,817.

What about someone who knows Python and Java but not JavaScript?

```
df['CompTotal'][(df['Python'] == 1) &
               (df['JavaScript'] == 0) &
               (df['Java'] == 1)].mean()
```

Here we get a result of $162,737.

Finally, what about someone who knows Java and JavaScript but not Python?

```
# Java and Javascript, not Python
df['CompTotal'][(df['Python'] == 0) &
               (df['JavaScript'] == 1) &
               (df['Java'] == 1)].mean()
```

This results in $140,867.

Solution

```
filename = '../data/so_2021_survey_results.csv'
df = pd.read_csv(filename,
    usecols=['LanguageHaveWorkedWith',
             'LanguageWantToWorkWith',
             'Country', 'CompTotal'])

df['LanguageHaveWorkedWith'
    ].str.split(';').explode().value_counts().index

have_worked_with = df['LanguageHaveWorkedWith'
    ].str.split(';').explode(
    ).value_counts().head(10).index

want_to_work_with = df['LanguageWantToWorkWith'
    ].str.split(';').explode(
    ).value_counts().head(10).index

want_to_work_with.intersection(have_worked_with)
have_worked_with[~have_worked_with.isin(want_to_work_with)]

all_languages = df['LanguageHaveWorkedWith'
```

```
    ].str.split(';').explode()

df[['Country']].join(all_languages).groupby('Country'
    ).agg(pd.Series.mode)

df['LanguageHaveWorkedWith'].str.split(';').str.len().mean()
df['LanguageHaveWorkedWith'].str.split(';').str.len().max()

df['LanguageHaveWorkedWith'][
    df['LanguageHaveWorkedWith'].str.count(';') == 38].count()

(
    df
    .loc[df['CompTotal'] >= 2_000_000]
    ['CompTotal']
    .count()
)

df = (
    df
    .loc[df['CompTotal'] < 2_000_000]
)

df = (
    pd.concat(
    [df,
    df['LanguageHaveWorkedWith']
    .str.get_dummies(
        sep=';')], axis='columns')

df['CompTotal'][(df['Python'] == 1) &
                (df['JavaScript'] == 1) &
                (df['Java'] == 1)].mean()

df['CompTotal'][(df['Python'] == 1) &
                (df['JavaScript'] == 0) &
                (df['Java'] == 1)].mean()

df['CompTotal'][(df['Python'] == 0) &
                (df['JavaScript'] == 1) &
                (df['Java'] == 1)].mean()
```

You can explore a version of this in the Pandas Tutor at http://mng.bz/4JvR.

Beyond the exercise

- When developers are stuck (as indicated in the column NEWStuck), what are the three things they're most likely to do?
- What proportion of the survey respondents marked their gender as Man? Does that proportion seem similar to your real-life experiences?
- On average, what proportion of their years coding have been done professionally?

Summary

In this chapter, we looked at various ways pandas lets us work with textual data, especially via the `str` accessor. The combination of Python's rich string methods along with the various ways pandas lets us manipulate series and data frames gives us a great deal of flexibility and lets us ask a wide variety of sophisticated questions that aren't directly numerical. Many data sets, such as the ones we looked at in this chapter, contain a mix of numeric and textual data, and being able to work with the text alongside the numbers is especially useful.

Dates and times

10

Programming languages' core data structures reflect the types of information we work with on a regular basis. It makes sense that we'll have numbers, because we use numbers a lot. We use lots of text, so strings make sense, as well. And of course we need collections of various sorts, so every language provides some of those—in the case of Python, we have lists, tuples, dictionaries, and sets, for starters.

Modern programming languages also support another type of data, one that we (as people) use on a regular basis but that wasn't part of the programming canon when I started my career: dates and times. It seems obvious in retrospect that dates and times, which are such essential parts of our lives, should be a main part of our programming languages. But it turns out that dealing with dates and times is hard, with all sorts of tricky problems—from leap years, to time zones, to the odd data structures we need to computerize a calendar that wasn't exactly designed with computers in mind.

Both the Python language and pandas handle time data with two different data structures. The first is a *timestamp*, also known as a *datetime* in many languages and systems. A timestamp refers to a specific point in time that you can point to using a calendar. A timestamp happens once and only once—when you were born, when your plane will take off, when you and your date will meet at a restaurant, or when the meeting was scheduled to end. You can describe a timestamp with a particular year, month, day, hour, minute, and second.

A second, complementary data type is the *timedelta*, known in some systems as an *interval*. A timedelta represents a time span—the distance between two timestamp objects. So a meeting's scheduled start and end can be represented as timestamps, but the time the meeting takes is a timedelta (figure 10.1).

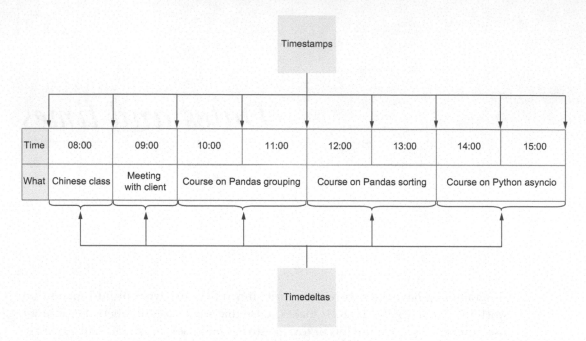

Figure 10.1   My schedule, illustrated with timestamps and timedeltas

Not surprisingly, lots of the data we want to analyze contains time and date information. And thus it's good to know that pandas can handle dates and times flexibly. We can read data in from files, turning columns into timestamps. We can also convert existing values—both individual values and series objects—into timestamps. We can perform calculations with timedeltas and perform comparisons with them.

But pandas goes further than that, allowing us to use date and time information in indexes. This makes it easier to search for data that took place during specific periods. Even better, we can perform *resampling*, which is most easily described as *grouping by time periods*.

This chapter's exercises all take advantage of these capabilities in pandas to explore information that has to do with dates and times. Along the way, you'll get experience working with a variety of date formats and input types, as well as producing reports based on those types.

Table 10.1   What you need to know

Concept	What is it?	Example	To learn more
pd.to_datetime	If passed a series of strings, returns a series of Timestamp objects	pd.to_datetime (s['when'])	http://mng.bz/6D2D

Table 10.1 **What you need to know** *(continued)*

Concept	What is it?	Example	To learn more
`pd.to_timedelta`	If passed a series of strings, returns a series of `Timedelta` objects	`pd.to_timedelta(s ['how_long'])`	http://mng.bz/o1Er
`pd.read_csv`	Returns a new data frame based on CSV input	`df = pd.read_csv ('myfile.csv')`	http://mng.bz/nW8g
`time.strftime`	Produces a string based on a time value	`time.strftime(a_time, a_format)`	http://mng.bz/vn5J
`time.strptime`	Parses a string into a time object	`time.strptime (time_string)`	http://mng.bz/4D2a
`df.to_csv`	Writes a CSV file based on a data frame	`df.to_csv('mydata .csv')`	http://mng.bz/QPNw
`df.resample`	Performs a time-based `groupby` operation on a specified period of time	`df.resample('1M')`	http://mng.bz/XN6G
`s.diff`	Returns a new series with the same index as s but whose values indicate the difference between that value and the previous value	`s.diff()`	http://mng.bz/yQnG
`s.pct_change`	Returns a new series with the same index as s but whose values indicate the *percentage* difference between that value and the previous value	`s.pct_change()`	http://mng.bz/MBj7

Creating datetime and timedelta objects

As we've repeatedly seen, pandas largely avoids built-in Python data structures in favor of its own types or those defined by NumPy. This is also the case when it comes to dates and times: to represent a specific point in time, we use the `Timestamp` class instead of either the `datetime.datetime` class that comes with Python or the `np.datetime64` class that comes with NumPy.

The standard way to create `Timestamp` objects is with the module-level function `to_datetime`, which takes a variety of argument types. If passed a single argument, it returns one `Timestamp`. For example, we can get the current date and time by passing it the string `'now'`:

```
pd.to_datetime('now')
```

(continued)

It's far more common and useful to call `pd.to_datetime` on an existing series of strings containing date and time information. For example:

```
s = Series(['1970-07-14', '1972-03-01', '2000-12-16',
    '2002-12-17', '2005-10-31'])
pd.to_datetime(s)
```

This code returns a new series:

```
0    1970-07-14
1    1972-03-01
2    2000-12-16
3    2002-12-17
4    2005-10-31
dtype: datetime64[ns]
```

Don't be confused by the indication that the `dtype` is `datetime64`, a type from NumPy; the values are all of type `Timestamp`, a pandas type.

In this example, the strings we feed to `to_datetime` are unambiguous and easy to parse. But what if we have slightly different strings, using month names instead of numbers?

```
s = Series(['1970-Jul-14', '1972-Mar-01', '2000-Dec-16',
    '2002-Dec-17', '2005-Oct-31'])
pd.to_datetime(s)
```

Actually, this works fine: that's because `pd.to_datetime` is fairly smart and flexible and can parse a number of different date formats. So this format works, as does this one:

```
s = Series(['14-Jul-1970', '01-Mar-1972', '16-Dec-2000',
    '17-Dec-2002', '31-Oct-2005'])
pd.to_datetime(s)
```

But what if we pass dates that are more ambiguous? For example, what if the months are all numbers?

```
s = Series(['14-07-1970', '01-03-1972', '16-12-2000',
    '17-12-2002', '31-10-2005'])
pd.to_datetime(s)
```

Once again, it works fine. However, sometimes dates are less obvious and human culture and tradition play a role. For example, take the following:

```
s = Series(['01/03/1972', '05/12/1995'])
pd.to_datetime(s)
```

Should pandas interpret these dates as March 1 or January 3, and as December 5 or May 12? By default, ambiguous date formats are assumed to have the month first, as in the United States. However, you can override that by passing `dayfirst=False` to `pd.to_datetime`:

```
s = Series(['01/03/1972', '05/12/1995'])
pd.to_datetime(s, dayfirst=False)
```

These examples have only included dates, but we can include time information, as well:

```
s = Series(['1970-07-14 8:00', '1972-03-01 10:00 pm',
    '2000-12-16 12:15:28', '2002-12-17 18:17', '2005-10-31 23:51'])
pd.to_datetime(s)
```

This code returns

```
0    1970-07-14 08:00:00
1    1972-03-01 22:00:00
2    2000-12-16 12:15:28
3    2002-12-17 18:17:00
4    2005-10-31 23:51:00
dtype: datetime64[ns]
```

Notice that we sometimes include seconds and in one case indicate a.m./p.m. rather than using a 24-hour clock. Pandas tries hard to understand all these formats and interpret them as well as possible.

What if we have several series representing the year, month, and date? We can use `pd.to_datetime` to get a new `Timestamp` series based on those inputs. This is especially useful if we're trying to create a `Timestamp` column from a data frame:

```
df = DataFrame([s.split('-')
                for s in ['14-07-1970', '01-03-1971',
                    '16-12-2000', '17-12-2002',
                    '31-10-2005']],
        columns='day month year'.split())
pd.to_datetime(df[['year', 'month', 'day']])
```

This code results in

```
0    1970-07-14
1    1971-03-01
2    2000-12-16
3    2002-12-17
4    2005-10-31
dtype: datetime64[ns]
```

All this is fine, but it ignores a common use case: loading a CSV file in which one or more columns are datetime information. How can we ensure that these columns are interpreted as `Timestamp` data and not as strings? We need to tell pandas to do this, using the `parse_dates` parameter in the `read_csv` function. We can pass a list of columns, either as names (strings) or as integers (indexes). For example:

```
pd.read_csv(filename,
        parse_dates=['birthday', 'anniversary'])
```

(continued)

We can pass various parameters to influence the parsing process. One of them is `dayfirst`, which works as we saw earlier to indicate that the dates being read start with days (as in Europe) rather than with months (as in the United States).

Once we have a `Timestamp` series, we can use the `dt` accessor to retrieve different parts of each object. For example:

```
s.dt.month          # month number
s.dt.month_name     # month name
s.dt.hour           # hour
s.dt.day_of_week    # day of week
s.dt.is_leap_year   # is it a leap year?
```

Some of these attributes return numbers, and others return boolean values. You can retrieve the full list of attributes via the `dt` accessor at http://mng.bz/j1wa.

Finally, I mentioned at the start of this chapter that when we work with dates and times, we need two distinct data types. We've spent some time looking at the first one: timestamps. But what about timedeltas, also known as intervals? We can generally say

```
datetime - datetime = interval
datetime + interval = datetime
datetime - interval = datetime
```

In other words, given two datetime objects, we can get an interval object representing the time between them. For example, given a birth date and a death date, we can calculate the length of someone's life. And given a datetime and an interval, we can get the datetime on the other side of that interval. For example, given a meeting start time and its length, we can find out when it ends—or similarly, if given a meeting end time and its length, we can calculate when it started.

Pandas allows us to perform precisely this type of calculation. For example, if we have two timestamp series, subtracting one from the other gives us a `timedelta` series. For example:

```
s = Series(['1970-07-14 8:00', '1972-03-01 10:00 pm',
            '2000-12-16 12:15:28', '2002-12-17 18:17',
            '2005-10-31 23:51'])
s = pd.to_datetime(s)
pd.to_datetime('2021-July-01') - s
```

The subtraction operation is broadcast to every element in `s`, returning a series of `timedelta64` objects:

```
0    18614 days 16:00:00
1    18018 days 02:00:00
2     7501 days 11:44:32
3     6770 days 05:43:00
4     5721 days 00:09:00
dtype: timedelta64[ns]
```

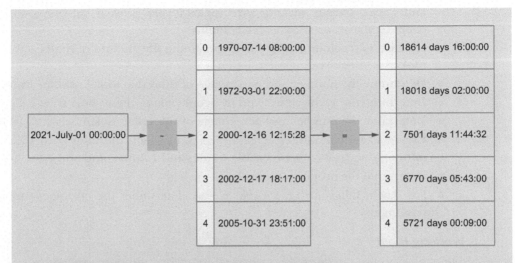

Subtracting a timestamp from a timestamp gives us a timedelta.

To create a `timedelta` object or series, we can also call `pd.to_timedelta` much as we can call `pd.to_timestamp`. The function's argument is typically a string or series of strings, each describing a time span, such as `'1 hour'` or `'2 days'`.

The pieces of a `timedelta` can be retrieved using the `components` attribute. For example:

```
pd.to_timedelta('2 days 3:20:10').components
```

This returns

```
Components(days=2, hours=3, minutes=20, seconds=10,
           milliseconds=0, microseconds=0, nanoseconds=0)
```

If we have a timedelta object, we can use the `days`, `seconds`, `microseconds`, and `nanoseconds` attributes to retrieve those calculations.

Now that you've seen how you can create and retrieve from `timestamp` and `timedelta` objects, you're all set to work through the exercises in this chapter, which use these skills to answer questions about a number of data sets.

EXERCISE 39 ■ Short, medium, and long taxi rides

We have already looked at taxi rides and have even (in exercise 30) looked at short, medium, and long taxi rides. However, in that exercise, we considered the distance traveled. In this exercise, we look at taxi rides from the perspective of how much time the ride took. Specifically, I want you to

1 Load taxi data from July 2019 into a data frame, using only the columns tpep_pickup_datetime, tpep_dropoff_datetime, passenger_count, trip_distance,

and `total_amount`, making sure to load `tpep_pickup_datetime` and `tpep_dropoff_datetime` as `datetime` columns.

2 Create a new column, `trip_time`, containing the amount of time each taxi ride took as a `timedelta`.

3 Determine the number and percentage of rides that took less than 1 minute.

4 Determine the average fare paid by people taking these short trips.

5 Determine the number and percentage of rides that took more than 10 hours.

6 Create a new column, `trip_time_group`, in which the values are `short` (< 10 minutes), `medium` (≥ between 10 minutes and 1 hour), and `long` (> 1 hour).

7 Determine the proportion of rides in each group.

8 For each value in `trip_time_group`, determine the average number of passengers.

Working it out

This exercise starts similarly to many others involving the taxi data. But whereas we were previously willing to let pandas determine the `dtype` of each column on its own, here we need to tell it to parse two of the columns as `Timestamp` objects. We could, of course, have imported them as text (i.e., the default) and then run `pd.to_timestamp` on them, but the following approach makes the process easier and cleaner. We can say

```
filename = '../data/nyc_taxi_2019-07.csv'

df = (
    pd
    .read_csv(filename,
              usecols=['tpep_pickup_datetime',
                       'tpep_dropoff_datetime',
                       'trip_distance',
                       'passenger_count',
                       'total_amount'],
              parse_dates=['tpep_pickup_datetime',
                           'tpep_dropoff_datetime'])
)
```

Notice that we need to include the two timestamp columns, `tpep_pickup_datetime` and `tpep_dropoff_datetime`, both in the `usecols` list and in the `parse_dates` list. In addition, this only works without any additional hints or tuning because the taxi dates are all stored in an unambiguous format of YYYY-MM-DD.

We can double-check that the columns have been interpreted correctly by invoking the `dtypes` method on our data frame:

```
df.dtypes
```

The result makes it clear that the parsing succeeded:

```
tpep_pickup_datetime      datetime64[ns]
tpep_dropoff_datetime     datetime64[ns]
```

```
passenger_count                 float64
trip_distance                   float64
total_amount                    float64
dtype: object
```

If we had not parsed the two timestamp columns, they would be listed as object, which as we've seen indicates that pandas is leaving them as Python objects—most often, as strings.

With these timestamp columns in place, we can create a new timedelta column called trip_time by subtracting the pickup time from the dropoff time:

```
df['trip_time'] = (
    df['tpep_dropoff_datetime'] -
    df['tpep_pickup_datetime']
)
```

With this timedelta column in place, we can now ask questions about our data. For example, how many of the taxi rides in July 2019 took less than 1 minute?

To answer this, we need to perform a comparison with our trip_time column. We could create a timestamp object with pd.to_timestamp, but it turns out that pandas takes pity on us and allows us to compare a timestamp column with a string by doing the conversion behind the scenes:

```
df['trip_time'] < '1 minute'
```

This returns a new boolean series indicating when the trip took less than 1 minute. We can (as always) apply the boolean series to df.loc as a mask index, getting only those short trips:

```
df.loc[
    df['trip_time'] < '1 minute',       Row selector, for trips that
    'trip_time'                         took less than 1 minute
    ].count()                           Column selector, asking
                                        for only trip_time
             Returns the number
             of non-NaN rows
```

We find that 70,212 taxi rides were less than 1 minute long. This seems like a large number of taxi rides to be taking so little time, but New York is a big city. What percentage of rides does this represent? We can find out by dividing this into the total number of rides in our data set:

```
df.loc[
    df['trip_time'] < '1 minute',
    'trip_time'
    ].count() / df['trip_time'].count() * 100
```

Just over 1% of taxi rides take less than a minute. That seems high to me, but maybe people enjoy taking a taxi for one or two blocks when they're in New York.

How much, on average, did people pay for those super-short taxi rides? To calculate that, we apply the mask index to `total_amount` and then calculate the mean (figure 10.2):

```
df.loc[
    df['trip_time'] < '1 minute',
    'total_amount'
    ].mean()
```

The result? More than $30! The only thing odder about so many people taking 1-minute taxi rides is the fact that they had to pay more than $30 for the privilege.

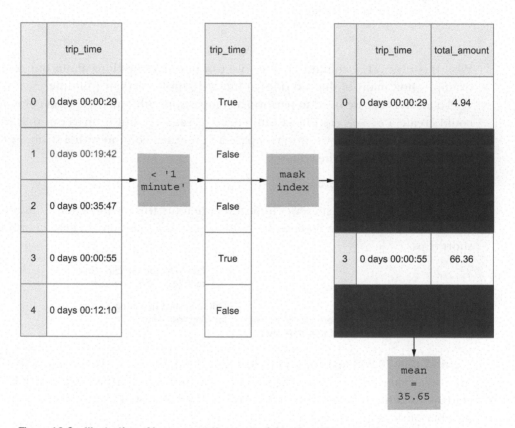

Figure 10.2   Illustration of how we got the mean of rides less than one minute long

Next, I asked you to find taxi rides that took more than 10 hours. I cannot imagine spending 10 hours in the back of a New York City taxi (or any other taxi, for that matter), but I thought it might be interesting to determine just how many such rides exist in this data set. Once again, we compare the `trip_time` column to a string:

```
df['trip_time'] > '10 hours'
```

We apply the resulting boolean series as a mask index and get all the long rides, which we then count:

```
df.loc[df['trip_time'] > '10 hours', 'trip_time].count()
```

Our data set contains 16,698 rides that took more than 10 hours. Seems high to me, but maybe it's a reasonable percentage. Let's calculate that:

```
df.loc[df[
    'trip_time'] > '10 hours',
    'trip_time].count() / df['trip_time'].count() * 100
```

These rides constitute only 0.2% of all taxi rides. Even so, that means 2 out of every 1,000 taxi rides in New York take more than 10 hours.

Next, we want to group taxi rides into three categories: short, medium, and long. To do that, we can use `pd.cut`, a method we've already used to perform a similar task. But for this to work, we need to pass a `bins` value to `pd.cat` consisting of values that can be compared with our series.

Our intermediate cut points are 10 minutes and 1 hour: we call "short" trips those up to 10 minutes long, "medium" trips between 10 minutes and 1 hour, and "long" trips longer than 1 hour. However, `pd.cut` won't let us use strings to compare with our `timedelta` column. We thus need to create a Python list (or pandas series) of `timedelta` objects. We do this with a list comprehension, a standard Python technique that is used more rarely by data analysts:

```
[pd.to_timedelta(arg)
 for arg in ['0 seconds', '10 minutes',
             '1 hour', '100 hours']]
```

In short, this list comprehension does the following:

1. Iterates over a list of strings
2. Converts each string to a `timedelta`
3. Returns a list of four `timedelta` objects based on the strings

We can then pass this list to `pd.cut`:

```
df['trip_time_group'] = (
    pd.cut(
        df['trip_time'],
        bins=[pd.to_timedelta(arg)
            for arg in ['0 seconds',
                        '10 minutes',
                        '1 hour',
                        '100 hours']],
        labels=['short', 'medium', 'long'])
)
```

Notice that to have three labels, we need four cut points, or *bins* as they're known here. And although we don't have to provide labels, we definitely should do so. The result of invoking `pd.cut` is a new series, which we then assign to `df['trip_time_group']`.

With those categories in place, we can perform a `groupby` query to see if there's any substantial difference in the number of passengers between short, medium, and long trips:

```
df.groupby('trip_time_group')['passenger_count'].mean()
```

Although short and medium trips both have average passenger counts of 1.5, there's a slightly larger average (1.7) for longer trips. That may imply that trips longer than 1 hour have more passengers, although it's hard to say why.

Solution

```
filename = '../data/nyc_taxi_2019-07.csv'

df = pd.read_csv(filename,
            usecols=['tpep_pickup_datetime',
                'tpep_dropoff_datetime',
                'trip_distance', 'passenger_count',
                'total_amount'],
            parse_dates=['tpep_pickup_datetime',
                'tpep_dropoff_datetime'])
```

Loads the file, parsing two columns as timestamps

Counts trips less than 1 minute long

```
df['trip_time'] = df['tpep_dropoff_datetime'
    ] - df['tpep_pickup_datetime']
```

Subtracts one timestamp from another, assigning to a new timedelta column

```
df.loc[df['trip_time'] < '1 minute', 'trip_time'].count()
df.loc[df['trip_time'] < '1 minute', 'trip_time'
    ].count() / df['trip_time'].count()_ 100
df.loc[df['trip_time'] < '1 minute', 'total_amount'].mean()
```

Calculates the percentage of trips less than 1 minute long

Applies the boolean index to the amount and takes the mean

```
df.loc[df['trip_time'] > '10 hours', 'trip_time'].count()
df.loc[df['trip_time'] > '10 hours', 'trip_time'
    ].count() / df['trip_time'].count()_ 100
```

Calculates the percentage of trips more than 10 hours long

Counts trips more than 10 hours long

```
df['trip_time_group'] = (
    pd.cut(
        df['trip_time'],
        bins=[pd.to_timedelta(arg)
            for arg in ['0 seconds',
                '10 minutes',
                '1 hour',
                '100 hours']],
        labels=['short', 'medium', 'long'])
)
```

Uses a list comprehension with to_timedelta to create bins

Assigns three labels for four edges in pd.cut

```
df.groupby('trip_time_group')['passenger_count'].mean()
```

What was the mean number of passengers for short, medium, and long trips?

You can explore a version of this in the Pandas Tutor at http://mng.bz/W1og.

Beyond the exercise

- The data set you loaded is supposed to be for July 2019. How many trips are not from July 2019? That is, how many records are in the wrong file?
- What was the mean trip time for each number of passengers?
- Load taxi data from July 2019 and 2020. For each year, and then for each number of passengers, what was the mean amount paid?

EXERCISE 40 ■ Writing dates, reading dates

In the previous exercise, we saw how easily we can read a CSV file into pandas, even if it includes date and time information. Generally speaking, we can tell the `parse_dates` keyword argument which columns should be passed to `pd.to_datetime`, and we don't have to think about it any more. Sometimes, though, we're forced to deal with nonstandard date and time formats. We may be asked to write data using a particular format or (even more commonly) to read data that doesn't conform to a standard that pandas recognizes.

Fortunately, we can customize the ways in which datetime information is written to disk as well as how it is parsed when we read it into pandas. In this exercise, we'll practice doing exactly that:

1 Load taxi data from July 2019 into a data frame, using only the columns `tpep_pickup_datetime`, `passenger_count`, `trip_distance`, and `total_amount`, making sure to load `tpep_pickup_datetime` as `datetime`.

2 Export this data frame to a tab-delimited CSV file. However, the datetime information should be written in the format `day/month/year HHh:MMm:SSs`. That is,

- The day should be a two-digit number.
- The month should be a two-digit number.
- The year should be a four-digit number.
- The hours should be a two-digit number, using a 24-hour clock, followed by the letter `h`.
- The minutes should be a two-digit number followed by the letter `m`.
- The seconds should be a two-digit number followed by the letter `s`.
- Read the CSV file you just created into a data frame. Be sure to parse the datetime column appropriately.

Using this weird format, the datetime February 3, 2023 at 10:11:12 is formatted as

`03/02/23 10h:11m:12s`

Working it out

This exercise is meant to give you some practice exporting and importing CSV files using alternative date formats. Most of the times I've had to read (or write) CSV files, dates have been in standard formats that pandas could parse without trouble. But there are always oddball logfiles that need parsing, typically written by custom programs, that use nonstandard formats. The good news is, we can use a custom format when working with CSV files.

I've had occasion to use this functionality in pandas just to translate files from one datetime format to another. In other words, I used pandas not for data analysis but instead as a very fancy date-translation service. That may feel like using a sledgehammer to swat a fly, but it got the job done and required me to write almost no code.

We started the exercise by importing New York taxi data from July 2019, including the `tpep_pickup_datetime` column. To ensure that `tpep_pickup_datetime` is treated as a datetime column, we specify `parse_dates` to `read_csv`:

```
filename = '../data/nyc_taxi_2019-07.csv'
df = pd.read_csv(
    filename,
    usecols=['tpep_pickup_datetime',
             'trip_distance',
             'passenger_count',
             'total_amount'],
    parse_dates=['tpep_pickup_datetime'])
```

With the data frame in place, we can export the data to a CSV file containing only these four columns, but with the oddball datetime format that we used above. In theory, we could create a new column based on `tpep_pickup_datetime` but with the format we want and then export that new column to the CSV file. But it turns out pandas is one step ahead of us here, allowing us to specify the format in which datetime columns are written by passing a value to the `date_format` parameter.

The format is specified using `%` signs, using the format specifiers from `time` `.strftime` and described at http://mng.bz/84DK. Our output can contain any combination of hours, minutes, months, days, time zones, and other elements. The format I described for the output is unusual in that dates are specified as `%d/%m/%Y`, meaning two digits for the day, two digits for the month, and four digits for the year, followed by a space character, and then the time in 24-hour format, but with `h` after the hours, `m` after the minutes, and `s` after the seconds. We can specify that as follows:

```
'%d/%m/%Y %Hh:%Mm:%Ss'
```

We can then write to our CSV file as follows:

```
df.to_csv('ex40_taxi_07_2019.csv',
          sep='\t',
          columns=['tpep_pickup_datetime', 'passenger_count',
                   'trip_distance', 'total_amount'],
          date_format='%d/%m/%Y %Hh:%Mm:%Ss')
```

In this code, we write to the file named ex40_taxi_07_2019.csv and specify (with the `sep` keyword argument) that we will use tabs to separate the fields. Pandas uses the

date_format parameter to indicate how all datetime columns (only tpep_pickup_
datetime, in our case) should be written.

Given that we're going to use this special datetime format in a number of places in
our program, it's wiser to define it as a global string variable, dt_format. Then we can
access that variable both within our call to df.to_csv and also later, in our date-pars-
ing function. In such a case, the code looks like this:

```
dt_format='%d/%m/%Y %Hh:%Mm:%Ss'

df.to_csv('ex40_taxi_07_2019.csv',
        sep='\t',
        columns=['tpep_pickup_datetime',
                'passenger_count',
                'trip_distance',
                'total_amount'],
        date_format=dt_format)
```

Once the file is written, I asked you to import it back into pandas, into a new data
frame, and then to check that the reloaded tpep_pickup_datetime column remains a
datetime column despite its weird date format.

> **NOTE** Previous to pandas 2.0, you were encouraged to handle odd date for-
> mats in read_csv by passing a function to the date_parser keyword argu-
> ment. That has been deprecated in favor of passing a string to date_format.

We can do that by invoking df.read_csv, specifying the filename, separator, columns,
which column requires parsing as a date, and the date format (dt_format) we defined
earlier:

```
df = pd.read_csv('ex40_taxi_07_2019.csv',
        sep='\t',
        usecols=['tpep_pickup_datetime',
                'passenger_count',
                'trip_distance',
                'total_amount'],
        parse_dates=['tpep_pickup_datetime'],
        date_format=dt_format)
```

Solution

```
filename = '../data/nyc_taxi_2019-07.csv'          ⟵┐ Reads in the CSV file, including
df = pd.read_csv(filename,                           │  the datetime column
            usecols=['tpep_pickup_datetime',
                'trip_distance',
                'passenger_count', 'total_amount'],
            parse_dates=['tpep_pickup_datetime'])
```

Specifies the format for
reading and writing
```
└──▷ dt_format='%d/%m/%Y %Hh:%Mm:%Ss'

                                                      ┐ Writes the
df.to_csv('ex40_taxi_07_2019.csv',          ⟵────────┘  CSV file
        sep='\t',
```

```
          columns=['tpep_pickup_datetime',
                   'passenger_count',
                   'trip_distance',
                   'total_amount'],
          date_format=dt_format)

import time
                                    ┌─ This function takes a string argument
def parse_weird_format(s):      ◄───┘  and returns a datetime object.
    return pd.to_datetime(s, format=dt_format)

df = (
    pd
                                          ┌─ Reads the CSV file, parsing
    .read_csv('ex40_taxi_07_2019.csv',  ◄─┘  dates with our function
              sep='\t',
              usecols=['tpep_pickup_datetime',
                       'passenger_count',
                       'trip_distance',
                       'total_amount'],
          parse_dates=['tpep_pickup_datetime'],
          date_format=dt_format)      ◄──┐ date_format expects a string
)                                        └ it can use for parsing
```

You can explore a version of this in the Pandas Tutor at http://mng.bz/E9Mq.

Beyond the exercise

- Export the `tpep_pickup_datetime` date in Unix time—i.e., the number of seconds since 1 January 1970. This is an integer value.
- Read the data frame from this question back into a data frame. Read the `tpep_pickup_datetime` column into a string column, and use `pd.to_datetime` to convert it into a datetime column.
- Compare the speed of parsing time in `read_csv` versus doing so in a separate `to_datetime` step.

Time series

We have seen that a data frame's index can be an integer or string. But things get really exciting when we set a timestamp column to be our index. In the pandas world, we call that a *time series*. When we create a time series, we can take advantage of a number of useful pandas features.

First, let's create a time series. We create a data frame with the dates and designations of NASA's Apollo program missions, grabbed from Wikipedia:

```
all_dfs = pd.read_html('https://en.wikipedia.org/wiki/Apollo_program')
df = all_dfs[2].copy()[['Date', 'Designation']]
```

Here is what the Wikipedia page looks like for me, with the table we want to retrieve:

Main article: Canceled Apollo missions

Several missions were planned for but were canceled before details were finalized.

Mission summary [edit]

For a more comprehensive list, see List of Apollo missions.

Designation	Date	Launch vehicle	CSM	LM	Crew
AS-201	Feb 26, 1966	AS-201	CSM-009	None	None
AS-203	Jul 5, 1966	AS-203	None	None	None
AS-202	Aug 25, 1966	AS-202	CSM-011	None	None
AS-204 (Apollo 1)	Feb 21, 1967	AS-204	CSM-012	None	Gus Grissom Ed White Roger B. Chaffee
Apollo 4	Nov 9, 1967	AS-501	CSM-017	LTA-10R	None
Apollo 5	Jan 22–23, 1968	AS-204	None	LM-1	None
Apollo 6	Apr 4, 1968	AS-502	CM-020 SM-014	LTA-2R	None
Apollo 7	Oct 11–22, 1968	AS-205	CSM-101	None	Wally Schirra Walt Cunningham Donn Eisele
Apollo 8	Dec 21–27, 1968	AS-503	CSM-103	LTA-B	Frank Borman James Lovell William Anders
Apollo 9	Mar 3–13, 1969	AS-504	CSM-104 *Gumdrop*	LM-3 *Spider*	James McDivitt David Scott Russell Schweickart
Apollo 10	May 18–26, 1969	AS-505	CSM-106 *Charlie Brown*	LM-4 *Snoopy*	Thomas Stafford John Young Eugene Cernan
Apollo 11	Jul 16–24, 1969	AS-506	CSM-107 *Columbia*	LM-5 *Eagle*	Neil Armstrong Michael Collins Buzz Aldrin
Apollo 12	Nov 14–24, 1969	AS-507	CSM-108 *Yankee Clipper*	LM-6 *Intrepid*	C. "Pete" Conrad Richard Gordon Alan Bean
Apollo 13	Apr 11–17, 1970	AS-508	CSM-109	LM-7	James Lovell Jack Swigert

Wikipedia page about the Apollo program

Some of the dates describe a single day (e.g., "Jul 5, 1966") but others have ending dates, as well (e.g., "Jan 22–23, 1968"). We remove the ending dates where they appear in the text, to create a series of Apollo launch dates:

```
df['Date'] = pd.to_datetime(df['Date'].str.replace(
        '(-.+)?,', '', regex=True))
```

We then set the Date column to be the data frame's index:

```
df = df.set_index('Date')
```

From this point on, df is a time series. We can see this by looking at df.index:

```
DatetimeIndex(['1966-02-26', '1966-07-05',
               '1966-08-25', '1967-02-21',
               '1967-11-09', '1968-01-22',
               '1968-04-04', '1968-10-11',
```

(continued)

```
                '1968-12-21', '1969-03-03',
                '1969-05-18', '1969-07-16',
                '1969-11-14', '1970-04-11',
                '1971-01-31', '1971-07-26',
                '1972-04-16', '1972-12-07'],
              dtype='datetime64[ns]', name='Date', freq=None)
```

The index contains a number of `datetime` objects. With this in place, we can retrieve a row on a particular date, just as we would with a normal index:

```
df.loc['1970-04-11']
```

Better yet, we can specify the smaller (i.e., more specific) parts of a date. That is, we can leave out the day, thus retrieving all values in a single month:

```
df.loc['1970-07']
```

Or we can specify just a year, thus getting all missions in that year:

```
df.loc['1971']
```

Date	Designation
1966-02-26	AS-201
1966-07-05	AS-203
1966-08-25	AS-202
1967-02-21	AS-204 (Apollo 1)
1967-11-09	Apollo 4
1968-01-22	Apollo 5
1968-04-04	Apollo 6
1968-10-11	Apollo 7
1968-12-21	Apollo 8
1969-03-03	Apollo 9
1969-05-18	Apollo 10
1969-07-16	Apollo 11
1969-11-14	Apollo 12
1970-04-11	Apollo 13
1971-01-31	Apollo 14
1971-07-26	Apollo 15
1972-04-16	Apollo 16
1972-12-07	Apollo 17

`df.loc['1971']`

Date	Designation
1971-01-31	Apollo 14
1971-07-26	Apollo 15

Retrieving rows of a time series via the year

We can also retrieve a set of rows with a slice by specifying starting and ending dates:

```
df.loc['1968-07-01':'1972-08-31']
```

Perhaps the most interesting and powerful feature of a time series is *resampling*. Resampling is similar to a `groupby` query, except that instead of producing one result per value of a categorical column, we get one result per chunk of time, starting at the earliest point in time and ending with the latest one. For example, resampling allows us to retrieve the mean value for every day, or every 2 weeks, or every 6 months, or every year of a data frame. For example, we can determine how many missions there were in every 6-month period covered by our data set:

```
df.resample('6M').count()
```

If the data is numeric, we can also run other aggregation methods, such as `mean` and `std`.

EXERCISE 41 ■ Oil prices

In this exercise, we work with a CSV file containing oil prices—specifically, West Texas Intermediate oil prices. These prices have been reported and updated daily, at least in our data set, from January 2, 1986 through the present day. (I constructed the CSV file using a Python program downloaded from https://github.com/datasets/oil-prices, which retrieves publicly available oil-price information from the US government.) In this exercise, we'll look at historical oil prices, using the datetime functionality in pandas to make such queries easier. Specifically, I want you to

1 Import the wti-daily.csv file into a data frame in which the `Date` column is treated as a datetime value and is set to be the index.
2 Answer these questions:
   - What was the average price of a barrel of oil in June 1992?
   - What was the average price of a barrel of oil in all of 1987?
   - What was the average price from September 2003 through July 2014?
3 Show the price of oil at the end of each quarter in the data set.
4 For each year in the data set, show the average price.
5 On which date were oil prices the highest? When were they the lowest?

Working it out

We've already seen that by using the `dt` accessor, we can retrieve various parts of a datetime column. With that tool at our disposal, we can query our data in all sorts of ways. But we've also seen that certain queries can be easier to read and write when we change the index. This is particularly true when we set the index to be a datetime value. In this exercise, we explore a number of these functions while looking at historical oil prices.

The first task, as always, is to load the data from a CSV file into a data frame. In this case, the CSV file contains only two columns named Date and Price. In loading the CSV file into memory, we ask pandas to treat the Date column as (not surprisingly) a datetime value. We also ask it to make that column the index, via the index_col parameter:

```
filename = '../data/wti-daily.csv'

df = pd.read_csv(filename,
                 parse_dates=['Date'],
                 index_col=['Date'])
```

With that in place, we can make some queries. For starters, we want to determine the average price of oil during the month of June 1992. As usual, we can retrieve items from the data frame by using the loc accessor along with the index value that's of interest to us. But because it's a time series, we can provide a subset of the date, removing more specific parts to match a larger number of rows. We can thus say

```
df.loc['1992-06-15']
```

and get back the row for June 15, 1992. (If there were more than one row, we would get all of them back. But we know that each date in this data set is unique.) However, we're interested in all days in June 1992. We can thus say

```
df.loc['1992-06']
```

By leaving off the day, pandas matches and retrieves all rows in which the date is sometime in June 1992. To get the mean price during that period, we can say

```
df.loc['1992-06'].mean()
```

We get a result of just over $22.38.

I similarly asked you to find the mean price during 1987. Just as we can leave off the day to find all rows from a particular year and month, we can leave off the day and month to get all rows from a particular year:

```
df.loc['1987'].mean()
```

This retrieves all rows with a year of 1987. We then run mean on the Price column, which returns a number just over $19.20.

Next, I asked you to find the average price from September 2003 through July 2014. The easiest way to do this, when we have a time series, is to use a slice. Normally, Python slices are specified as a starting value and then 1 past the final value. For example, if we have a sequence (string, list, or tuple) named s and request s[10:20], the slice retrieves values from the index 10 up to (but not including) 20.

Slices with a time series are similar, but as with other non-numeric indexes in pandas, we *include* the end of the slice. We can specify the date on which we want to start and also the date on which we want to end:

```
df.loc['2003-09':'2014-07']
```

This retrieves all rows from `df` starting September 1, 2003, and going through July 31, 2014. We can then run `mean` on the values we get back:

```
df.loc['2003-09':'2014-07'].mean()
```

This returns a value of just over $76.45.

Next, I asked you to find the price of oil at the end of each quarter in the data set. Pandas makes this easy to do with the `is_quarter_end` attribute on the `dt` accessor for `datetime` series. In our case, the `datetime` values aren't exactly in a series; they're on our index. How can we invoke `is_quarter_end` on our datetime index?

It turns out that we can invoke it directly on the index, getting a boolean series back:

```
df.index.is_quarter_end
```

This boolean series can then be applied as a mask index to `df`:

```
df.loc[df.index.is_quarter_end]
```

The result is a one-column data frame whose index values are the final days of each quarter, regardless of whether it's the 30th or 31st of the month in question.

I also asked you to find the mean price of oil for each year in our data set. This is most easily accomplished by using `resample`, which is a kind of `groupby` but for time series: it lets us run an aggregation method (e.g., `mean`) for all the values in a given time period. If the time period doesn't exist in the data frame or is cut off, it still appears in the output to ensure that we have all the periods from start to finish.

When we run `resample`, we tell it what time-period granularity we want, giving a number and a letter representing the measurement. For example, we can run our aggregation method on a weekly basis with `1W` or on a bimonthly basis with `2M`. In this exercise, I asked to see annual average prices, which means specifying `1Y`. The resulting query is

```
df.resample('1Y').mean()
```

The result from a `resample` query is always a data frame in which the index contains the values from the end of each period. The index in our result thus starts at `1986-12-31` and goes through `2021-12-31`. Note that even if we only have partial values for a year, we get the average amount for that year.

Finally, I asked you to determine on which dates we had the historically highest and lowest oil prices. There are numerous ways to accomplish this, but I think it's easiest to sort the values in the `Price` column and then retrieve the first and last values from the resulting sorted series. Remember that we can retrieve more than one value by passing a list of indexes to `loc` or `iloc` and that if we use `iloc` (which retrieves by position), we can ask for index 0 (the first item) and −1 (the final item):

```
df['Price'].sort_values().iloc[[0, -1]]
```

You may be surprised that the lowest price of oil in this data set is −$36.98, meaning you could get paid to accept a barrel of oil. If this sounds odd, you're right; it was the result of a dramatic drop in oil demand at the start of the Covid-19 pandemic. There wasn't enough storage space for the oil that had already been extracted from the ground, resulting in this bizarre situation. Look it up—it's just one of the many economic oddities of the pandemic.

Note that if we want the dates on which the minimum and maximum values were found but not the prices themselves, we can use

```
df['Price'].agg(['idxmin', 'idxmax'])
```

The `idxmin` and `idxmax` return the index corresponding to the minimum and maximum values, respectively. The `agg` method lets us invoke more than one aggregation method. So this query asks to see the indexes for the lowest and highest values in `Price`. We get the indexes (i.e., dates) but not the values themselves.

Solution

```
filename = '../data/wti-daily.csv'

df = pd.read_csv(filename,
                 parse_dates=['Date'],
                 index_col=['Date'])

df.loc['1992-06'].mean()
df.loc['1987'].mean()
df.loc['2003-09':'2014-07'].mean()
df.loc[df.index.is_quarter_end]
df.resample('1Y').mean()
df['Price'].sort_values().iloc[[0, -1]]
```

You can explore a version of this in the Pandas Tutor at http://mng.bz/NVlE.

Beyond the exercise

- Use `resample` to find, for each quarter, the mean and standard deviations in price.
- In which quarter did you see the biggest increase in mean price from the previous quarter?
- What was the biggest percentage increase in oil prices across quarters?

EXERCISE 42 ▪ Best tippers

We've looked at New York taxi data a number of times, and now we'll use our time-related knowledge to study them again. This time, we'll try to understand when people tip their taxi drivers more generously. (If you're not from the United States, you may not be familiar with the custom of tipping, often 15% or 20%, in addition to whatever a taxi meter says you officially need to pay. In many other countries, this practice is unexpected, rare, or even illegal.) In particular, I'd like you to

1   Import the taxi info from both January and July 2019. Include the following columns: `tpep_pickup_datetime`, `passenger_count`, `trip_distance`, `fare_amount`,

extra, mta_tax, tip_amount, tolls_amount, improvement_surcharge, total_amount, and congestion_surcharge.

2 Create a new column, pre_tip_amount, with all the payment columns except total_amount and tip_amount. (Note that total_amount is the sum of all the other payment columns, including tip_amount. It should be equivalent to calculating total_amount - tip_amount.)

3 Create a new column, tip_percentage, showing the percentage of pre_tip_amount that the tip was.

4 Answer these questions:

– What was the mean tip percentage across all trips in the data set?

– How many times did people tip more than the pretip amount?

– On which day of the week do people tip the greatest percentage of the fare, on average?

– At which hour do people tip the greatest percentage?

– Do people typically tip more in January or July?

– What was the 1-day period in our data set when people tipped the greatest percentage?

Working it out

In this exercise, we ask the same question—when do people tip taxi drivers the most?—in a number of different ways. All of them use the extensive support for dates and times that pandas offers.

For starters, we load the data from both January and July 2019. As we've done before, we use a list comprehension along with pd.read_csv. This creates a list of data frames that we can turn into a single data frame with pd.concat:

```
filenames = ['../data/nyc_taxi_2019-01.csv',
             '../data/nyc_taxi_2019-07.csv']

all_dfs = [pd.read_csv(one_filename,
            usecols=['tpep_pickup_datetime',
                    'passenger_count',
                    'trip_distance',
                    'fare_amount','extra','mta_tax',
                    'tip_amount','tolls_amount',
                    'improvement_surcharge',
                    'total_amount','congestion_surcharge'],
            parse_dates=['tpep_pickup_datetime'])
          for one_filename in filenames]

df = pd.concat(all_dfs)
```

I asked you to include a large number of columns when creating the data frame so we can calculate the tip percentage more accurately. I considered not asking you to specify usecols but rather to read all the data anyway—but as tempting as it may be to do that, it's not a good habit to get into. You should specify the columns you want in your data frame; otherwise, you'll find yourself running out of memory when you work with large data sets.

With our data frame in place, we want to calculate the pretip amount—that is, the amount on which the tip is based—for each ride. It's not always obvious what should (and shouldn't) be included in the tip. For example, do we include tolls for bridges and tunnels in our calculation? How about the surcharge that's sometimes added because the streets of New York are extra congested during those hours? For our purposes, we included all these fees and charges.

I thus asked you to create a new column, `pre_tip_amount`, that is the sum of six columns. How can we do that?

One possibility is to explicitly name those columns and add them together:

```
df['pre_tip_amount'] = (df['fare_amount'] +
                        df['extra'] +
                        df['mta_tax'] +
                        df['tolls_amount'] +
                        df['improvement_surcharge'] +
                        df['congestion_surcharge'])
```

This will certainly work, but it seems wordy. Perhaps there's a way to name the columns and sum them. The `sum` method would seem to be a perfect way to do this, except that it sums the rows rather than the columns. But wait! Many pandas methods allow us to specify the axis on which they run—and sure enough, `sum` is one of them. We can thus sum our selected columns by specifying `axis='columns'`:

```
df['pre_tip_amount'] = df[['fare_amount',
                           'extra',
                           'mta_tax',
                           'tolls_amount',
                           'improvement_surcharge',
                           'congestion_surcharge']
          ].sum(axis='columns')
```

Notice that we select our six columns with a list of strings. We then run `sum` on these columns, producing a new pandas series. We assign this series back to `df['pre_tip_amount']`.

With that in hand, we're ready to create another column, `tip_percentage`, which contains the percentage of the pretip charge the user added as a tip:

```
df['tip_percentage'] = df['tip_amount'] / df['pre_tip_amount']
```

Our data frame now has all the information we need to answer our questions about tipping in New York taxis. For starters, what was the mean tipping rate across all taxi rides in our data set? We can find that by running the `mean` method on our `tip_percentage` column:

```
df['tip_percentage'].mean()
```

The answer is 13%. That seems low to me, so perhaps we're calculating the pretip base amount differently than others do. But maybe the data set is more complex than a straight percentage. For example, does anyone tip more than 100%? We can find out:

```
(df['tip_percentage'] > 1).value_counts()
```

Here, we use `value_counts` to find how many people tipped more than 100% of the pretip amount. By applying `value_counts` to a boolean series, we're able to determine how often the `True` value is returned, meaning how often our condition is met.

The number of people giving above-and-beyond tips isn't overwhelming. But it's not zero, either, which came as a surprise to me. However, this number will skew the average tip upward. Perhaps there are people who aren't tipping at all, which will skew things downward. Let's take a look, calculating the percentage of riders who don't tip:

```
(df['tip_percentage'] == 0).value_counts(normalize=True)
```

Again, we use `value_counts`—but this time, we pass it `normalize=True` to get a percentage answer. And the results are surprising, at least to me: about 32% of taxi riders in New York don't tip at all! This almost certainly has an effect on the mean tipping rate.

Next, we were curious to know whether people tip more on any particular day of the week. To do this, we combine `groupby` with the `dt` accessor's `day_of_week` attribute, which returns the integer for the day of the week, with Monday being 0 and Sunday being 6. You may think we need to define a new `day_of_week` column in our data frame so we can run a `groupby` on it. But no, the pandas developers make it possible to run a `groupby` not only on a column but also on the result we get back from `dt.day_of_week`:

```
df.groupby(df['tpep_pickup_datetime'].dt.day_of_week)
```

For each day of the week, we want to get the mean tip percentage. We thus run the following query:

```
df.groupby(df['tpep_pickup_datetime'].dt.day_of_week
    )['tip_percentage'].mean()
```

This gives us values, one for each day of the week. Just to make sure we get the right data, we then sort the resulting values from highest to lowest:

```
df.groupby(df['tpep_pickup_datetime'].dt.day_of_week
    )['tip_percentage'].mean().sort_values(ascending=False)
```

Much to my surprise, the tipping percentages aren't that different from one another. I was sure, before analyzing this data, that people tip more on weekends, but the data doesn't support that. On the contrary, it shows that people tip the least on Fridays and Saturdays and the most on Tuesdays and Wednesdays. However, the difference isn't that great, so I'm not sure if we can draw significant conclusions. Certainly if I were a taxi driver deciding which shifts to take, the tip amount on a given day wouldn't make much difference. (And besides, one-third of passengers aren't going to tip anything, right?)

But maybe the hour of the day makes a difference: that is, perhaps people tip better in the mornings or afternoons. I thus asked you to create such a query, to find out at which hour of the day people tip the most on average:

```
df.groupby(df['tpep_pickup_datetime'].dt.hour
    )['tip_percentage'].mean().sort_values(ascending=False)
```

The query in this case is similar to the previous one. Here, however, we get more interesting results: people tip about 11% early in the morning (between 3:00 and 6:00 a.m.) and nearly 14% at night (from 8:00 to 11:00 p.m.). We see similar, if slightly lower, rates from 7:00 to 9:00 a.m.—so if you're unsure whether to take the 5:00 a.m. or 9:00 a.m. slot as a taxi driver, I'd suggest, based on average tips alone, choosing the latter.

Let's ask another question, which our data set can help us answer: do people tip more during the winter or the summer? (Or is there no difference?) We have data from both January and July, which should provide useful insights. We can say

```
df.groupby(df['tpep_pickup_datetime'].dt.month
    )['tip_percentage'].mean().sort_values(ascending=False)
```

The highest tips (20% on average) are given in May, followed by August, March, and September, respectively.

But wait a moment: our data set is supposed to contain data from January and July. How did other months get in there? The answer, of course, is that no data set is completely clean. Whether the dates are wrong, were reported late, or were otherwise scrambled along the way, our data contains information from other months. If we only compare January with July from this data set, we see a slight difference between the months, with tipping in January at 13.7% but in July at 12.1%. Whether that's because of summer tourists (who may—I'm just guessing—tip less) or people feeling more open with their cash during the winter months, I'm not sure.

Next, I asked what one-day period in the data set had the highest average percentage of tipping. This type of problem is most easily solved with a time series, meaning we use a datetime value as the index:

```
df = df.set_index('tpep_pickup_datetime')
```

With that in place, we can use `resample` with an argument of `1D` (i.e., one day) to find the day on which people tipped the most. First, we find the mean tipping percentage for each day in the time series:

```
df.resample('1D')['tip_percentage'].mean()
```

That works, but we'd like to sort these values so we can find the highest-tipping day. We do this by running `sort_values` on our results and then listing only the top 10 dates:

```
df.resample('1D')['tip_percentage'
    ].mean().sort_values(ascending=False).head(10)
```

The results include zero days from either January or July. Let's try this again but first get rid of dates that aren't in January or July:

```
df = pd.concat([df['2019-01-01':'2019-01-31'],
        df['2019-07-01':'2019-07-31']])
df.resample('1D')['tip_percentage'].mean().sort_values(
      ascending=False).head(10)
```

Having cleaned the data from non-January/July rows, we can see that all 10 of the highest-tipping days are in January. In our data sample, at least, people are more likely to tip better in the winter than in the summer. We can double-check by resampling at one-month granularity:

```
df.resample('1M')['tip_percentage'].mean().dropna()
```

Because we have only two months of data, but they're in January and July, using `resample` means we get NaN values for February, March, April, May, and June. We thus remove those with `dropna`. And we see that the average tipping rate in January is 13.7%, whereas in July it's 12.1%—a finding I hadn't anticipated.

Solution

```
filenames = ['../data/nyc_taxi_2019-01.csv',
          '../data/nyc_taxi_2019-07.csv']
                                                    Runs read_csv
                                                    on each filename
all_dfs = [pd.read_csv(one_filename,           ←─┘
          usecols=['tpep_pickup_datetime',
                  'passenger_count',
                  'trip_distance',
                  'fare_amount','extra',
                  'mta_tax','tip_amount',
                  'tolls_amount',
       Our list          'improvement_surcharge',
  comprehension          'total_amount','congestion_surcharge'],
 returns a list of      parse_dates=['tpep_pickup_datetime'])
    data frames.  ──▷   for one_filename in filenames]
                                              Combines the list of data
                                              frames into a single one
   df = pd.concat(all_dfs)                ←─┘

df['pre_tip_amount'] = df[['fare_amount', 'extra',
                      'mta_tax', 'tolls_amount',
                      'improvement_surcharge',
                      'congestion_surcharge']].sum(    Creates the column
              axis='columns')                     ←─  pre_tip_amount

df['tip_percentage'] = df[                     Calculates the
    'tip_amount'] / df['pre_tip_amount']    ←─ tip percentage
                                           What was the mean tip
df['tip_percentage'].mean()             ←─ percentage across all trips?

(df['tip_percentage'] > 1).value_counts()    ←─┐ How many trips tipped
                                                 more than 100%?
(df['tip_percentage'] == 0).value_counts(
```

```
        normalize=True)                     ◁────┐ What percentage of taxi
df.groupby(df[                                   │ riders give no tip at all?
    'tpep_pickup_datetime'].dt.day_of_week)[
    'tip_percentage'].mean().sort_values(ascending=False)
```

> Grouping by the day of week, calculates the mean tip percentage and then sorts ◁──────

```
df.groupby(df[
    'tpep_pickup_datetime'].dt.hour)[
    'tip_percentage'].mean().sort_values(
        ascending=False).head(5)        ◁──┘
```

> Grouping by the hour of the day, calculates the mean tip percentage and then sorts

```
df.groupby(df[
    'tpep_pickup_datetime'].dt.month)[
        'tip_percentage'].mean().sort_values(
            ascending=False)            ◁──┐
```

> Grouping by month, finds the mean tip percentage

```
df = df.set_index('tpep_pickup_datetime')   ◁──┐
```

> Sets the data frame's index, making it a time series

```
df.resample('1D')[
    'tip_percentage'].mean().sort_values(
        ascending=False).head(10)      ◁──┐
```

> Finds, for each day, the mean tip percentage

```
df = pd.concat([df['2019-01-01':'2019-01-31'],
        df['2019-07-01':'2019-07-31']])   ◁──┐
```

> Excludes dates that aren't from January or July 2019

```
df.resample('1D')[
    'tip_percentage'].mean().sort_values(
        ascending=False).head(10)
```

You can explore a version of this in the Pandas Tutor at http://mng.bz/lW42.

Beyond the exercise

- You saw that 32% of riders don't tip at all. Of those who *do*, what percentage do they tip, on average?
- How many of the rides in the data set, supposedly from January and July 2019, are from outside of those dates?
- Looking only at dates in January and July, in what week did passengers tip the greatest percentage?

Summary

In this chapter, we explored various ways pandas lets us examine data that includes a date-and-time component. We saw how to read datetime information into a data frame, extract datetime information from an existing column, break such a column apart, and interpret odd datetime formats. We also learned to create and work with a time series—a data frame in which a datetime column serves as our index—and how to query it in various ways, including resampling, letting us run aggregation methods over particular time periods.

Visualization 11

Data analysis, as you've seen throughout this book, is largely about numbers. A typical pandas data frame contains columns and rows full of numbers, and data analysis involves lots of mathematical methods and statistical techniques.

That's fine, except that we humans are typically bad at understanding large collections of numbers. We're generally much better at comprehending visual depictions of numbers, especially if we're trying to understand relationships among our data. So, although we often think of visualization as a way to explain technical ideas in simple terms to non-experts, the fact is that visualization can also be helpful for the experts working on a problem. Seeing a chart or graph can help us put the numbers in perspective, improve our understanding of a problem we're working on, and thus inform the very analysis that created the visualization.

The 900-pound gorilla in the world of Python data visualization is Matplotlib. There's no doubt that Matplotlib is powerful—but it's also overwhelming to many people. Fortunately, pandas provides a visualization API that allows us to create plots from our data without having to use Matplotlib explicitly. We thus get the best of both worlds: the ability to plot information in our data frame, without having to learn too much about Matplotlib's API. However, if and when you need more power, Matplotlib is there, under the hood.

In this chapter, we'll look at how to visualize data using the pandas wrapper for Matplotlib. We'll explore a number of different plots that can help make your data come alive.

We'll also spend some time looking at Seaborn, a popular alternative to Matplotlib. There are a number of such alternatives; some (like Seaborn) are wrappers around the Matplotlib library, and others are full-blown alternatives written from the ground up. It's worth learning what your options are so you can find a system with which you feel comfortable. I've grown to like Seaborn's API as well as its ability to create attractive plots with little or no customization.

This chapter also provides you with the opportunity to explore one of Jupyter's best features: the fact that it keeps images inline (figure 11.1). The ability to have data, code, and plots in the same document is a game-changer for many projects, making it possible for data scientists to both share information and get input from less technical colleagues.

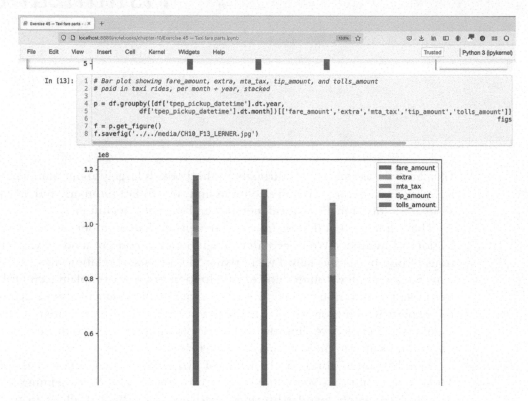

Figure 11.1   Screenshot of a Jupyter notebook combining code and plots

Table 11.1   What you need to know

Concept	What is it?	Example	To learn more
pd.read_csv	Returns a new data frame based on CSV input	df = df.read_csv('myfile.csv')	http://mng.bz/a1az
df.groupby	Allows us to invoke one or more aggregate methods for each value in a particular column	df.groupby('year')	http://mng.bz/gBGl
df.loc	Retrieves selected rows and columns	df.loc[:, 'passenger_count'] = df['passenger_count']	http://mng.bz/pPNG

Table 11.1 **What you need to know** *(continued)*

Concept	What is it?	Example	To learn more
`df.plot`	Plotting object for a data frame	`df.plot.box()`	http://mng.bz/Ox8n
`df.corr`	Produces a data frame describing correlations among each pair of numeric columns	`df.corr()`	http://mng.bz/Y1oN
`s.quantile`	Gets the value at a particular percentage of the values	`s.quantile(0.25)`	http://mng.bz/GyYq
`df.join`	Joins two data frames based on their indexes	`df.join(other_df)`	http://mng.bz/zXva
`pandas.plotting .scatter_matrix`	Creates scatter plots comparing every pair of numeric columns	`pandas.plotting.scat ter_matrix`	http://mng.bz/OKqx
Matplotlib	Python library for plotting data	`import matplotlib .pyplot as plt`	http://mng.bz/9D6l
Seaborn	Python library for plotting data	`import seaborn as sns`	http://mng.bz/jPKx
`df.reset_index`	Gets a data frame identical to our current one, but with a new numeric index starting at 0	`df.reset_index(drop= True)`	http://mng.bz/Wz50
`pd.concat`	Returns a list of data frames combined as a single new data frame	`df = pd.concat(df1, df2)`	http://mng.bz/8r5P

EXERCISE 43 ▪ Cities

Back in exercise 20, we worked with a JSON file describing the 1,000 largest cities in the United States. In this exercise, we look at the same file—but instead of printing the analysis as a bunch of numbers, we visualize some of the most interesting numbers and trends in the file. Specifically, I want you to

1. Load data from cities.json into a data frame.
2. Create a bar plot showing how many of the top 1,000 cities are in each state. There should be one vertical bar per state (with a few extra for nonstates such as Washington, DC). The plot should be ordered such that the state with the fewest cities in this list is on the left and the state with the most cities is on the right.
3. Create a bar plot comparing the growth of all cities in the state of Pennsylvania. There should be one vertical bar per city, ordered with the slowest-growing city on the left and the fastest-growing city on the right.

4 Create a pie plot showing how much each Massachusetts city in the list contributes to the overall population. (And no, I'm not trying to say that 100% of the population of that state resides in large cities.) There should be one pie segment per city in the list, and its size should indicate how much it contributes to the total.

5 Create a scatter plot of the cities, putting the longitude on the *x* axis and latitude on the *y* axis. What does the resulting plot look like?

Working it out

Matplotlib offers a wide variety of plotting formats, and we use this exercise to explore a number of them, trying different techniques to understand our data in a variety of ways. Visualization isn't just about choosing a type of plot; we often need to clean, arrange, and modify the data before we can do so.

First, I asked you to create a bar plot showing how many of the top 1,000 cities in the United States are in each state. The data frame we create from the JSON has several columns, one of which is state. We use that column, along with a call to groupby, to find the number of cities per state:

```
df.groupby('state').count()
```

This works, but it gives a result for every column in the data frame. Because we're only interested in the number of cities, we can choose a single column—in this case, the city column:

```
df.groupby('state')['city'].count()
```

With that in place, we can create a bar plot. But wait: the question asks for the bar to be sorted from the smallest value to the largest. This means before producing the plot, we need to sort the values in the series returned by the groupby call. Fortunately, sorting a series is easily done with sort_values:

```
(
    df
    .groupby('state')['city'].count()
    .sort_values()
)
```

With that in place, we can produce our bar plot:

```
(
    df
    .groupby('state')['city'].count()
    .sort_values()
    .plot.bar()
)
```

NOTE Another way to invoke this plot would be to invoke plot as a function, passing kind='bar' as a keyword argument. I prefer the other syntax, but either is considered standard and acceptable.

This works, but with 50 states (plus Washington, DC), we end up with a plot that's small. We thus pass the `figsize` keyword argument to `bar`, which is in turn passed to the Matplotlib backend. By giving `figsize` a value of `(10, 10)`, we can set it to be a 10-inch by 10-inch square:

```
(
    df
    .groupby('state')['city'].count()
    .sort_values()
    .plot.bar(figsize=(10,10))
)
```

It's probably not particularly surprising that California has the most large cities, but the sheer number (and thus very tall bar in our plot) was still striking to me when producing this plot (figure 11.2).

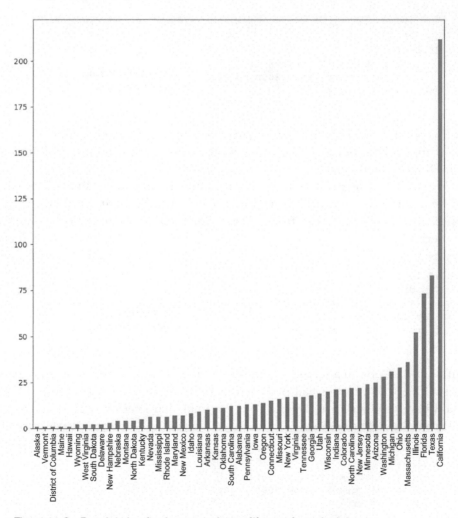

Figure 11.2   Bar plot showing how many large cities are in each state

Next, I asked you to create a bar plot showing growth in Pennsylvania cities, sorted from lowest to highest. For this task, we took data from the `growth_from_2000_to_2013` column, along with the `city` column, all from rows in which `state` equals to `'Pennsylvania'`. I decided it would be easiest to turn these rows and columns into a separate, smaller data frame using `df.loc`:

```
df.loc[df['state']=='Pennsylvania',          ←──┐ Row selector: only rows
       ['city','growth_from_2000_to_2013']    ←─┐  describing Pennsylvania cities
      ]                                          │ Column selector: only two columns,
                                                   the city name and its growth
```

As we've seen on many occasions, we select rows in which the state is equal to `'Pennsylvania'` and then the two columns that are of interest. Then, because we want to show the city names in our plot's x index, we make it the index of the data frame:

```
(
    df.loc[
        df['state']=='Pennsylvania',
        ['city','growth_from_2000_to_2013']]    Sets the city name
    .set_index('city')                      ←──┘ to be the index
)
```

At this point, it would be nice to produce the plot. But there's a problem: the growth is a string ending with a `'%'` sign. If we want to plot it, we need to turn it into a number. How can we do that?

We could use the `str` accessor to run a method on our string. But before we can do so, we need to turn our data frame into a series. That's because `str` only works on a series. Fortunately, the index from a data frame remains when we extract one column as a series:

```
(
    df.loc[
        df['state']=='Pennsylvania',
        ['city','growth_from_2000_to_2013']]
    .set_index('city')                       Retrieves the
    ['growth_from_2000_to_2013']         ←──┘ growth column
)
```

With our data now in a series, we can remove the `'%'` in a variety of ways. I decided to use `str.replace`, turning all occurrences of `'%'` into the empty string, `''`. But we could have used a slice to keep all but the final character or `str.rstrip` to remove `'%'` from the right side. Using `str.replace`, we end up with the following code:

```
(
    df.loc[
        df['state']=='Pennsylvania',
        ['city','growth_from_2000_to_2013']]
    .set_index('city')
```

```
    ['growth_from_2000_to_2013']
    .str.replace('%', '')
)
```
←— Removes the % sign from each growth string

The result is still a series of strings. However, these strings can all be turned into floating-point values using `astype`:

```
(
    df.loc[
        df['state']=='Pennsylvania',
        ['city','growth_from_2000_to_2013']]
    .set_index('city')
    ['growth_from_2000_to_2013']
    .str.replace('%', '')
    .astype(np.float16)
)
```
←—| Gets a float16 column from the growth string

We now have every city in Pennsylvania along with its growth percentage. We can plot it, but before doing so, I asked you to sort the values from lowest to highest. Once again, we invoke `sort_values`:

```
(
    df.loc[
        df['state']=='Pennsylvania',
        ['city','growth_from_2000_to_2013']]
    .set_index('city')
    ['growth_from_2000_to_2013']
    .str.replace('%', '')
    .astype(np.float16)
    .sort_values()
)
```

And with that in place, we create a bar plot, setting a size of `(10, 10)` to see it more easily in our notebook (figure 11.3):

```
(
    df.loc[
        df['state']=='Pennsylvania',
        ['city','growth_from_2000_to_2013']]
    .set_index('city')
    ['growth_from_2000_to_2013']
    .str.replace('%', '')
    .astype(np.float16)
    .sort_values()
    .plot.bar(figsize=(10,10))
)
```

Next, I asked you to find all cities in Massachusetts and create a pie plot with all these cities. This will allow us to see what proportion of the urban population of Massachusetts lives in each city. Remember that a pie plot takes all the values, sums them, and produces a pie "slice" of that item's proportion of the total.

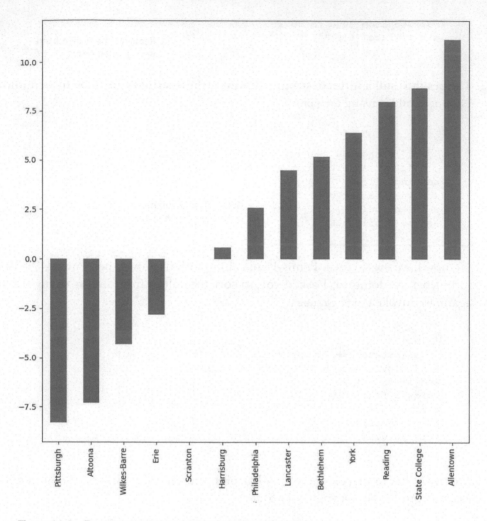

Figure 11.3   Bar plot showing growth in Pennsylvania cities

We first need to get names and populations of cities in Massachusetts. We can do that using the following query:

```
(
    df
    .loc[                                    Row selector: Only
                                             cities in Massachusetts
        df['state'] == 'Massachusetts',      Column selector: Two
        ['city','population']]                columns, city and population
    .set_index('city')                       Uses the city name
    ['population']                           as the index
)                          Retrieves only
                           the population column
```

This is similar to what we did for Pennsylvania: we retrieved only two columns (`city` and `population`) from the data frame and only for those rows in which the state was

Massachusetts. We set the index of our data frame to be `city` and then retrieved the only remaining column, `population`, as a series.

Next, we draw a pie plot based on this data, giving it a size of 10 inches by 10 inches:

```
(
    df
    .loc[
        df['state'] == 'Massachusetts',
        ['city','population']]
    .set_index('city')
    ['population']
    .plot.pie(figsize=(10,10))
)
```

Sure enough, we see that Massachusetts has many different cities—but of the urban population in the state, Boston clearly dominates, followed distantly by Worcester and Springfield (figure 11.4).

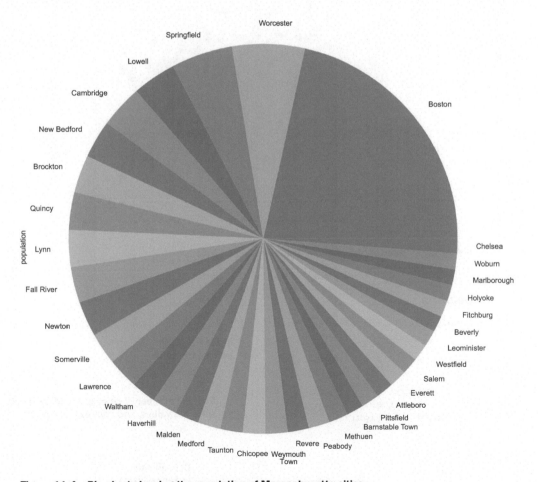

Figure 11.4 Pie chart showing the population of Massachusetts cities

Finally, I asked you to create a scatter plot with the longitude and latitude of the 1,000 cities in the data frame. We can do that by invoking `plot.scatter` on the data frame, indicating which column should be used for the *x* axis and which should be used for the *y* axis:

```
df.plot.scatter(x='longitude', y='latitude')
```

What does the scatter plot look like? Well, we're plotting the 1,000 most populous cities in the United States, which means the plot will look like . . . a map of the United States, at least the most densely populated areas (figure 11.5).

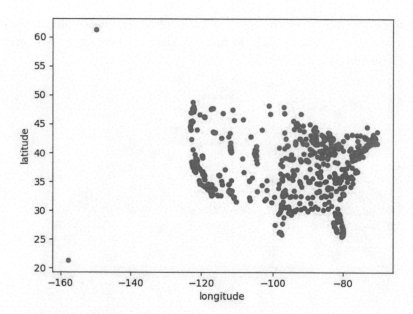

Figure 11.5   Scatter plot of cities' longitude and latitude

Solution

```
filename = '../data/cities.json'
df = pd.read_json(filename)        ◁──┐ Reads the JSON
                                      │ into a data frame
(
    df
    .groupby('state')['city'].count()
    .sort_values()                    ┌── Gets the number of cities grouped by state,
    .plot.bar(figsize=(10,10))   ◁──┘   sorts the values, and creates a bar plot
)

(
    df.loc[                          ┌── Gets all cities
        df['state']=='Pennsylvania', ◁──┘  in Pennsylvania
```

```
        ['city','growth_from_2000_to_2013']]          Only columns city and
    .set_index('city')                                growth_from_2000_to_2013
    ['growth_from_2000_to_2013']
    .str.replace('%', '')                 Removes
    .astype(np.float16)                   the % sign
    .sort_values()
    .plot.bar(figsize=(10,10))          Turns into a float, sorts values,
)                                       and creates a bar plot


(
    df
    .loc[
        df['state'] == 'Massachusetts',     Gets all cities in Massachusetts,
        ['city','population']]              columns city and population
    .set_index('city')
    ['population']                  Creates a pie plot of
    .plot.pie(figsize=(10,10))      the cities' populations
)
                                            Creates a scatter plot from
df.plot.scatter(x='longitude', y='latitude')    cities' longitude and latitude
```

Beyond the exercise

Now that you've gotten your feet wet with visualization, let's create some more plots:

- Create a histogram of the growth rates among cities in both Texas and Michigan.
- Create a histogram of the growth rates among cities in both Texas and California.
- Create a bar plot from the average growth per state.

Box-and-whisker plots

When I took introductory statistics in graduate school, the professor started to tell us about plots. I was wondering why he felt the need to explain plots that we had seen since middle school—line plots, bar plots, and even pie plots. But then he got to box-plots, more formally known as *box-and-whisker plots*, and I was intrigued.

We frequently use the `describe` method to describe data. The `describe` method includes the *Tukey five-number summary*—minimum, 0.25 quartile, median, 0.75 quartile, and maximum—along with the mean and standard deviation, which together help us understand our data.

The "Tukey" in this name refers to John Tukey, a famous mathematician and statistician. Tukey developed not only the five-number summary but also a graphical depiction of that summary: the boxplot. (He also invented the words *bit*, for *binary digit*, and *software*, which . . . well, if you're reading this book, you probably know what software is.)

For example, let's create a simple series:

```
s = Series([10, 15, 17, 20, 25])
```

(continued)

We can get all the descriptive statistics, including the five-number summary with
`s.describe()`:

```
count     5.00000
mean     17.40000
std       5.59464
min      10.00000
25%      15.00000
50%      17.00000
75%      20.00000
max      25.00000
dtype: float64
```

A boxplot shows us this five-figure summary, but in graphical form. We can create boxplots in pandas using `plot.box` on a series (for a single plot) or a data frame (for
one plot for each numeric column). We create a boxplot from `s` with

```
s.plot.box()
```

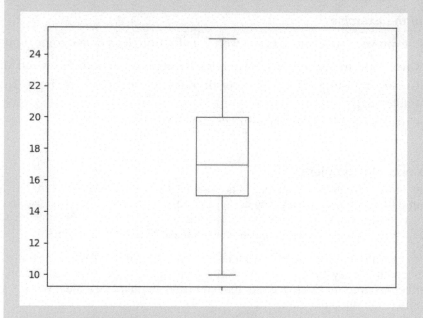

Boxplot from our series s

The central "box" in the boxplot has three parts:

- The top of the box indicates the 75% value.
- The middle line, often highlighted in a different color, indicates the median, the
  50% value.
- The bottom of the box indicates the 25% value.

Extending above and below the box are two lines, sometimes known as *whiskers*. The top whisker ends at the maximum value, and the bottom whisker ends at the minimum value. Thus, at a glance, we get a graphical depiction of the five-figure summary.

A boxplot often has circles above and below the whiskers. These represent the outliers, defined in the case of our boxplots to be 1.5 * IQR (interquartile range) below the first quartile (25% mark) or 1.5 * IQR above the third quartile (75% mark).

For example, here's another series:

```
s = Series([-20, 10, 15, 17, 20, 25, 40])
```

The descriptive statistics are as follows:

```
count     7.000000
mean     15.285714
std      18.273061
min     -20.000000
25%      12.500000
50%      17.000000
75%      22.500000
max      40.000000
dtype: float64
```

And the boxplot?

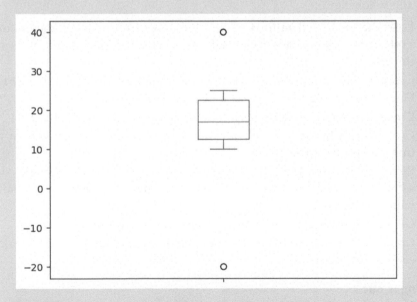

Boxplot from our series s with outliers

Boxplots allow us, at a glance, to better understand our data. They can be especially useful when it comes to comparing data sets; we can quickly see if they're on the

(continued)

same scale and whether (and where) they overlap. Plotting the different columns from a data frame can be particularly useful when creating machine-learning models, when having all the data in the same range increases the model's accuracy. Note that if you put all the columns in the same boxplot, they share a *y* axis, which is perfect for checking that they're in the same range. You can, however, have a separate *y* axis for each column if you pass `subplots=True` to your call:

```
df.plot.box(subplots=True)
```

Note that nowhere in the boxplot do we see the mean value. I personally think that's a shame, because the mean can also be a useful measure, imperfect though it may be.

EXERCISE 44 ■ Boxplotting weather

One of the phrases I often use when teaching data analytics is that you need to "know your data." And one of the best ways to know your data is with a boxplot. In this exercise, we use boxplots to understand the weather during the winter of 2018–2019, using data in three different US cities. We start with Chicago and then add Los Angeles and Boston to emphasize the differences between these locations (and to assure Chicago residents that yes, their winters really are that cold).

Do the following:

1 Load the weather data for Chicago. We only care about three columns: `date_time`, `min temp`, and `max temp`. Make `date_time` the index, and set the names of the min and max temp columns to `mintemp` and `maxtemp`.

2 Create a boxplot of Chicago's minimum temperatures during this period.

3 Find the values that are represented as dots on that boxplot.

4 Create a boxplot of Chicago's minimum temperatures in February.

5 Create a side-by-side boxplot of Chicago's minimum and maximum temperatures in February and March.

6 Read in data from Los Angeles and Boston, as well. Create a single data frame with data from all three cities, along with a new `city` column containing the name of the city.

7 Get descriptive statistics for `mintemp` and `maxtemp` grouped by city.

8 Create side-by-side boxplots showing minimum and maximum temperatures for each of the three cities.

Working it out

In this exercise, we combine techniques we've seen previously: specifically, using `read_csv` with a variety of parameters, combining several CSV files into a single data frame, and using a `datetime` column as an index. But the main point of this exercise is to create a number of different boxplots and, in so doing, better understand the shape and nature of our data.

First, I asked you to load Chicago weather into a data frame, using the `date_time` column as the index of type `datetime`. I also asked you to load the columns with the minimum and maximum temperatures found on each day. We do that using the following code:

```
filename = '../data/chicago,il.csv'
df = pd.read_csv(filename,
                 usecols=[0, 1,2],
                 header=0,
                 names=['date_time','mintemp', 'maxtemp'],
                 parse_dates=['date_time'],
                 index_col=['date_time'])
```

We've used each of these options to `read_csv` in the past, but here we use them all at once. For starters, we indicate that we're interested in only the first three columns. In previous exercises, we often referred to these columns by name, using the names provided by the index. But here, we refer to the columns by number. That's because we want to give them names of our own, specified in the `names` parameter. We thus choose them by number and rename them in `names`. We also indicate that `date_time` should be parsed as a `datetime` column and used as the index of the data frame. Finally, just to be on the safe side, we pass `header=0` to indicate that the first row of the file contains headers and thus shouldn't be treated as data.

At the conclusion of this process, we end up with a data frame with 728 rows and 2 columns. The values start at midnight on December 12, 2018, and end at 9:00 p.m. on March 11, 2019, with new measures taken every three hours.

I then asked you to create a boxplot for the minimum temperatures found in Chicago throughout the period in the data frame. We can do this by running the following code (figure 11.6):

```
df['mintemp'].plot.box()
```

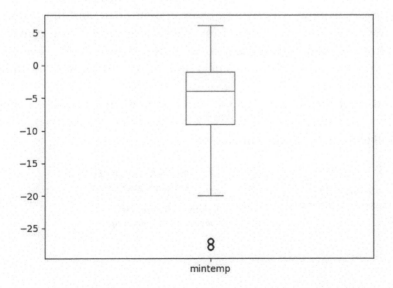

**Figure 11.6
Boxplot of minimum
temperatures in Chicago**

A boxplot is supposed to visualize the five-number summary: minimum, 0.25, median, 0.75, and maximum. The result shows us that most of the temperatures were between −20 and 5 degrees Celsius. However, we also see a number of circles at the bottom of the plot, indicating outlier values. In the pandas implementation of boxplots, outliers are defined as those at least 1.5 * IQR below the 0.25 mark or at least 1.5 * IQR above the 0.75 mark. Just to double check that the plot is showing them correctly, I asked you to find those values:

```
iqr = df['mintemp'].quantile(0.75) - df['mintemp'].quantile(0.25)

(
    df.loc[
        df['mintemp'] < df['mintemp'].mean() - (iqr_ 1.5),
        'mintemp'
        ]
)
```

Sure enough, we see a number of temperature readings (on January 30 and 31) when the temperature was −27 and −28 degrees Celsius—not only cold, but unusually cold, even for a Chicago winter. Our boxplot is thus right to show them as outliers.

Next, I asked you to create a boxplot for Chicago's minimum temperatures in February. We solve this as follows:

```
(
    df
    .loc[
        '01-Feb-2019':'28-Feb-2019',     ⟵┘ Row selector in
                                            February 2019
        'mintemp']    ⟵┐ Column selector
    .plot.box()          of mintemp
)
```

Our row selector is the slice from February 1 through February 28. Here we take advantage of the fact that our data frame's index contains date and time values and that we can always use a slice to retrieve rows. We choose the `mintemp` column and feed the resulting one-column data frame to `plot.box` (figure 11.17). The median temperature during February 2019 was −5 degrees Celsius, which does indeed sound right for a Chicago winter.

Next, I asked you to create boxplots for both minimum and maximum temperatures in February and March. We again use a slice to select the appropriate rows, stretching from February 1 through March 30:

```
(
    df
    .loc['01-Feb-2019':'30-Mar-2019',     ⟵┘ Row selector, all of
                                             February and March
        ['mintemp','maxtemp']]    ⟵┐ Column selector, both
    .plot.box()                      mintemp and maxtemp
)
```

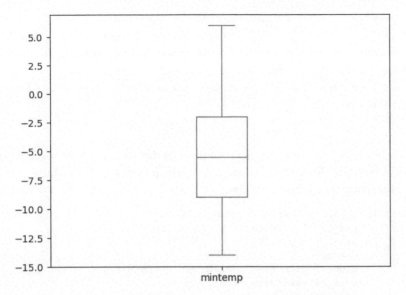

Figure 11.7 Boxplot for minimum Chicago temperatures in February

Once again, we select rows using a slice. But the column selector needs to be a list of strings: the names of the columns that we want to plot. We then pass these to `plot.box` and get two boxplots displayed on the same scale, next to one another (figure 11.8).

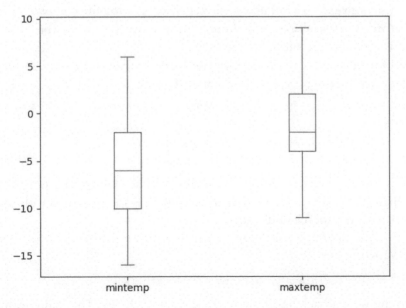

Figure 11.8 Boxplot for minimum and maximum Chicago temperatures in February and March

Having experienced, if only on paper, the cold Chicago winter, I thought it would be nice to add data from two other cities. I thus asked you to read data from Los Angeles and Boston as well, creating a single data frame from all three of the CSV files. To distinguish data from the various cities, I asked you to add a `city` column with the city's name as you read them in. Because `df` already contains information for Chicago, we set that value right away:

```
df['city'] = 'Chicago'
```

To load the other data, we use a `for` loop—typical in day-to-day Python programming, but unusual in pandas. Here, the loop runs not over a series or data frame but rather over a list of filenames containing city data:

```
for city_stem in ['los+angeles,ca', 'boston,ma']:
    new_df = pd.read_csv(f'../data/{city_stem}.csv',
                usecols=[0, 1,2],
                header=0,
                names=['date_time','maxtemp', 'mintemp'],
            parse_dates=['date_time'],
            index_col=['date_time'])
    new_df['city'] = city_stem.split(',')[0].replace('+', ' ').title()
    df = pd.concat([df, new_df])
```

Let's break down what we do here:

1   We set up a list with the filenames (minus the `'csv'` suffix) over which we want to run.

2   We use a `for` loop to iterate over those filenames.

3   We reuse the `read_csv` call that we used earlier, passing the complete filename.

4   As before, we select specific columns, indicating that `date_time` should be parsed as a `datetime` and set to the index.

5   We add a value to `city` for each of the loaded cities using a bunch of string methods to convert `city_stem` into a useful string:

   – We use `str.split` on `city_stem`, getting a list—from which we take the initial part.

   – We replace the character `'+'` with a space, `' '`.

   – We invoke `str.title`, capitalizing each word.

Finally, we use `pd.concat` to add the new data frame to the existing one. The end result is a single data frame with weather data from all three cities and with the `city` column indicating the source of the data.

With this data loaded, I asked you to get descriptive statistics for `mintemp` and `maxtemp`, grouped by city:

```
df.groupby('city')[['mintemp', 'maxtemp']].describe()
```

The data frame we get back has three rows, one for each city. The columns are in a multi-index, with all measurements for `mintemp` and then all measurements for maxtemp. But although these details may be interesting and useful, they're not as compelling as a boxplot. I thus asked you to create a boxplot showing minimum and maximum temperatures for all three cities, grouped together. We solve it as follows:

```
(
    df
    .plot.box(column=['mintemp', 'maxtemp'],
              by='city')
)
```

This produces two side-by-side boxplots, one for mintemp and the second for maxtemp. In each plot, we see the five-number summary for each city, side by side (figure 11.9). It isn't a surprise to find that although Boston's winter months are warmer than Chicago's, Los Angeles is far warmer than either of them.

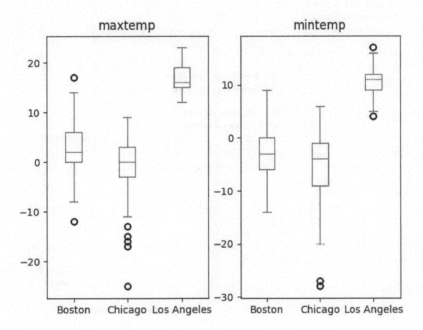

Figure 11.9 Boxplot for minimum and maximum temperatures in several cities

Solution

```
filename = '../data/chicago,il.csv'
df = pd.read_csv(filename,
                 usecols=[0, 1,2],          Loads only        Explicitly tells pandas
                 header=0,                  three columns     that the first line
                                                              contains header info
  Names the three
  columns we load →  names=['date_time','maxtemp', 'mintemp'],
                 parse_dates=['date_time'],       The date_time column should
    Sets date_time → index_col=['date_time'])     be parsed as a datetime.
    to be an index
```

```
df['mintemp'].plot.box()                                    ⟵──────────────────┐

iqr = df['mintemp'].quantile(0.75) - df['mintemp'].quantile(0.25)              │
                                                            Creates a boxplot of
(                                                           min temp in Chicago │
    df.loc[
        df['mintemp'] < df['mintemp'].mean() - (iqr * 1.5),
        'mintemp'
        ]
)         ⟵──┐ Finds the outliers, assuming
             │ 2.5*std above/below mean

(
    df
    .loc['01-Feb-2019':'28-Feb-2019',
    'mintemp']
    .plot.box()
)         ⟵──┐ Boxplot of February
             │ min temp in Chicago
(
    df
    .loc['01-Feb-2019':'30-Mar-2019',
        ['mintemp','maxtemp']]
    .plot.box()                  Boxplot of Feb–March
)               ⟵────────────┘   min+max temps in Chicago

                              New column, city, all
df['city'] = 'Chicago'   ⟵──┘ with 'Chicago' values

                                                     Loads additional
for city_stem in ['los+angeles,ca', 'boston,ma']:  ⟵─┘ cities
    new_df = pd.read_csv(f'../data/{city_stem}.csv',    ⟵──┐
                usecols=[0, 1,2],                          Loads the CSV for
                header=0,                                  each new city
                names=['date_time','mintemp', 'maxtemp'],
                parse_dates=['date_time'],
                index_col=['date_time'])
    new_df['city'] = city_stem.split(',')[0].replace('+', ' ').title()  ⟵──┐
    df = pd.concat([df, new_df])
                                                     Uses Python string
                                                     methods to set the
df.groupby('city')[['mintemp', 'maxtemp']].describe()  ⟵─  city name from
                                                     the filename
(                               Gets descriptive
    df                          statistics for
    .plot.box(column=['mintemp', 'maxtemp'],   temps by city
            by='city')
)         ⟵──┐ Boxplot of min and
             │ max temps by city
```

Adds the new data frame to the existing ones ⟵ (points to `df = pd.concat([df, new_df])`)

Beyond the exercise

- Rather than starting with data from Chicago, begin with an empty data frame and use a `for` loop to load data from all three cities.
- For each city, calculate the mean and median for `mintemp` and `maxtemp`. Are they the same (or even close)? If they're different, in which direction are they pulled?

- Create a line plot showing the minimum temperatures in each city. The *x* axis should show dates, the *y* axis should show temperatures, and each line should represent a different city.

EXERCISE 45 ■ Taxi fare breakdown

We've looked at New York City taxi fares a number of times in this book. This time, we're going to look at this data set visually, plotting the data from a variety of perspectives. It's hard to exaggerate not just how much of an effect a good plot can have when presenting it to others, but how much better it can help you understand the data set yourself. You'll see new relationships in the data and know how to answer questions you already asked as well as what new questions you should be asking.

I'd like you to do the following:

1 Load data from all four NYC taxi files into a single data frame. We need a bunch of different columns: `tpep_pickup_datetime`, `passenger_count`, `trip_distance`, `fare_amount`, `extra`, `mta_tax`, `tip_amount`, `tolls_amount`, `improvement_surcharge`, `total_amount`, and `congestion_surcharge`.

2 Create a bar plot showing how many rides took place during each month and year of our data set. (It's fine if there are "holes" in the bar plot.)

3 Create a bar plot showing the total amount paid in taxi rides for every year and month of the data set.

4 Create a bar plot showing `fare_amount`, `extra`, `mta_tax`, `tip_amount`, and `tolls_amount` paid in taxi rides per month and year, with the various components stacked in a single bar per year/month.

5 Create a bar plot showing `fare_amount`, `extra`, `mta_tax`, `tip_amount`, and `tolls_amount` paid in taxi rides per number of passengers, stacked in a single bar per number of passengers.

6 Create a histogram showing the frequency of each tipping percentage between (and including) 0% and 50%.

Working it out

This exercise is all about visualizing our taxi data. To make the data more interesting and varied, I asked you to load all four of the CSV files I've made available: from January 2019, July 2019, January 2020, and July 2020. We load them, as we've done before, most recently in exercise 42, via a list comprehension:

```
filenames = ['../data/nyc_taxi_2019-01.csv',
             '../data/nyc_taxi_2019-07.csv',
             '../data/nyc_taxi_2020-01.csv',
             '../data/nyc_taxi_2020-07.csv']

all_dfs = [pd.read_csv(one_filename,
           usecols=['tpep_pickup_datetime',
                    'passenger_count',
```

```
            'trip_distance',
            'fare_amount',
            'extra',
            'mta_tax',
            'tip_amount',
            'tolls_amount',
            'improvement_surcharge',
            'total_amount',
            'congestion_surcharge'],
    parse_dates=['tpep_pickup_datetime'])
for one_filename in filenames]
```

In this case, we pass `usecols` the list of columns I asked for in the question. We also pass `parse_dates` a single value, the column `tpep_pickup_datetime`. (In this exercise, I didn't see a need for us to have the dropoff datetime.) This create a list of data frames, which we can then concatenate into a single data frame using `pd.concat`:

```
df = pd.concat(all_dfs)
```

With our data frame in place, we can now begin to perform our analysis.

I first asked you to create a bar plot showing how many rides there were in each year and month of our data set. To do this, we run a `groupby`, grouping by two columns—first by year, and then by month:

```
(
    df
    .groupby([df['tpep_pickup_datetime'].dt.year,
              df['tpep_pickup_datetime'].dt.month])
)
```

This, of course, gives us a `groupby` object on which we can perform the query. For this part of the exercise, I asked you to find the total amount paid in each year-month period of our data set. We run the query as follows:

```
(
    df
    .groupby([df['tpep_pickup_datetime'].dt.year,
              df['tpep_pickup_datetime'].dt.month])
    ['total_amount'].sum()
)
```

This produces a numeric result, showing the total amount paid for each year-month combination of our data set. Given that we only loaded four files, each supposedly containing one month of data, it may seem strange that we have data from other months and years. Some of that data may not have been stored in New York's databases when it was first created. Or the computer wasn't set to the right date. Or the data may be corrupt. Likely it's a combination of these and other factors; even in a fully automated system, you shouldn't be surprised to have some bad data.

I then asked you to create a bar plot from this data:

```
(
    df
```

```
        .groupby([df['tpep_pickup_datetime'].dt.year,
                  df['tpep_pickup_datetime'].dt.month])
        ['total_amount'].sum()
        .plot.bar(figsize=(10,10))
)
```

The call to `plot.bar` creates the bar plot based on the data frame we get from the groupby (figure 11.10). That data frame's index serves as the plot's *x* axis and the values determine the *y* axis, which we allow to be generated automatically.

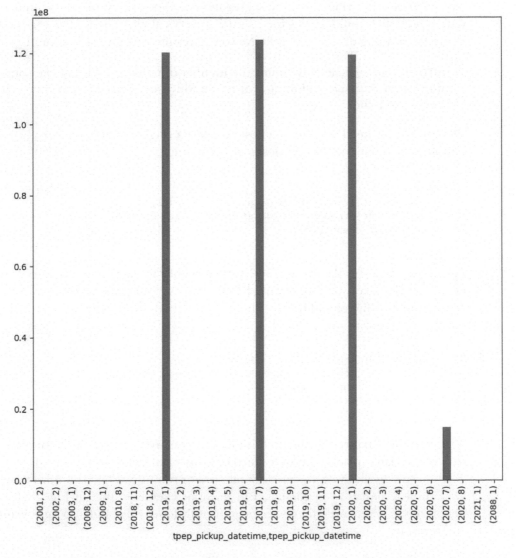

Figure 11.10   Bar plot showing how much money was paid to taxis in each month and year

Next, I asked you to create a bar plot showing, again for every year-month combination, the number of taxi rides per month. Once again, we start with a groupby query:

```
(
    df
    .groupby([df['tpep_pickup_datetime'].dt.year,
              df['tpep_pickup_datetime'].dt.month])
    ['passenger_count'].count()
    .plot.bar(figsize=(10,10))
)
```

Here, we're not interested in totaling the receipts but rather in counting the rows. Although we could run count, the aggregation method that counts rows, on the entire data frame, that would give us the count for every column. (So if a data frame has 10 columns, running df.count() will give you 10 results, one for each column.)

> **NOTE** Because count only counts the number of non-NaN values, it can sometimes come in handy, allowing you to see which columns contain more (or fewer) NaN values.

We don't really need that. So we chose to select a single column, passenger_count—although we really could have chosen any of them:

```
(
    df
    .groupby([df['tpep_pickup_datetime'].dt.year,
              df['tpep_pickup_datetime'].dt.month])
    ['passenger_count'].count()
)
```

Finally, we take this data frame and turned it into a bar plot. As before, we called plot.bar with a keyword argument of figsize=(10, 10), ensuring that the image is a 10-inch square (figure 11.11):

```
(
    df
    .groupby([df['tpep_pickup_datetime'].dt.year,
              df['tpep_pickup_datetime'].dt.month])
    ['passenger_count'].count()
    .plot.bar(figsize=(10,10))
)
```

Although the *x* axis is the same in this plot and the previous one, and although we see bars in the same places, the values are obviously different. Moreover, although July 2019 was the month with the greatest amount of revenue, it had the third-most rides. We can also see (as we've discussed in previous exercises) that in July 2020—at the height of the pandemic—there were significantly fewer rides and also significantly less taxi revenue.

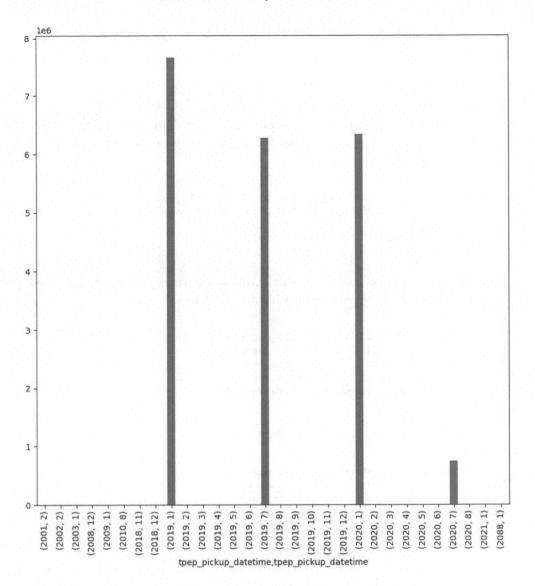

Figure 11.11   Bar plot showing how many taxi rides occurred per month and year

We've generally talked about the `total_amount` column when it comes to taxi revenue. But `total_amount` is the final dollar figure that a taxi passenger has to pay at the end of the ride. Although passengers don't often think about this, that fare can be broken down into a number of different pieces. In this question, I asked you to plot the amount of revenue each month in the data set and to break that bar down into segments, thus allowing us to see how much of each month's revenue came from each source.

Once again, we use `groupby` on the year and month columns:

```
(
    df.groupby([df['tpep_pickup_datetime'].dt.year,
                df['tpep_pickup_datetime'].dt.month])
)
```

Because we want to produce the plot with input from five columns—`fare_amount`, `extra`, `mta_tax`, `tip_amount`, and `tolls_amount`—we name them in a list of column names after the `groupby`:

```
(
    df.groupby([df['tpep_pickup_datetime'].dt.year,
                df['tpep_pickup_datetime'].dt.month])
    [['fare_amount','extra','mta_tax',
      'tip_amount','tolls_amount']]
)
```

We then run the `sum` method, which gives us a separate sum for each of these five columns in each of the months for which we have data:

```
(
    df.groupby([df['tpep_pickup_datetime'].dt.year,
                df['tpep_pickup_datetime'].dt.month])
    [['fare_amount','extra','mta_tax',
      'tip_amount','tolls_amount']].sum()
    .plot.bar(stacked=True, figsize=(10,10))
)
```

Finally, we ask pandas to create a bar plot:

```
(
    df.groupby([df['tpep_pickup_datetime'].dt.year,
                df['tpep_pickup_datetime'].dt.month])
    [['fare_amount','extra','mta_tax',
      'tip_amount','tolls_amount']].sum()
    .plot.bar(stacked=True, figsize=(10,10))
)
```

However, there's a difference between our previous calls to `plot.bar` and this one: normally we would get a separate plot for each column for each month. But because we specified `stacked=True`, we get all the bars for a given month stacked on top of one another. Moreover, each portion of the bar is in a different color, and pandas provides a legend, as well. In this way, we can see visually not just how much revenue taxis brought in each month but also how much of that revenue came from the fare itself, as opposed to taxes, tips, and tolls (figure 11.12). We can see that although the fare is by far the greatest proportion of the total taxi revenue, tips constitute a fairly large proportion, followed by `extra` charges, taxes, and tolls.

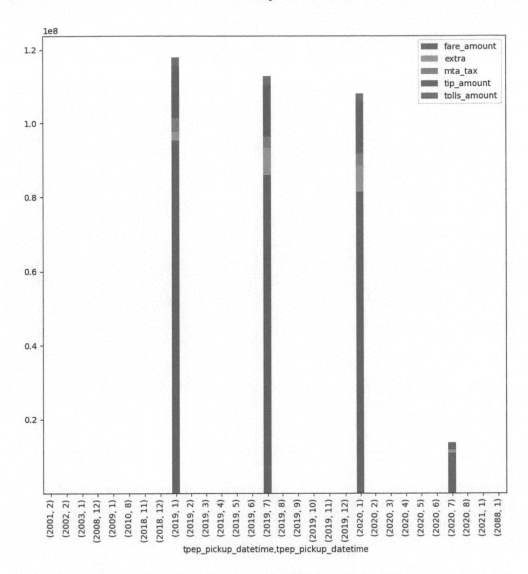

Figure 11.12   Stacked bar plot showing the relative components that go into the total fare per year and month

Next, I asked for a similar stacked bar plot with the same five columns as components in each bar. However, rather than grouping by the year and month, I asked you to group by the `passenger_count` column. We can do that with a query similar to the previous one, grouping on `passenger_count` rather than by year-month combination (figure 11.13):

```
(
    df
```

```
    .groupby(df['passenger_count'])
    [['fare_amount','extra','mta_tax',
      'tip_amount','tolls_amount']].sum()
    .plot.bar(stacked=True, figsize=(10,10))
)
```

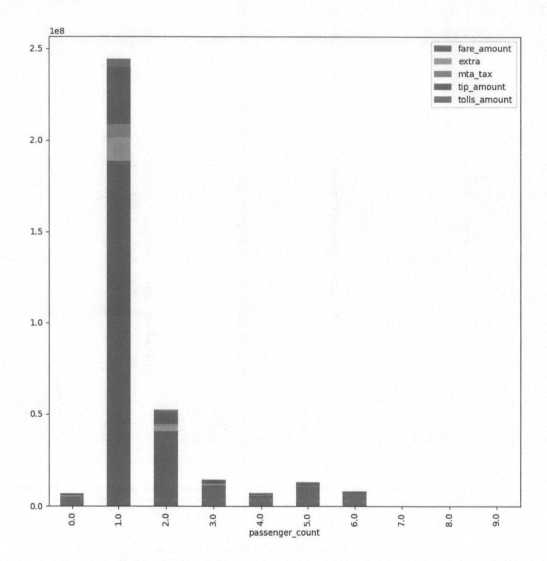

Figure 11.13   Stacked bar plot showing the relative components that go into the total fare per number of passengers

Finally, I asked you to create a histogram showing the frequency of each tipping percentage between (and including) 0 and 50. To do this, we need to find the tipping percentage for each ride and keep only those between 0 and 50. The easiest thing would be to create a new column, `tip_percentage`, by dividing `tip_amount` by `fare_amount`. But the real world includes all sorts of surprises, including `NaN` values and records in which the `fare_amount` is equal to zero—thus giving us an infinite (known as `np.inf`) value. To avoid this, we first get rid of any ride in which the fare was less than or equal to 0:

```
df = df[df['fare_amount'] > 0]
```

Then we create a new column, `tip_percentage`, knowing we won't get any `np.inf` values:

```
df['tip_percentage'] = df['tip_amount'] / df['fare_amount']
```

Finally, we plot all the values less than or equal to 50%:

```
(
    df
    .loc[
        df['tip_percentage'] <= .50,      ←── Row selector
        'tip_percentage']   ←── Column selector
    .plot.hist()
)
```

The resulting histogram has a huge bar—the largest—for 0% tips, indicating that a plurality of New York taxi riders don't tip at all. But other than that bar, we see a fairly normal distribution, centered around 20% or 25% (figure 11.14).

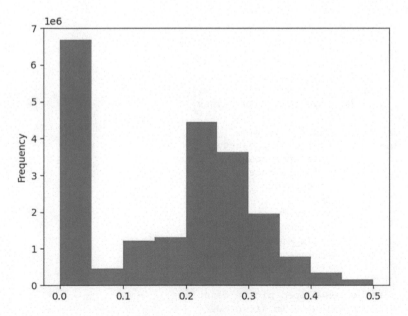

Figure 11.14 Histogram showing, across all rides, what nonzero percentage New York riders tip

We can create this histogram another way, using method chaining along with `.loc`, `assign`, and `lambda`:

```
(
    df
    .loc[lambda df_: df_['fare_amount'] > 0]
    .assign(tip_percentage =
            lambda df_: df_['tip_amount'] / df_['fare_amount'])
    .loc[lambda df_: df_['tip_percentage'] <= 0.5,
        'tip_percentage']
    .plot.hist()
)
```

It's easiest to understand this code if you read it one line at a time:

1. We use `.loc` to find all rows of `df` where `fare_amount` is more than 0. We use a `lambda` here, along with a temporary variable of `df_`, which is typical when chaining methods because it ensures that we're working with the data frame we get rather than the original `df`.
2. We use `assign` to create a new column, `tip_percentage`. Its value is the result of running a function, defined with `lambda`, that takes each row and divides `tip_amount` by `fare_amount`. The column created by `assign` isn't actually added to `df`; it's only on the data frame we're building via method chaining.
3. We again use `.loc` to keep only those rows where `tip_percentage` is less than 0.5. But here we use the two-argument value of `.loc`, filtering rows via the `lambda` and columns by explicitly naming the one we want: `tip_percentage`.
4. We call `plot.hist` and get a histogram.

Solution

```
filenames = ['../data/nyc_taxi_2019-01.csv',
             '../data/nyc_taxi_2019-07.csv',
             '../data/nyc_taxi_2020-01.csv',
             '../data/nyc_taxi_2020-07.csv']

all_dfs = [pd.read_csv(one_filename,
           usecols=['tpep_pickup_datetime',
                    'passenger_count',
                    'trip_distance',
                    'fare_amount',
                    'extra',
                    'mta_tax',
                    'tip_amount',
                    'tolls_amount',
                    'improvement_surcharge',
                    'total_amount',
                    'congestion_surcharge'],
           parse_dates=['tpep_pickup_datetime'])
           for one_filename in filenames]

df = pd.concat(all_dfs)
```

```
(
    df
    .groupby([df['tpep_pickup_datetime'].dt.year,
             df['tpep_pickup_datetime'].dt.month])
    ['total_amount'].sum()
    .plot.bar(figsize=(10,10))
)

(
    df
    .groupby([df['tpep_pickup_datetime'].dt.year,
             df['tpep_pickup_datetime'].dt.month])
    ['passenger_count'].count()
    .plot.bar(figsize=(10,10))
)

(
    df.groupby([df['tpep_pickup_datetime'].dt.year,
               df['tpep_pickup_datetime'].dt.month])
    [['fare_amount','extra','mta_tax','tip_amount','tolls_amount']].sum()
    .plot.bar(stacked=True, figsize=(10,10))
)

(
    df
    .groupby(df['passenger_count'])
    [['fare_amount','extra','mta_tax',
      'tip_amount','tolls_amount']].sum()
    .plot.bar(stacked=True, figsize=(10,10))
)

df = df[df['fare_amount'] > 0]
df['tip_percentage'] = df['tip_amount'] / df['fare_amount']

df.loc[df['tip_percentage'] <= .50,
    'tip_percentage'].plot.hist()

(
    df
    .loc[lambda df_: df_['fare_amount'] > 0]
    .assign(tip_percentage = lambda df_: df_['tip_amount'] / df_['fare_amount
      '])
    .loc[lambda df_: df_['tip_percentage'] <= 0.5,
        'tip_percentage']
    .plot.hist()
)
```

Beyond the exercise

- Create a bar plot showing the average distance traveled per day of the week in July 2020. The *x* axis should show the name of each day.
- Create a scatter plot with the taxi data from July 2020, comparing trip_distance with total_amount. Ignore all rides in which either value was less than or equal to 0 or greater than 500.

- Create a scatter plot with the taxi data from July 2020, comparing `trip_distance` with `passenger_count`. Ignore all rides in which `trip_distance` was less than or equal to 0 or greater than 500.

Correlation isn't causation. But what is it?

No matter where you are in your data-analysis career, you're bound to hear someone say "correlation isn't causation." What does that mean? Moreover, what *is* correlation?

Loosely speaking, two measurements are correlated when movement in one is generally accompanied by movement in another. If the measurements rise and fall together, they're considered positively correlated. If one goes up when the other goes down (and vice versa), they're said to be negatively correlated.

In addition to being positive or negative, correlation can be weak or strong. There's probably a strong correlation between your annual income and the size of your house. There's probably a weak correlation between your annual income and your shoe size. (Although to be fair, higher income correlates with better nutrition and better health, so the correlation may be stronger than you'd expect.)

Let's take a simple example. The more electric power you use, the higher your electric bill. If you use more electricity, your bill goes up. If you use less electricity, your bill goes down. We can thus say that your electric consumption and your electric bill are positively correlated.

Here's another example: the wealthier you are, the more likely you are to own a private jet. If you're a multibillionaire, you probably have a jet or several. (At least, that's what I've learned from watching *Succession*.) So we can say that as your income goes up, the number of private jets you own goes up. And as your income goes down, the number of private jets you can afford to keep on hand will probably go down, as well.

It's very tempting, when we see data that is correlated, to say that one thing causes another. And in some cases, that's certainly true: we can safely say that your higher electric bill is caused by greater consumption.

But just because two data points are correlated doesn't mean one causes the other. And even if one does, you have to be careful to determine just what causes what. For example, if there is a causal relationship between private-jet ownership and billionaire status, perhaps I should buy a private jet. That'll raise the likelihood of my becoming a billionaire, right?

There are numerous examples of correlations without causation. For some terrific examples, check out the Spurious Correlations website by Tyler Vigen: https//tylervigen.com/spurious-correlations.

This difference between correlation and causation was most famously used by the tobacco industry. True, they said, people who smoke cigarettes are more likely to have cancer. But just because there's a correlation doesn't mean it's a causal effect. Can we really know whether cigarettes cause cancer? After many studies and many years, it became clear that the answer is "yes": we can know, and the effect is causal.

Finding a causal relationship is hard and generally requires doing an experiment. You divide the population into two parts, giving one half the treatment and the other half no treatment (or a placebo). Then you measure the difference in effects on the two populations.

Fortunately, in the world of data analytics, we're often less interested in causation than in finding correlations. If I find that my online store gets more sales between 12:00 noon and 1:00 p.m., I don't really care what's causing it—but I do want to know about it and take advantage of it.

This raises the question, though: What exactly does it mean for two sets of numeric values to be correlated? Let's take two sets of numbers, the high and low temperatures for the city of Modi'in over the coming week:

```
df = DataFrame(
        {'high':[19,21,24,17,14,16,16,19,16,16,15,16,18,18],
         'low':[12,9,11,12,11,11,10,8,10,8,8,6,6,7]})
```

What would correlation mean?

- If the columns are positively correlated, days with the highest high temperatures will also have the highest low temperatures. And days with the lowest high temperatures will have the lowest low temperatures.
- If the columns are negatively correlated, days with the highest high temperatures will have the lowest low temperatures. And days with the lowest high temperatures will have the highest low temperatures.

If the two are strongly correlated, a large change in one is accompanied by a large change in the other. If they're weakly correlated, a large change in one will be accompanied by a small change in the other.

The most common measurement for correlation, and what we use in this book, is called *Pearson's correlation coefficient* and is often abbreviated as *r*. It's a number between –1 (indicating the strongest possible negative correlation) and 1 (indicating the strongest possible positive correlation), with 0 indicating no correlation. A correlation is always calculated between two data sets, which in the case of pandas means two different columns.

We can find the correlation for the expected high and low temperatures with the `corr` method:

```
df.corr()
```

The result is a data frame in which each of our original column names appears both as a column and a row. Along the diagonal, where columns meet themselves, there will always be a value of 1.0, indicating (not very usefully) that a column has a perfect positive correlation with itself. More interesting is the intersection between different column names, showing the correlation between each of those pairs of columns. In this case, our data frame only has two columns, so the result is underwhelming:

```
        high        low
high    1.000000    0.105603
low     0.105603    1.000000
```

(continued)

We see that there is a correlation of 0.105603 between our high and low tempera-tures, meaning there's a positive correlation between the two, but a very weak one. With more data over a longer period of time, we would probably find a higher correla-tion. In fact, we can do that by loading the weather data for New York City, with 728 weather measurements:

```
filename = '../data/new+york,ny.csv'

df = pd.read_csv(filename, usecols=[1, 2],
                 header=0,
                 names=['high', 'low'])
```

If we run `df.corr()` on this data frame, we see a different type of result:

```
high      low
high  1.000000  0.874205
low   0.874205  1.000000
```

This is a very strong positive correlation. It raises the question, how can it be that in one data set the correlation is very strong, whereas in another one it's very weak?

There are numerous possible answers. Perhaps Modi'in's temperatures are harder to predict. Perhaps the data we input was from a particularly turbulent time with a high degree of variability. But I think the real reason is that the sample from Modi'in is extremely small, with only 13 data points. It's hard to establish any correlations based on such a small sample.

Why are we interested in correlation? First and foremost, because it can inform our understanding and thus our behavior. If I know that my store gets a huge number of requests at lunchtime each day, perhaps I'll provision additional servers during that time. Or perhaps I'll offer discounts outside of that window to encourage sales during otherwise dead times.

We can also use correlations to hint at underlying similarities and relationships in our data. If two things are correlated, perhaps there's some behavior that explains the connection between the two. If that behavior or relationship isn't obvious, it can point to a topic worth investigating or understanding better.

Although correlations are normally measured mathematically, it's often possible to see correlations via a scatter plot. In such a plot, we choose one column as the *x* axis and a second column as the *y* axis. We then plot each of the points. We cannot expect to see a perfect diagonal line, but such a line starting at (0,0) and moving up and to the right points to a strong positive correlation in the columns. One that starts high up on the *y* axis and moves down to the right indicates a strong negative correla-tion. Using a scatter plot is a great way to better understand the data. In pandas, we can create such a plot based on a data frame with the `plot.scatter` method:

```
df.plot.scatter(x='high', y='low')
```

In this case, we see a strong positive correlation matching the numeric calculations we performed earlier.

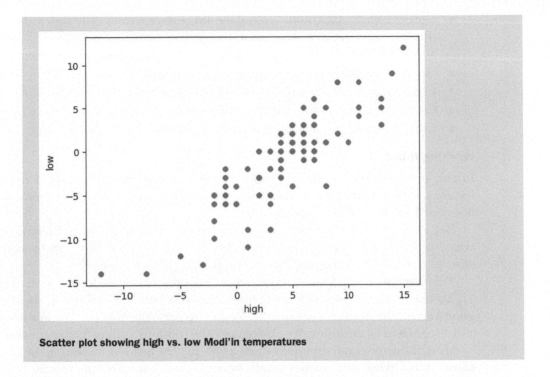

Scatter plot showing high vs. low Modi'in temperatures

EXERCISE 46 ▪ Cars, oil, and ice cream

In this exercise, we'll try to answer a question that has probably occurred to you on many occasions: when the price of oil goes up, do people drive their cars more or less? And while we're at it, we'll also attempt to answer another question: whether the price of ice cream is correlated with the price of oil.

This exercise will not only try to identify these correlations but also use many of the techniques we've discussed in the book so far, including parsing dates, selecting appropriate rows and columns, removing bad data, and joining data frames. Specifically, I want you to

1. Load the oil data (wti-daily.csv, as in exercise 41) into a data frame. Set the names of the columns to `date` and `oil`, with the `date` column parsed as a date and set to be the index.

2. Load historical ice cream prices in the United States (for a half gallon, aka 1.9 liters) into a separate data frame from the file `ice-cream.csv`. Set the column names to be `date` and `icecream`. The `date` column should be parsed as a date and set to be the index.

3. Set the `icecream` column to be a floating-point value, removing any rows that stop you from accomplishing that.

4. Load historical US "miles traveled per month" data (from the file miles-traveled .csv) into a separate data frame. Name the columns `date` and `miles`, parsing `date` as a date and setting it to be the index.

5 Create a single data frame from these three data frames. The index should be the date, and the new data frame should have three columns: oil, icecream, and miles. Only dates that are common to all three should be included.

6 Get the numeric correlations among the columns.

7 Create a scatter plot looking at the relationship between oil and icecream.

8 Create a scatter plot looking at the relationship between oil and miles.

9 Create a scatter matrix among all three columns.

Working it out

In this exercise, we take three distinct data sets, merge them to make a new data frame, and then find correlations among the various columns. And the results are . . . not what I was expecting, to say the least.

Before we can calculate the correlations, we have to load the data. I always like to create separate data frames and join them. This lets us do things step by step and ensures that we can debug, improve, and rerun our steps more easily.

The first data frame I asked you to create is similar to one we looked at in exercise 41. To make our join operation run more smoothly later, I asked you to standardize some parts of the naming. For example, we want to parse the date column as a datetime and also set it to be the index. We also rename the columns, calling them date and oil.

Most of the time, and especially when a CSV file has headers indicating the column names, I like to use those names in calls to read_csv. That makes the function call easier to read and debug. But when we want to rename the columns with the names parameter, we need to describe them numerically. Moreover, to avoid having the header row read as data, we need to indicate which row contains the header (0, in this case), effectively causing it to be ignored.

In the end, we load the oil data as follows:

```
oil_filename = '../data/wti-daily.csv'
oil_df = pd.read_csv(oil_filename,
                     parse_dates=[0],
                     header=0,
                     index_col=0,
                     names=['date', 'oil'])
```

A brief check (with oil_df.head() and oil_df.dtypes) shows that we successfully created the data frame with the correct dtype. With the oil data in hand, it's time to create the next data frame based on the monthly ice cream price data from the US government.

This file is in a format very similar to the oil data, in a CSV file containing two columns. The first column is a date—the final date of each month, when the ice cream pricing data is recorded. We can thus load it with our usual combination of keyword arguments:

```
ice_cream_filename = '../data/ice-cream.csv'
ice_cream_df = pd.read_csv(ice_cream_filename,
                           parse_dates=[0],
                           index_col=0,
                           header=0,
                           names=['date','icecream'])
```

However, running `ice_cream_df.dtypes` shows that the `icecream` column didn't load as a floating-point value. Rather, it loaded as `object`. That's usually a good sign that one or more values tripped up the system that pandas uses to identify and assign dtypes on CSV files. We can see where the problem is by trying to turn the column into an `np.float64` value:

```
ice_cream_df['icecream'].astype(np.float64)
```

Sure enough, it fails, telling us that it choked on a line containing nothing more than . instead of a price.

We decide to keep only those lines of `ice_cream_df` that contain at least one digit, on the assumption that such values can be turned into a floating-point value. First, we create a boolean series based on `ice_cream_df['icecream']` with `True` wherever the value contains at least one digit. We do this using `str.contains` along with a regular expression, making sure to pass `regex=True`. We then convert the resulting value to `np.float64` using `astype`:

```
ice_cream_df = (
    ice_cream_df
    .loc[ice_cream_df['icecream'].str.contains(r'\d', regex=True)]
    .astype(np.float64)
)
```

Notice that we use a raw string (i.e., a string with an r before the opening quote). Raw strings are Python's way of automatically doubling backslashes, thus ensuring that Python doesn't predigest our backslashes before they get to the regular expression engine.

Next, I asked you to create a data frame containing the US government's report on total miles traveled during each calendar month. My naive assumption was that when oil prices are high, people will drive less, but that when they're low, they'll drive more. We create the new data frame using arguments similar to those we've already seen:

```
miles_filename = '../data/miles-traveled.csv'
miles_df = pd.read_csv(miles_filename,
                       parse_dates=[0],
                       index_col=0,
                       header=0,
                       names=['date', 'miles'])
```

With these three data frames in place, it's time to join them. We've already seen how we can join two data frames using the `join` method. But here I asked you to join three data frames. How can we do that?

The answer, once you see it, is straightforward: we join two data frames, getting a new one. We join this new data frame with the third to get a final new one. As long as all the data frames share an index, we should be fine:

```
df = oil_df.join(ice_cream_df).join(miles_df)
```

If we do things this way, we discover a hitch: oil price data was recorded once per day, as opposed to the ice cream and travel data, which were recorded once per month. Joining our data frames this way will result in a new row for each index value in `oil_df` and NaN values in all but one row per month.

There are a few ways to solve this problem. One is to perform the join as we did previously and use `dropna` to remove all NaN-containing rows:

```
df = oil_df.join(ice_cream_df).join(miles_df).dropna()
```

A second method would be to perform the join on `ice_cream_df`, thus constraining the index values:

```
df = ice_cream_df.join(oil_df).join(miles_df)
```

But my preferred solution is to use an inner join, meaning our index will only contain values that existed in all three data frames. We can do this by passing the keyword argument `how='inner'` to each call to `join`:

```
df = (
    oil_df
    .join(ice_cream_df, how='inner')
    .join(miles_df, how='inner')
)
```

The result is a data frame whose index contains 275 distinct values, from April 1986 through December 2021. With all these values in place, we can (finally) start to look for correlations in our data. First, we can run `corr` on our data frame to find the correlations across all columns:

```
df.corr()
```

The resulting data frame has three columns (`oil`, `icecream`, and `miles`) and identical rows. The intersection of the column names gives us the correlation, ranging from –1 to 1. We can see that oil prices and the number of miles traveled per month are positively correlated, with a value of 0.64. The correlation between gas prices and ice cream prices is not only positive but much larger, at 0.77.

But the biggest correlation of all is between the price of ice cream and the number of miles driven per month, with a value of 0.818. That's a large correlation factor, indicating that whenever ice cream prices decline, people drive less and vice versa.

Can we realistically say that there is a causal relationship here? I highly doubt it; I don't think you are likely to drive more because you ate more ice cream or that you eat more ice cream because you drove more. A more likely explanation, at least to me, is that people both drive more and eat more ice cream in the summer months and that both prices rise when there's more demand. I haven't done any serious analysis to see if this is the case, but it seems more likely than either random chance or a causal effect.

Next, I asked you to produce two scatter plots. The first is between `oil` and `ice-cream` (figure 11.15):

```
df.plot.scatter(x='oil', y='icecream')
```

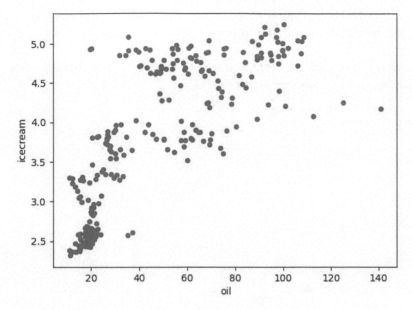

Figure 11.15 Scatter plot comparing oil prices and ice cream consumption

The second scatter plot I asked you to make is between `oil` and `miles` (figure 11.16):

```
df.plot.scatter(x='oil', y='miles')
```

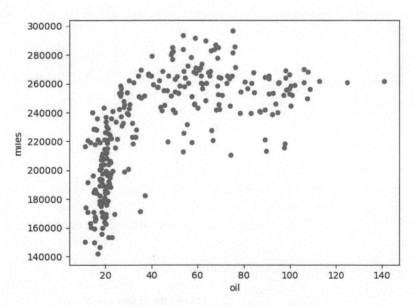

Figure 11.16 Scatter plot comparing oil prices and miles driven

Although you may be able to identify from these scatter plots whether there is a positive correlation here, I think the output from `corr()` gives a much clearer indication of the strength of that correlation.

Finally, I asked you to create a single scatter matrix plot, showing all numeric columns plotting against one another (figure 11.17):

```
from pandas.plotting import scatter_matrix
scatter_matrix(df)
```

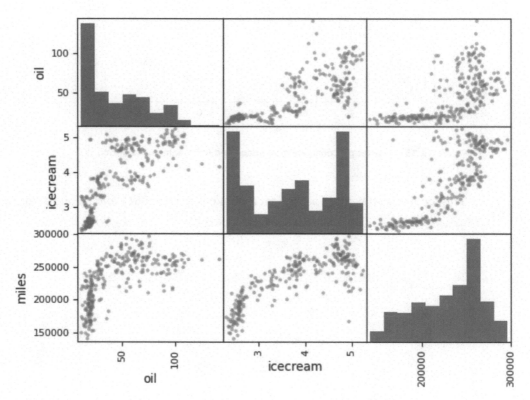

Figure 11.17   Scatter matrix

The scatter matrix is a great way to get a quick look at all the correlations in a data set. The diagonal, which always contains 1.00 values in the call to `df.corr()`, is a histogram in the scatter matrix, indicating the distribution of values in each column.

Solution

```
oil_filename = '../data/wti-daily.csv'
oil_df = pd.read_csv(oil_filename,
                     parse_dates=[0],
                     header=0,        ◁──┐ Ignores the header row because
                                           we are naming the columns
```

```
                    ┌──▷   index_col=0,
Sets the index      │         names=['date', 'oil'])  ◁──────┐ Names the two
based on column 0   │                                          │ columns in the file
ice_cream_filename = '../data/ice-cream.csv'
ice_cream_df = pd.read_csv(ice_cream_filename,
                           parse_dates=[0],
                           index_col=0,
                           header=0,
                           names=['date','icecream'])


ice_cream_df = (
    ice_cream_df
    .loc[ice_cream_df['icecream']                    ┌── Uses a regular expression to exclude
        .str.contains(r'\d', regex=True)]  ◁─────────┘   rows lacking even one digit
    .astype(np.float64)          ◁───┐ Sets the dtype
)                                    └─ to be np.float64

miles_filename = '../data/miles-traveled.csv'
miles_df = pd.read_csv(miles_filename,
                       parse_dates=[0],
                       index_col=0,
                       header=0,
                       names=['date', 'miles'])


df = (
    oil_df
    .join(ice_cream_df, how='inner')        ┌── Performs two inner joins, creating a
    .join(miles_df, how='inner')  ◁─────────┘   single data frame with three columns
)
                       ┌── Gets a correlation matrix
df.corr()  ◁───────────┘   comparing all columns

                                             ┌── Creates a scatter plot
df.plot.scatter(x='oil', y='icecream')  ◁────┘   of oil vs. ice cream
df.plot.scatter(x='oil', y='miles')

from pandas.plotting import scatter_matrix   ┌── Creates scatter plots of
scatter_matrix(df)  ◁────────────────────────┘   all possible combinations
```

Beyond the exercise

- Is the month correlated with any of these three values?
- Create a scatter plot of `icecream` versus `miles`.
- Instead of using an inner join, you could remove all rows from `oil_df` that weren't on the final day of the month. How could you do that?

Seaborn

Matplotlib is without a doubt the leading plotting system for Python. Many people find it hard to learn and use, however, which has led to the creation of several alternatives. One of the best-known, Seaborn (http://seaborn.pydata.org), was written by data scientist Michael Waskom and acts as an API on top of Matplotlib.

(continued)

So far, this book has focused on the pandas plotting API, which (like Seaborn) uses Matplotlib to produce its plots. The pandas API tries to simplify things, papering over much of the configuration that needs to happen to create a plot but otherwise keeping Matplotlib's approach and API intact. By contrast, Seaborn rethinks how plotting should be done, replacing the original Matplotlib and pandas calls with a distinct set of functions and parameters.

Just as we typically `import numpy as np` and `import pandas as pd`, we also import Seaborn with an alias:

```
import seaborn as sns
```

Whereas pandas visualization is done via the `plot` attribute followed by the type of plot we want to create, Seaborn is organized more conceptually around the different types of insights we may be trying to draw from our plots. We can choose from four functions defined within `sns`:

- To visualize relationships among numeric columns, use `sns.relplot`.
- To visualize relationships that include categorical columns, use `sns.catplot`.
- To understand the distribution of data, use `sns.displot`.
- To visualize regression models, use `sns.regplot`.

To explore this more fully, let's load the temperature and precipitation data from our weather CSV files:

```
import glob

all_dfs = []

all_filenames = glob.glob('../data/*,*.csv')


for one_filename in all_filenames:
    print(f'Loading {one_filename}...')
    city, state = one_filename.removeprefix('../data/').
        removesuffix('.csv').split(',')
    one_df = pd.read_csv(one_filename,
                    usecols=[1, 2, 19],
                    names=['max_temp', 'min_temp', 'precipMM'],
                    header=0)
    one_df['city'] = city.replace('+', ' ').title()
    one_df['state'] = state.upper()
    all_dfs.append(one_df)

df = pd.concat(all_dfs)
```

We've already seen how line and scatter plots can give us insights into the relationship between two numeric columns. Seaborn puts both of them in its `relplot` function. Let's first look at how we can create a scatter plot for min versus max temperatures in Chicago:

```
sns.relplot(x='max_temp',
            y='min_temp',
            data=df.loc[df['city'] == 'Chicago'])
```

Our call to `sns.relplot` includes three mandatory keyword arguments:

- `x` indicates which column from our data frame is used for the *x* axis.
- `y` indicates which column from our data frame is used for the *y* axis.
- `data` is a data frame containing both of those columns.

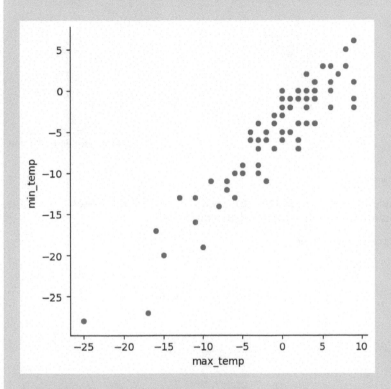

Scatter plot with Chicago weather

In this case, we provide only a subset of the data from `df` so we only see Chicago weather. But what if we want to see all the data from all the cities?

```
sns.relplot(x='max_temp',
            y='min_temp',
            data=df)
```

The good news is that this is much easier to write. But the bad news is that it's not nearly as useful. We've mixed all the weather reports from all the cities! Fortunately, Seaborn provides a number of different ways to make the data more useful and interesting.

(continued)

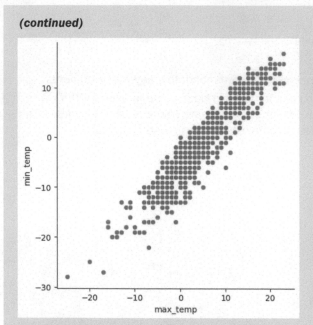

Scatter plot with all cities

For example, we can ask Seaborn to use a different color for each city by passing a column name to the `hue` keyword argument:

```
sns.relplot(x='max_temp',
            y='min_temp',
            data=df,
            hue='city')
```

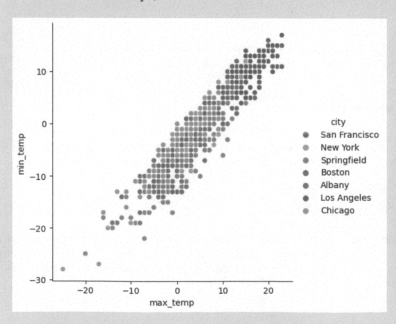

Scatter plot with all cities, with a different hue per city

We can have each city's dots use a different marker, as well, by giving the same `city` argument to the `style` parameter:

```
sns.relplot(x='max_temp',
            y='min_temp',
            data=df,
            hue='city', style='city')
```

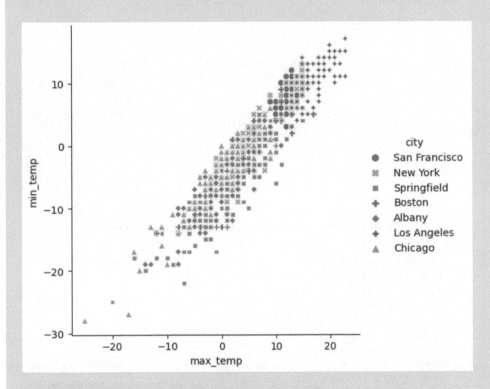

Scatter plot with all cities, with a different hue and marker per city

We don't have to use the same categorical data for `hue` and `style`. For example, we can set the `hue` per state:

```
sns.relplot(x='max_temp',
            y='min_temp',
            data=df,
            hue='state', style='city')
```

(continued)

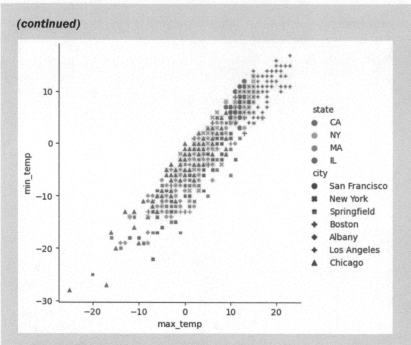

Scatter plot with all cities, with a different hue per state and marker per city

However, it's messy to see all these plots on the same axes. We can ask Seaborn to do the visual equivalent of a `groupby`, with one plot per value of `city`. There are two different ways to do this, actually, by setting `row` (i.e., each row is a different value for the named column) or `col` (i.e., each column is a different value for the named column). For example:

```
sns.relplot(x='max_temp',
            y='min_temp',
            data=df,
            hue='state',
            row='city')
```

Although scatter plots are extremely useful, we can also see the relationship between two numeric columns with line plots. The most obvious difference between the two kinds of plots is that Seaborn draws a line between the dots. For example:

Put each city on a different row.

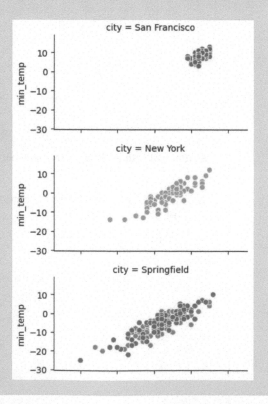

```
sns.relplot(x='max_temp',
            y='min_temp',
            data=df,
            hue='state', kind='line')
```

This call is fine, *except* it won't work. In my case, I got both a warning from pandas and an error message from Seaborn. Both of them told me they could not handle my data frame as it stood, because its index contained nonunique values.

We can fix this easily with `reset_index`:

```
df = df.reset_index(drop=True)
```

Note that we pass `drop=True` to avoid having the old index added as a column to the data frame. We're happy to throw out the old index and replace it with a new one, so we pass `drop=True`.

With a new index in place, we can again ask Seaborn to create our line plot:

```
sns.relplot(x='max_temp',
            y='min_temp',
            data=df,
            hue='state', kind='line')
```

The good news is that we see all the values, and thanks to our value for `hue`, we have a different-colored line for each state. The bad news is that two of the cities in our data set are from the same state. And besides, it's hard to read this plot, with all the data squashed.

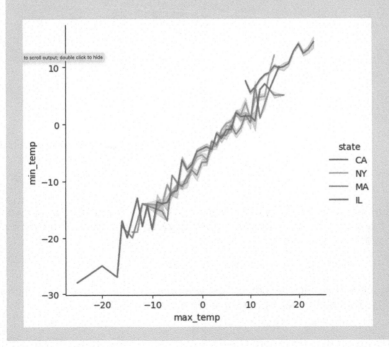

Line plot with temperatures per city

(continued)

We can once again ask Seaborn to put each city in a separate row:

```
sns.relplot(x='max_temp',
            y='min_temp',
            data=df,
            hue='state',
            kind='line',
            row='city')
```

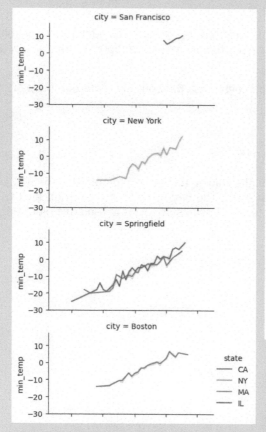

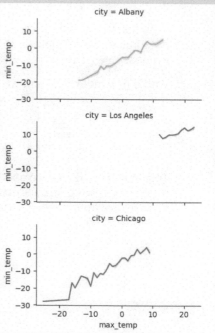

Line plot with temperatures per city, one city per row

Seaborn supports a wide variety of other plots, as well. For example, what if we want to see all the values of `max_temp` for a given city? You can think of this as a set of one-dimensional scatter plots:

```
sns.catplot(x='city', y='max_temp', data=df)
```

Notice how the *x* axis is for the categories, whereas the *y* axis describes which value we're seeing. This plots each of the values in the data set.

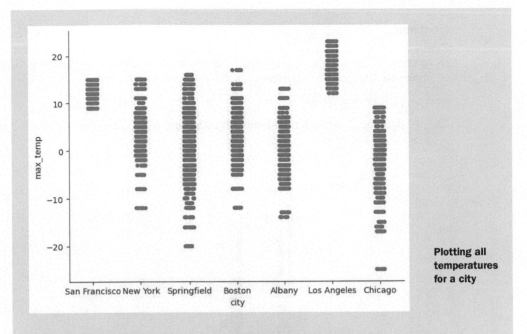

Plotting all temperatures for a city

If we instead want to summarize our data, we can ask for a boxplot, instead:

```
sns.catplot(x='city', y='max_temp', data=df, kind='box')
```

This shows a boxplot for each of the cities' values of `max_temp`, all side by side on the same *y* axis.

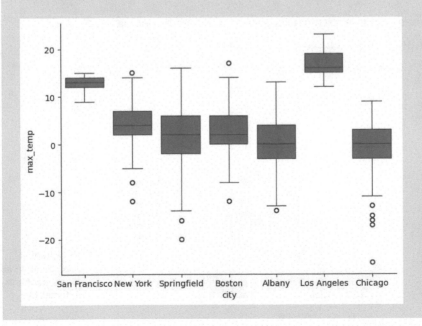

Boxplot for `max_temp` in each city

(continued)

Finally, Seaborn offers the chance to create histograms. Because histograms allow us to understand the distribution of our data, we use the `sns.displot` function. For example, we can get a histogram of all maximum temperatures:

```
sns.displot(x='max_temp', data=df)
```

This, of course, shows the distribution of all values of `max_temp`.

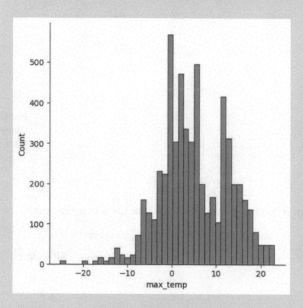

Histogram of `max_temp` in all cities

We can also give each city its own colored bars by setting `hue`:

```
sns.displot(x='max_temp', data=df, hue='city')
```

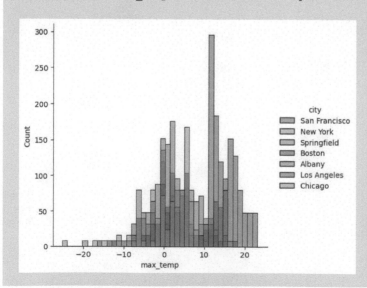

Histogram of `max_temp` in all cities, each city in a different hue

And we can see them in a single column, with only one city per row, by saying

```
sns.displot(x='max_temp', data=df, hue='city', row='city')
```

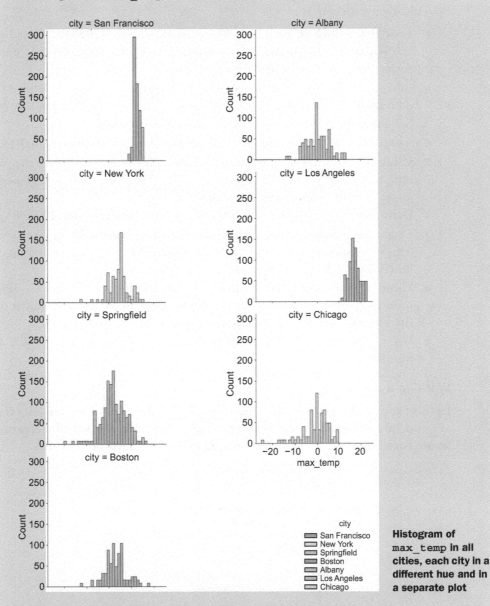

Histogram of `max_temp` in all cities, each city in a different hue and in a separate plot

These are just some of Seaborn's many capabilities. If you're interested in seeing everything Seaborn can do, I strongly recommend checking out the documentation at https://seaborn.pydata.org. I've grown to really like the Seaborn approach to visualization—not only does it produce very nice-looking plots, but I find the API easier to understand and work with than many others.

EXERCISE 47 ▪ Seaborn taxi plots

In this exercise, we're going to revisit our New York City taxi data from 2020, creating some visualizations with Seaborn rather than with the built-in pandas plotting system. Specifically, I want you to

1   Load data from NYC taxis in 2020 (i.e., both nyc_taxi_2020-01.csv and nyc_taxi_2020-07.csv), only loading the columns `tpep_pickup_datetime`, `passenger_count`, `trip_distance`, and `total_amount`.

2   Add `month` and `year` columns from `tpep_pickup_datetime`. Keep only those data points in which the year is 2020 and the month is either January or July.

3   Set a new numeric range index numbered starting at 0.

4   Assign `df` to a random sample of 1% of the elements in the original `df`.

5   Using Seaborn, create a scatter plot in which the *x* axis shows `trip_distance` and the *y* axis shows `total_amount`, with the plot colors set by `passenger_count`. Use the 1% sample of the data.

6   Determine why there are colors for `passenger_count` values of 1.5, 4.5, and 7.5.

7   Create a line plot showing the distance traveled on each day of January and July. The *x* axis should be the day of the month, and the *y* axis is the average trip distance. There should be two lines, one for each month.

8   Using Seaborn, show the number of trips taken on each day (1–31) of both months (January and July). The *x* axis should refer to the day of the month, and the *y* axis should show the number of trips taken.

9   Using Seaborn, create a boxplot of `total_amount` with one plot for each month.

Working it out

In this exercise, I asked you to create plots of 2020 New York City taxi data from January and July and then to use Seaborn to plot that data. We start by creating a data frame based on the 2020 taxi files, loading four of our favorite columns:

```
filenames = ['../data/nyc_taxi_2020-01.csv',
             '../data/nyc_taxi_2020-07.csv']

all_dfs = [pd.read_csv(one_filename,
           usecols=['tpep_pickup_datetime',
                    'passenger_count',
                    'trip_distance',
                    'total_amount'],
           parse_dates=['tpep_pickup_datetime'])
          for one_filename in filenames]

df = pd.concat(all_dfs)
```

Notice that we once again use `parse_dates` to turn the `tpep_pickup_datetime` column into a `datetime` column, leaving the three others to be detected as floating-point values. This code creates a list of data frames using a list comprehension. The list is passed to `pd.concat`, which returns a new data frame that combines all the input data frames.

I then asked you to create three new columns from various parts of each row's date:

```
df['year'] = df['tpep_pickup_datetime'].dt.year
df['month'] = df['tpep_pickup_datetime'].dt.month
df['day'] = df['tpep_pickup_datetime'].dt.day
```

I asked you to ensure that all the data we look at is from January or July 2020. As we've seen, the taxi data is "dirty," including a number of rows from other years and months. To avoid having our plots come out odd looking, I thought it would be wise to remove rows that aren't from January and July 2020. We can do that by using a combination of mask indexes:

```
df = df.loc[(df['month'].isin([1, 7])) &
            (df['year'] == 2020)]
```

Next, I asked you to ensure that the new data frame's index doesn't contain duplicate values—something that is almost certainly the case at this point, given that we created `df` from two previous data frames. We can check whether a data frame's index contains repeated values with the code:

```
df.index.is_unique
```

If this returns `True`, the values are already unique. If not, some Seaborn plots will give you errors. We could renumber the index on our own, but why work so hard when pandas includes this functionality? We can just say

```
df = df.reset_index(drop=True)
```

Yes, this is the same `reset_index` that we've used before to get rid of a "special" index we've created, such as from a data column. By passing `drop=True`, we tell `reset_index` not to make the just-ousted index column a regular column in the data frame but rather to drop it entirely.

We could begin to plot our data. But the data set is large, with many millions of data points. To speed up our plotting, albeit at the cost of some accuracy, I asked you to keep a random 1% of the original `df`'s values and assign it to `df`:

```
df = df.sample(frac=0.01)
```

We're now finally ready to plot our data with Seaborn. First, I asked you to create a scatter plot comparing `trip_distance` (*x* axis) with `total_amount` (*y* axis) on the `df` containing 1% of our original data:

```
sns.relplot(x='trip_distance',
            y='total_amount',
            data=df,
            hue='passenger_count')
```

The `relplot` function shows relationships among numeric columns, and the default way to do that is with a scatter plot. Here, we tell `relplot` the following:

- The *x* axis should use values from the `trip_distance` column.
- The *y* axis should use values from the `total_amount` column.
- We use `df` as our data frame.
- We use `passenger_count` as the basis for coloring the lines and dots.

Sure enough, this works, giving us a nice scatter plot (figure 11.18).

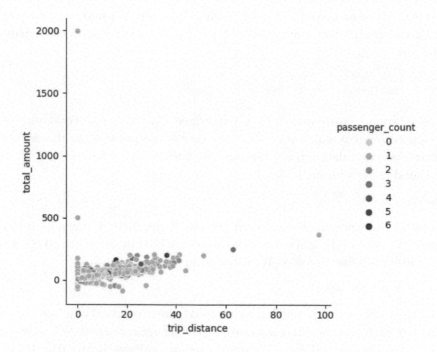

Figure 11.18   Scatter plot comparing `trip_distance` **with** `total_amount`

Next, I asked you to show a line plot in which the *x* axis indicates days of the month (1–31) and the *y* axis shows the value of `trip_distance` on that date. As before, we use `relplot` to get that plot:

- The *x* axis is from the `day` column.
- The *y* axis is from the `trip_distance` column.
- We have to indicate that `kind='line'` to get the line plot.
- We say that data comes from the `df` data frame.
- We color each of the lines by month.

```
sns.relplot(x='day', y='trip_distance', kind='line',
        data=df, hue='month')
```

By asking Seaborn to use separate colors for each value of month, we are able to plot two different lines on the same chart.

Notice, though, that there are gray lines around each plot. Those indicate the *confidence interval* for each calculation. Confidence intervals are a statistical tool to indicate how likely a value is to fall within a certain range. We can disable the confidence intervals by passing ci='None' on a relplot (figure 11.19):

```
sns.relplot(x='day', y='trip_distance', kind='line',
          data=df, hue='month', ci=None)
```

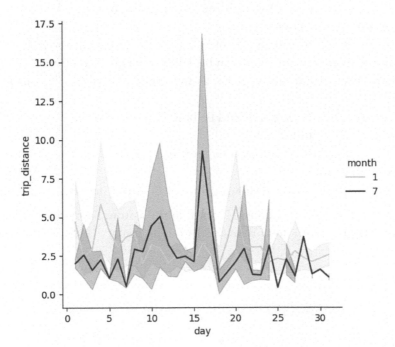

Figure 11.19
Line plot showing
`trip_distance` **per**
day, separated by month

Next, I asked you to show the number of trips taken on each day of these months. This requires another line plot:

- The *x* axis is the day of each month.
- The *y* axis reflects how many trips were taken on that day.
- We have to indicate that kind='line' to get a line plot.

But wait a second: how will we get the number of trips taken each day? To do that, we need to use the count aggregation method. And indeed, here I suggest getting data back not from df but rather from the result of a groupby on df. If we count by both month and day and count in the year column, we have access to month and day and also to the number of rides per day. (Using year is weird because we aren't counting the year—but we need to pick a column.) After performing this groupby, we reset the index, making month and day back into regular columns from which they can be retrieved:

```
sns.relplot(x='day', y='year', hue='month', kind='line',
            data=df.groupby(['month', 'day'])[['year']].count()
            .reset_index(), ci=None)
```

This is a complex query, and it's used in a complex plot. So let's walk through it a step at a time:

1 We want to know how many rides there were on each day of each month. That requires `groupby(['month', 'day'])`.

2 We run the `count` aggregation method on the `groupby` object.

3 The result gives us a count for each remaining column in the data frame. We only need one, and we choose `year`.

4 We run `reset_index` to take `month` and `day`, which are part of the index of the aggregation data frame, and put them back into the main data frame.

5 We pass the result from `reset_index` as the argument to `data` in our call to `relplot`.

6 We tell `relplot` that the *x* axis should be based on `day` and the *y* axis should be based on `year`, the count of rides.

7 We tell `relplot` to distinguish between months by color.

8 We ask for a line plot.

9 We ask for `ci='None'` to avoid showing any confidence intervals.

We then see, rather dramatically (figure 11.20), that there were fewer rides per day in July (in the middle of the pandemic) than there were in January (before it started).

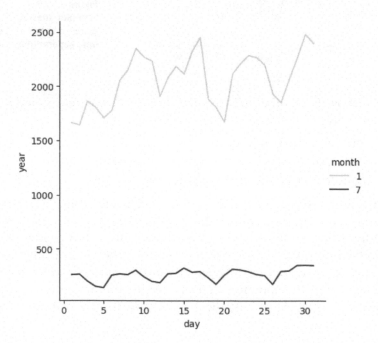

Figure 11.20   Line plot showing `trip_distance` **per day, separated by month**

Finally, we ask to see a boxplot of the `total_amount` column, separated by month. Boxplots are, in the world of Seaborn, categorical plots because they allow us to compare the distribution of values across multiple categories. We thus need to use the `catplot` function:

- The *x* axis is the categories we're comparing: `month`.
- The *y* axis is the values we want to see graphically: `total_amount`.
- We're looking at data from `df`.
- We want to see a boxplot and thus specify `kind='box'`.

The code is as follows (figure 11.21)

```
sns.catplot(x='month', y='total_amount', data=df, kind='box')
```

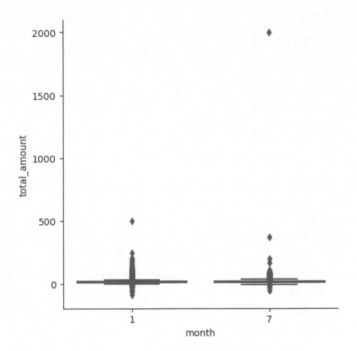

Figure 11.21 Boxplot for `total_amount` per month

The mean values for `total_amount` weren't that different in January and July of 2020. And sure enough, we can see this numerically:

```
df.groupby('month')['total_amount'].mean()
```

Solution

```
filenames = ['../data/nyc_taxi_2020-01.csv', '../data/nyc_taxi_2020-07.csv']

all_dfs = [pd.read_csv(one_filename,
           usecols=['tpep_pickup_datetime', 'passenger_count',
               'trip_distance', 'total_amount'],
```

```
                    parse_dates=['tpep_pickup_datetime'])
                    for one_filename in filenames]

df = pd.concat(all_dfs)

df['year'] = df['tpep_pickup_datetime'].dt.year
df['month'] = df['tpep_pickup_datetime'].dt.month
df['day'] = df['tpep_pickup_datetime'].dt.day

df = df.loc[(df['month'].isin([1, 7])) & (df['year'] == 2020)]

df = df.reset_index(drop=True)

df = df.sample(frac=0.01)

sns.relplot(x='trip_distance', y='total_amount', data=df,
            hue='passenger_count')

sns.relplot(x='day', y='trip_distance', kind='line',
            data=df, hue='month', ci=None)

sns.relplot(x='day', y='year', hue='month', kind='line',
            data=df.groupby(['month', 'day'])[['year']].count()
            .reset_index(), ci=None)

sns.catplot(x='month', y='total_amount', data=df, kind='box')
```

Beyond the exercise

- Load NYC taxi data from both 2019 and 2020, January and July. Remove data from outside of those years and months. Now display the number of trips on each day of the month in four separate graphs: the top row in 2019 and the bottom row in 2020, the left column for January and the right column for July.
- Add a `trip_length` column for short, medium, and long trips, as we did in exercise 7. Show the trip distance per day of month in three plots alongside one another, with one for each category.
- Create a bar plot showing how many rides take place in each hour (0–24) in each month (January and July). Each month should appear in a different color, and they should appear side by side with January on the left and July on the right.

Summary

Visualization is a key part of data science. We often think of it as a way to help non-experts to better understand our data, but it's also a powerful way to better understand our own data, getting insights from a new perspective. In this chapter, we saw a number of the ways pandas can perform visualizations using a simplified API to Matplotlib. We also saw, in the final exercise, how the Seaborn package can create attractive plots using data frames with its own separate API on top of Matplotlib.

Performance

12

It's hard to fathom just how powerful modern computers are. They perform billions of calculations per second, allowing us to have video chats with people around the world, predict the weather with incredible accuracy, and search through entire libraries of documents in the blink of an eye. An office worker from 100 years ago would be awestruck by how much data we can process and how little time it takes us to do so.

But let's be honest: when were you last satisfied by your computer's speed? If you're like me, you spend very little time amazed by the speed with which our computers operate and a lot of time frustrated by how long they take to do things.

I often say that Python is the perfect language for an age in which computers are cheap and people are expensive. By that, I mean Python optimizes for programmer productivity, often at the expense of efficient execution. Things aren't all bad; the fact that pandas uses NumPy under the hood makes it far faster and slimmer than would be the case with standard Python objects. The more we stay in the high-powered world of NumPy and away from built-in Python objects, the better it will be.

Beyond that general rule of thumb, though, there are numerous techniques for keeping your pandas data frames slim and your queries fast. Many of these come down to the simple rule of only using the data you need for a data frame. Because pandas keeps all data in memory, less data means faster processing and results.

In this chapter, we'll explore a number of topics having to do with pandas performance. We'll talk about how to measure the memory usage of a data frame and why pandas sometimes lies to us about it. We'll see how we can measure how much time it takes to perform tasks using `timeit`. We'll look at saving memory by using categories. And we'll explore how to speed up performance using PyArrow, the

Python implementation of the Arrow library, both for loading CSV files and as a back-end replacement for NumPy.

By the end of this chapter, you'll understand many of the problems surrounding pandas performance as well as how you can (and should) address them.

Table 12.1   What you need to know

Concept	What is it?	Example	To learn more
`df.info`	Gets information about a data frame, including its memory usage	`df.info()`	http://mng.bz/D4eE
`df.memory_usage`	Gets information about a data frame's memory usage	`df.memory_usage (deep=True)`	http://mng.bz/lWjy
Categorical data	Pandas documentation for categorical data	`df['a'].astype('cat egorical')`	http://mng.bz/BmaJ
`df.to_feather`	Writes a data frame to feather format	`df.to_feather('myda ta.feather')`	http://mng.bz/d1pQ
`pd.read_feather`	Creates a data frame based on a feather-formatted file on disk	`df = pd.read_ feather('mydata .feather')`	http://mng.bz/rWIX
`pd.read_csv`	Returns a new data frame based on CSV input	`df = df.read_csv ('myfile.csv')`	http://mng.bz/V1r5
`pd.read_json`	Returns a new data frame based on JSON input	`df = df.read_json ('myfile.json')`	http://mng.bz/x4qB
`time.perf_counter`	Gets the number of seconds (useful for timing programs)	`time.perf_ counter()`	http://mng.bz/AonW
`df.query`	Writes an SQL-like query	`df.query('v > 300')`	http://mng.bz/ZqBZ
`df.eval`	Performs actions and queries on a data frame	`df.eval('v + 300')`	http://mng.bz/Rx9P
`pd.eval`	Performs a variety of pandas actions in an evaluated string	`pd.eval('df.v > 300')`	http://mng.bz/2D9X
`timeit`	Python module for benchmarking code speed, and a Jupyter "magic command" for invoking it	`%timeit 3+2`	http://mng.bz/1qKg
`isin`	Checks whether a value is in a Python sequence	`df['a'].isin([10, 20, 30])`	http://mng.bz/PzOP
`pd.CategoricalDtype`	Returns a new categorical dtype	`pd.CategoricalDtype (['a', 'b', 'c', 'd'])`	http://mng.bz/Jgev

Saving memory with categories

Let's say we want to work with data from our Olympics CSV file:

```
filename = '../data/olympic_athlete_events.csv'
df = pd.read_csv(filename)
```

How much memory does this data set consume? That's an important question when working with pandas, because all our data needs to fit into memory. We can find out by running the `memory_usage` method on our data frame:

```
df.memory_usage()
```

This returns a series telling us how many bytes are consumed by each column. (The column names from `df` constitute the index of the returned series.) We can get the total memory usage by summing the values:

```
df.memory_usage().sum()
```

On my computer, this comes up as 32,534,048 bytes or just over 31 MB of RAM.

But you know what? This number is completely wrong. That's because pandas, by default, ignores the size of any Python objects contained in a data frame. Given that these objects are generally strings and can be any length, the difference between the actual memory usage and what is reported here can be big.

We can tell pandas to include all the objects in its size calculation by passing the `deep=True` keyword argument:

```
df.memory_usage(deep=True).sum()
```

On my computer, the same data frame gives me a result of 186,408,012 bytes, or about 182 MB of RAM—five times the originally calculated amount.

But wait: this is a lot of memory, and the data set is relatively small. A much larger data set will obviously consume much more memory, potentially more than I can fit into my computer. How can I cut down the size of the data set, thus allowing me to potentially work with more data? We've already talked about several of them in past chapters:

- Limit which columns are imported, by passing a value to `usecols`
- Explicitly specify the `dtype` for each column, allowing us to choose types with fewer bits while simultaneously speeding up the loading of data

However, the majority of the memory is being used by strings. We can see this by running `df.memory_usage(deep=True).sort_values()`. The columns using the most memory contain strings, not numbers. This means we need to somehow reduce the size or number of the text strings in our data frame.

One way to do this is with a special pandas data type known as a *category*. In the case of a category, each distinct string value is stored a single time and then referred to multiple times. This replacement is completely transparent to us, as users of the data frame: we can continue to pretend that the column contains strings, including use of the `str` accessor to apply string methods to every element of the column.

(continued)

We've often used `astype` to create a new series based on an existing one. We can do the same thing to create a new categorical column based on one containing text strings.

We demonstrate this using the `Games` column, which contains a different string for each time the Olympics were held. Running `df['Games'].value_counts()` `.head(10)` gives the following output:

```
Games
2000 Summer    13821
1996 Summer    13780
2016 Summer    13688
2008 Summer    13602
2004 Summer    13443
1992 Summer    12977
2012 Summer    12920
1988 Summer    12037
1972 Summer    10304
1984 Summer     9454
Name: count, dtype: int64
```

In other words, the string `2000 Summer` appears in the `Games` column 13,821 times. By creating a category, we can create a single string with that value, assign an integer to represent that string, and then store the integer in the column rather than the string (or, more accurately, a reference to the Python string object containing that value). Assuming that the integer is smaller than the reference, this can save a lot of memory.

Ten rows from `Games`, before and after being turned into a category

We can create our category this way:

```
df['Games'].astype('category')
```

However, this doesn't do anything useful, because it doesn't store our new series anywhere. It's often easiest to just assign the newly created categorical series back to the original column, replacing it with an equivalent-but-slimmer version:

```
df['Games'] = df['Games'].astype('category')
```

How much memory does that action save us? We can find out by running `memory_usage` again:

```
df.memory_usage(deep=True).sum()
```

Sure enough, memory usage has gone down to 168,248,812 bytes, or more than 160 MB. In other words, we've trimmed 15 MB of storage from our data frame simply by turning the `Games` column from a string into a category.

Which columns should we attack first? Well, we want those in which the same strings are often repeated. Consider this code:

```
(df.count() / df.nunique()).sort_values(ascending=False)
```

Here, we divide the number of non-null rows in each column by the number of distinct values in that column. The higher the number, the more times the same string is repeated, and thus the greater the memory savings we can achieve by switching the column to a category. We then use `sort_values(ascending=false)` to sort the rows in order of priority.

I decided to choose all categories with a `dtype` of `object` in which a value is repeated at least 100 times. This leads to the following code:

```
for column_name in ['Sex', 'Season', 'Medal', 'City', 'Games',
                    'Sport', 'NOC', 'Event', 'Team']:
    print(column_name)
    df[column_name] = df[column_name].astype('category')
```

The result? A data frame that's just over 33 MB in size. After only a handful of lines of code that took several seconds to execute, we've cut the memory requirement to about 20% of its original value. That seems like an extremely worthwhile use of our time.

But wait a second: this method creates the category based on the data that's already in the series. What if we know the series may include other values in the future, even if they're not in the original data set? Here's a simple example:

```
s = Series(['a', 'b', 'c', 'a', 'b', 'c', 'c', 'c']).astype('category')
```

We now try to set one of the values to `'d'`:

```
s.loc[7] = 'd'
```

This fails with a `TypeError` exception, telling us that we cannot set a value that wasn't included in the category.

(continued)

We can solve this problem by creating the category before creating the series (or column of the data frame), including all possible values it may contain. Then we can ask pandas not to create the category with `astype` but rather to assign the specific category type that we've defined, with all its values. Let's first see how this may work with the earlier series:

```
abcd_category = pd.CategoricalDtype(['a', 'b', 'c', 'd'])
s = Series(['a', 'b', 'c', 'a', 'b',
    'c', 'c', 'c']).astype(abcd_category)
s.loc[7] = 'd'  # Success!
```

In this code, we create a new category with all its values by calling `pd.Categorical-Dtype`. Then, when we call `astype`, we pass the category we created rather than asking pandas to create a new, anonymous category. We can do the same in our Olympics data frame:

```
medals_category = pd.CategoricalDtype(['Gold', 'Bronze', 'Silver'])
df['Medal'] = df['Medal'].astype(medals_category)
```

EXERCISE 48 ▪ Categories

We've explored New York City's parking tickets on several previous occasions in this book, but we were always concerned by how much memory the full data set would require. Indeed, if I load the entire data set onto my computer, it uses a *lot* of memory—about 18 GB. We'd like to crunch that down to a much smaller number by turning many of the columns into categories.

NOTE Because I realize that not everyone reading this book has many gigabytes of RAM to spare, you'll limit the number of columns you load for this exercise. If you are fortunate enough to have such a computer, though, I encourage you to load the entire data set into memory and pare the columns down using the same techniques. If you're like me, you'll be amazed by how much memory categories can save you. If your computer cannot load even the subset of columns I specify for this exercise, feel free to cut them down even further.

1 Read the NYC parking violations data into a data frame. Only load the following columns: `Plate ID`, `Registration State`, `Vehicle Make`, `Vehicle Color`, `Vehicle Body Type`, `Violation Time`, `Street Name`, and `Violation Legal Code`.
2 Determine how much memory is being used by the data frame you've created.
3 Turn each column into a category.
4 Answer these questions:
   – What types are your columns now?
   – How much memory does your data consume now?

– How much memory have you saved thanks to using categories?

Working it out

This exercise has fewer steps than many of the recent ones we've done, for two reasons. First, I want to show you how easily we can create and work with categories. Second, when we're dealing with large amounts of memory, even the fastest and most tricked-out computers can take a while to calculate things.

With that in mind, let's go through the code and see what we can do. First, we load the data set, limiting ourselves to the eight columns I asked for:

```
filename = '../data/nyc-parking-violations-2020.csv'

df = pd.read_csv(filename,
                 usecols=['Plate ID',
                          'Registration State',
                          'Vehicle Make',
                          'Vehicle Color',
                          'Vehicle Body Type',
                          'Violation Time',
                          'Street Name',
                          'Violation Legal Code'])
```

You'll likely get a `DtypeWarning` from pandas because one or more columns have mixed types. We've seen this warning before, and we'll soon be turning this column into a category, so we can ignore this warning.

Next, I asked you to calculate how much total memory the data frame is using. There are actually two ways to do this. The first is to run the `memory_usage` method, passing the keyword argument `deep=True`. This returns a series in which the index contains the data frame's column names and the values show how much memory is being used by each column:

```
df.memory_usage(deep=True)
```

On my computer, I get the following result:

```
Index                       128
Plate ID               798282162
Registration State     737248306
Vehicle Body Type      758166224
Vehicle Make           768611575
Violation Time         774726961
Street Name            879156216
Violation Legal Code   515644296
Vehicle Color          735089399
dtype: int64
```

According to this report, each column requires more than half a gigabyte of RAM. Even in our modern era of cheap, plentiful RAM, this is still a large data set—and given the alternative, there's no reason for us to use all this memory.

I want to remind you that it's important to always use `deep=True` if you truly want to know the size of your data frame. If we hadn't passed `deep=True`, we would have gotten something like this:

```
Index                        128
Plate ID                99965872
Registration State      99965872
Vehicle Body Type       99965872
Vehicle Make            99965872
Violation Time          99965872
Street Name             99965872
Violation Legal Code    99965872
Vehicle Color           99965872
dtype: int64
```

Notice how all the columns, aside from the index, have the same size: 99,965,872 bytes—basically 100 MB. Not a small amount of memory, but far less than the actual size of our data, whose size we calculated using `deep=True`.

Why does pandas not run `deep=True` all the time? Because instead of just checking the size of the memory allocated by the NumPy backend, pandas has to go through each object in Python and ask for its size. That can take substantially longer, so we have to ask for it explicitly.

Calling `memory_usage` returns a series: the size of each column. We can add the values using `sum`:

```
df.memory_usage(deep=True).sum()
```

On my computer, the result is 5,966,925,267, or about 6 GB.

Next, I asked you to turn each of these columns into a category. Remember that given a column named `colname`, we can turn it into a category with

```
df['colname'] = df['colname'].astype('category')
```

When we do this, pandas removes NaN values in the column, looks at the remaining unique values, builds a new category object from it, and then uses that category to assign values. Although the values still appear to be there, as before, pandas has replaced them with much-smaller integers, storing each string a single time.

Before transforming the columns into categories, we keep track of how much memory our original version of the data frame is using:

```
orig_mem = df.memory_usage(deep=True).sum()
```

Next, we do the transformation itself, using a `for` loop. You may be surprised to see this suggestion, given that I often point out that if you're using a `for` loop in pandas, you're almost certainly doing something wrong. But that's if you're trying to perform a calculation on each row; for such purposes, pandas has a lot of functionality that is generally faster than any loop. Because so much of the backend data uses NumPy, pulling the data into Python data structures uses significantly more memory than taking advantage of its vectorized, compiled, and optimized systems.

But this case is different: we're interested in performing one vectorized operation per column. There isn't any vectorizing to be done across the columns. For this reason, a `for` loop is perfectly reasonable. The index object we get back from `df.columns` is iterable, allowing us to get each column name, one at a time. We thus write

```
for one_colname in df.columns:
    print(f'Categorizing {one_colname}...')
    df[one_colname] = df[one_colname].astype('category')
    print('\tDone.')
```

Notice that we put two calls to `print` inside the `for` loop: once before starting the transformation and once after. This is because the creation of a category can take some time, and it would be useful to know when pandas is starting to work on a column and when it has finished. In addition, if something goes wrong while creating the columns, we know exactly where we were when the problem took place.

After performing this transformation, we want to get confirmation that things changed. By retrieving `dtypes` on our data frame, we can see precisely what type each column has:

```
df.dtypes
```

Sure enough, pandas shows that all the columns have been changed to have `category` types. But what effect does that have on the memory usage? As before, we can ask for a deep memory check:

```
new_mem = df.memory_usage(deep=True).sum()
```

This time, on my computer, I get the value 574,455,678—still half a gigabyte of RAM, but a far cry from the original value of 6 GB. In other words, we have cut down our memory usage by about 90%! And indeed, if we perform a quick calculation

```
new_mem / orig_mem
```

we get a result of 0.096, meaning we are indeed using approximately 10% of the original data frame's memory while still using the same data and enjoying the same benefits from it.

How much memory?

The `df.info` method returns a summary of information about the data frame, including the total memory usage. By default, it doesn't do a "deep" memory check; in such cases, and if there are object columns, the memory is returned with a + sign following the number. You can avoid the + and get a precise calculation by passing `memory_usage='deep'` as a keyword argument to `info`:

```
df.info(memory_usage='deep')
```

This gives you a summary of the total memory used.

Solution

```
filename = '../data/nyc-parking-violations-2020.csv'

df = pd.read_csv(filename,
        usecols=['Plate ID', 'Registration State',
                'Vehicle Make', 'Vehicle Color',
                'Vehicle Body Type', 'Violation Time',
                'Street Name', 'Violation Legal Code'])

orig_mem = df.memory_usage(deep=True).sum()

for one_colname in df.columns:
    print(f'Categorizing {one_colname}...')
    df[one_colname] = df[one_colname].astype('category')
    print('\tDone.')

df.dtypes()

new_mem = df.memory_usage(deep=True).sum()

print(new_mem /  orig_mem)
```

Gets the memory usage of each column, sums them, and stores the result in orig_mem

Goes through each column in df

Turns each column into a category column

Gets the dtype of each column

Gets the memory usage of each column after categorization and stores it in new_mem

Shows how much memory we are using now

Beyond the exercise

- Without calculating: Of the columns you loaded, which would make less sense to turn into categories? Once you've thought about it, calculate how many repeated values are in each column and determine (more formally) which would give the biggest improvement when using categories.

- In exercise 25, we saw that the vehicle makes and colors were far from standardized, with numerous misspellings and variations. If you were to standardize the spellings before creating categories, would that have any effect on the memory savings you gain from categorization? Why or why not?

- Read only the first 10,000 lines from the CSV file, but all columns. Show the 10 columns that will most likely benefit greatest from using categories.

Apache Arrow

For nearly all of this book, I've assumed that pandas acts as something of a wrapper around NumPy. Sure, it provides a great deal of functionality, but the actual storage is handled by NumPy, which means the `dtype` of a column is nearly always defined by NumPy. The major exceptions are strings (stored as an `object` dtype) and categories (discussed elsewhere in this chapter).

An open source project known as Apache Arrow may change all that. Arrow is designed to be a highly efficient in-memory storage mechanism for data. Some basic facts about Arrow:

- Arrow works not only with pandas but also with other languages and systems such as R and Apache Spark.

- The Python bindings for Arrow are known as PyArrow.
- Arrow has its own data types, similar to but distinct from those defined by NumPy.
- Arrow's types are nullable, meaning if we have an integer column with a single NaN value, the column's dtype doesn't need to change to a floating-point type.
- Arrow supports two file formats, feather and parquet, which are binary, thus consuming less disk space and taking less time to read and write.
- Arrow can also read and write CSV files.

Let's start with this final point: by default, pandas reads CSV files using its own internal engine. We can speed up the loading of CSV files by asking pandas to instead use PyArrow:

```
df = pd.read_csv(filename, engine='pyarrow')
```

I've found that using the PyArrow engine for loading CSV is 20 times faster than the built-in engine. Unless you're working with very small data sets, it's probably worth always using this option with read_csv.

What about Arrow's binary formats? The feather format, as I mentioned, combines compression and binary storage to give us smaller files that are faster to read and write than either CSV or JSON.

To write a pandas data frame to a feather-formatted file, we can use the to_feather method, which works similarly to to_csv and to_json:

```
df.to_feather('mydata.feather')
```

We can similarly read from a feather-formatted file into a data frame using the pd.from_feather method, which works similarly to from_csv and from_json:

```
df = pd.from_feather('mydata.feather')
```

As of pandas 2.0, there is also experimental support for using PyArrow for backend storage, rather than NumPy. When we read a CSV file into pandas, we can specify that it should use PyArrow by passing the dtype_backend='pyarrow' keyword argument:

```
df = pd.read_csv(filename, dtype_backend='pyarrow')
```

If you check the dtypes attribute on your data frame, you'll find that the types are all from PyArrow and not from NumPy.

Note that the use of dtype_backend is separate from the engine used to read the CSV file. You can use one or both of these keyword arguments.

The use of PyArrow as a pandas backend is still experimental as of this writing, and it's also not guaranteed to be faster. In some experiments that I ran just after pandas 2.0 was released, simple comparisons were faster with PyArrow, but more sophisticated queries, such as grouping and joins, took longer than the NumPy backend. I have no doubt that this will improve over time, but for now you shouldn't assume that PyArrow will always be faster. That said, it's worth doing some experiments to see how it works on your data and your queries.

EXERCISE 49 ■ Faster reading and writing

Each file format has its own advantages and disadvantages, among them being the speed with which you can read and write data. Given a data frame, is it faster to write it as a CSV, JSON, or feather file? (If you read the side bar on Apache Arrow and feather, you may have a good sense of the answer.) How much of a difference is there? And is there a significant difference in speed when reading CSV, JSON, and feather files into a data frame?

To understand that, I'm asking you to do the following:

1   Load the New York parking data CSV file into a data frame.
2   Write the data frame out to the filesystem in each of three different formats: CSV, JSON, and feather. Time the writing of each format, and print the format along with the number of seconds it took to write to it.
3   Check the size of the files you've created.
4   Read each file you created into a data frame. Once again, time how long the loading takes and print that timing alongside the format name.

NOTE   The New York parking data set is large and may overwhelm computers with less than 32 GB of free memory. If you're working on such a computer, I encourage you to use the `usecols` keyword parameter to reduce the number of columns read into the data frame at the start of the exercise. You may see less of a difference between writing to and then reading from the various formats, but at least you'll be able to finish the exercise.

Working it out

The first thing I asked you to do was load the New York parking violations data set for 2020. We'll assume that your computer has enough memory to load the entire thing, which we do as follows:

```
filename = '../data/nyc-parking-violations-2020.csv'
df = pd.read_csv(filename, low_memory=False)
```

Notice that we pass the `low_memory=False` keyword argument. This tells pandas that we have enough RAM that it can look through all the rows in the data set when trying to determine what `dtype` to assign to each column.

With the data frame in place, we can begin writing to different formats, timing how long each takes. But, of course, that means we need some way to keep track of time. Python's `time` module, part of the standard library, provides a number of different methods that could theoretically be used, but it's generally considered best to use `time.perf_counter()`. This function uses the highest-resolution clock available and returns a float indicating a number of seconds. The number returned by `perf_counter` should not be relied on for calculating the current date and time; but within the same program, it can be used to measure the passage of time, which is precisely what we want to do.

NOTE Python's standard library also includes the `timeit` module (http://mng.bz/67OA), which includes a number of utilities for benchmarking. I'm generally a big fan of `timeit`, and we'll use it in exercise 50. But `timeit` runs code several times and reports the mean time after those runs. In this case, where the code will take a long time to run, we run it a single time—and thus opt to use `perf_counter`.

We want to try writing to CSV, JSON, and feather formats. In theory, we could write code that looks like this:

```
df.write_json('parking-violations.json')
df.write_csv('parking-violations.csv')
df.write_feather('parking-violations.feather')
```

But, of course, we want to determine how long each one takes. So we add some benchmarking code above and below each format:

```
start_time = time.perf_counter()        ← Gets the time at the
df.write_json('parking-violations.json')    start of the JSON run
end_time = time.perf_counter()                 ← Gets the time at
total_time = end_time - start_time               the end of the run
print(f'\tWriting JSON: {total_time=}')   ← Calculates
                                             the run time

start_time = time.perf_counter()        ← Repeats
df.write_csv('parking-violations.csv')     for CSV
end_time = time.perf_counter()
total_time = end_time - start_time
print(f'\tWriting CSV: {total_time=}')

start_time = time.perf_counter()        ← Repeats
df.write_feather('parking-violations.feather')  for JSON
end_time = time.perf_counter()
total_time = end_time - start_time
print(f'\tWriting feather: {total_time=}')
```

This code works and does the job. But it also violates an important rule of programming: "Don't repeat yourself," often abbreviated DRY. We're basically doing the same thing three times. If we can consolidate that code into a loop, our code will be cleaner, easier to read, easier to debug, and easier to extend. But how can we do that? After all, we're calling three different methods.

This is where some knowledge and understanding of Python, not just pandas, comes in handy: we can create a dictionary in which the keys are the file formats and the values are the methods we want to use to write the data frame. That's right—we can store any Python object, including a function or method—as the value in a dict. We can thus say

```
root = 'parking-violations'
write_methods = {'JSON': df.to_json,
        'CSV': df.to_csv,
```

```
          'feather': df.to_feather
      }

for one_format, method in write_methods.items():
    print(f'Saving in {one_format}')
    start_time = time.perf_counter()
    method(f'parking-violations.{one_format.lower()}')
    end_time = time.perf_counter()

    total_time = end_time - start_time
    print(f'\tWriting {one_format}: {total_time=}')
```

The `for` loop here iterates over the dict, getting each key (a string, stored in `one_format`) and value (`method`, containing the method to be run) from the `write_methods` dict. We print the current format, just for debugging purposes, and then run `time.perf_counter()`, getting back the current time (more or less) in seconds. We then invoke `method` on the filename via an f-string. After writing the file to disk, we call `time.perf_counter()` again, storing the difference in `total_time`, which we then print.

On my computer, I get the following results from running this code:

```
Saving in JSON
        Writing JSON: total_time=46.29149689315818
Saving in CSV
        Writing CSV: total_time=114.35314526595175
Saving in feather
        Writing feather: total_time=7.929971480043605
```

In other words, it took about 114 seconds (nearly two minutes) to write our data frame to a CSV file. It took 46 seconds to write the same data to JSON. But it took just under 8 seconds—about 14 times faster!—to write the same data to feather. If that doesn't convince you to consider using feather, I'm not sure what will.

Notice that for this code to work, we have to define `df`, the data frame, *before* the `write_methods` dictionary is defined. We also use `one_format.lower()` to take the format name and ensure that it is only in lowercase letters.

How big are the files we've created? We again rely on Python's standard library. We've seen the `glob.glob` function in previous exercises; here we use it to retrieve all filenames that start with the value of our `root` variable. But we then want to get the size of each file, something we can do easily with `os.stat`. This function returns a special data structure that's modeled on Unix's `stat` functionality. In Python, we can get the size of the file in bytes by retrieving the `st_size` attribute from the value we get back from `os.stat`:

```
for one_filename in glob.glob(f'{root}*'):
    print(f'{one_filename:27}: {os.stat(one_filename).st_size:,}')
```

Inside the f-string, we use two tricks to adjust the way the values are formatted:

- We tell the f-string to pad `one_filename` with spaces so each filename uses 27 characters. This help ensure that the results line up.

- We tell the f-string to add commas before every three digits in the integer it displays, making them more readable.

The result, on my computer, is

```
parking-violations.json    : 8,820,247,015
parking-violations.csv     : 2,440,860,181
parking-violations.feather : 1,466,535,674
```

We can see here that the CSV file is about 2 GB in size, the JSON file is about 8 GB (!), and Apache Arrow's feather format is just over 1 GB. This isn't the only reason writing feather files is faster, but it's certainly one of them; at the end of the day, pandas has to write one-eighth as much data to disk.

However, I also wanted you to benchmark reading these files back from the filesystem. We use the same technique as before: creating a dictionary (this time called `read_methods`) containing the file extensions and the methods we want to run. The code is as follows:

```
read_methods = {'JSON': pd.read_json,
        'CSV': pd.read_csv,
        'feather': pd.read_feather
        }

for one_format, method in read_methods.items():
    print(f'Reading from {one_format}')
    start_time = time.perf_counter()
    df = read_methods[one_format](
        f'parking-violations.{one_format.lower()}')
    end_time = time.perf_counter()

    total_time = end_time - start_time
    print(f'\tReading {one_format}: {total_time=}')
```

As before, we iterate over a dictionary, getting each key (a string, stored in `one_format`) and value (`method`) from the `read_methods` dict. We print the current format and then run `time.perf_counter()`. We retrieve the appropriate read method with `read_methods[one_format]` and invoke the method we get on the appropriate filename. After reading the file into a data frame, we call `time.perf_counter()` again, storing the difference in `total_time`, which we then print.

If you're like me, you'll likely get the `DtypeWarning` we've previously discussed. (As a reminder, this warning crops up when pandas is trying to figure out the type of data contained in a column, doesn't read all the rows to avoid using too much memory, and then worries that it may guess the `dtype` incorrectly. This doesn't happen in other formats because the type of data we're reading into each column is more explicit.) For our purposes, we can ignore it, in no small part to avoid having to worry about which method and which format are being read. But the benchmarking results are as follows:

```
Reading from JSON
        Reading JSON: total_time=469.92014819500037
```

```
Reading from CSV
        Reading CSV: total_time=35.20077076088637
Reading from feather
        Reading feather: total_time=9.132312984904274
```

This time the JSON file takes the longest to read into memory, at a hefty 469 seconds, or nearly 8 minutes. In second place, and taking less than 10% of the time, is CSV, at 35 seconds. But the speed champion remains feather, taking just over 9 seconds.

From this simple demonstration, it seems pretty clear that Apache Arrow and its feather format are significantly faster for reading and writing than both CSV and JSON. This doesn't mean you can or should move everything to feather—but it has a number of clear advantages, both in terms of speed and in its footprint on the filesystem.

Solution

```
import glob
import os

filename = '../data/nyc-parking-violations-2020.csv'
df = pd.read_csv(filename, low_memory=False)

root = 'parking-violations'
write_methods = {'JSON': 'to_json',        ◁─── Dict of formats
        'CSV': 'to_csv',                        and methods
        'feather': 'to_feather' }

for one_format, method in write_methods.items():   ◁─── Iterates over formats
    print(f'Saving in {one_format}')                    and write methods
    start_time = time.perf_counter()
    method(f'parking-violations.{one_format.lower()}')   ◁─── Invokes the method
    end_time = time.perf_counter()                            on the filename

    total_time = end_time - start_time
    print(f'\tWriting {one_format}: {total_time=}')
                                                   Goes through each
for one_filename in glob.glob(f'{root}*'):     ◁─── filename we created
    print(f'{one_filename:27}: {os.stat(one_filename).st_size:,}')   ◁─────

read_methods = {'JSON': 'read_json',                  Uses os.stat to display
        'CSV': 'read_csv',                             the size of each file
        'feather': 'read_feather' }

for one_format, method in read_methods.items():   ◁─── Iterates over formats
    print(f'Reading from {one_format}')                and read methods
    start_time = time.perf_counter()
    df = read_methods[one_format](
        f'parking-violations.{one_format.lower()}')   ◁─── Invokes the
    end_time = time.perf_counter()                          appropriate read
                                                            method for the format
    total_time = end_time - start_time
    print(f'\tReading {one_format}: {total_time=}')
```

Beyond the exercise

- If you read the CSV file using the `pyarrow` engine, do you see any speedup? That is, can you read CSV files into memory any faster if you use a different engine?
- If you specify the dtypes to `read_csv`, does it take more time or less than without doing so?
- How much memory does the data frame use with a NumPy backend versus a PyArrow backend?

Speeding things up with eval and query

Over the course of this book, I've emphasized a number of techniques that you should use to speed up your pandas performance:

- Never use standard Python iterations (`for` loops and comprehensions) on a series or data frame.
- Take advantage of broadcasting.
- Use the `str` accessor for anything string related.
- Use the smallest `dtype` you can without sacrificing accuracy.
- Avoid double square brackets when setting and retrieving values.
- Load only those columns that you really need for your analysis.
- Columns with repeated values should be turned into categories.
- Use a binary format, such as feather, for data you'll repeatedly save or load.

Even after using all these techniques, we may find that our queries are still running slowly or using lots of memory. This often occurs when performing an arithmetic operation on two columns, each of which contains many rows. A related problem is when broadcasting an operation on a scalar and a series. Although pandas takes advantage of the high-speed calculations in NumPy, much of the work is still done within the Python language, which is slower to execute than C.

Another problem occurs when creating a boolean series for use as a mask index based on several conditions. It's certainly convenient to use `&` and `|` to combine conditions with logical "and" and "or," but behind the scenes, pandas has to create multiple boolean series, which are then combined. If we have 1 million rows in your original column, combining three conditions creates at least 3 million rows in temporary series before combining and applying them together.

We can avoid these problems, as well as make our queries more readable, using the `query` method that I introduced back in chapter 2, as well as two versions of the more general `eval` method. These reduce the memory required in queries using `|` and `&` and can often execute expressions in a library known as `numexpr`. The combination of reduced memory and increased speed can sometimes give dramatically faster results while also using fewer resources.

However, it's important to understand that these methods are not cure-alls for performance problems:

- Using them on small data frames with fewer than 10,000 rows will often result in slower performance, not faster performance.

(continued)

- Often, the bottleneck in performance is in the assignment or retrieval of elements, not in the calculation. There won't be a speed boost in such cases.
- You'll need to install the `numexpr` package from PyPI and then explicitly tell pandas to use it. If you don't make this explicit, pandas will use its default Python-based engine for parsing the query string, resulting in no speedup.
- Anything that doesn't involve calculations, comparisons, and boolean operators will either raise an exception or run at the standard (non-enhanced) speed.

Let's start by looking at the `query` for data frames. We'll then talk about two versions of `eval` that are part of the same family.

Given a data frame `df`, the method `df.query` allows us to describe which rows you we want to get back from `df`. The description is passed as an SQL-like string in which the columns can be named as if they were variables. The result of the query is a data frame, a subset of `df`, with all the columns from `df` and those rows for which the comparison returned a `True` value. For example, given a data frame `df` with numeric columns `a` and `b` in which we want all rows where `a` is greater than 100 and `b` is less than 700, we would normally say

```
np.random.seed(0)
df = DataFrame(np.random.randint(0, 1000, [5,5]),
               index=list('vwxyz'),
               columns=list('abcde'))

df.loc[((df['a'] > 100) &
        (df['b'] < 700))]
```

But using `df.query`, we can instead write

```
df.query('a > 100 & b < 700')
```

The version using `query` will sometimes run faster, but it will almost always use less memory. That's because it doesn't need to create two separate, temporary boolean series, one for `a > 100` and another for `b < 700`. We may not see these boolean series when running a traditional query, but they're there and can use a great deal of memory without us realizing it. I should add that some people prefer to use `df.query` for all their pandas work because of its readability and reduced memory use.

A related data frame method is `df.eval`, which allows us to retrieve from a data frame (as in `df.query`) as well as perform other actions, including broadcasting and assigning. For example:

```
df.eval('(a + b) * 3')
```

This code adds columns `a` and `b` and multiplies the new series by 3 via broadcasting. The returned value is a series. What if we were to pass the same code we used before, with `df.query`?

```
df.eval('a > 100 & b < 700')
```

This returns a boolean series. Whereas `df.query` applies that boolean series to `df`, `df.eval` returns the boolean series itself and allows us to apply it if and when we want to do so. We can even add a new column (or update an existing one) by assigning to a column name:

```
df.eval('f = d + e - c')
```

Using a triple-quoted string, we can perform multiple assignments with `df.eval`:

```
df.eval('''
f = d + e - c
g = a * 2
h = a * b
''')
```

In general, `df.eval` can be used for either conditions or assignments. However, when we pass a triple-quoted string to `df.eval`, it is only for assignments; conditions aren't allowed.

The third and final method that allows us to use less memory, speed up computation, and write more readable queries is `pd.eval`. Notice that this is a top-level function in the `pd` namespace rather than a method we run on a specific data frame. We can use `pd.eval` instead of `df.eval`, although we need to explicitly state the name of the data frame we're working on. For example, we can say

```
pd.eval('df[df.a > 100 & df.b < 700]')
```

When using `pd.eval`, you'll probably want to use the dot syntax to reference columns, rather than the square-bracket syntax that I have generally used in this book, to avoid too much syntactic messiness. To retrieve column `a` from data frame `df`, we say `df.a` rather than `df['a']`. This also means column names cannot contain spaces.

This code returns all rows of `df` in which `a` is greater than 100 and `b` is less than 700, as before. However, we have written the query as a string, which is passed to `numexpr`. That package will, as we've seen, use less memory and (usually) result in better performance. Note that a call to `df.eval` is translated into a call to `pd.eval`, which means you can probably get better performance if you just call `pd.eval`. That said, the convenience of the syntax in `df.eval` is hard to beat.

As with `df.eval`, we can assign to one or more columns in the string we pass to `pd.eval`. But because we're invoking `pd.eval`, the data frame on which the assignment should take place isn't known to the system. We must set it by passing the `target` keyword argument. The assignment is reflected in the data frame that is returned:

```
pd.eval('f = df.d + df.e - df.c', target=df)
```

So, when should you use each of these? Again, the biggest wins are likely to be with compound queries (using `&` and `|`) on large data frames. The larger the data frame and the more complex the query, the bigger the speed boost you may see—but even if you don't, you'll almost certainly be using less memory.

(continued)

Meanwhile, here's a quick recap on each of these three functions:

- To retrieve selected rows from a data frame, use df.query.
- To assign multiple columns or to perform either queries or assignments on a data frame, use df.eval.
- To work on multiple data frames, use pd.eval. But it doesn't handle multiline assignments, and the syntax makes it uglier.

EXERCISE 50 ▪ "query" and "eval"

In this exercise, we'll look through New York parking tickets one final time, running queries using the traditional df.loc accessor and also using df.query and df.eval. For each of these questions, I'd like you to run the query via timeit, allowing us to compare the executing time needed for the various types of queries. Specifically, I'd like you to

1 Load the New York parking data CSV file into a data frame. You'll only need the following columns: Plate ID, Registration State, Plate Type, Feet From Curb, Vehicle Make, and Vehicle Color.

2 Rename the columns to pid, state, ptype, make, color, and feet. (This will make it easier to use df.eval.)

3 Find all cars whose registration state is from New York (NY), New Jersey (NJ), or Connecticut (CT) using .loc.

4 Find all cars whose registration state is New York, New Jersey, or Connecticut using df.query.

5 How much faster is it to use query?

6 Use isin to search for the states. How does this technique compare?

7 Perform each of the following queries using df.loc, df.query, and df.eval, all within timeit. In each case, which type of query runs the fastest?
   - Find cars from New York.
   - Find cars from New York with passenger (PAS) plates.
   - Find white cars from New York with passenger (PAS) plates.
   - Find white cars from New York with passenger (PAS) plates that were parked > 1 foot from the curb.
   - Find white Toyota-brand cars from New York with passenger (PAS) plates that were parked > 1 foot from the curb.

8 Which type(s) of query appears to run the fastest?

Working it out

In this exercise, I want you to learn several things:

1 How to formulate the same query using .loc, df.query, and df.eval

2 How to use timeit to time your queries and thus compare their relative speeds

3 What may lead a query to be slower

4 Some of the syntactic problems associated with alternative query mechanisms

The first thing I asked you to do was load a number of columns from the New York parking-ticket dataset, much as we've often done in this book:

```
df = pd.read_csv(filename,
    usecols=['Plate ID', 'Registration State',
        'Plate Type',
        'Vehicle Make', 'Vehicle Color', 'Feet From Curb'])
```

There is nothing inherently wrong with loading the data this way. However, when we use `pd.query` and `pd.eval`, it's often annoying to have column names that include spaces. Yes, we can use backticks, but it's more convenient to give them names that allow us to treat them as variables inside the query string. So although there's nothing technically wrong with loading the data as we do here, we then want to set the headers to be single-word names. We can do that by assigning a list of strings to `df.columns`:

```
df.columns = ['pid', 'state', 'ptype', 'make', 'color', 'feet']
```

You may be thinking that it would be more effective to set these names as part of the call to `read_csv`. After all, `read_csv` has a `names` parameter, which takes a list of strings that are assigned to the newly created data frame. However, things get tricky if we want to rename the columns (with `names`) and also load a subset of the columns (with `usecols`). That's because passing a value to `names` means we need to use those names rather than the original ones from the file when choosing columns in `usecols`. And we can only do that if we name all the columns, which is annoying.

Actually, there is another way to do it: we can specify which columns we want by passing a list of integers to `usecols`. Pandas selects the columns at those indexes. We can then assign them names by passing a value to the `names` parameter. Here's how to do that:

```
df = pd.read_csv(filename,
            usecols=[1, 2, 3, 7, 33, 37],
            names=['pid', 'state', 'ptype',
                'make', 'color', 'feet'])
```

Will this work? Yes, it will, and in many cases it may be the preferred way to go. However, I have two problems with it. First, I find it somewhat annoying to find the integer positions for the columns we want to load. And second, when I ran this code on my computer, I got the "low memory" warning that we've sometimes seen in previous examples. I thus decided to avoid the annoyance of finding the desired columns' numeric locations and the low-memory warning and to use the two-step column renaming that appears in the solution.

With our data frame in place, we can start to perform some queries. One of the main points of this exercise is to get comfortable timing queries, to find out how quickly they run. Python provides the `timeit` module, which we can use in standard programs, but Jupyter provides a special `%timeit` magic method that can be used inside Jupyter cells. We can say

```
%timeit myfunc(2, 3, 4)
```

In this example, `timeit` runs `myfunc(2,3,4)` a number of times, reporting the mean execution time along with the variation it detects. Just how many loops `timeit` runs is determined by the code speed; something that takes a fraction of a second may run hundreds or even thousands of times, whereas something that takes more than a few seconds may be run only a handful of times.

> **NOTE** When using the `%timeit` magic command in Jupyter, don't forget: your code must be written on a single line, just after the `%timeit` magic command. If you have more than one line, wrap it into a function and invoke that function. Or use the related `%%timeit` command, which works on an entire cell rather than a single line. Also, if you're timing a function, don't forget to put `()` after the function's name.

For the first task, I asked you to find all rows in `df` that were for parking tickets issued in New York (`'NY'`), New Jersey (`'NJ'`), or Connecticut (`'CT'`), using both the traditional `loc` accessor and the `query` method. I also asked you to time each of these for comparison.

We start with the traditional `.loc` accessor, combining three separate queries:

```
%%timeit

df.loc[(df['state'] == 'NY') |
       (df['state'] == 'NJ') |
       (df['state'] == 'CT')]
```

On my computer, this query took 1.84 seconds. (As usual, the timing will vary slightly with each run.)

Consider everything that pandas has to do for this query:

- Compare each element in `df['state']` with `'NY'`
- Compare each element in `df['state']` with `'NJ'`
- Compare each element in `df['state']` with `'CT'`
- Perform an "or" operation on the first two (New York and New Jersey) boolean series
- Perform an "or" operation on the result of this "or" and the Connecticut series
- Apply that final boolean series to `df.loc` as a mask index

There's no doubt that with so many rows, each comparison will take some time. Moreover, the "or" operations, resulting in a single boolean series, will also take a while. Using the `query` method won't help with the first part; we still need to perform the comparisons. However, by using `query`, we can dramatically reduce the number of "or" operations involved. That's because `query` uses the `numexpr` backend to perform such operations, which does them far more efficiently. How much more? Here's how we rewrite things to use `query`:

```
%timeit df.query("state == 'NY' or state == 'NJ' or state == 'CT'")
```

On my computer, using `query` took only 1.03 seconds, about 0.8 seconds (or 45%) less than the original query. That's a pretty dramatic speed improvement and points to how much `query` can improve performance for certain queries.

However, the comparisons with each of the three state abbreviations also takes some time. Can we cut down on the number of comparisons? Yes, if we use the `isin` method on our column to search for a match within a Python list:

```
%timeit df.loc[df['state'].isin(['NY', 'NJ', 'CT'])]
```

This query took even less time than the previous one, clocking in at 0.77 seconds on my computer. That represents a 58% speedup from the original query.

But wait: maybe we can enjoy an even greater speedup if we use `query` and `isin` together. Let's give it a try:

```
%timeit df.query('state.isin(["NY", "NJ", "CT"])')
```

Unfortunately, this didn't seem to improve things; it took 0.80 ms on my computer—still better than the original queries, but not as good as simply using `isin`.

From this small comparison, we see that optimization of queries is rarely a matter of always using one particular technique. It requires thinking about what we're doing, considering what pandas is doing behind the scenes, and then performing some tests to check our assumptions. That said, we can conclude at least two things from these queries. First, if you're combining queries with | or &, you'll likely get a decent improvement by using `query` rather than `loc`, thanks to the speedups provided by `numexpr`. Second, using `isin` will almost always be faster than combining multiple queries because you're making a single comparison per row, rather than three.

Following this first set of queries, I asked you to perform a number of increasingly complex queries, each in three different ways: using the traditional `loc` accessor, then using `df.query`, and finally using `df.eval`. I did this not only to give you some practice building queries in different ways and comparing the time each takes but also to see that the improvements using `query` and `eval` become more pronounced as the query becomes more complex.

For starters, I asked you to find all parking tickets given to cars with New York license plates. Here are the three queries together:

```
%timeit df.loc[(df['state'] == 'NY')]
%timeit df.query('state == "NY"')
%timeit df[df.eval('state == "NY"')]
```

On my computer, these gave me timings of 903 ms, 733 ms (19% faster), and 758 ms (17% faster), respectively. We thus already see that `loc` is the slowest of the three, with the use of `df.query` and `df.eval` coming in almost the same.

But wait—the result of df.eval is a boolean series, which we then apply to df. Perhaps, instead of using a mask index on df, we should do so on df.loc. Using %timeit, we can find out pretty quickly:

```
%timeit df.loc[df.eval('state == "NY"')]
```

Sure enough, we get the fastest result, albeit by just a hair, when using df.loc here: 729 ms. In other words, it would seem that selecting via df.loc and a mask index gives better performance than just df and a mask index—something I've seen elsewhere, too. The rest of my solutions in this exercise all use df.loc for a fairer comparison.

Next, I asked you to find passenger cars (i.e., with ptype equal to 'PAS') from New York. Here are the three solutions:

```
%timeit df.loc[((df['state'] == 'NY') & (df['ptype'] == 'PAS'))]
%timeit df.query('state == "NY" & ptype == "PAS"')
%timeit df.loc[df.eval('state == "NY" & ptype == "PAS"')]
```

I got timings of 1.27 seconds for the traditional use of df.loc versus 965 ms for df.query (24% faster) and 924 ms for df.eval (27% faster). Here we use & to combine the two boolean series we get back from each comparison. Although we were able to speed up our "or" query using isin, there isn't an exact equivalent for "and" queries.

Next, I asked you to expand the query further, thus narrowing the potential results, looking for white passenger cars from New York that had been ticketed. Again, we can compare the queries:

```
%%timeit
df.loc[((df['state'] == 'NY') &
                (df['ptype'] == 'PAS') &
                (df['color'] == 'WHITE'))]

%%timeit
df.query(
    'state == "NY" & ptype == "PAS" & color == "WHITE"')

%%timeit
df.loc[df.eval(
    'state == "NY" & ptype == "PAS" & color == "WHITE"')]
```

This time, I got timings of 1.34 seconds, 728 ms for df.query (45% faster), and 727 ms for df.eval (also 45% faster). We can see that adding another condition slows the traditional query a bit but actually results in faster queries when using the numexpr backend. I'm not sure why this is the case, except that perhaps numexpr is only activated once the query reaches a certain size threshold.

Next, I asked you to find tickets for white passenger cars from New York that were parked more than 1 foot from the curb. Here are the queries:

```
%%timeit
df.loc[((df['state'] == 'NY') & (df['ptype'] == 'PAS') &
                (df['color'] == 'WHITE') & (df['feet'] > 1))]
```

```
%%timeit
df.query('state == "NY" & ptype == "PAS" &
                    color == "WHITE" & feet > 1')

%%timeit
df.loc[df.eval('state == "NY" & ptype == "PAS" &
                    color == "WHITE" & feet > 1')]
```

In this case, I got timings of 1.31 seconds for the traditional query, 712 ms for df.query (45% faster), and 706 ms for df.eval (46% faster). Again, we can see that when the queries are complex, using the numexpr backend gives us a big speed advantage.

Finally, I asked you to find tickets given to white Toyota passenger cars with license plates from New York state that were parked more than 1 foot from the curb. Here is how we write those queries:

```
%%timeit
df.loc[((df['state'] == 'NY') &
               (df['ptype'] == 'PAS') &
               (df['color'] == 'WHITE') &
               (df['feet'] > 1) &
               (df['make'] == 'TOYOT'))]

%%timeit
df.query('state == "NY" & ptype == "PAS" &
                color == "WHITE" & feet > 1 &
                make == "TOYOT"')

%%timeit
df.loc[df.eval('state == "NY" & ptype == "PAS" &
                color == "WHITE" & feet > 1 &
                make == "TOYOT"')]
```

I got timings of 1.75 seconds for the traditional query, 896 ms for df.query (49% faster), and 899 ms for df.eval (48% faster). The added condition slowed all the queries, but the numexpr backend continued to prove its worth, giving us the same answer at nearly twice the speed.

Does this mean it's always worth using df.query or df.eval? I know there are pandas users who would say "yes," given that even in the simplest of cases, we see a speedup. And in the most complex cases, the speedup is dramatic. So you could argue that because it doesn't matter much for simple queries on a short data set but it matters a lot for complex queries on large ones, you should always use these techniques.

However, focusing on speed before you've thought hard about the problem and potential bottlenecks can be misleading. Remember that df.query returns all the columns from a data frame—so if a data frame contains more columns than we want to get back, it may end up using lots of memory unnecessarily. By contrast, df.loc provides not only a row selector but also a column selector for more flexibility. I thus tend to use df.loc for my queries while I'm still putting them together. When I'm done, I can then experiment with these techniques to see how to reduce memory and speed things up.

Solution

```
filename = '../data/nyc-parking-violations-2020.csv'
df = pd.read_csv(filename,
                 usecols=['Plate ID', 'Registration State',
                          'Plate Type', 'Feet From Curb',
                          'Vehicle Make', 'Vehicle Color'])
df.columns = ['pid', 'state', 'ptype',
              'make', 'color', 'feet']

%timeit df.loc[(df['state'] == 'NY') |
               (df['state'] == 'NJ') |
               (df['state'] == 'CT')]
%timeit df.query("state == 'NY' or
                  state == 'NJ' or
                  state == 'CT'")
%timeit df.loc[df['state'].isin(['NY', 'NJ', 'CT'])]

%timeit df.loc[(df['state'] == 'NY')]
%timeit df.query('state == "NY"')
%timeit df.loc[df.eval('state == "NY"')]

%timeit df.loc[((df['state'] == 'NY') &
               (df['ptype'] == 'PAS'))]
%timeit df.query('state == "NY" & ptype == "PAS"')
%timeit df.loc[df.eval('state == "NY" & ptype == "PAS"')]

%timeit df.loc[((df['state'] == 'NY') &
               (df['ptype'] == 'PAS') &
               (df['color'] == 'WHITE'))]

%timeit df.query(
    'state == "NY" & ptype == "PAS" & color == "WHITE"
    ')
%timeit df.loc[df.eval(
    'state == "NY" & ptype == "PAS" & color == "WHITE"')
    ]

%timeit df.loc[((df['state'] == 'NY') &
               (df['ptype'] == 'PAS') &
               (df['color'] == 'WHITE') &
               (df['feet'] > 1))]

%timeit df.query(
    'state == "NY" & ptype == "PAS" & color == "WHITE" & feet > 1'
    )

%timeit df.loc[df.eval('state == "NY" & ptype == "PAS" &
                        color == "WHITE" & feet > 1')]

%timeit df.loc[((df['state'] == 'NY') &
               (df['ptype'] == 'PAS') &
               (df['color'] == 'WHITE') &
               (df['feet'] > 1) &
               (df['make'] == 'TOYOT'))]
%timeit df.query(
    ('state == "NY" & ptype == "PAS" & color == "WHITE"' +
```

```
    '& feet > 1 & make == "TOYOT"')
    )
%timeit df.loc[df.eval(
    ('state == "NY" & ptype == "PAS" & color == "WHITE"' +
    '& feet > 1 & make == "TOYOT"')
    )]
```

Beyond the exercise

In this exercise, we ran a number of queries using plain ol' `.loc` as well as `df.query` and `df.eval`, comparing their performance times. Here are some additional challenges for you to try along these lines:

- In `df.query`, you can use the words `and` and `or`, rather than the symbols `&` and `|`, thanks to the `numexpr` library. Rewrite the final query using the words. Does this change the speed at all?
- I prefer measuring distance in meters rather than feet. I thus want to find all cars that were ticketed when they were more than 1 meter from the curb. (Every 1 meter is 3.28 feet.) Perform this query using the traditional `df.loc` and also using `df.query`. Which one runs faster?
- What if you modify the query to look for cars that are more than 1 meter from the curb and for which the state is New York? Which query runs faster and by how much?

Summary

Calculations and analysis with pandas are much faster than they would be in pure Python. Even so, when you're working with a large data set, you'll often want or need to reduce the memory footprint of your data frame and use techniques that can improve performance. In this chapter, we reviewed a number of techniques you can use to speed up your queries and also use fewer resources:

- Choosing columns carefully
- Reducing memory usage with categories
- Reading data from feather format rather than CSV
- Speeding up complex queries with `df.query` and `df.eval`

If you've reached this part of the book, congratulations! You've successfully gone through all 50 exercises! I have no doubt that if you've made it this far, you have a much better, deeper understanding of pandas, what it can do, and how you can use it in a variety of situations. You should feel good about yourself and confident about your ability to use pandas at work.

But before you stop reading: the next chapter contains a large project in which I'll ask you to use all the techniques from this book to analyze a large real-world data set. I hope you'll take the time to do the project, which will help cement the lessons you've learned and help you use pandas even more effectively in the future.

Final project

Congratulations! You've finished all the exercises in this book. If you've gone through each one—and especially if you've gone through the "Beyond the exercise" questions—I'm sure you have improved your pandas skills a lot.

But before you go, I want to give you a final project. We'll explore the "college scorecard," a data set assembled by the US Department of Education about post-secondary (i.e., after high school) educational programs. The college scorecard allows us to see what programs schools offer, how many students they admit, what those students pay in tuition and fees, how many students graduate, and how much they can expect to earn after graduation. From looking at this data, we can better understand many different aspects of university education in the United States. I should add that with a data set this large and rich, there are many different questions that you could ask. After you finish answering the questions I pose here, I strongly suggest that you also explore the data set on your own, asking (and answering) questions that you think are interesting and relevant.

Problem

Here is what I'd like you to do:

1 Create a data frame (`institutions_df`) from the college scorecard cohorts-institutions CSV file (Most-Recent-Cohorts-Institution.csv.gz). You only need to load the following columns: `OPEID6`, `INSTNM`, `CITY`, `STABBR`, `FTFTPCTPELL`, `TUITIONFEE_IN`, `TUITIONFEE_OUT`, `ADM_RATE`, `NPT4_PUB`, `NPT4_PRIV`, `NPT41_PUB`, `NPT41_PRIV`, `NPT45_PUB`, `NPT45_PRIV`, `MD_EARN_WNE_P10`, and `C100_4`.

2 Load the CSV file for fields of study (FieldOfStudyData1718_1819_PP.csv.gz) into another data frame (`fields_of_study_df`). Here, load the columns `OPEID6`, `INSTNM`, `CREDDESC`, `CIPDESC`, and `CONTROL`.

3 Answer the following questions:
  - What state has the greatest number of universities in this database?
  - What city, in which state, has the greatest number of universities in this database?
  - How much memory can you save if you set the `CITY` and `STABBR` columns in `institutions_df` to be categories?
  - Create a histogram showing how many bachelor programs universities offer.
  - Determine which university offers the greatest number of bachelor programs.
  - Create a histogram showing how many graduate (master's and doctoral) programs universities offer.
  - Determine which university offers the greatest number of different graduate (master + doctoral) programs.

4 Answer these questions:
  - How many universities offer bachelor's degrees but not master's or doctorates?
  - How many universities offer master's and doctoral degrees but not bachelor's?
  - How many institutions offer bachelor's degrees whose name contains the term "Computer Science"?
  - The `CONTROL` field describes the types of institutions in the database. How many of each type offer a computer science program?

5 Create a pie chart showing the different types of institutions that offer CS (short for "computer science") degrees.

6 Determine the minimum, median, mean, and maximum tuitions for an undergrad CS degree. (We define this as a bachelor's program with the phrase "Computer Science" in the name.) When comparing tuition, use `TUITIONFEE_OUT` for all schools.

7 Describe the tuition again, but grouped by the different types of universities (`CONTROL`).

8 Determine the correlation between admission rate and tuition cost. How would you interpret this?

9 Create a scatter plot with tuition on the *x* axis, admission rate on the *y* axis, and median earnings after 10 years are used for colorizing. Use the "Spectral" colormap. Where do the lowest-paid graduates show up on the graph?

10 Determine which universities are in the top 25% of tuition and also the top 25% with Pell grants (i.e., government assistance to lower-income students). Print only the institution name, city, and state, ordered by institution name.

11 NPT4_PUB indicates the average net price for public institutions (in-state tuition) and NPT4_PRIV for private institutions. NPT41_PUB and NPT45_PUB show the average price paid by people in the lowest income bracket (1) versus the highest income bracket (5) at public institutions. NPT41_PRIV and NPT45_PRIV show the average price paid by people in the lowest income bracket (1) versus the highest income bracket (5) at private institutions. At how many institutions does the bottom quintile receive money (i.e., the value is negative)?

12 Determine the average proportion that the bottom quintile pays versus the top quintile at public universities.

13 Determine the average proportion that the bottom quintile pays versus the top quintile at private universities?

14 Let's try to figure out which universities offer the best overall return on investment (ROI) (across all disciplines):

- For which schools in the cheapest 25% do their students have the top 25% of salaries 10 years after graduation?
- How about private institutions?
- Is there a correlation between admission rates and completion rates? That is: If a school is highly selective, are students more likely to graduate?
- Ten years after graduating, from what kinds of schools (private, for-profit, private nonprofit, or public) do people earn, on average, the greatest amount?
- Do people who graduate from "Ivy Plus" schools (the Ivy League as well as MIT, Stanford, and the University of Chicago) earn more than the average private-school university graduate? If so, how much more?
- Do people studying at universities in particular states earn, on average, more after 10 years?

15 Create a bar plot for the average amount earned, per state, sorted by ascending pay.

16 Create a boxplot for the earnings by state.

Column names and meanings

The column names in the two CSV files we're examining in this chapter are terse, as shown in tables 13.1 and 13.2.

Table 13.1 Column names in the "Cohorts and institutions" file

Column name	Explanation	Sample value
OPEID6	Unique ID (integer) for each educational institution	1002
INSTNM	Institution name	"Alabama A & M University"
CITY	Institution's city	"Normal"

Table 13.1 Column names in the "Cohorts and institutions" file *(continued)*

Column name	Explanation	Sample value
STABBR	Institution's state name (abbreviated)	"AL"
FTFTPCTPELL	Percentage of Pell-grant recipients	0.6925
TUITIONFEE_IN	In-state tuition	10024.0
TUITIONFEE_OUT	Out-of-state tuition	18634.0
ADM_RATE	Admission rate	0.8965
NPT4_PUB	Net price (for public institutions; NaN if a private institution)	15529.0
NPT4_PRIV	Net price (for private institutions; NaN if a public institution)	NaN
NPT41_PUB	Average price paid by people in the lowest income bracket (for public institutions; NaN if a private institution)	14694.0
NPT41_PRIV	Average price paid by people in the lowest income bracket (for private institutions; NaN if a public institution)	NaN
NPT45_PUB	Average price paid by people in the highest income bracket (for public institutions; NaN if a private institution)	20483.0
NPT45_PRIV	Average price paid by people in the highest income bracket (for private institutions; NaN if a public institution)	NaN
MD_EARN_WNE_P10	Median income for graduates 10 years following graduation	36339.0
C100_4	Completion rates after four years	0.1052

Table 13.2 Column names in the "Fields of study" file

Column name	Explanation	Sample value
OPEID6	Unique ID (integer) for each educational institution	1002
INSTNM	Institution name	"Alabama A & M University"
CREDDESC	Degree being offered	"Bachelors Degree"
CIPDESC	Education program	"Agriculture, General."
CONTROL	What type of institution is this?	"Public"

Working it out

As I said, the college scorecard data set includes a large number of facts and figures about American higher education, describing both the institutions and the students who learn there. To answer this set of questions, we only need to look at two CSV files: (1) information about the most recent cohorts of students who enrolled at and graduated from these institutions and (2) the fields of study that each institution offers. Some of our questions require just one of these data sources, and others require that we combine them into a single data frame.

CREATE A DATA FRAME FROM THE COLLEGE SCORECARD COHORTS-INSTITUTIONS CSV FILE

To start, I asked you to load each of the CSV files into a data frame. You may have noticed that the files I've provided have a .csv.gz suffix. This means they are compressed with gzip—but you don't need to uncompress them before loading because pandas is smart enough to automatically do so when we run `read_csv`. Load the first data frame as follows, defining `institutions_df`:

```
institutions_filename = '../data/Most-Recent-Cohorts-Institution.csv.gz'
institutions_df = pd.read_csv(institutions_filename,
                usecols=['OPEID6',
                         'INSTNM', 'CITY', 'STABBR',
                         'FTFTPCTPELL', 'TUITIONFEE_IN',
                         'TUITIONFEE_OUT', 'ADM_RATE',
                         'NPT4_PUB', 'NPT4_PRIV',
                         'NPT41_PUB', 'NPT41_PRIV',
                         'NPT45_PUB', 'NPT45_PRIV',
                         'MD_EARN_WNE_P10', 'C100_4'])
```

LOAD THE CSV FILE FOR FIELDS OF STUDY INTO ANOTHER DATA FRAME

We load the other CSV file with information about fields of study for the last few years as follows, assigning it to `fields_df`:

```
fields_filename = '../data/FieldOfStudyData1718_1819_PP.csv.gz'
fields_of_study_df = pd.read_csv(fields_filename,
                usecols=['OPEID6', 'INSTNM',
                         'CREDDESC', 'CIPDESC', 'CONTROL'])
```

With these two data frames defined and in memory, we can start performing some queries.

WHAT STATE HAS THE GREATEST NUMBER OF UNIVERSITIES IN THIS DATABASE?

First, I wanted to know which state has the greatest number of universities in this database. This is a classic example of when to use grouping. We can group on the STABBR (state abbreviation) column, running the `count` method. This will tell us how often each state appears in the data set. We also have to provide a second column, which is where the count is reported. The choice doesn't matter, so we go with OPEID6, the unique ID used for each institution:

```
(
    institutions_df
```

```
        .groupby('STABBR')['OPEID6'].count()
)
```

This query tells us how often each state appears in the data set. But we're interested in finding which states have the greatest number of universities. To find that, we sort the series by the values we get back in descending order. The first row in this series is, by definition, the state with the largest number—which we retrieve using head(1):

```
(
    institutions_df
    .groupby('STABBR')['OPEID6'].count()
    .sort_values(ascending=False)
    .head(1)
)
```

According to this data, California has the greatest number of universities—a large number, at 705.

WHAT CITY, IN WHICH STATE, HAS THE GREATEST NUMBER OF UNIVERSITIES IN THIS DATABASE?

I then decided to ask a slightly different question: which city has the greatest number of universities? At first glance, it may seem that this query is identical to the previous one, grouping by the CITY column rather than STABBR. But that would combine cities of the same name in different states, combining Springfield, Illinois with Springfield, Massachusetts. The solution requires that we group by two columns: first STABBR and then CITY. The combination allows us to find which city, in which state, has the greatest number of universities:

```
(
    institutions_df
    .groupby(['STABBR', 'CITY'])['OPEID6'].count()
    .sort_values(ascending=False)
    .head(1)
)
```

Once again, we ask for the count method to be run on OPEID6 because we need to count on a nongrouping column. And again we sort in descending order and grab the top value. The answer is New York City, with 81 institutions of higher learning.

HOW MUCH MEMORY CAN WE SAVE IF WE SET THE CITY AND STABBR COLUMNS IN INSTITUTIONS_DF TO BE CATEGORIES?

Considering that both state and city names are text data and that they repeat so often, it makes sense to consider how much memory we may save by turning the STABBR and CITY columns into categories. But as always when trying to optimize, we should measure before and after taking such an action, to know whether our efforts were worthwhile.

I thus asked you to determine how much memory our data frame was already using. The easiest way to find this is to run memory_usage on a data frame. Don't forget to pass the deep=True keyword argument. This returns the total memory usage of each column, including the objects to which it refers. (As we saw in chapter 12, that argument can make a huge difference!) Here's how we can calculate that and then print it:

```
pre_category_memory = (
    institutions_df
    .memory_usage(deep=True)
    .sum()
)

print(f'{pre_category_memory:,}')
```

First, we calculate the total memory usage and assign it to pre_category_memory. Then, to print the number with commas between the digits—and yes, we're showing off here—we print it in an f-string, using a single comma (,) as the format specifier after the colon (:).

We then turn both the STABBR and CITY columns into categories:

```
institutions_df['CITY'] = (
    institutions_df['CITY']
    .astype('category')
)

institutions_df['STABBR'] = (
    institutions_df['STABBR']
    .astype('category')
)
```

Now that this has been done, how much memory did we save?

```
post_category_memory = (
    institutions_df
    .memory_usage(deep=True)
    .sum()
)

savings = pre_category_memory - post_category_memory
print(f'{savings:,}')

savings = pre_category_memory - post_category_memory
print(f'{savings:,}')
```

On my computer, the savings is calculated as 579,371 bytes—meaning we reduced memory usage by approximately one-third by turning these two columns into categories. Not a bad gain for a few seconds of coding, I'd say.

CREATE A HISTOGRAM SHOWING HOW MANY BACHELOR'S PROGRAMS UNIVERSITIES OFFER.
Next, I asked you to create a histogram indicating how many programs are offered by each university. That is, we'd like to know how many universities offer 10 programs, how many offer 20, how many offer 30, and so forth.

To create such a histogram, we first need to count the number of different bachelor's programs each university offers. We start by looking at fields_of_study_df and retrieving only those rows for which the CREDDESC value is 'Bachelors Degree':

```
(
    fields_of_study_df
    .loc[fields_of_study_df['CREDDESC'] == 'Bachelors Degree']
```

With that in hand, we can run `groupby` on the `INSTNM` (institution name) column. This means our aggregation method (`count`, in this case) runs once for each distinct value of `INSTNM`. To avoid getting a result for each column, we restrict our output to `CIPDESC`:

```
(
    fields_of_study_df
    .loc[fields_of_study_df['CREDDESC'] == 'Bachelors Degree']
    .groupby('INSTNM')['CIPDESC'].count()
    .plot.hist()
)
```

This returns a series in which the index contains the institution name and the value contains the number of bachelor-level degrees offered by each institution. Finally, we can feed that into the histogram-plotting method (figure 13.1):

```
(
    fields_of_study_df
    .loc[fields_of_study_df['CREDDESC'] == 'Bachelors Degree']
    .groupby('INSTNM')['CIPDESC'].count()
    .plot.hist()
)
```

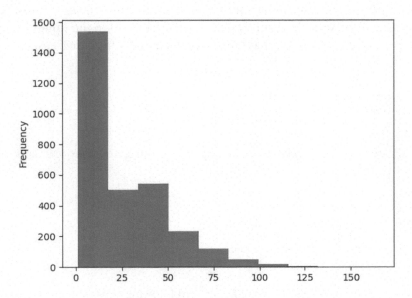

Figure 13.1
Histogram showing how many schools offer different numbers of bachelor's programs

The result shows that a very large number of institutions (more than 1,400!) offer fewer than 20 bachelor-level programs, fewer than 600 institutions offer between 20 and 50 programs, and 200 or fewer institutions offer more than 50 programs.

WHICH UNIVERSITY OFFERS THE GREATEST NUMBER OF BACHELOR'S PROGRAMS?

Now that we've counted the number of programs offered by each institution in this data set, we can ask which universities offer the greatest number of programs. We already have their counts, thanks to the `groupby` we ran before. We can thus rerun that query, sorting the resulting values in descending order and keeping only the top 10 results:

```
(
    fields_of_study_df
    .loc[fields_of_study_df['CREDDESC'] == 'Bachelors Degree']
    .groupby('INSTNM')['CIPDESC'].count()
    .sort_values(ascending=False)
    .head(10)
)
```

When I ran this, I found that the institution with the greatest number of programs was Westminster College (with 165 bachelor-level programs), followed by Pennsylvania State University's main campus (141) and the University of Washington's Seattle campus (137).

CREATE A HISTOGRAM SHOWING HOW MANY GRADUATE (MASTER'S AND DOCTORAL) PROGRAMS UNIVERSITIES OFFER.

Now that we've counted bachelor's programs, how about graduate programs offering either a master's or doctoral degree? That query is trickier because we can no longer compare `CREDDESC` with a single string. Rather, we need to check if the value is one of two different strings. For that, we use the `isin` method, which takes a list of strings and returns `True` if the value in that row matches one or more of the values in the list.

To start, we can get all schools that offer master's and doctoral degrees:

```
(
    fields_of_study_df
    .loc[fields_of_study_df['CREDDESC']
        .isin(["Master's Degree", "Doctoral Degree"])]
)
```

With that in hand, we can repeat our `groupby` query, using `count` as our aggregation method:

```
(
    fields_of_study_df
    .loc[fields_of_study_df['CREDDESC']
        .isin(["Master's Degree", "Doctoral Degree"])]
    .groupby('INSTNM')['CIPDESC'].count()
)
```

Finally, having grouped by `INSTNM` using `count` and knowing how many programs each institution offers, we can create the histogram (figure 13.2):

```
(
    fields_of_study_df
    .loc[fields_of_study_df['CREDDESC']
        .isin(["Master's Degree", "Doctoral Degree"])]
    .groupby('INSTNM')['CIPDESC'].count()
    .plot.hist()
)
```

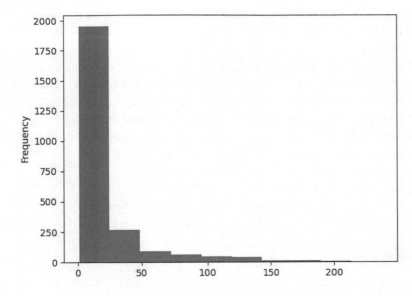

Figure 13.2 Histogram showing how many schools offer different numbers of graduate programs

Here we see that the vast majority of schools offer fewer than 25 different graduate programs, with more offering fewer than 50. The number of schools offering more than 50 master's and doctoral degrees declines even more precipitously, although a handful offer more than 200.

WHICH UNIVERSITY OFFERS THE GREATEST NUMBER OF DIFFERENT GRADUATE (MASTER + DOCTORAL) PROGRAMS?

I next asked you to find just which schools offer the greatest number of different graduate programs. As before, this means sorting the results from our groupby and count:

```
(
    fields_of_study_df
    .loc[fields_of_study_df['CREDDESC']
        .isin(["Master's Degree", "Doctoral Degree"])]
    .groupby('INSTNM')['CIPDESC'].count()
    .sort_values(ascending=False)
    .head(10)
)
```

The University of Washington's Seattle campus has the most programs (237), followed by Penn State's main campus (230) and New York University (226).

> **NOTE** The number of programs a university offers at any level shouldn't be taken as an indication of how good the university is or whether the program is appropriate for you. Especially when it comes to graduate studies, the important thing is whether the specific program is good for you and (perhaps even more importantly) whether your advisor is someone you can trust to help you through the program. So don't take these questions as anything other than a numeric exercise; I'm certainly not trying to imply that the more programs a university offers, the better it is.

HOW MANY UNIVERSITIES OFFER BACHELOR'S DEGREES BUT NOT MASTER'S OR DOCTORATES?

Although the universities I attended all offered degree programs at all levels, some focus exclusively on either undergraduate or graduate education. I asked you to find how many universities offer bachelor's degrees but not master's or doctorates, followed by the reverse—how many offer master's or doctoral degrees but not bachelor's.

To answer these questions, we first find all schools offering bachelor's programs and those offering master's and doctoral programs. These queries are identical to what we did before. However, here we store them in two separate variables so we can make calculations based on them:

```
ug_schools = (
    fields_of_study_df
    .loc[fields_of_study_df['CREDDESC'] == 'Bachelors Degree',
    'INSTNM']
)

grad_schools = (
    fields_of_study_df
    .loc[fields_of_study_df['CREDDESC']
        .isin(["Master's Degree", "Doctoral Degree"]),
    'INSTNM']
)
```

Both `ug_schools` and `grad_schools` are pandas series with the values containing the names of the universities. However, because we retrieved the university names from `fields_of_study_df`, there are plenty of repeats, with one row for each program offered by the institution. We will leave things as they are rather than apply the `unique` method because `apply` returns a NumPy array and we want to use some additional pandas functionality.

Now that we have defined these two series, how can we determine which schools offer bachelor's degrees but not master's or doctoral degrees? We can again rely on `isin`. That is, to find all undergraduate institutions that are also graduate schools, we can say

```
ug_schools.isin(grad_schools)
```

This code returns a boolean series. But we want the opposite of this: the undergraduate schools that are *not* graduate schools. So we use ~ to flip the logic:

```
~ug_schools.isin(grad_schools)
```

This gives the opposite boolean series from what we had before. If we apply that boolean series to `ug_schools`, we get the rows corresponding to undergraduate schools that aren't graduate schools:

```
ug_schools[~ug_schools.isin(grad_schools)]
```

However, there is a problem with this result: the school names are repeated. This is where we can use the `drop_duplicates` method, getting distinct values back:

```
ug_schools[~ug_schools.isin(grad_schools)].drop_duplicates()
```

We can retrieve `size` from the result:

```
ug_schools[~ug_schools.isin(grad_schools)].drop_duplicates().size
```

The database has 923 undergraduate schools that don't offer graduate degrees.

HOW MANY UNIVERSITIES OFFER MASTER'S AND DOCTORAL DEGREES BUT NOT BACHELOR'S?

We can apply similar logic to this to flip the question around:

```
grad_schools[~grad_schools.isin(ug_schools)].drop_duplicates().size
```

The result is 404 institutions that offer master's and doctoral degrees but don't offer bachelor's degrees.

HOW MANY INSTITUTIONS OFFER BACHELOR'S DEGREES WHOSE NAME CONTAINS THE TERM "COMPUTER SCIENCE"?

Next, I thought it would be interesting to determine how many institutions offer bachelor's degrees in computer science. Every institution calls its department and degree something slightly different, which means we'll likely miss many possibilities. But if we look for programs containing the term `'Computer Science'`, how many will we find?

First, we need to find all those rows in which `CIPDESC` contains the string `'Computer Science'`:

```
fields_of_study_df['CIPDESC'].str.contains('Computer Science')
```

But that isn't enough because we're specifically looking for bachelor's programs in computer science. We thus need to have two conditions joined with `&`:

```
fields_of_study_df['CIPDESC'].str.contains('Computer Science') &
    fields_of_study_df['CREDDESC'] == 'Bachelors Degree'
```

This combined query returns a boolean series. We can then apply that boolean series to `fields_of_study_df` with `.loc`:

```
(
    fields_of_study_df
    .loc[(fields_of_study_df['CIPDESC']
        .str.contains('Computer Science')) &
        (fields_of_study_df['CREDDESC'] == 'Bachelors Degree')]
)
```

The thing is, we're not interested in all the columns. We just want to see the institution names so we can count them. We can do this by adding a column selector to `.loc`, indicating that we want to see `INSTNM`:

```
(
    fields_of_study_df
    .loc[(fields_of_study_df['CIPDESC']
        .str.contains('Computer Science')) &
        (fields_of_study_df['CREDDESC'] == 'Bachelors Degree'),
        'INSTNM']
)
```

This returns a series of 824 institution names. But, as before, the names aren't necessarily unique, given that there may be more than one degree program with "Computer Science" in its name. For this reason, we take the results, invoke `unique()` on them, and then get the size of the resulting array:

```
(
    fields_of_study_df
    .loc[(fields_of_study_df['CIPDESC']
            .str.contains('Computer Science')) &
            (fields_of_study_df['CREDDESC'] == 'Bachelors Degree'),
            'INSTNM']
    .unique()
    .size
)
```

The result, on my system, is 762.

HOW MANY TYPES OF INSTITUTIONS IN THE DATABASE OFFER A COMPUTER-SCIENCE PROGRAM?
The college scorecard data set puts each university into one of four categories listed in the `CONTROL` column: public, private and nonprofit, private and for-profit, or foreign. In my next question, I asked you to show how many institutions of each type offer computer science as a bachelor-level degree.

We start with our previous query before the call to `unique`:

```
(
    fields_of_study_df
    .loc[(fields_of_study_df['CIPDESC']
            .str.contains('Computer Science')) &
        (fields_of_study_df['CREDDESC'] == 'Bachelors Degree'),
    ['CONTROL','INSTNM']].groupby('CONTROL').count()
)
```

We then run a `groupby` on `CONTROL` because we want to know how many institutions of each type offer undergraduate CS programs. For this to work, our column selector needs to include not just `INSTNM`, as before, but also `CONTROL`:

```
fields_of_study_df.loc[(fields_of_study_df[
        'CIPDESC'].str.contains('Computer Science')) &
        (fields_of_study_df['CREDDESC'] ==
            'Bachelors Degree'), ['CONTROL',
            'INSTNM']].groupby('CONTROL')
```

This query gives us a `groupby` object on which we can then invoke `count`:

```
fields_of_study_df.loc[(fields_of_study_df[
        'CIPDESC'].str.contains('Computer Science')) &
        (fields_of_study_df['CREDDESC'] ==
            'Bachelors Degree'),
            ['CONTROL', 'INSTNM']].groupby('CONTROL').count()
```

With this query, I find 32 foreign universities, 18 private for-profit universities, 501 private nonprofit universities, and 273 public universities, all offering undergraduate CS programs.

CREATE A PIE CHART SHOWING THE DIFFERENT TYPES OF INSTITUTIONS THAT OFFER CS DEGREES.
Seeing this information in a table, however accurate, isn't as striking as a graphical display would be. I thus asked you to take these results and put them into a pie chart. Fortunately, that's easy. We start with this query and then retrieve only the INSTNM column:

```
(
    fields_of_study_df
    .loc[(fields_of_study_df['CIPDESC']
            .str.contains('Computer Science')) &
        (fields_of_study_df['CREDDESC'] == 'Bachelors Degree'),
    ['CONTROL','INSTNM']]
    .groupby('CONTROL').count()['INSTNM']
)
```

That returns a single series of values along with the index (i.e., the different institution categories). We can turn that into a pie chart by invoking .plot.pie() at the end (figure 13.3):

```
(
    fields_of_study_df
    .loc[(fields_of_study_df['CIPDESC']
            .str.contains('Computer Science')) &
        (fields_of_study_df['CREDDESC'] == 'Bachelors Degree'),
    ['CONTROL','INSTNM']]
    .groupby('CONTROL').count()['INSTNM']
    .plot.pie()
)
```

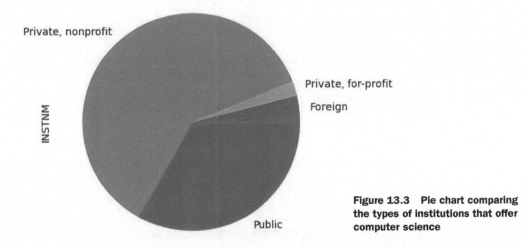

Figure 13.3 Pie chart comparing the types of institutions that offer computer science

Next, we want to start looking at the cost of getting a computer science degree from an American university. To do this, we first need to find all universities at which computer science is taught at the undergraduate level. This query is identical to one we've already seen, except that we're looking for three different columns: OPEID6 (a unique

ID number for each university in the system), CONTROL (the category of institution we've already seen), and INSTNM (the name of the institution):

```
comp_sci_universities = (
    fields_of_study_df
    .loc[(fields_of_study_df['CIPDESC']
            .str.contains('Computer Science')) &
        (fields_of_study_df['CREDDESC'] == 'Bachelors Degree'),
    ['OPEID6','CONTROL','INSTNM']]
)
```

The good news is that we now have these rows and have put them into a new data frame, comp_sci_universities. However, the index contains the same values we had in fields_of_study_df. This isn't inherently bad, except that to answer our questions, we need to join this data frame with institutions_df. Joining requires that the indexes match up. For that reason, we modify our creation of comp_sci_universities so it sets the index to be OPEID6:

```
comp_sci_universities = (
    fields_of_study_df
    .loc[(fields_of_study_df['CIPDESC']
            .str.contains('Computer Science')) &
        (fields_of_study_df['CREDDESC'] == 'Bachelors Degree'),
    ['OPEID6','CONTROL','INSTNM']]
    .set_index('OPEID6')
)
```

Now let's make sure institutions_df has the index we need to join them:

```
institutions_df[['OPEID6', 'TUITIONFEE_OUT']].set_index('OPEID6')
```

Note that this doesn't change institutions_df; rather, it returns a new data frame with OPEID6 as its index.

Now that we have two data frames with a common index, we can join them:

```
(
    comp_sci_universities
    .join(institutions_df[['OPEID6', 'TUITIONFEE_OUT']]
        .set_index('OPEID6'))
)
```

But this query gives us the entire new data frame. We don't really want that; we only need the TUITIONFEE_OUT column:

```
(
    comp_sci_universities
    .join(institutions_df[['OPEID6', 'TUITIONFEE_OUT']]
        .set_index('OPEID6'))
    ['TUITIONFEE_OUT']
)
```

The result of this query, short as it is, packs a real punch: we retrieve the tuition at each university with an undergraduate CS program in the data set.

WHAT ARE THE MINIMUM, MEDIAN, MEAN, AND MAXIMUM TUITIONS FOR AN UNDERGRAD CS DEGREE?

I asked you to find the minimum, median, mean, and maximum values for tuition. We could, of course, calculate each of these individually. But when we want to perform a number of aggregate calculations, the easiest thing to do is invoke `describe`, which gives them all:

```
(
    comp_sci_universities
    .join(institutions_df[['OPEID6', 'TUITIONFEE_OUT']]
        .set_index('OPEID6'))
    ['TUITIONFEE_OUT']
    .describe()
)
```

DESCRIBE THE TUITION AGAIN, BUT GROUPED BY THE DIFFERENT TYPES OF UNIVERSITIES

Next, I asked you to describe the tuition again, but grouped by the different types of universities (i.e., the CONTROL column). We can accomplish this by invoking `groupby('CONTROL')` on the result of the join, retrieving TUITIONFEE_OUT, and then invoking `describe` on the result:

```
comp_sci_universities.join(institutions_df[
    ['OPEID6', 'TUITIONFEE_OUT']].set_index('OPEID6')).groupby(
        'CONTROL')['TUITIONFEE_OUT'].describe()
```

However, I find two problems with this result. First, foreign-owned universities give results of 0 or NaN for each column. Second, it's weird to have the university types in the index and the results from `describe` in the columns. Both of these are problems of aesthetics, but if we're already playing with the data, let's see how we can clean it up.

We can use `dropna` to remove the Foreign row, the only one in which we have any NaN values:

```
(
    comp_sci_universities
    .join(institutions_df[['OPEID6', 'TUITIONFEE_OUT']]
        .set_index('OPEID6'))
    .groupby('CONTROL')['TUITIONFEE_OUT'].describe()
    .dropna()
)
```

What about my preference that the values of `describe` be in the rows rather than the columns? We can transpose rows and columns in a pandas data frame with the `transpose` method:

```
(
    comp_sci_universities
    .join(institutions_df[['OPEID6', 'TUITIONFEE_OUT']]
        .set_index('OPEID6'))
    .groupby('CONTROL')['TUITIONFEE_OUT'].describe()
```

```
    .dropna()
    .transpose()
)
```

However, because this is used so often, we can instead invoke it with T:

```
(
    comp_sci_universities
    .join(institutions_df[['OPEID6', 'TUITIONFEE_OUT']]
          .set_index('OPEID6'))
    .groupby('CONTROL')['TUITIONFEE_OUT'].describe()
    .dropna()
    .T
)
```

NOTE Whereas `transpose` is a method and needs to be invoked with parentheses after its name, `T` is a Python property and should *not* have parentheses. Using `T()` will result in an error. They are otherwise equivalent to one another.

WHAT IS THE CORRELATION BETWEEN ADMISSION RATE AND TUITION COST? HOW WOULD YOU INTERPRET THIS?

We often hear that the most expensive universities are also the hardest to get into. Is this true? Do we see a correlation in the data? To find out, we can invoke `corr` on `institutions_df`, looking at the `ADM_RATE` and `TUITIONFEE_OUT` columns:

```
institutions_df[['ADM_RATE', 'TUITIONFEE_OUT']].corr()
```

As always, a correlation of 0 means there's no correlation between the two values, 1 means they're perfectly aligned, and –1 means they're completely opposite. In this case, we see a correlation of –0.3: slightly negative. This means as the tuition fee goes up, the admission rate goes (slightly) down—which does indeed describe many American universities. Another way to say this is that the universities that are hardest to get into are, in general, also more expensive.

CREATE A SCATTER PLOT WITH TUITION ON THE X AXIS AND ADMISSION RATE ON THE Y AXIS. WHERE DO THE LOWEST-PAID GRADUATES SHOW UP ON THE GRAPH?

I asked you to create a scatter plot with the admission rate on the *y* axis and the tuition fee on the *x* axis:

```
institutions_df.plot.scatter(x='TUITIONFEE_OUT', y='ADM_RATE')
```

We can see that the plot (overall) starts in the top left and moves toward the bottom right. This aligns with our numeric correlation finding that higher admission rates are associated with lower tuition and vice versa.

However, I was intrigued by the fact that the college scorecard includes a column `MD_EARN_WNE_P10`, which shows the median income for graduates from each school 10 years following graduation. This allows us to ask and answer a number of different questions. For example, we have now seen that more-expensive schools are also harder to get into. However, is there a tangible benefit for that additional cost? Specifically, if you attend a more exclusive school, can you expect to earn more after graduation?

I thus asked you to modify this scatter plot, colorizing it using the Spectral colormap and drawing on the values in the `MD_EARN_WNE_P10` column (figure 13.4):

```
(
    institutions_df
    .plot.scatter(x='TUITIONFEE_OUT',
                  y='ADM_RATE',
                  c='MD_EARN_WNE_P10',
                  colormap='Spectral')
)
```

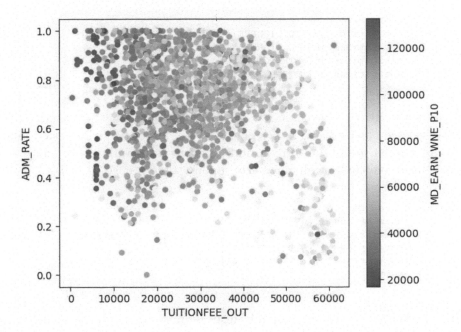

Figure 13.4   Scatter plot comparing tuition fees and admission rates

The Spectral colormap puts earnings of $20,000/year in red, $120,000/year in blue, and everything else in between. The closer to blue (darkest gray in bottom-right corner) the dots are colored, the higher the income. It's not a huge surprise that we see a great deal of red (darkest gray) in the top-left corner (i.e., less expensive, lower-admission schools with lower earnings), whereas yellows, greens, and blues are in the lower-right corner (i.e., more expensive, higher-admission schools with higher earnings). On average, it would seem, graduates from more exclusive schools do earn more.

WHICH UNIVERSITIES ARE IN THE TOP 25% OF TUITION AND ALSO THE TOP 25% WITH PELL GRANTS? I decided to probe expensive, exclusive schools further. First, I asked you to find schools that charge in the top 25% of tuition (i.e., the most expensive universities) that are also in the top 25% of schools offering Pell grants. Pell grants are awarded to students on the basis of financial need and provide a rough estimate of how many less-wealthy students are studying somewhere. We're thus looking to find, in simple terms, expensive schools that have a relatively high proportion of nonwealthy students.

To do that, we need to use `quantile(0.75)` on the `TUITIONFEE_OUT` column to determine the top quartile of tuition. We similarly need to run `quantile(0.75)` on the `FTFTPCTPELL` column, which contains the percentage of Pell-grant recipients at each school. We can then compare each institution's value for `TUITIONFEE_OUT` and `FTFTPCTPELL` against that 0.75 quantile, retrieving institutions that are above those thresholds in both:

```
(
    institutions_df
    .loc[(institutions_df['TUITIONFEE_OUT'] >
        institutions_df['TUITIONFEE_OUT'].quantile(0.75)) &
        (institutions_df['FTFTPCTPELL'] >
        institutions_df['FTFTPCTPELL'].quantile(0.75))]
)
```

This returns all rows in `institutions_df` where both `TUITIONFEE_OUT` and `FTFTPCTPELL` are above the 75th percentile. But we aren't really interested in all the columns; I asked you to show the institution name along with its city and state. For that, we need to include a column selector in our call to `.loc`:

```
(
    institutions_df
    .loc[(institutions_df['TUITIONFEE_OUT'] >
        institutions_df['TUITIONFEE_OUT'].quantile(0.75)) &
        (institutions_df['FTFTPCTPELL'] >
        institutions_df['FTFTPCTPELL'].quantile(0.75)),
        ['INSTNM', 'CITY', 'STABBR']]
)
```

Finally, I asked you to sort the output by institution name, which we can do by calling `sort_values` and specifying the `INSTNM` column:

```
(
    institutions_df
    .loc[(institutions_df['TUITIONFEE_OUT'] >
        institutions_df['TUITIONFEE_OUT'].quantile(0.75)) &
        (institutions_df['FTFTPCTPELL'] >
        institutions_df['FTFTPCTPELL'].quantile(0.75)),
        ['INSTNM', 'CITY', 'STABBR']]
    .sort_values(by='INSTNM')
)
```

IN HOW MANY INSTITUTIONS DOES THE BOTTOM QUINTILE RECEIVE MONEY?

Now let's look at university tuition from another perspective. The college scorecard tracks the net price for four-year public and private institutions (`NPT4_PUB` and

NPT4_PRIV, respectively). It then breaks the tuition payments down even further in additional columns, showing (for example) the average price paid by people in the lowest income bracket at public (NPT41_PUB) and private (NPT41_PRIV) universities.

At how many institutions, both public and private, does the average lowest-income-bracket student receive money rather than spend money? If we were merely interested in public institutions, we could find all those where the value of NPT41_PUB is less than 0 and then show their names:

```
(
    institutions_df
    .loc[((institutions_df['NPT41_PUB'] < 0) |
          (institutions_df['NPT41_PRIV'] < 0)),
    'INSTNM']
    .count()
)
```

Or if we were interested in private institutions, we would do the same for NPT41_PRIV:

```
institutions_df.loc[institutions_df['NPT41_PRIV'] < 0,
    'INSTNM'].count()
```

We could use | for an "or" condition, thus getting the values where either of these is less than 0:

```
institutions_df.loc[((institutions_df['NPT41_PUB'] < 0) |
                     (institutions_df['NPT41_PRIV'] < 0)),
                    'INSTNM'].count()
```

This gave me an answer of 12. However, there's another way to do this: we can add the values in NPT41_PRIV to those in NPT41_PUB with a fill_value of 0. Then we can simply check to see where NPT41_PUB is < 0:

```
institutions_df.loc[institutions_df['NPT41_PUB'].add(
    institutions_df['NPT41_PRIV'], fill_value=0) < 0,
    'INSTNM'].count()
```

This gives the same answer. Although I'm not convinced it's a better way to solve the problem, it shows that in pandas, there's always more than one option, and they often look different from one another.

WHAT IS THE AVERAGE PROPORTION THAT THE BOTTOM QUINTILE PAYS VERSUS THE TOP QUINTILE AT PUBLIC UNIVERSITIES?

I then asked you to show, for public universities, the average proportion that the bottom quintile pays versus the top quintile. To calculate this, we divide NPT41_PUB (the bottom quintile) into NPT45_PUB (the top quintile) and then take the mean:

```
(institutions_df['NPT41_PUB'] / institutions_df['NPT45_PUB']).mean()
```

We get a result of about 52%.

WHAT IS THE AVERAGE PROPORTION THAT THE BOTTOM QUINTILE PAYS VERSUS THE TOP QUINTILE AT PRIVATE UNIVERSITIES?

We can then repeat this for private universities:

```
(institutions_df['NPT41_PRIV'] / institutions_df['NPT45_PRIV']).mean()
```

It turns out that people in the bottom quintile at private universities pay about 71% of what the top quintile do. So not only do students pay more to attend private universities, but the poorest of them pay a higher percentage of their tuition fees than their public-university counterparts.

In looking at this data, we've seen that, overall, the schools with the highest-paid alumni are also the most expensive and the hardest to get into. But of course, that's only overall, in the aggregate.

FOR WHICH SCHOOLS IN THE CHEAPEST 25% DO THEIR STUDENTS HAVE THE TOP 25% OF SALARIES 10 YEARS AFTER GRADUATION?

To try to figure out which universities offer the best overall ROI, I asked you to find the schools whose tuitions are in the lowest 25% but whose 10-year alumni are in the highest 25% of salaries. First, let's look at public institutions:

```
(
    institutions_df
    .loc[(institutions_df['NPT4_PUB']
        <= institutions_df['NPT4_PUB'].quantile(0.25)) &
        (institutions_df['MD_EARN_WNE_P10']
        >= institutions_df['MD_EARN_WNE_P10'].quantile(0.75)),
        ['INSTNM', 'STABBR', 'CITY']]
    .sort_values(by=['STABBR', 'CITY'])
)
```

This query is a variation on what we've already done, looking for those public universities whose tuition is in the lowest quartile but whose 10-year alumni are earning in the highest quartile. In our column selector, we ask for only three columns: institution name, state, and city. That allows us to sort the results first by state and then by city. The result is a data frame with 22 rows whose universities are in California, Florida, New York, Texas, and New Mexico.

HOW ABOUT PRIVATE INSTITUTIONS?

What about private universities? We can run a similar query but using NPT4_PRIV rather than NPT4_PUB:

```
(
    institutions_df
    .loc[(institutions_df['NPT4_PRIV']
        <= institutions_df['NPT4_PRIV'].quantile(0.25)) &
        (institutions_df['MD_EARN_WNE_P10']
        >= institutions_df['MD_EARN_WNE_P10'].quantile(0.75)),
    ['INSTNM', 'STABBR', 'CITY']]
    .sort_values(by=['STABBR', 'CITY'])
)
```

This query returns 30 universities spread across a variety of states. Some well-known universities (e.g., Harvard, Stanford, and Princeton) are in there, along with smaller and lesser-known ones.

IS THERE A CORRELATION BETWEEN ADMISSION RATES AND COMPLETION RATES?

Next, I wanted to know if we could find any correlation between admission rates and completion rates. That is, if a school is highly selective, are its students more likely to graduate? We run the following query:

```
institutions_df[['C100_4', 'ADM_RATE']].corr()
```

Sure enough, we see a moderate negative correlation. That is, a school that accepts more people has a lower graduation rate. That shouldn't be a huge surprise; after all, for a school to accept more people, it likely has to take people who are bigger risks in terms of not finishing.

TEN YEARS AFTER GRADUATING, FROM WHAT KINDS OF SCHOOLS DO PEOPLE EARN, ON AVERAGE, THE GREATEST AMOUNT?

Next, I asked whether, on average, people earn more after graduating from a public or private university. That is, on average, how much do people earn for each value of the CONTROL column? Once again, we join institutions_df with fields_of_study_df—but only after doing a groupby on fields_of_study_df:

```
(
    institutions_df[['OPEID6', 'MD_EARN_WNE_P10']]
    .set_index('OPEID6')
    .join(fields_of_study_df
          .groupby('OPEID6')['CONTROL'].min())
    .groupby('CONTROL')
    .mean()
)
```

The result aligns with my expectations: that people who attend private for-profit universities end up earning less than those who attend public universities, who in turn end up earning less than those who attend private universities. Obviously, this is an aggregate measure—and I definitely know high earners who attended public universities and low earners who attended private ones. But data analytics is all about making generalizations, drawing conclusions that are incorrect for any individual but correct for the overall population.

DO PEOPLE WHO GRADUATE FROM "IVY PLUS" SCHOOLS EARN MORE THAN THE AVERAGE PRIVATE-SCHOOL UNIVERSITY GRADUATE?

Let's take this question of private universities to an extreme. People often want to get into the best-known universities on the assumption that they'll be able to earn more later on in life. Is this true? Does going to a famous, exclusive university mean you'll have a more lucrative career? I asked you to check the mean salary for graduates from what are sometimes known as "Ivy Plus" schools: the Ivy League as well as MIT, Stanford, and the University of Chicago.

To do this, we use `isin` in the column selector. Note that the universities' formal names are tricky to figure out, especially for "Columbia University in the City of New York." But here's the final query:

```
ivy_plus = ['Harvard University',
            'Massachusetts Institute of Technology',
            'Yale University',
            'Columbia University in the City of New York',
            'Brown University',
            'Stanford University',
            'University of Chicago',
            'Dartmouth College',
            'University of Pennsylvania',
            'Cornell University',
            'Princeton University']

(
    institutions_df
    .loc[institutions_df['INSTNM'].isin(ivy_plus),
         'MD_EARN_WNE_P10']
    .mean()
)
```

The answer to this query is just over $91,806/year, more than twice the average salary earned by all graduates of private universities—which was, as we saw, greater still than the amount earned by graduates of public or for-profit institutions.

DO PEOPLE STUDYING AT UNIVERSITIES IN PARTICULAR STATES EARN, ON AVERAGE, MORE AFTER 10 YEARS?

Finally, we want to compare post-graduation salaries, 10 years out, by state. That is, do your future earnings depend in part on the state in which you studied? For starters, we perform a `groupby` on the states (STABBR), looking at the mean salary of 10-year graduates:

```
institutions_df.groupby('STABBR')['MD_EARN_WNE_P10'].mean()
```

This gives the overall answer we want, but understanding such data is always easier when it's sorted. I thus asked you to sort the values in descending order:

```
(
    institutions_df
    .groupby('STABBR', observed=True)
    ['MD_EARN_WNE_P10'].mean()
    .sort_values(ascending=False)
)
```

CREATE A BAR PLOT FOR THE AVERAGE AMOUNT EARNED, PER STATE, SORTED BY ASCENDING PAY

Now I asked you to create a bar plot from the per-state salary averages (figure 13.5):

```
(
    institutions_df
    .groupby('STABBR', observed=True)
    ['MD_EARN_WNE_P10'].mean()
```

```
    .sort_values()
    .plot.bar(figsize=(20,10))
)
```

By sorting the values, we get (I believe) a more aesthetically pleasing, easy-to-read plot than would otherwise be the case. We can easily see that there is a big difference between how much people earn after graduating from schools in Massachusetts and Rhode Island as opposed to Arkansas and Mississippi. However, before we make a claim regarding the quality of universities in these respective states, we have to determine how many people still live in the states where they studied. After all, the cost of living in New England is significantly higher than in Arkansas and Mississippi, so it stands to reason that people living there will earn more—regardless of what university they attended.

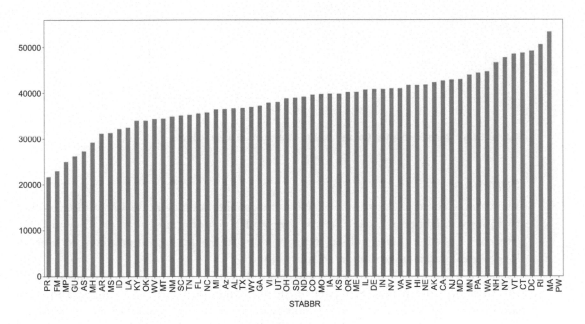

Figure 13.5   Bar chart showing the average amount earned per state

CREATE A BOXPLOT FOR THE EARNINGS BY STATE.

Finally, I asked you to create a box plot based on the per-state salary data so we can easily see the spread in visual form (figure 13.6):

```
(
    institutions_df
    .groupby('STABBR', observed=True)
    ['MD_EARN_WNE_P10'].mean()
    .plot.box()
)
```

The plot shows that most annual salaries are between $25,000 and $50,000, with the median being just under $40,000.

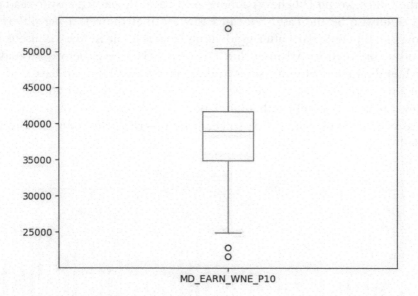

Figure 13.6   Boxplot showing the average salaries earned by graduates

Summary

You've now come to the true and actual end of the book. Thanks for joining me on this journey. I hope the exercises in this book, including all the extra "Beyond the exercise" questions, have helped improve your understanding of pandas and how to load, clean, and analyze data in a variety of ways.

Beyond the specific techniques I've covered in this book, I hope you've also begun to internalize the pandas perspective on data analysis. Pandas is a huge (and constantly growing) library, and there's no way for someone to know all of it. Understanding how pandas works means when you're faced with a new problem, you can guess how to solve it, even predicting what methods pandas will provide to do so.

I wish you the best of success in your use of pandas to analyze data in whatever you're doing. And I hope this book helped you to advance your skills in that area. If it did, please drop me a line at reuven@lerner.co.il! I'm always delighted to hear from people who have read my books.

index